Jaipur Quilts

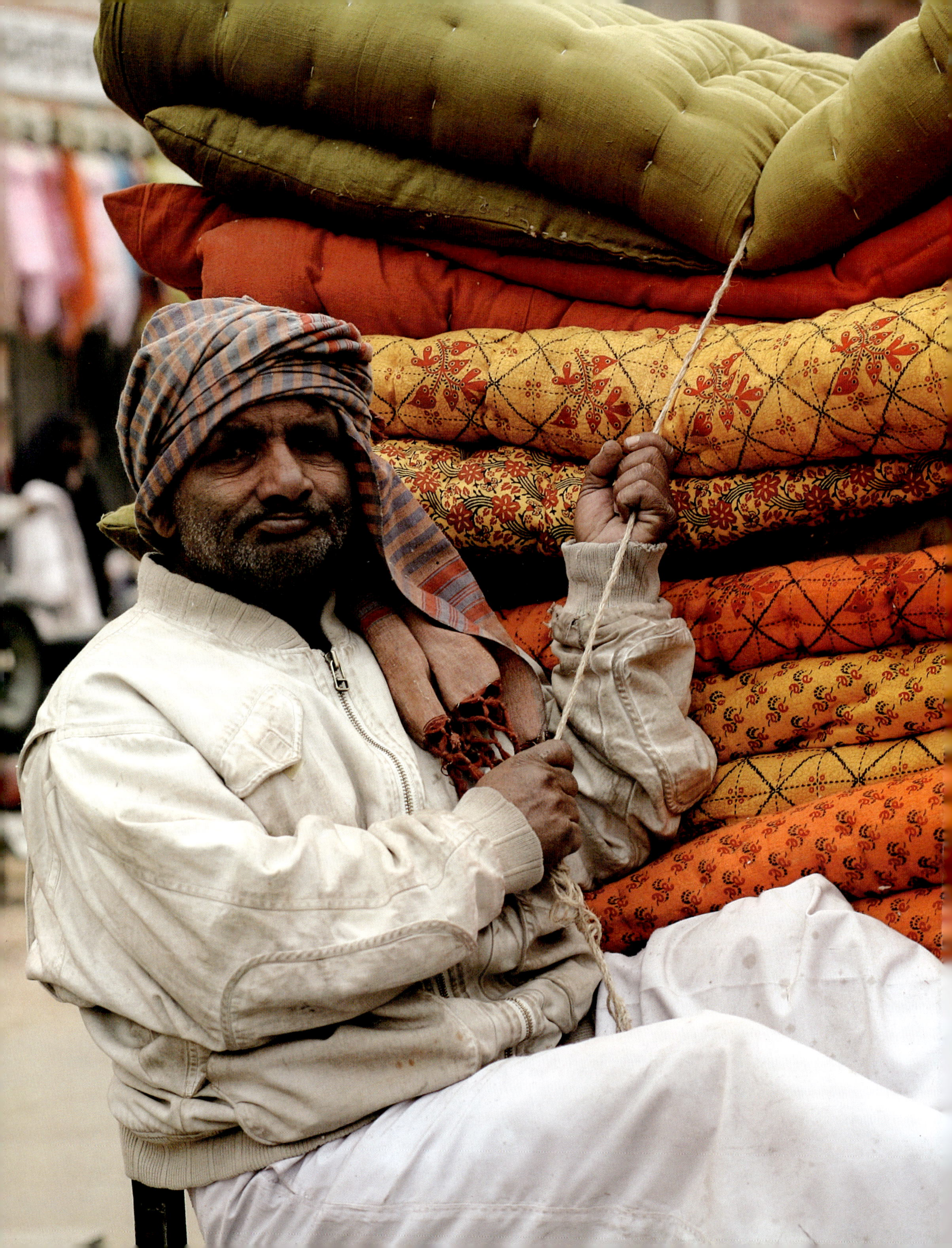

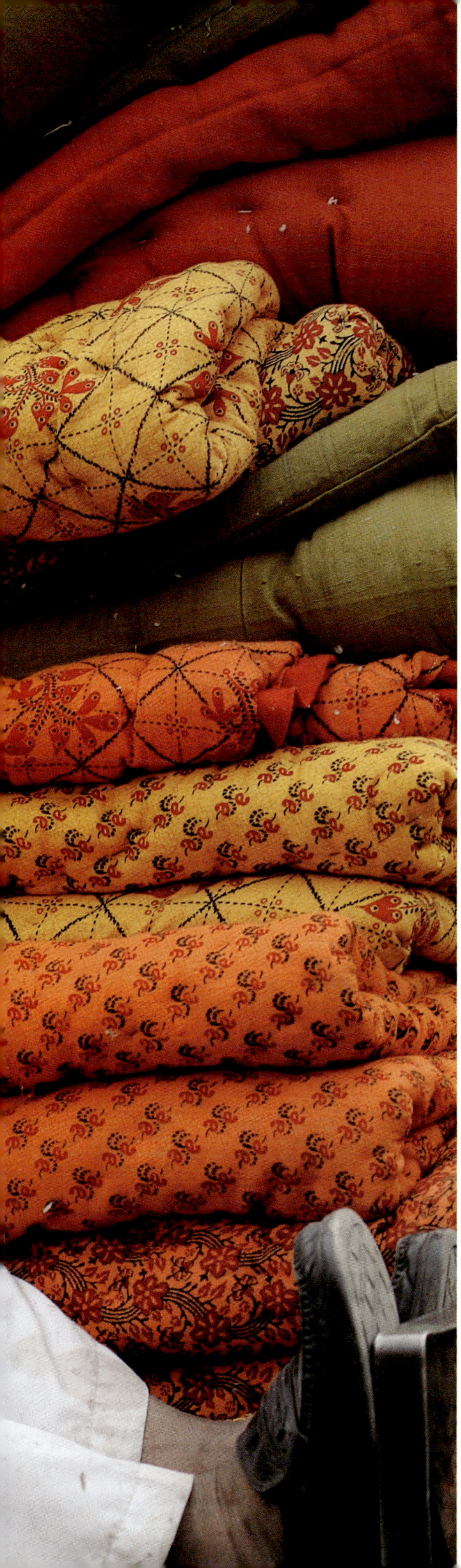

Jaipur Quilts

Krystyna Hellström

NIYOGI
BOOKS

Published by

NIYOGI BOOKS

Block D, Building No. 77,
Okhla Industrial Area, Phase-I,
New Delhi-110 020, INDIA
Tel: 91-11-26816301, 26818960
Email: niyogibooks@gmail.com
Website: www.niyogibooksindia.com

Editor: Mohua Mitra/Niyogi Books
Design: Nabanita Das, Ajoy Kumar Das/Niyogi Books
Cover Design: Maria Hegborn

ISBN: 978-81-920912-5-9
Publication: 2012
Reprint: 2023

Printed at: Niyogi Offset Pvt. Ltd., New Delhi, India

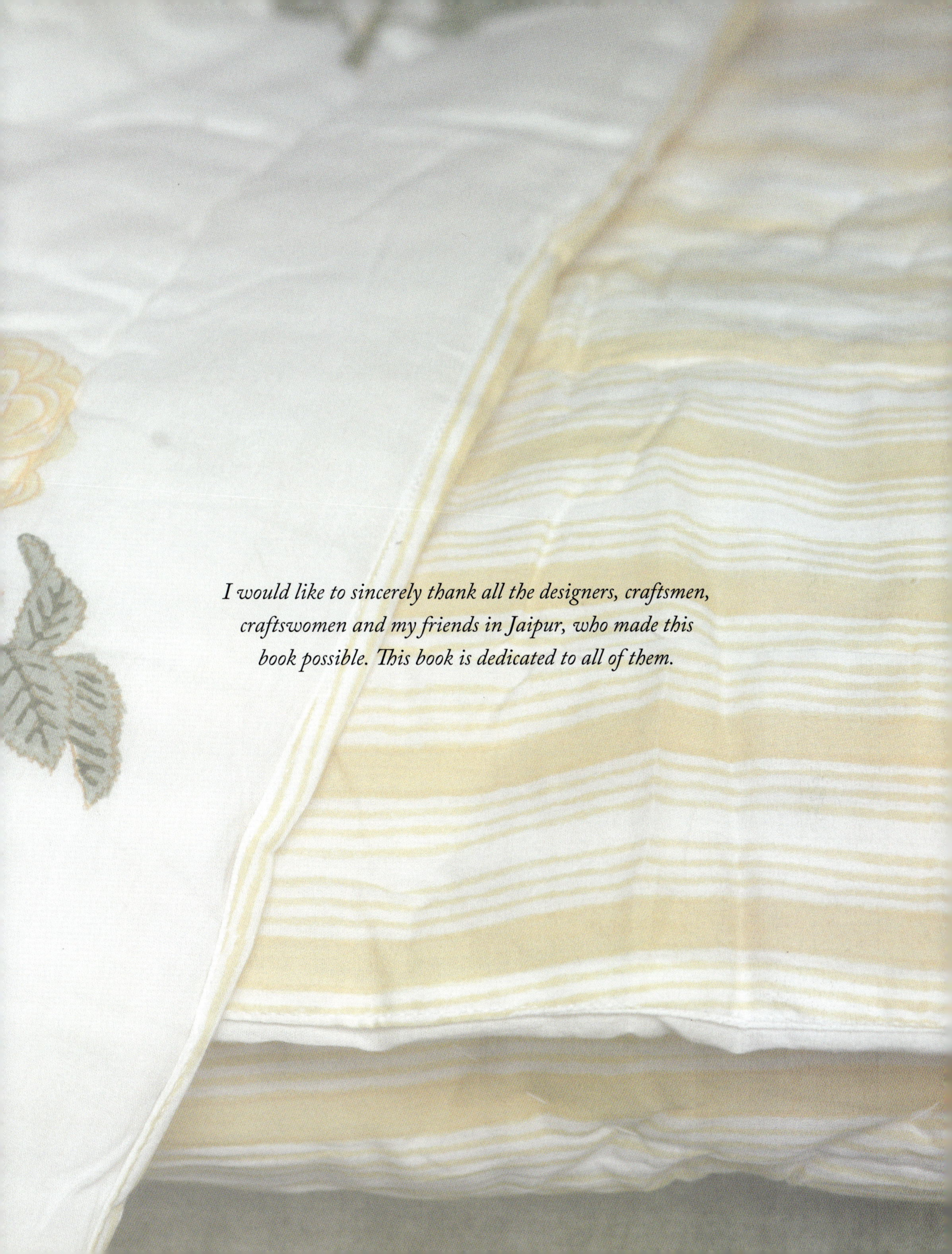

I would like to sincerely thank all the designers, craftsmen, craftswomen and my friends in Jaipur, who made this book possible. This book is dedicated to all of them.

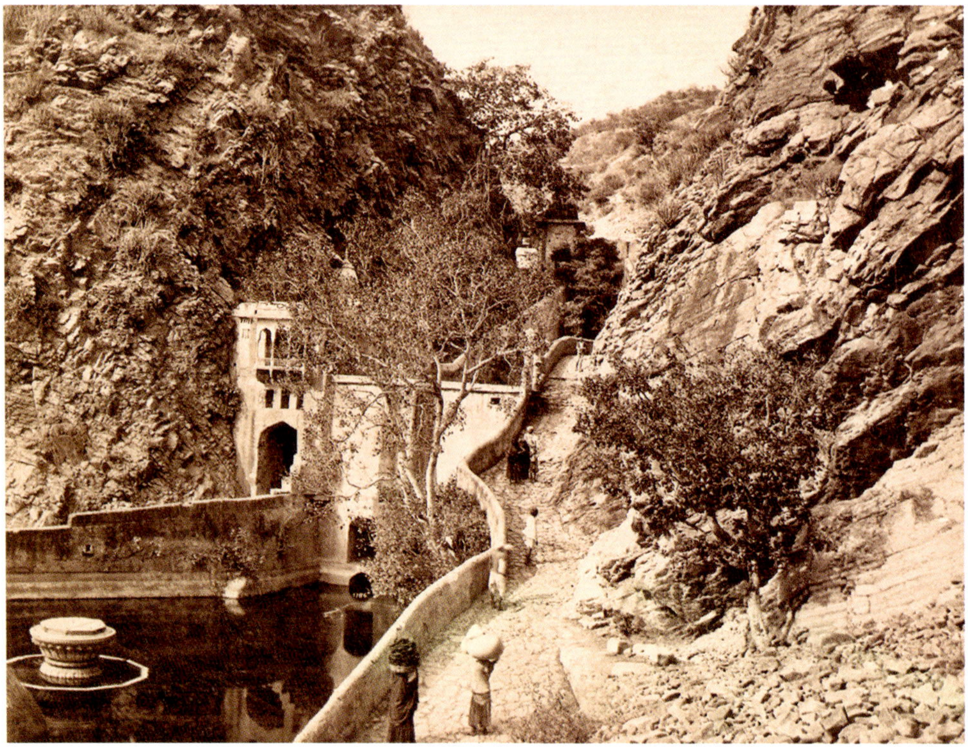

Galtaji, an old water tank in Jaipur

Galtaji is an ancient Hindu pilgrimage situated ten kilometres from Jaipur on the Jaipur-Agra highway near Sisodia Rani ka Bagh. It has temples, pavilions, natural springs and holy kund*s. It is believed that Saint Galav spent his life here in meditation. The main temple of Galtaji is built of pink stone. There are seven tanks and the Galta kund is considered to be the holiest. Pilgrims take the holy dip here on Makar Sankranti, a winter harvest festival celebrated in January*

Photo: Raja Deen Dayal
Courtesy: Subhash Sharma

Contents

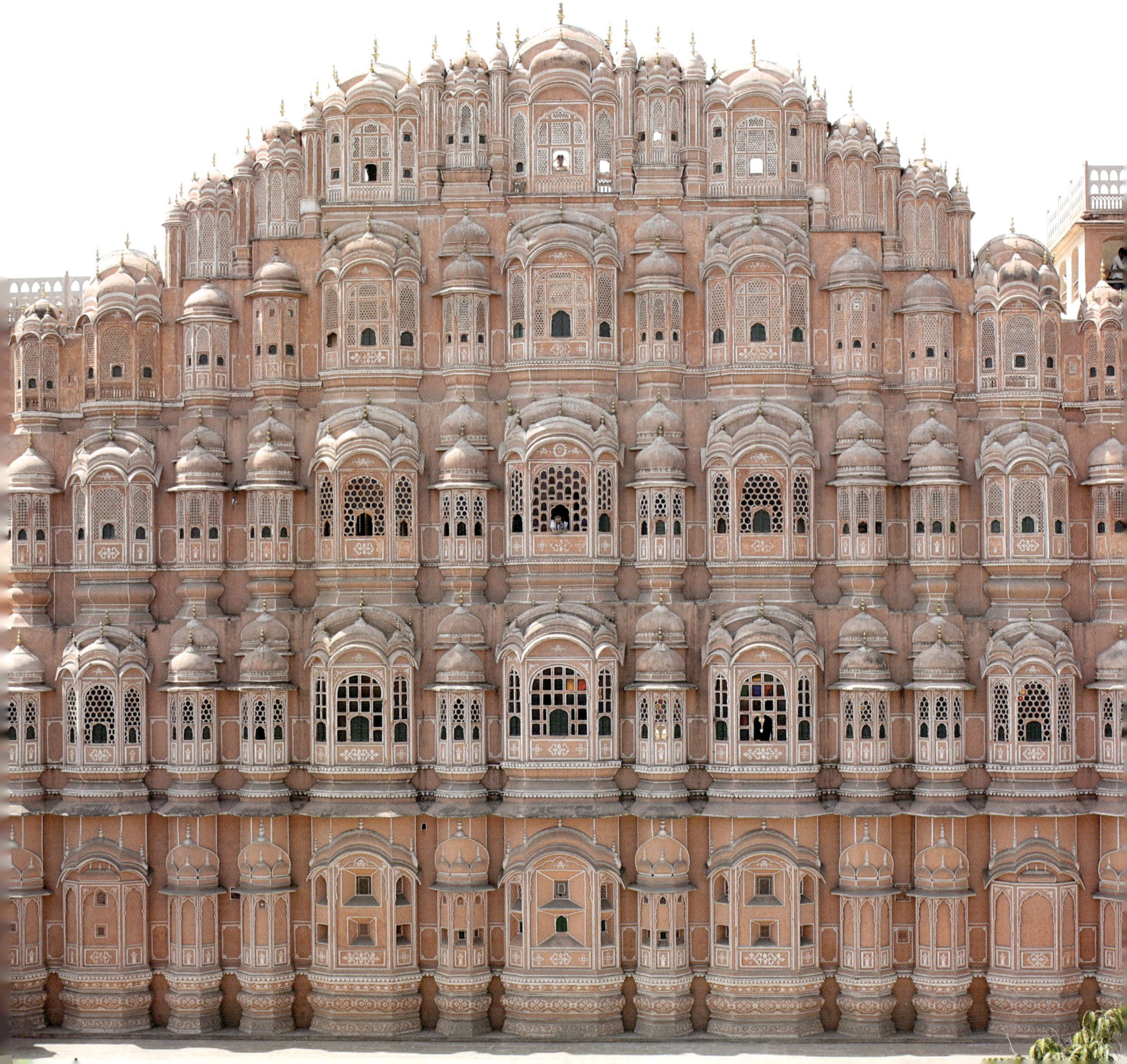

Foreword

Jaipur has been my home for many years now and I have watched the city grow and change over these last three decades. From a population of barely eight lakh in the 1970s, the city is now bursting at its seams with a population of thirty-seven lakh. The look and feel of the city has also changed over the years with the city's limits expanding and a lot of new buildings coming up in the new areas of the modern part of the city.

What hasn't changed too much, thankfully, is the character of the Walled City, better known and recognised as the Pink City. The eighteenth century look and feel of the planned city still impresses and attracts the visitor. Even after having written extensively about the city and its numerous attractions, I still felt that there was so much more to discover and so much more to record.

One area that has been a little neglected is the craft segment. Jaipur is recognised the world over for its wide range of arts and crafts giving it a well-deserved reputation as a shoppers' paradise. From jewellery to stoneware, from textiles to blue pottery... it's a long, long list.

Among the many handcrafted items that the Pink City is famous for, the *Jaipuri razai*, or the Jaipur quilt occupies an important place. Block-printed cotton fabric with some exquisite designs carefully filled with as little as 250 gm (or more) of cotton-wool that is spread evenly and stitched in traditional patterns... In fact their popularity and reach can be gauged by the number of framed photographs of celebrity customers, from high ranking politicians to film stars, that are displayed in shops in the old city.

Facing page: *Hawa Mahal, Jaipur*

Page 2-3: *Quilt seller on the streets of Jaipur*

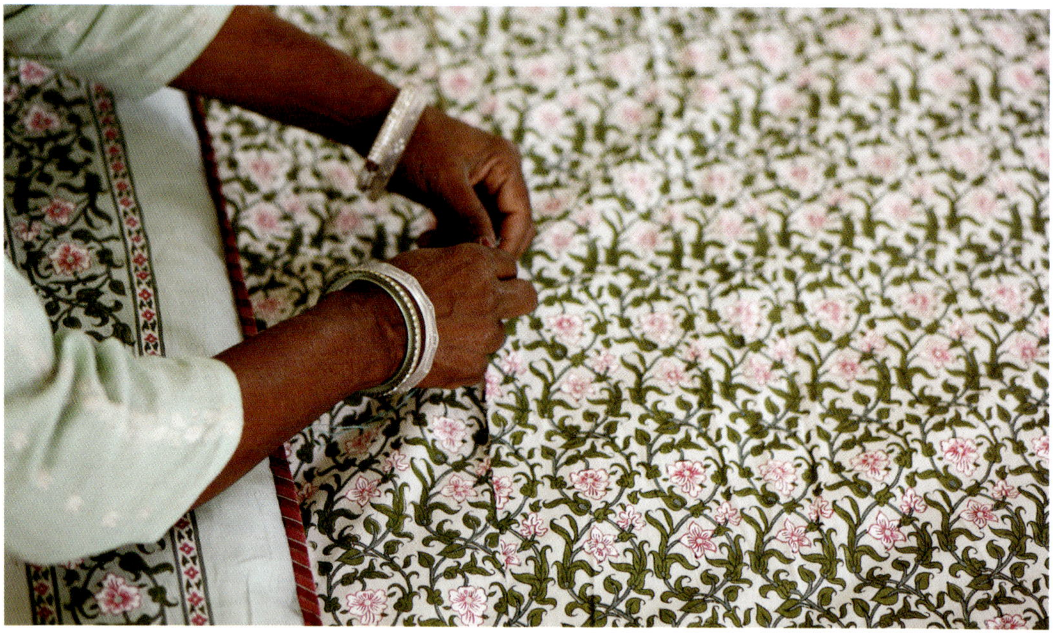

Closing the shell of a decorative quilt with floral motifs

When you read Krystyna's interesting account you'll look at these quilts a lot more carefully instead of taking them for granted as most people in Jaipur tend to do. We see them all the time, we use them regularly and we even gift them to our friends and relatives. In fact, they are so much a part of our daily lives that we don't always give them the importance or attention that they deserve. It took a Polish woman to set that right!

When Krystyna Hellström met me last year through a mutual friend and showed me her book on Jaipur quilts, I was pleasantly surprised and a little taken aback because despite having written so much about Rajasthan and several aspects of Jaipur, a book on the famed *Jaipuri razai* had never occurred to me!

Krystyna has had a long relationship with the quilts and quilt-makers of Jaipur and she has recorded her interactions with them in a very readable way. She has researched and documented this craft beautifully.

Jaipur Quilts is a very well-written and illustrated book and provides an in-depth look into the wonderfully creative world of the quilt-maker, touching upon the contributions of the block-printer, the filler to the craftsman who stitches intricate patterns on these beautifully designed and lightweight quilts.

This book will give readers a detailed look into a craft that they too may have just taken for granted.

Dharmendar Kanwar

Jaipur

Preface

Around 250 years ago, Sawai Jai Singh II, the ruler of Jaipur, brought the quilt makers from neighbouring hamlets to the Pink City and settled them down. Since then the Jaipur quilts have created a rich tradition for themselves. The two most popular varieties available in the market are cotton and velvet. New customer markets for the *Jaipuri razai* are opening up gradually.

My intention is to give the reader a general idea about Jaipur quilts and the tradition of quilting in the world. I have also made an effort to present to the reader a visual experience of the beauty of the quilts through some of my photographs. I have quoted some authors on subjects that I personally did not research or write and have freely rendered the authors' thoughts instead. Chandramani Singh was my guide on Jaipur textiles and she advised me to use the catalogue she wrote for the City Palace Museum–*Textiles and Costumes from the Maharaja Sawai Man Singh II Museum*–which was an important source of information. My task was to go to Jaipur and find some of the people who produce, design or collect the best of quilts, interview them and photograph the quilts and the people associated with their production and popularity. Building the concept and writing my book was like trying to solve a jigsaw puzzle—finding the correct pieces and fitting them in to slowly create the whole image. I am sure some pieces are still missing and perhaps the discerning reader can take up the task of completing the picture after reading this book.

Dear reader, thank you for picking up my book. I hope it will be useful and will let you spend a few moments pleasantly.

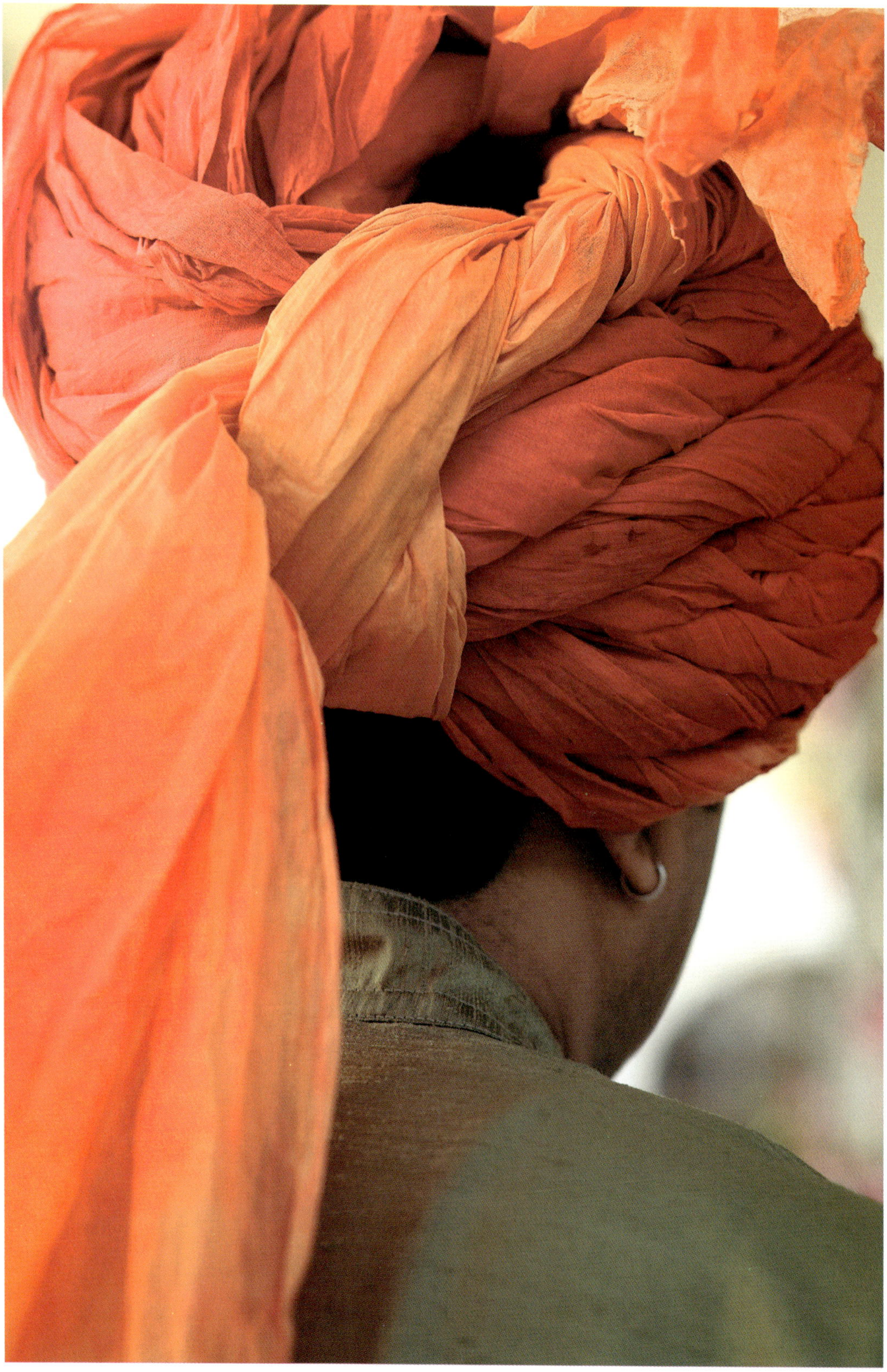

Introduction

One cold December evening in the early nineties, I stepped into an international bookshop in Stockholm in a rather gloomy mood. My eyes caught the new issue of *Architektur & Wohnen* with the title: *Creative India Discovered by Trendsetters.* I looked through the magazine and was taken aback by the pictures and stories about the people and the beautiful things it featured. The issue presented Charles Correa, one of the best Indian architects in contemporary times and one of his creations—the Jawahar Kala Kendra in Jaipur. This was a cultural centre dedicated to Jawaharlal Nehru, with galleries, a library, museum and a theatre.

Next in line was Asha Sarabhai, a minimalistic designer from Ahmedabad, with her famous boutique Egg in London, followed by Brigitte Singh, the French-born designer of exquisite clothes, quilts and textiles, living in close proximity to Jaipur. And finally there was the legendary Kitty Rae, who started the commercial production of quilts in Jaipur in 1963. What captured my attention was the adaptation of the *razai* or the Indian quilt–a traditional handicraft–to suit modern tastes and needs and the fresh new style created for a demanding international clientele.

The gloom disappeared magically and I decided to visit India. I wanted to meet the producers and to see and touch the beautiful objects, which enchanted me. It did not cross my mind that nobody was actually waiting for me in Jaipur. However, I guess my enthusiasm subsequently opened a few doors and I was able to achieve my goal in the end.

Facing page: *The most visible part of the men's outfits in Rajasthan is the colourful turban. It sits majestically atop their heads*

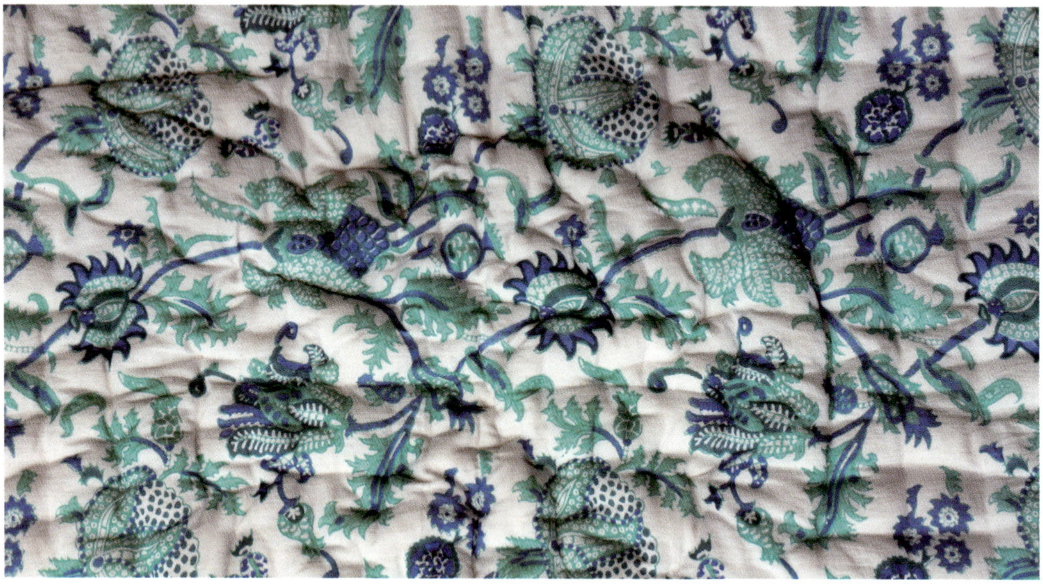

Kitty Rae quilt, with poppy and poppy fruits

I arrived in Jaipur, ready to explore and enjoy. The fact that a well-known designer had accorded me a rendezvous perhaps melted the heart of the manager of Diggi Palace Hotel in Jaipur. He actually found me a room in the fully booked hotel!

After a halting start things started to improve and over the years I made friends in Jaipur. Gradually, I also developed the opportunity to get to know a few quilt producers, printers, designers, jewellers and art dealers. I came to understand how rich the tradition of handicrafts was in Jaipur and see how talented even the lesser known artists and craftsmen were.

I often wished more people knew about Jaipur quilts. Although I met a few regular visitors to Jaipur who are somewhat addicted to these quilts, as I am, it is more like a secret society of quilt lovers who remain hidden from the public eye.

Slowly the thought of creating an album on quilts emerged, and Chandramani Singh, an Indian textile expert, promised to give me a helping hand. It seemed that there was an absence of documented material on the history of Jaipur quilts, at least in English or other languages, which I spoke. I contacted the Victoria & Albert (V&A) Museum in London and when I received the answer that the museum did not have anything on Jaipur quilts either, I decided to produce this book.

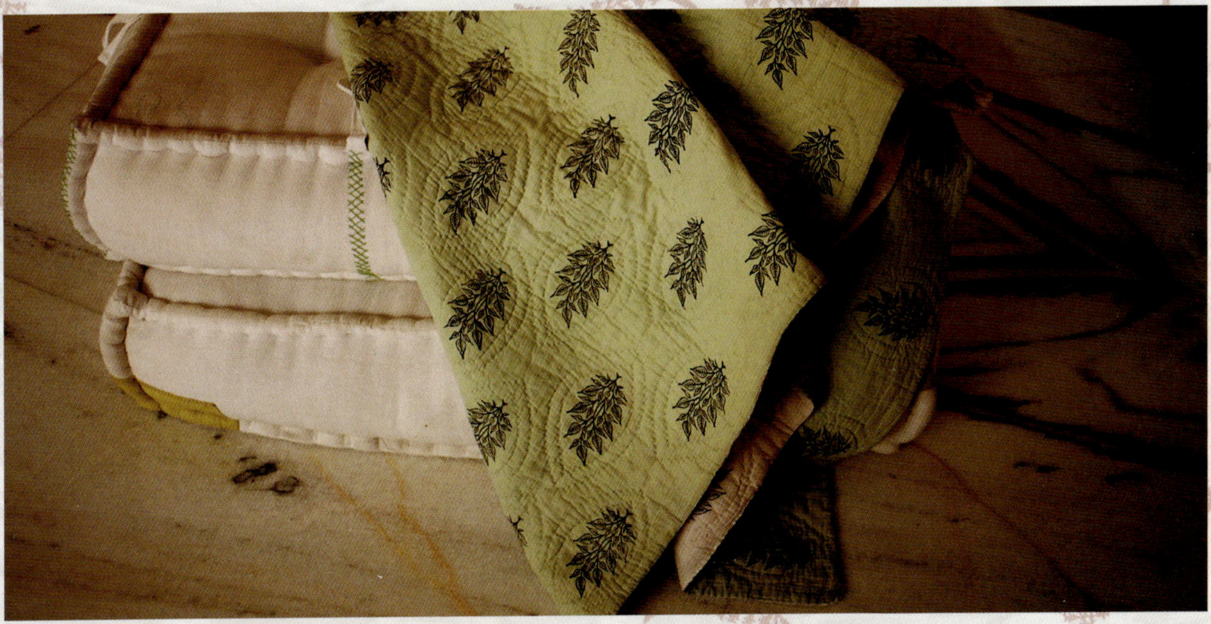

Quilt from Satayam's collection

Quilts are meant for everyday use and at the same time they are stylish pieces of traditional handicraft and art. They can be used as a blanket or duvet and also as bedcovers. The light cotton fabric breathes. Should one quilt not be enough, you can put several on top of each other and create layers of warmth. The patterns and colours may differ but they still look chic together. If a quilt is really thin, you can decorate your table with it, or even hang it as a curtain. It will keep the heat out in summer and lend the room warmth when the cold days come. You can wrap your favourite quilt around you when you watch television, read a book and also take it to the beach.

Jaipur quilts are made of very fine cotton fabric, called 'mulmul' and are filled with fluffed-up cotton wool. The air pockets make them warm, soft, light and fluffy. The soft cotton fabric cover has block-printed designs and is stitched usually by hand. The designs come in bright hues as well as muted pastel shades, using traditional motifs of flowers, leaves, plants and geometric shapes, often assimilating them in a stylised, contemporary form.

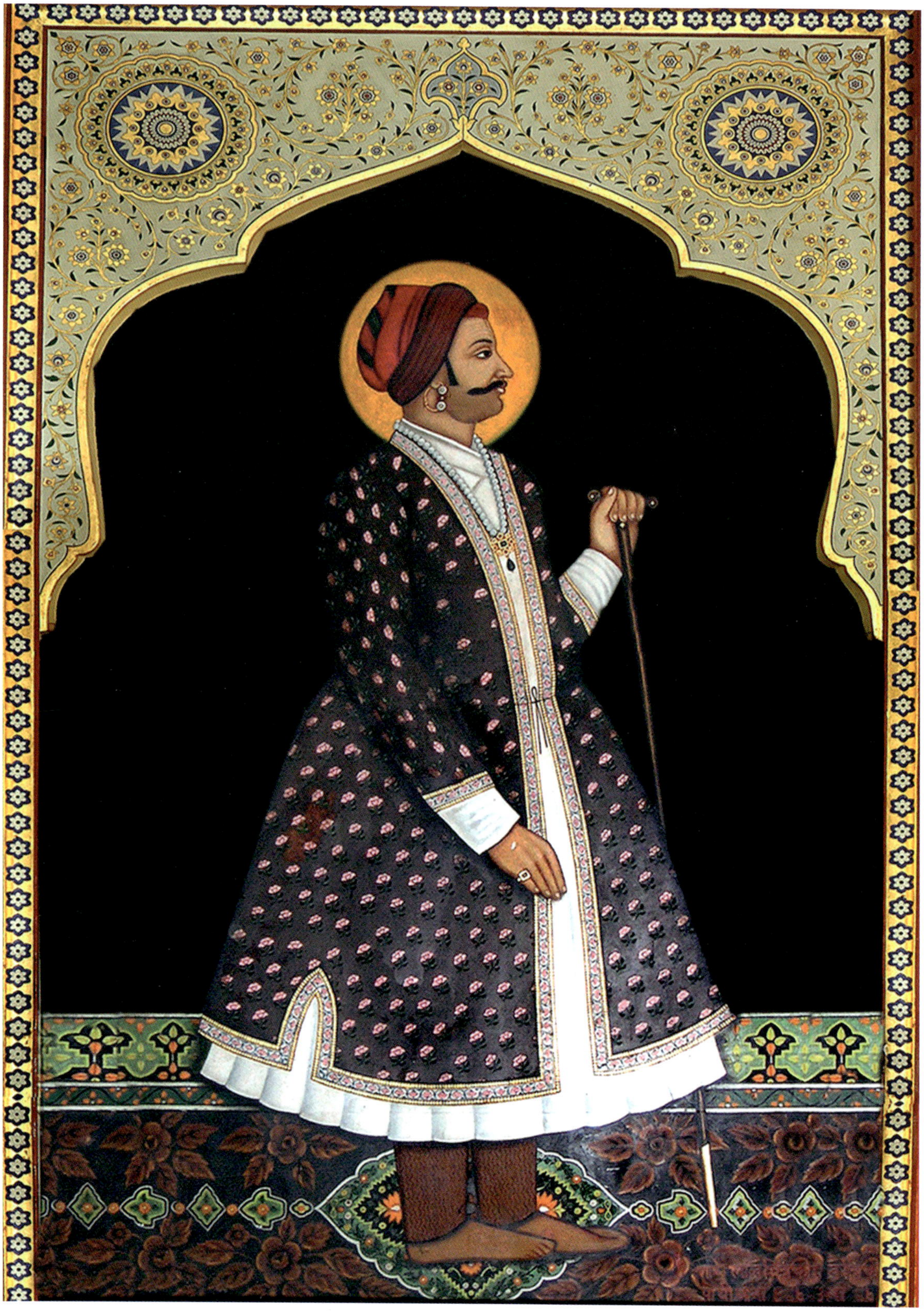

'A new future to create and the past to rediscover again is the right way to act'

—The Maharaja Sawai Jai Singh II

Jaipur: the Pink City

My love affair with the city of Jaipur, the Pink City began several decades ago. I was drawn into its history and culture shortly after and thus began my journey into the heart of the city; the charm of its people and places unfolding frame by frame; the secret behind the exquisite beauty of its crafts and handloom products–especially its exotic quilts–revealing itself in all its splendour.

As a tourist from the West, I was keen to know more, gather information and unveil the creative pattern of the mind that went into the making of such beautiful works of art.

Some amount of reticence on the part of the craftsmen and their general reluctance to talk much on the subject of creation and the creative process fuelled me on to a more intense quest which turned out to be a rather engaging journey to the rough-hewn lanes and little-known corners and edges of Jaipur, down the way of the quilt and its makers.

This historic city was founded in AD 1727 by the Maharaja Sawai Jai Singh II (1688–1743). It replaced Amber, which

Facing page: *Maharaja Sawai Jai Singh II Courtesy: Maharaja Sawai Man Singh II Museum Trust, the City Palace, Jaipur*

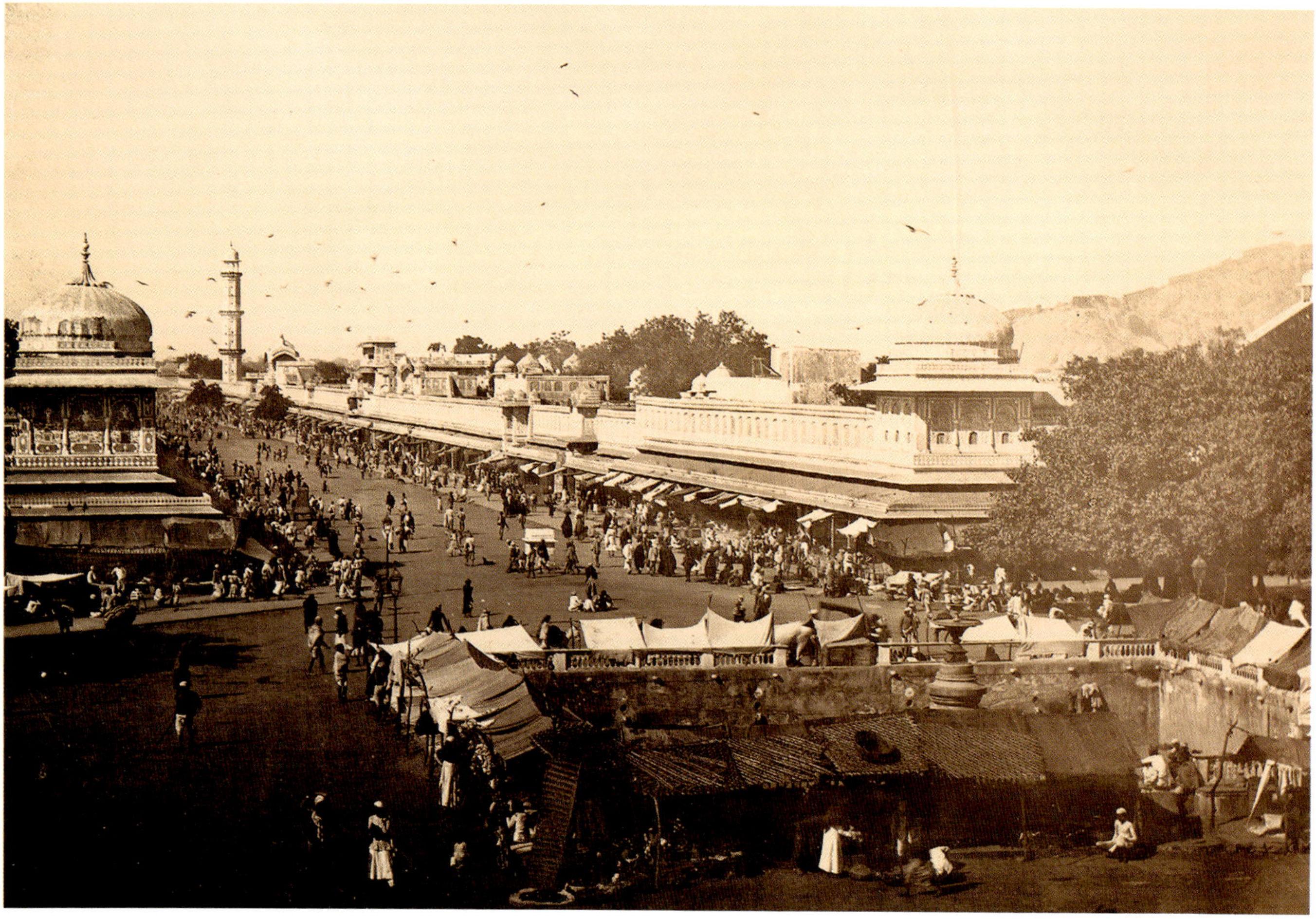

is situated 11 km outside Jaipur, as capital of the Kachawahas. The Kachawahas were Hindus and belonged to the warrior caste. However, they realised the importance of aligning themselves with the powerful Mughal Empire. They paid homage at the Mughal court and created marital alliances with the Mughal rulers. The Maharaja was born in Amber and became its ruler in 1699 at the age of eleven, after the death of his father. The Mughal emperor Aurangzeb bestowed upon him the title of 'Sawai' which meant being one and a quarter times superior to his contemporaries.

Tripolia Bazaar in the nineteenth century, still a popular landmark in Jaipur

Photo: Raja Deen Dayal
Courtesy: Subhash Sharma

The decision to move the capital from Amber to Jaipur was a carefully planned one, led by more reasons than one. Apart from the more subtle political motives behind the move, the more apparent were a rising population and a growing scarcity of water, which led the king to shift to Jaipur. Located in the semi-desert lands, this was the first planned city in India, built along geometrical lines and shapes and according to the tenets of the Vastu Shastra.

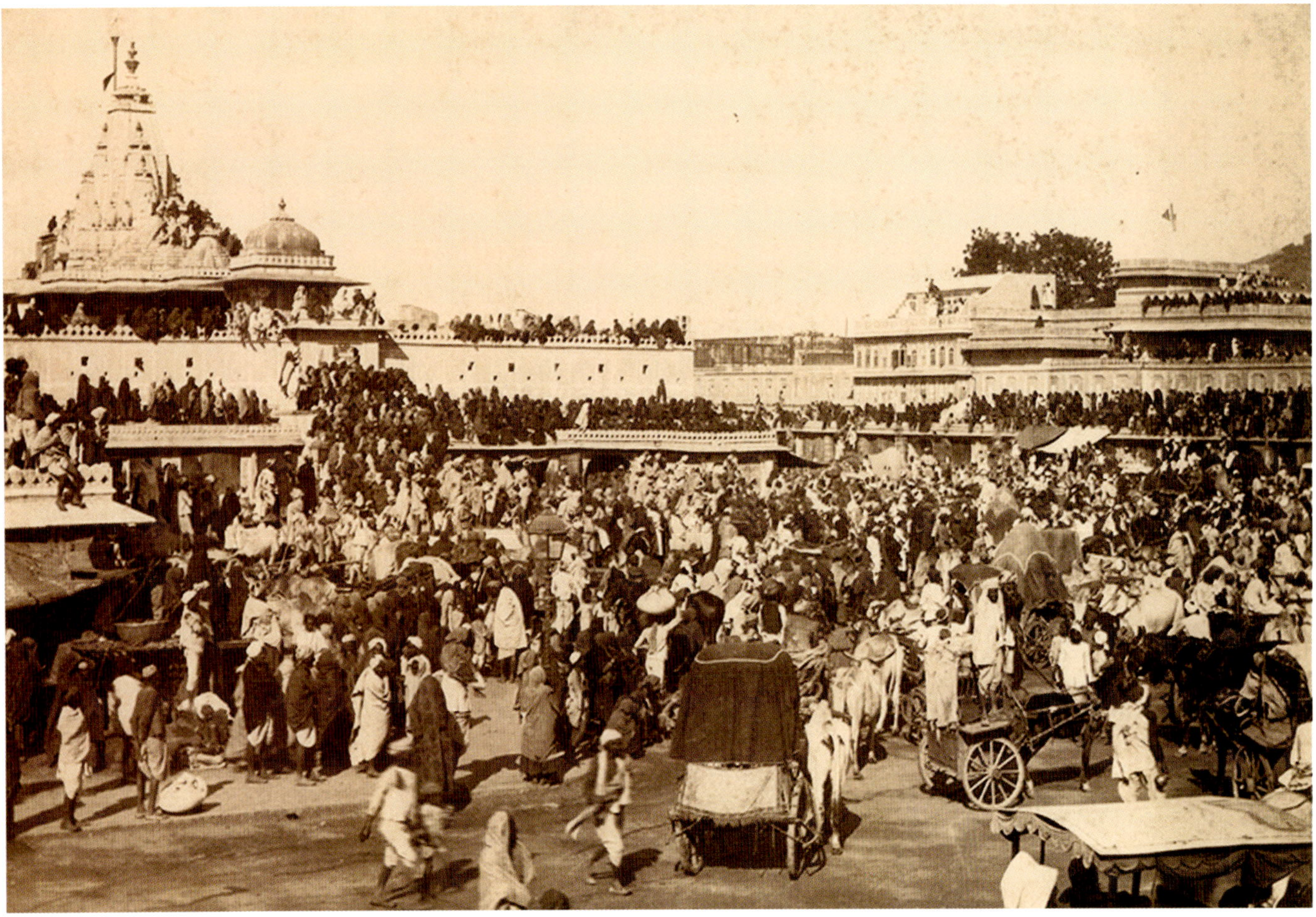

The city was built and designed by the Maharaja's court architect Vidyadhar Bhattacharya–a Brahmin scholar from Bengal–who originally kept accounts in the Royal Treasury. He was later promoted to the post of Chief Architect in the king's court and helped design the city and its buildings, including the royal palace. Elegant buildings and trees lined the streets. The city's culture and way of life was deeply influenced by the aesthetics and cultural thoughts of the neighbouring princely states. Merchants from all over India settled in this city. Quite a few of their havelis–the beautiful old houses–still stand, gracious but run-down. Tourists continue to be spellbound by their magnificence and beauty although sometimes, passing in a rickshaw, one wonders how great they would look if restored to their former grandeur!

Sawai Jai Singh II was not only a great builder but also a poet and astronomer. He had the famous Jantar Mantar observatory built in Jaipur,

Badi Chapur in the nineteenth century, Jaipur

Photo: Raja Deen Dayal
Courtesy: Subhash Sharma

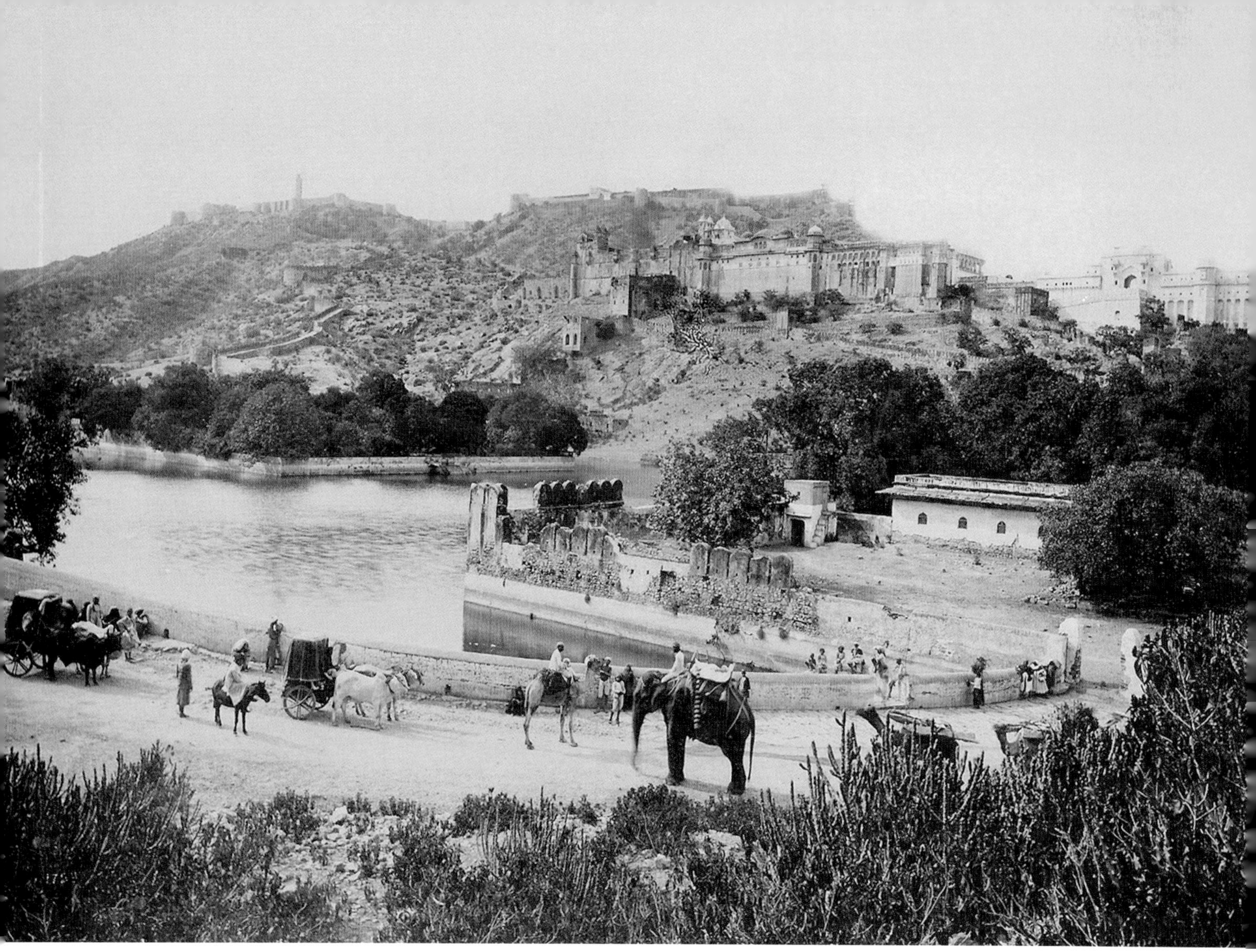

Amber Fort, Jaipur
Photo: Raja Deen Dayal
Courtesy: Subhash Sharma

Facing page: *Quilted fan from the antiquity collection of Subhash Sharma*

which is a collection of architectural and astronomical instruments. His interest in the arts and the sciences turned the royal court into an intellectual and artistic centre. His court attracted some of the most learned scholars, astronomers, writers and architects. The craftsmen he brought with him have descendants who are still active, living and working in and around Jaipur today.

As a consequence to it all, Jaipur grew to be a centre of Rajput arts and aesthetics and is known for its traditional art forms. Tourists down the ages have been lured to buy jewellery, clothes, quilts, fabric and other mementos, while on a trip to the city.

Jaipur has been the capital of Rajasthan since 1956. In March 1949, the city merged with the Rajput states of Jodhpur, Jaisalmer and Bikaner, to become Greater Rajasthan. Present day Rajasthan covers an area of 3,42,269 sq km and is the largest state of the Republic of India. With around 3.5 million inhabitants, it is one of the most popular tourist destinations in India and in the world.

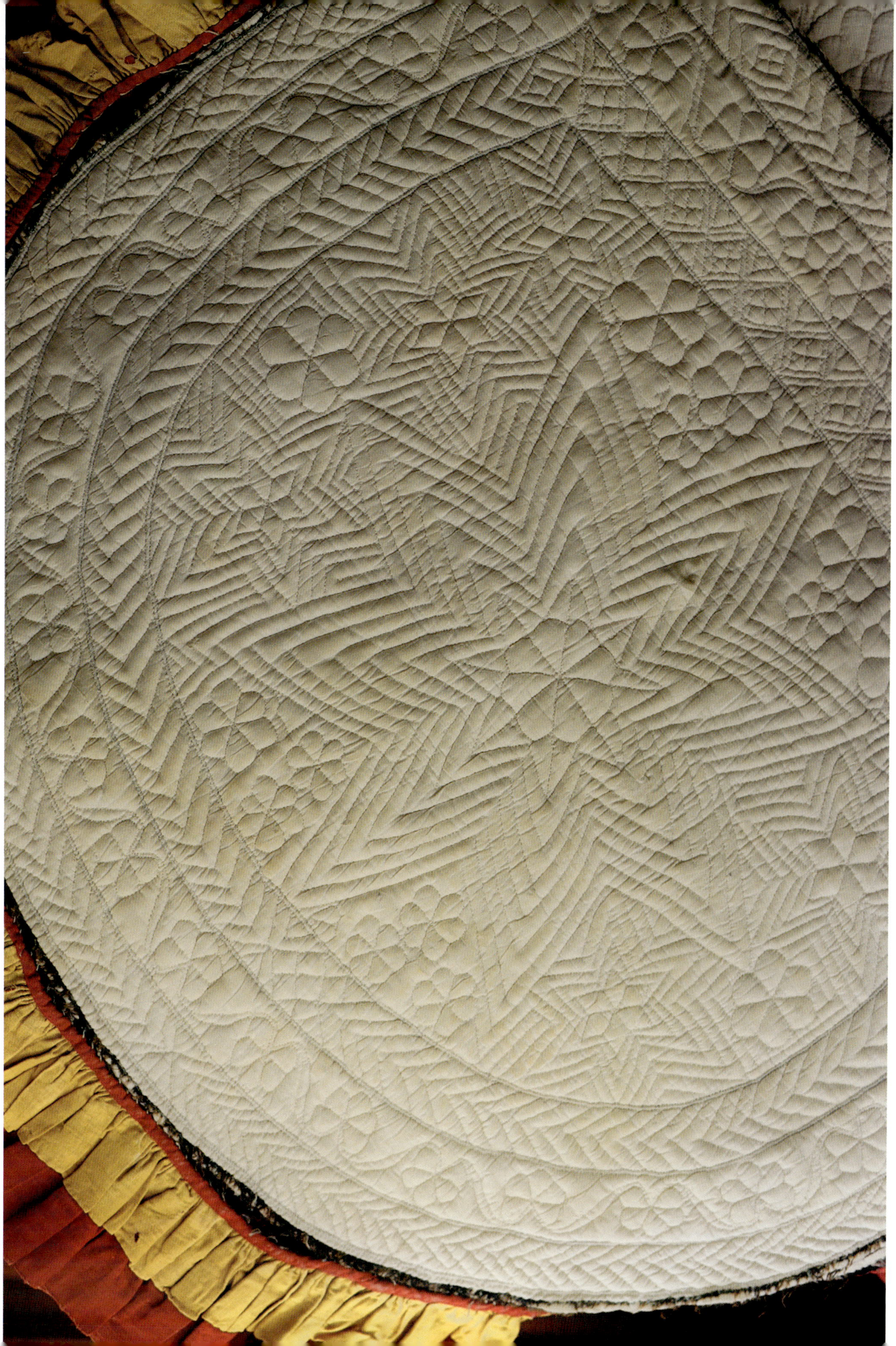

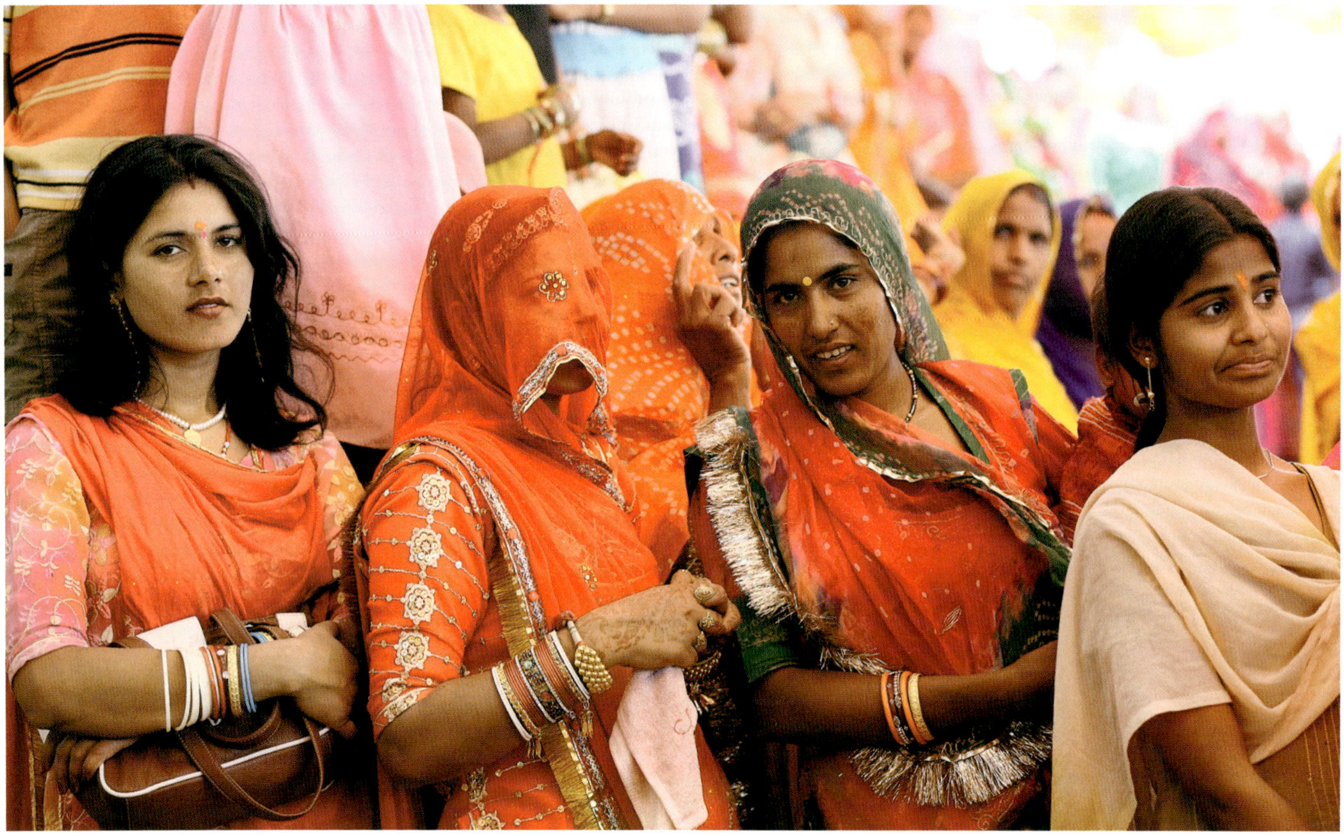

The city's craftsmen excel in brass and lacquer work, in *meenakari* and *kundan* jewellery designing and gem setting. The block prints and the 'bandhni' (tie-and-dye) prints; the 'gota' and the 'kinari' along with the famed 'zardozi' and 'zari' work reflect the bright and colourful Rajasthani culture. Rajasthani clothes are usually designed in bright colours like fuchsia, blue and orange. Women normally wear an ankle-length skirt and a top. A shawl or a light drape is used to cover the head, both for protection from the sun and maintenance of modesty. The most visible part of the traditional mens' outfit is the turban. The golden earrings that men wear make them look handsome and exotic.

The region appears to be more exotically oriental than other parts of India to a foreigner's eye. When you enter Rajasthan from Delhi on a bus for example, you can feel the change immediately. The landscape is dry and sandy, the people are handsome and the women's saris are very pretty. The city has interesting old temples,

The celebration of seventy weddings in the village of Diggi, onlookers and family members

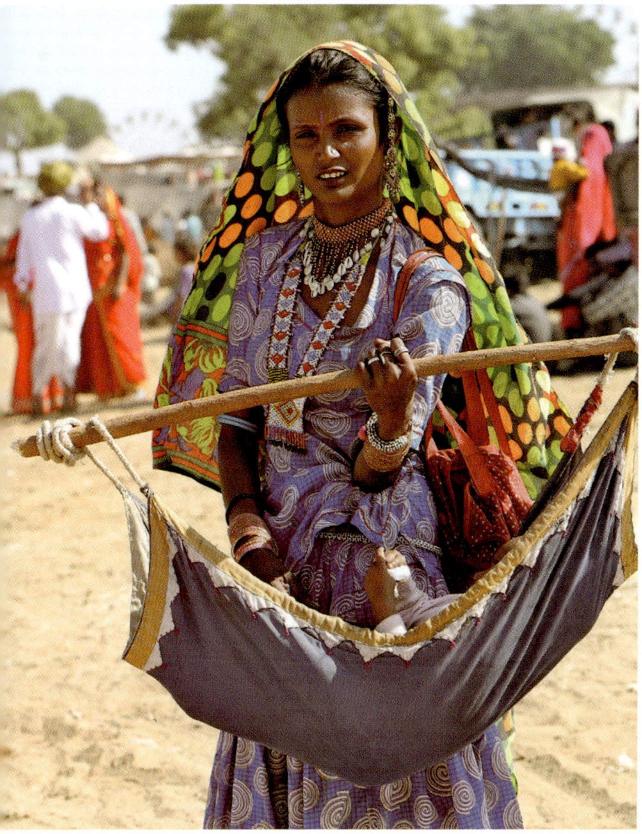

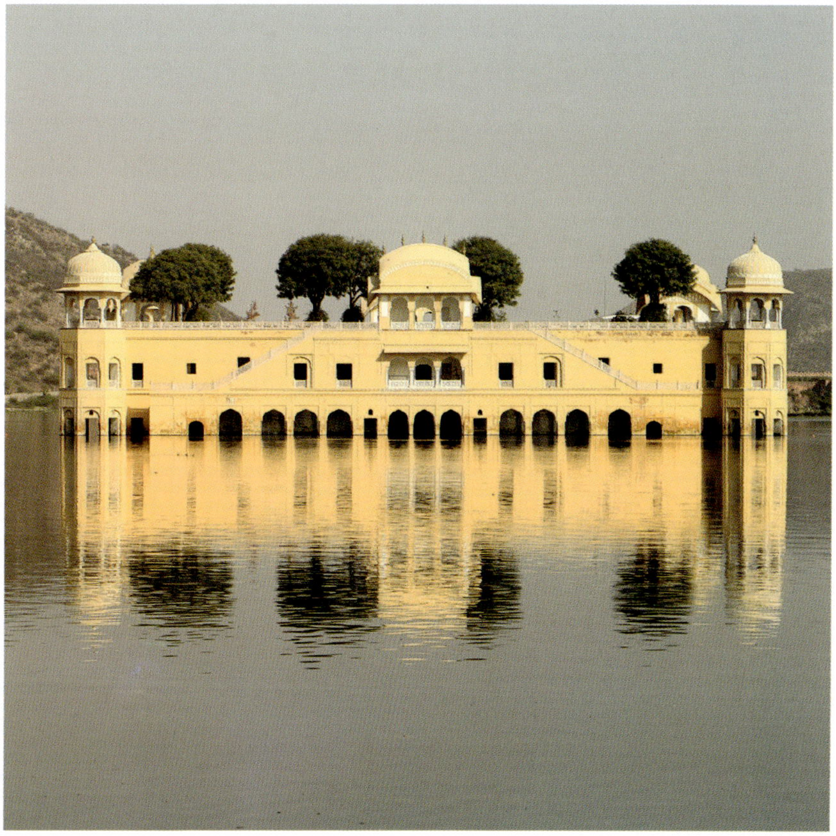

fairytale palaces and fabulous hotels. If you are interested in classy textiles and precious stones, Jaipur is surely your city.

The city is all about colours. The pink colour of the Pink City was used while the city was being built, to create an impression of the red sandstone buildings of Mughal cities. Its streets are full of life. As I passed by, rickshaws, dust from the desert, garlands of bright yellow marigold, bicycles, shops, carts laden with multi-coloured fruits, and moving frames of roadside temples, of vendors selling hot fried snacks and artisans lost in sculpting figurines out of marble slabs mingle to create one melting pot of visuals. And somehow, everybody looks incredibly good in Jaipur!

My tryst with Jaipur

I had been woven into the Jaipur fabric of life, ever since my first visit to the city 30 years ago. I do not recall any tuk tuk (auto rickshaw) from this visit to the city. Cycle rickshaws were my only means of transport at that time. They are soundless and environment-friendly vehicles. Travelling then, was quite a pleasant exercise and I enjoyed the peace and quiet about me while I moved across

Top : *Jal Mahal, Jaipur*

Top left: *Woman in tribal finery—an ankle-length skirt and a short top with her child in a makeshift hammock at the annual Pushkar fair*

the city, overwhelmed by its sights. Nothing much happened during this visit; I simply absorbed everything I saw around me. I had very high fever during my stay and was quite ill for a while but I did manage to see all the historical monuments that a first time visitor should see. I dutifully made the rounds of Amber Fort and Hawa Mahal, and I walked down the colourful and crowded bazaars, looking at the shops, savouring the unfamiliar but lovely atmosphere. I do remember buying some sarongs and not much else. Today I am amazed when I think of how little shopping I did on my first visit to Jaipur. The only business transaction I did at the time involved twenty-five pieces of mulmul printed with a paisley pattern and some gold print on it. I made sarongs out of the fabric, which I later carried to Mykonos in Greece. It seemed like an enormous order and made me feel very good about my busines capabilities.

I remember the flying peacocks in the garden of Khasa Kothi Hotel, where I stayed. There were other memorable events as well. One day I woke up and

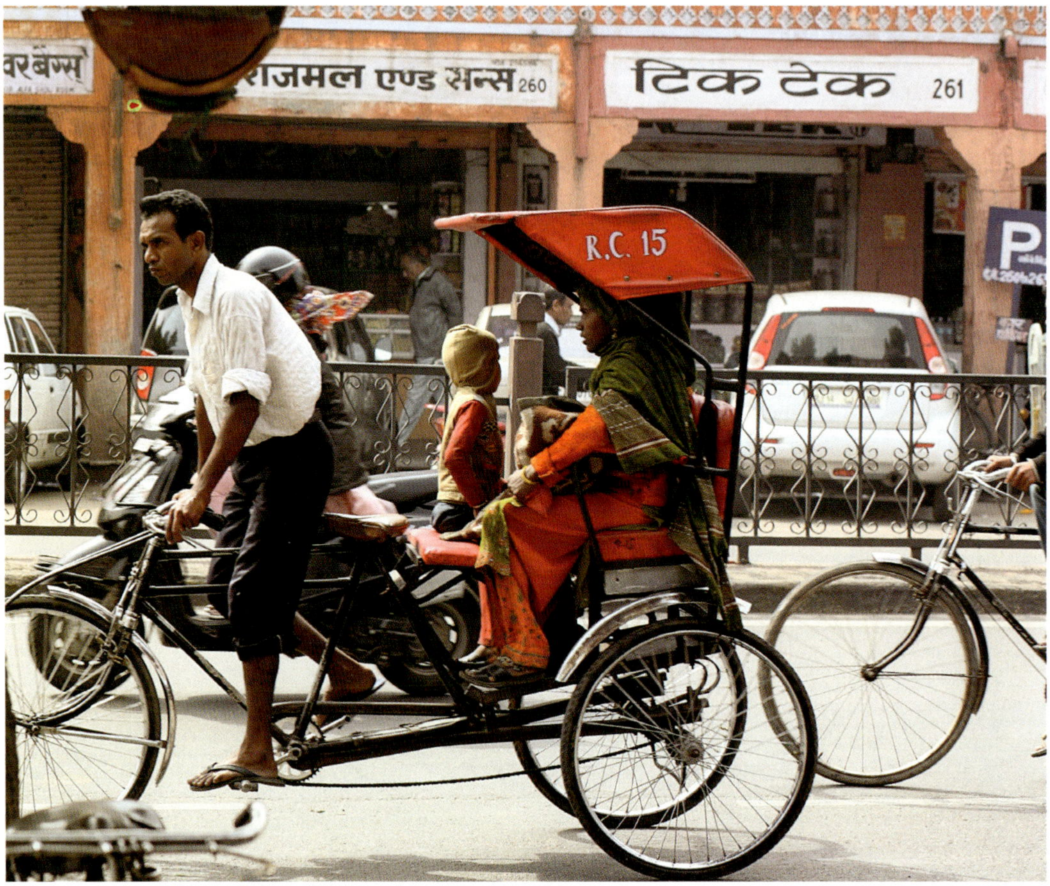

Cycle rickshaws are fast commuters in the Pink City

discovered an army man walking back and forth in front of my door carrying a big gun. I wondered for a moment whether I was under arrest but he turned out to be the guard of an Indian politician who happened to be my neighbour. Such incidents simply added more punch to my period of discovery.

I cruised the local bazaars as a practice and admired the wonderful textiles and art objects. It was almost like watching a play or a masquerade of sorts. I did not have a clue to what Jaipur really was, how many amazing and beautiful places it hid in its myriad corners, how many jewellers were strewn across the city, how many artists and artisans, marble carvers, wood carvers and sculptors, printers, embroiderers...the list was endless.

Coming back to Jaipur later always felt like returning to my hometown. Maybe it was my hometown, who knows... I once dreamed, before knowing Jaipur or Rajasthan and its ancient customs and rites that I lived in India, many years ago. I was sixteen years old and was dressed in a pink-red blouse and skirt with a drape over my head. I

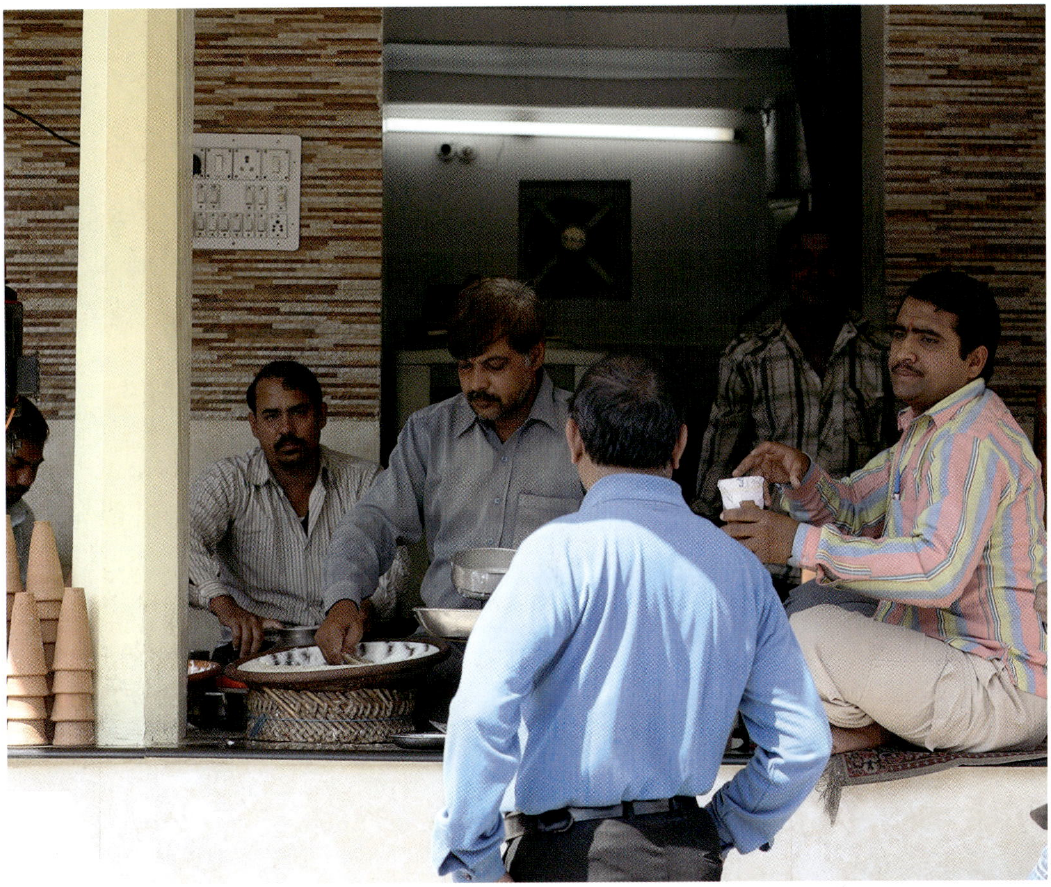

'Lassiwala' is a hotspot for both locals and tourists looking for good lassi *in Jaipur*

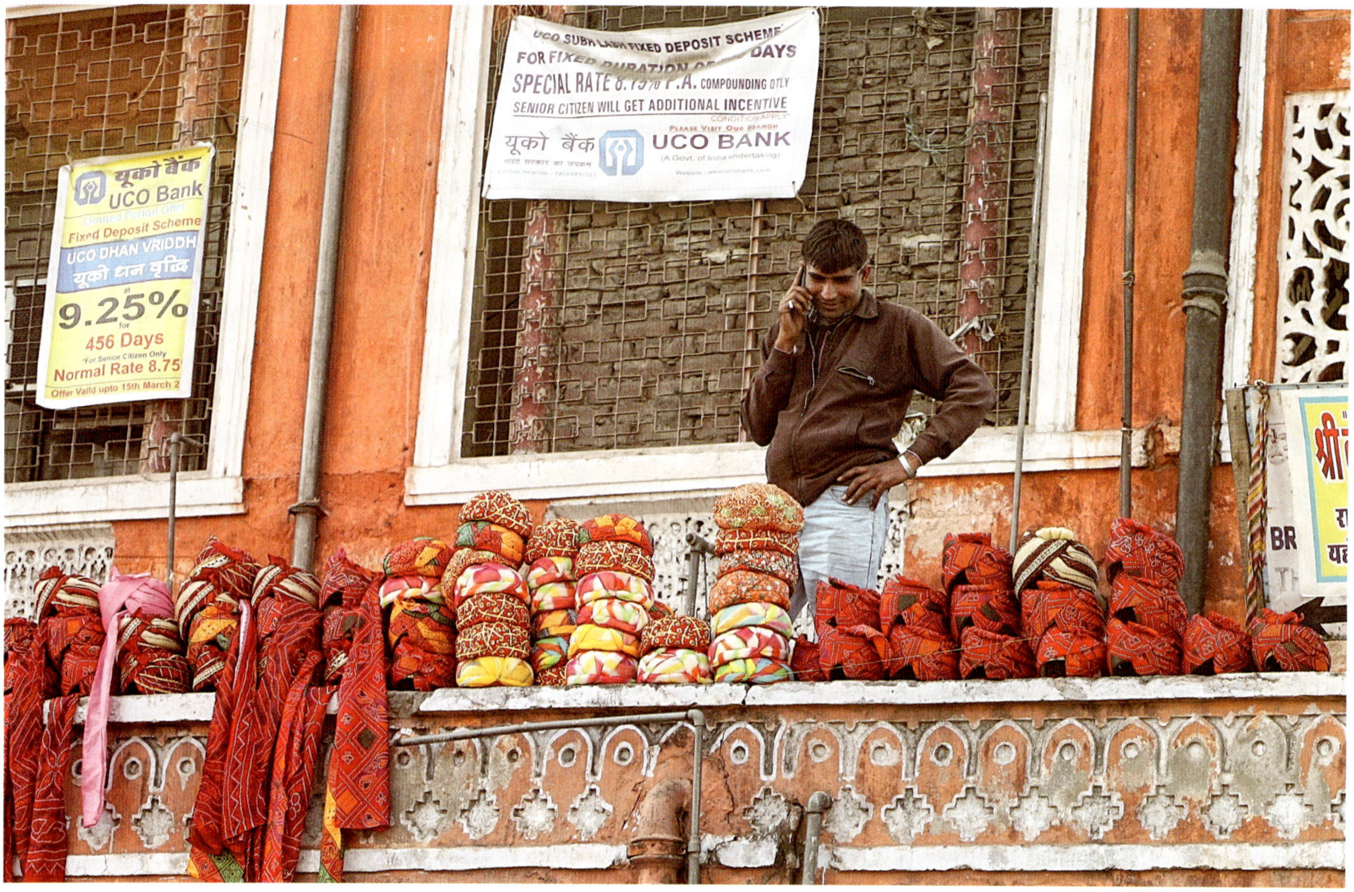

Colourful turbans on display by the roadside

was leaning against a pillar, looking at my dead husband, an older, handsome man. He was lying on a *lit de parade*. I knew that I was supposed to step into the pyre with my husband but I flatly refused...and woke up. Much later, I read about the ancient custom of 'sati' (the custom of self-immolation by the widow in her deceased husband's funeral pyre) in Rajasthan, which has long been abolished by the law of the land.

I began to discover Jaipur more consciously, on my subsequent visits. However, it never occured to me to use any guide-book. I met people and through them, the city unfolded. Today I see people coming to Jaipur for the first time and getting to know 'everything' about the city in two weeks! Shops, cargo services, hairdressers, factories... they have the names and contacts on the tips of their fingers. I am happy without this 'instant knowledge'; I would rather linger on my knowledge imbibed from walking the lanes and by-lanes of the city and watching life flow by. After all these years I still look around for something new that I may learn, for some new discovery.

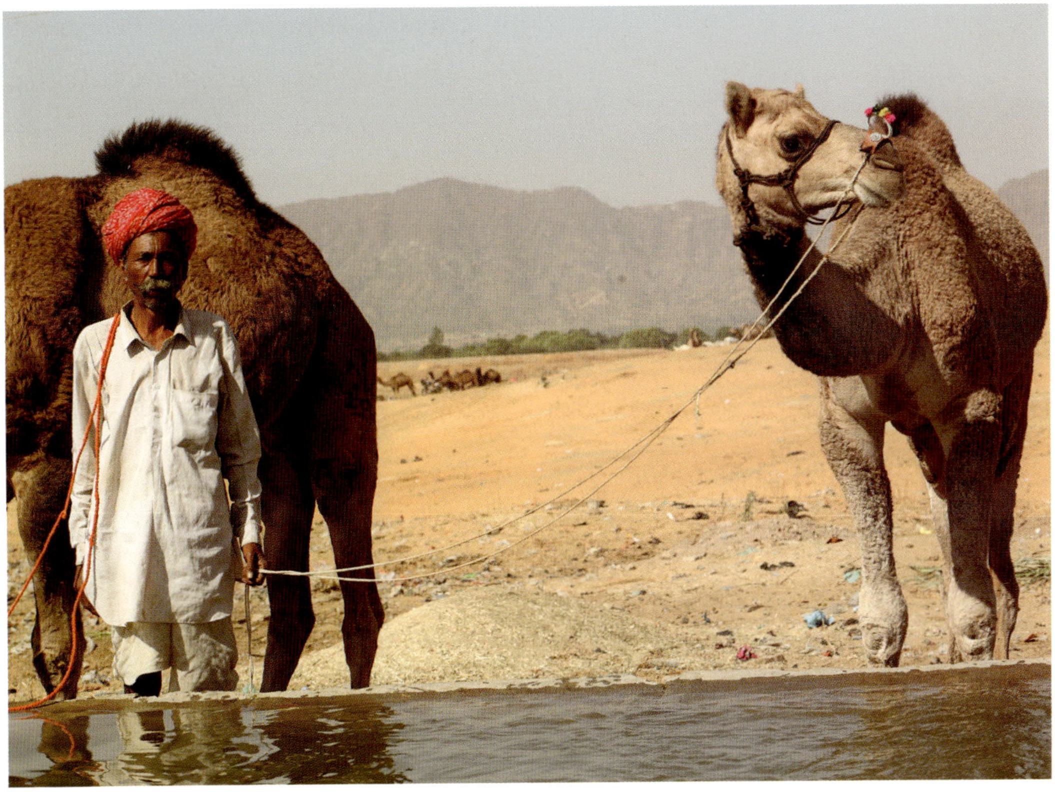

Arya Niwas Hotel where I usually stay when I am in Jaipur, is a popular, family-managed hotel located in the heart of the city. It is a renovated haveli, or mansion and the ambience has been carefully retained, most of the repainting having been done using natural colours. The charming little garden and the quiet in the air make for a pleasant stay.

The hotel was quite the 'centre of the world', as somebody once said in jest. There you could meet anybody from across the wide world. Business people from all over the world came and stayed at the hotel. I made friends with people from Croatia, South Africa, the United States, Greece, Ukraine, Taiwan… I could go on. This was a real Babel Tower. Some of my new acquaintances made jewellery, others designed and produced garments. There were dancers, photographers and yoga teachers among them too, with many an interesting life story to tell. Most of the visitors were extensive travellers. Some were owners of important trading companies but still hippies at heart. Honestly, it was quite a melee!

At breakfast every morning, I witnessed a certain kind of fashion show. People sat together and talked, admired or envied each others' outfits, exchanged

Camels out for a drink, against a rugged, semi-desert landscape near Pushkar

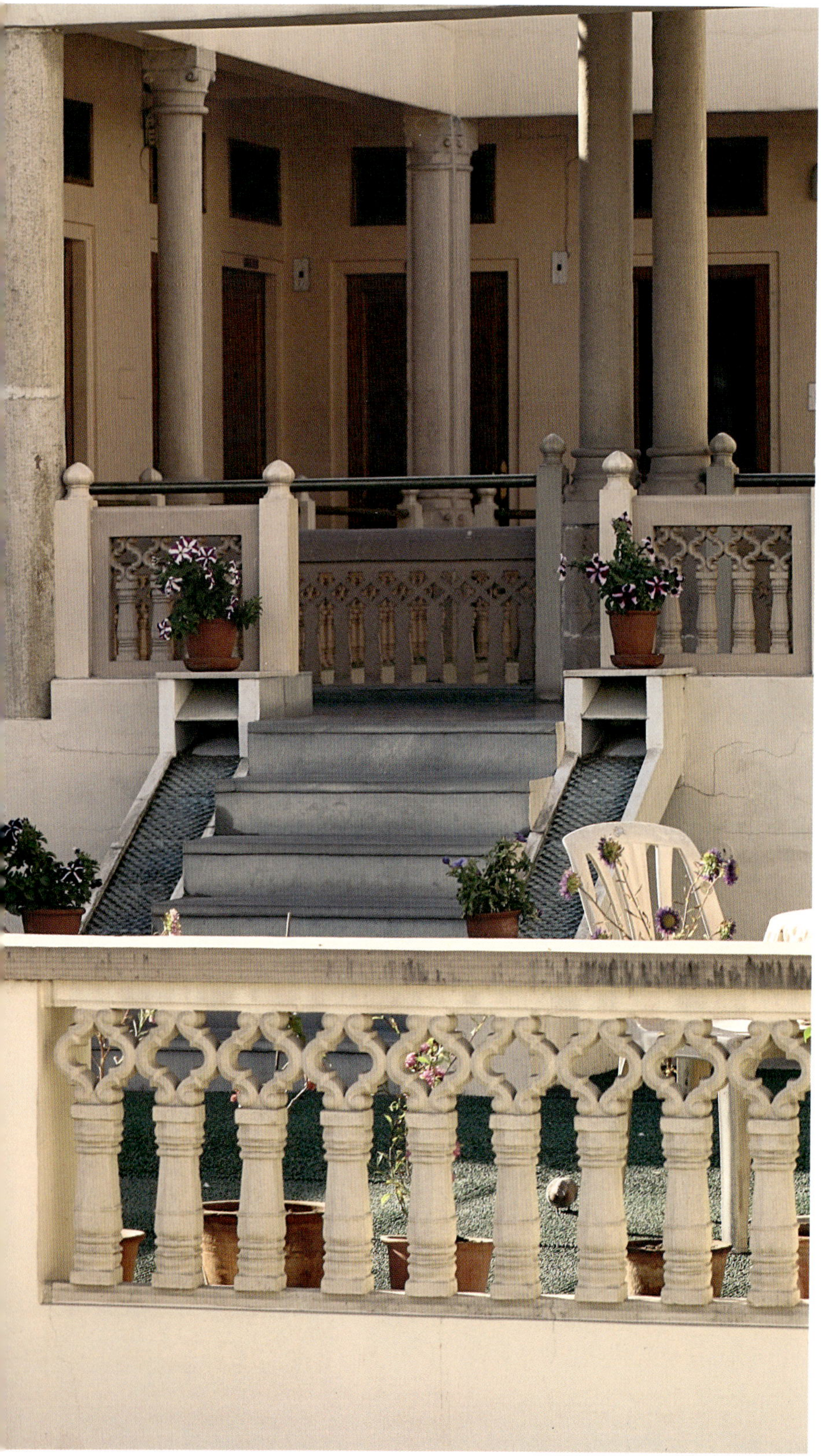

information about work experiences and production houses and complained about people who promised but did not show up with their samples in time. Here you learned about important landmarks and received helpful tip-offs—where to get the best massage, which rickshaw driver was clever and had the right addresses on the back of his palm. We discussed how the rickshaw drivers sometimes drove us crazy and how perhaps we did the same to them. But we co-existed; we were dependent on each other. We had 'our' tailors, dyers, shoemakers… some became dear friends, like my tailor, Nanag Ram Saini. His workshop was like an international club. My 'important' friends routinely asked me in jest, whether I had been to my tailor that day, and I most often than not, answered 'Yes'.

I made friends with several of my tailor's regular customers. There was an American lady who I thought resembled the animated movie version of the princess Pocahontas–the fabled Red Indian chief's daughter–with whom I struck a cordial note. There was a lady who came to Jaipur to play polo. She came to the tailor to get comfortable trousers stitched for horse riding. She also wanted specially tailored underwear embellished with lace for the same sport! I met a doctor who advised me on my broken finger and a journalist who worked for a large media house.

My tailor's 'guruji', as they called him, was a master tailor. He was ninety-six years old and lived alone. He visited my tailor every day and sat on a chair, always very smartly dressed and he was actually still very good looking. He sat quietly, deep in thought. Other people came because they liked my tailor–a very generous and friendly personage. I was often invited to lunch when I went there to try on a pair of trousers for example! We would sit 'comfortably' crouched in a small corner between the stairs and the porch and share food brought by his seamstress. He would then see me off courteously at the gate, hailing a rickshaw for me. I often stopped by Amrapali, the famous jeweller who also sold reasonably-priced but nonetheless beautiful pieces of jewellery. Unfortunately, it was difficult to resist the temptation. I finally realised that in Jaipur it was best perhaps, for your pocket, not to leave your hotel or step on to the road. As soon as you went out you found something you would love to buy. Excessive luggage at the airport on the return flight is a haunting bad dream I and others like me still have.

Another attraction of the city is Jaipur Polo. I like the graphic look of the two

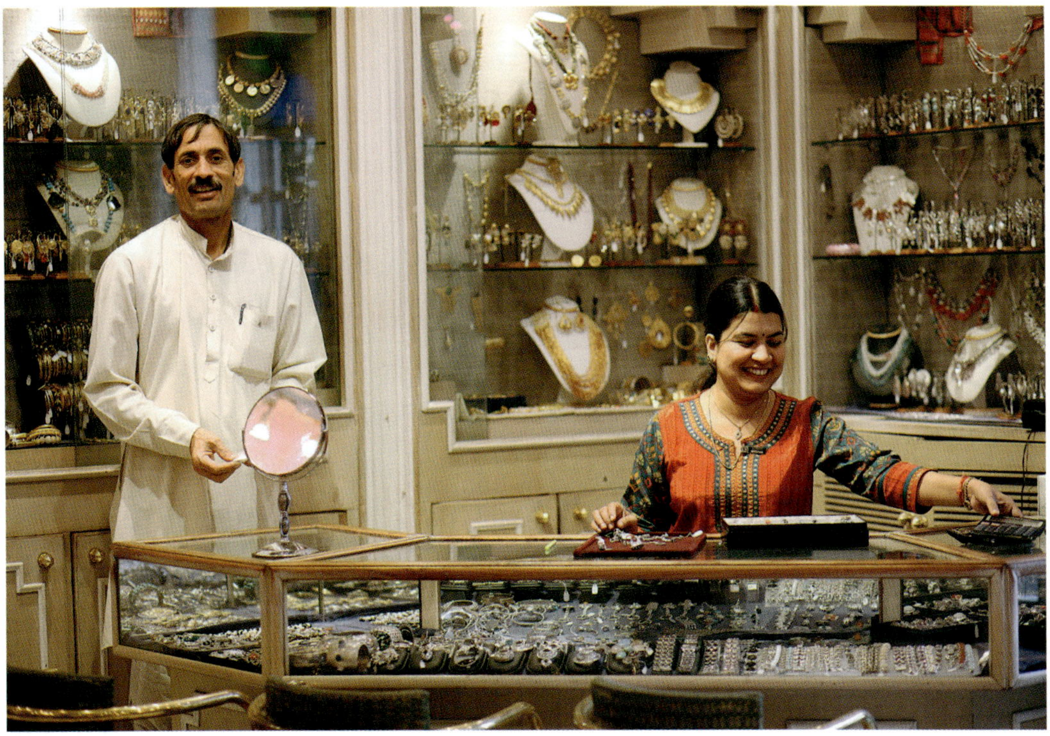

Jewellery display at Amrapali where filmstars from Hollywood and Bollywood are among its customers. Jaipur is a specialised centre for jewellery production, particularly Kundan *work. A large number of traditional jewellery is made here, studded with emerald, diamond, pearl, garnet, agate and lapis lazuli. An entire market called the Johari Bazaar is dedicated to jewellers*

Facing page: *Arya Niwas Hotel, Jaipur*

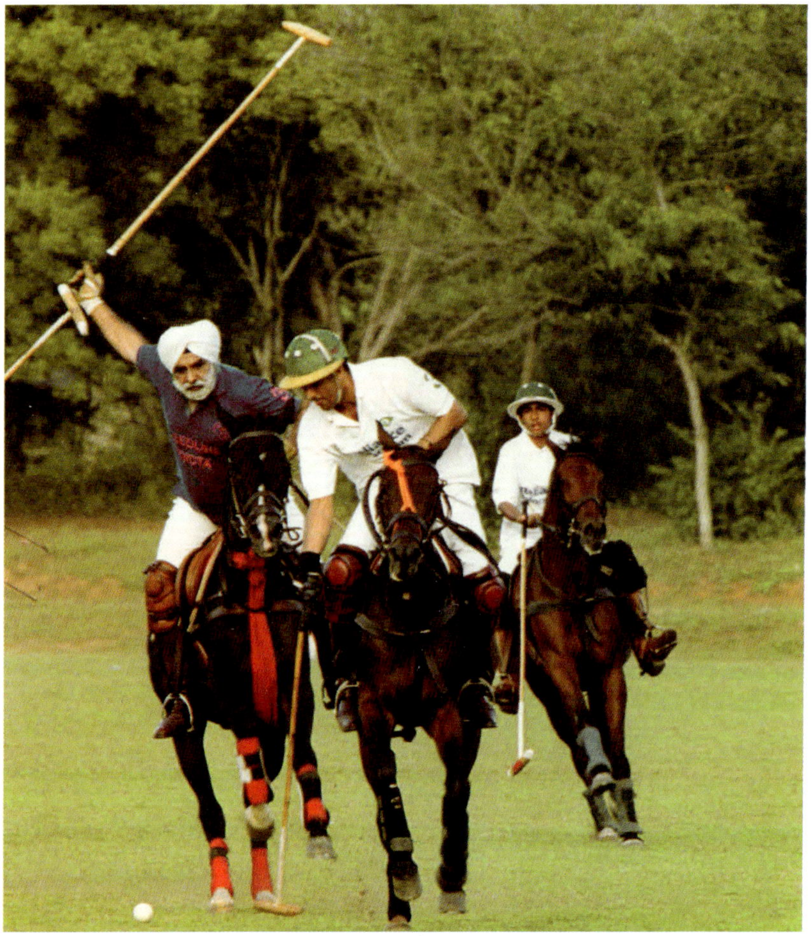

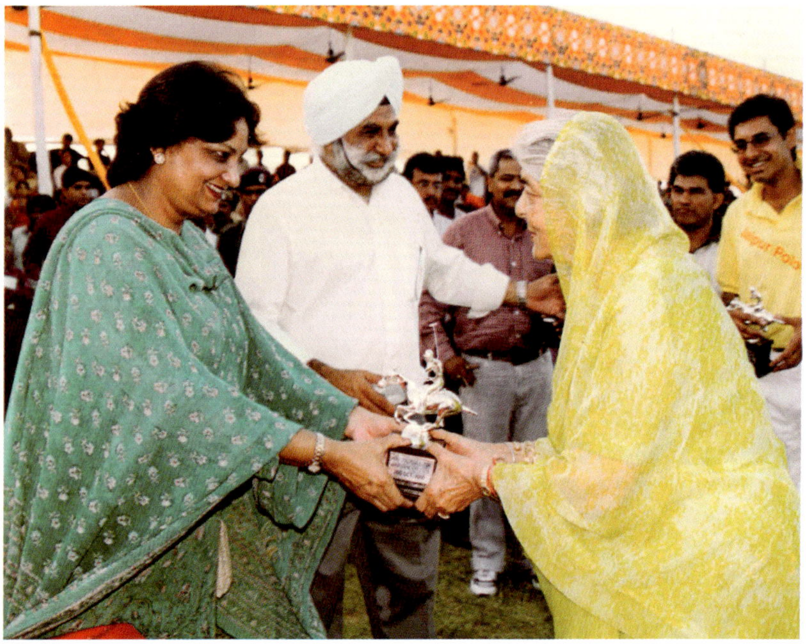

words. Jaipur and polo some how look good together. The first time I attended and watched a polo match in my life was in Jaipur. It was an amazingly casual and breezy affair. Elegant certainly, and a smart game with a royal air about it, but held without much fuss. I was pleasantly surprised by the fact that watching the match was free of cost! The Maharaja, Bhawani Singh comes by sometimes and sits next to you. I like the Jaipur polo ground because you sit quite near the game, which is a great feeling. I don't know much about polo, but it is exciting to watch the match and feel the speed, look at the horses and admire the players. The Jaipur Polo Team won the prestigious World Cup in 1933 and received other awards. The last ruling Maharaja of Jaipur–Sawai Man Singh II–was an eminent polo player and a notable sportsman. He met with an unfortunate accident playing polo in Cirencester, England and died the same day.

Opposite the polo grounds you have the fabulous Rambagh Palace Hotel, which was previously the late Maharaja's home. Built in 1835 on a modest scale, it was a royal guesthouse—a pleasure resort and hunting lodge. It was converted into a palace in 1925 and subsequently turned into the residence of the royal

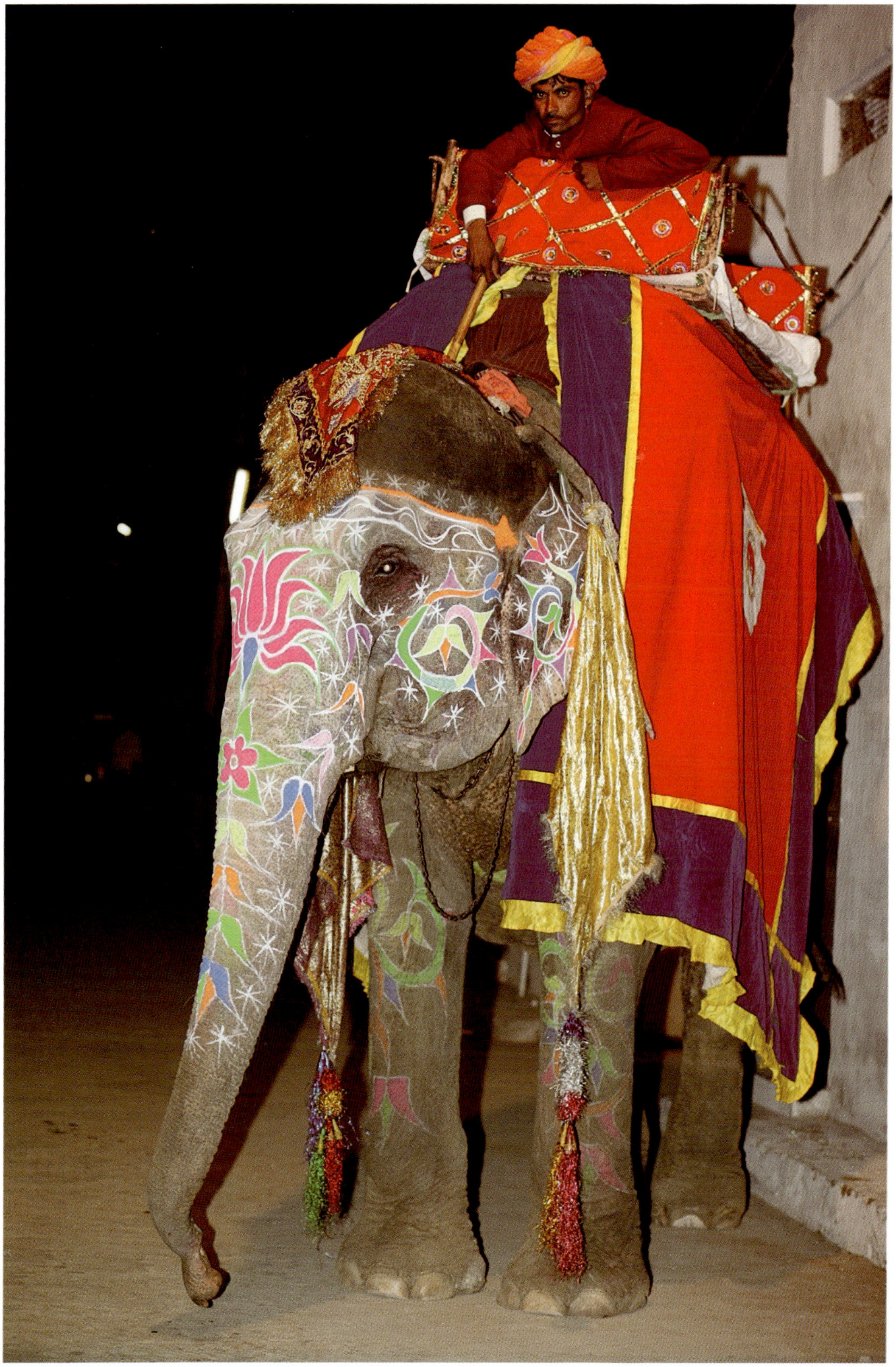

Painted elephant at the Diggi Palace Hotel in Jaipur

Facing page: *Polo match in progress at the Jaipur Polo Club. Capt. KS Garcha on horseback in turban is a recipient of the prestigious Arjuna Award, India's highest national award for outstanding sportspersons (above); HH Maharani Gayatri Devi distributing prizes at a polo match (below)*

Facing page courtesy (above and below): Capt. KS Garcha

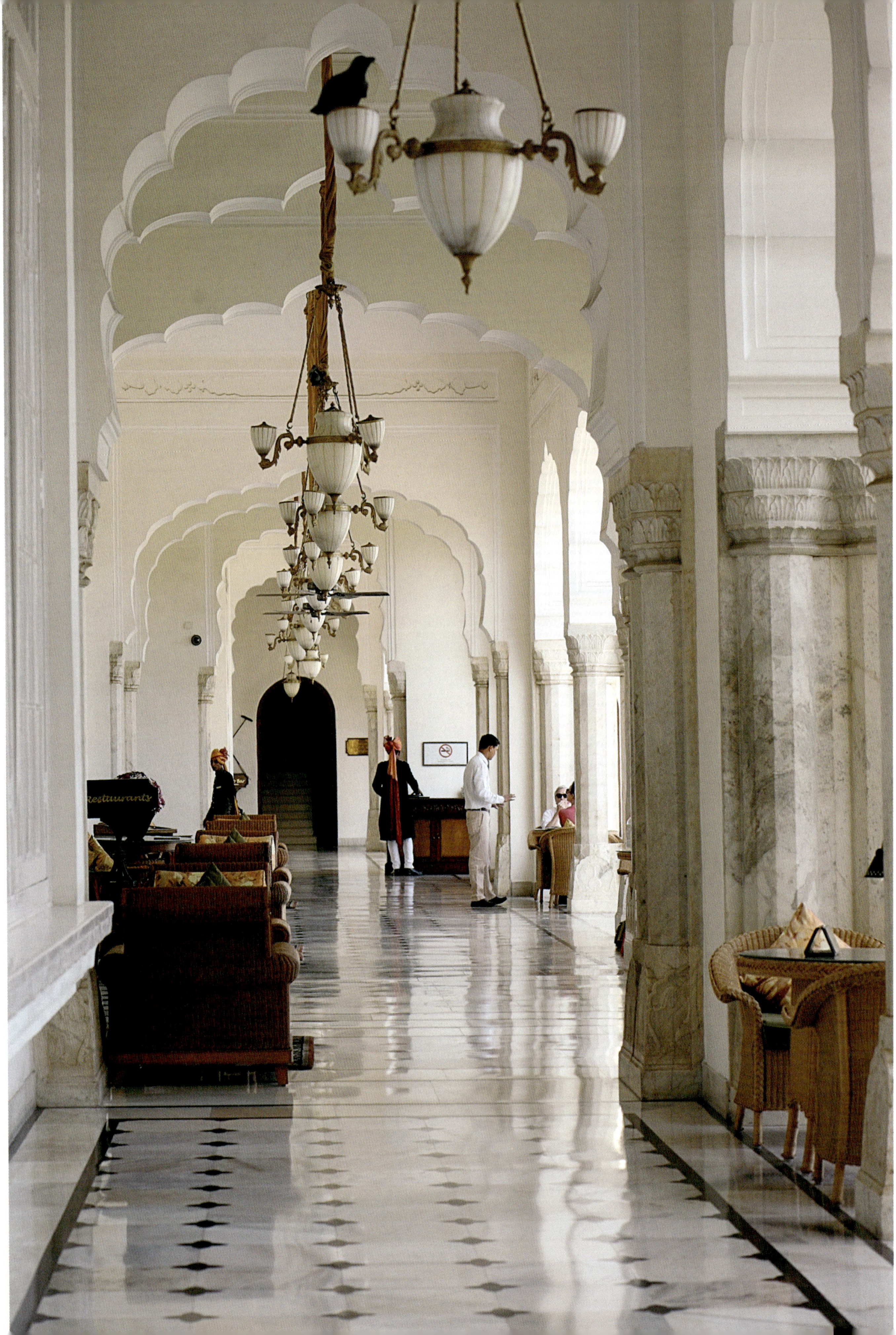
Restaurants

family. In 1957 the palace was converted into a luxury hotel by Maharaja Sawai Man Singh II.

It really is a wonderful place although some parts of it have been redone to make it better, an exercise which usually produces quite the opposite results, as we all know. However, it is still nice to go there for a cup of tea, breathe clean air in the garden and relax. It is considered the 'crown jewel'of the Taj Group of hotels.

Nowadays Jaipur is not a sleepy town any more. There are fairs, festivals, conferences and film shoots with famous movie stars. The Jaipur Literature Festival held usually in January every year at the Diggi Palace hotel has recently evolved as one of the most important literary festivals in Asia. I was recently invited to the National Convention of Interior Designers and Architects in Jaipur, where I was once again exposed to the fact that Jaipur has incredible craftsmen and artists who work for the most famous and sophisticated interior design projects in India and abroad. Over the years I have also made close friends in this town. They stay by me. Somehow, the name 'Jaipur' has a special warmth and opulence like the perfume of Boucheron.

But as with everything else, Jaipur is changing, tidying up. Camels, cows and buffaloes are disappearing from the streets where new glitzy buildings are coming up. The Pink City is now a city on the move.

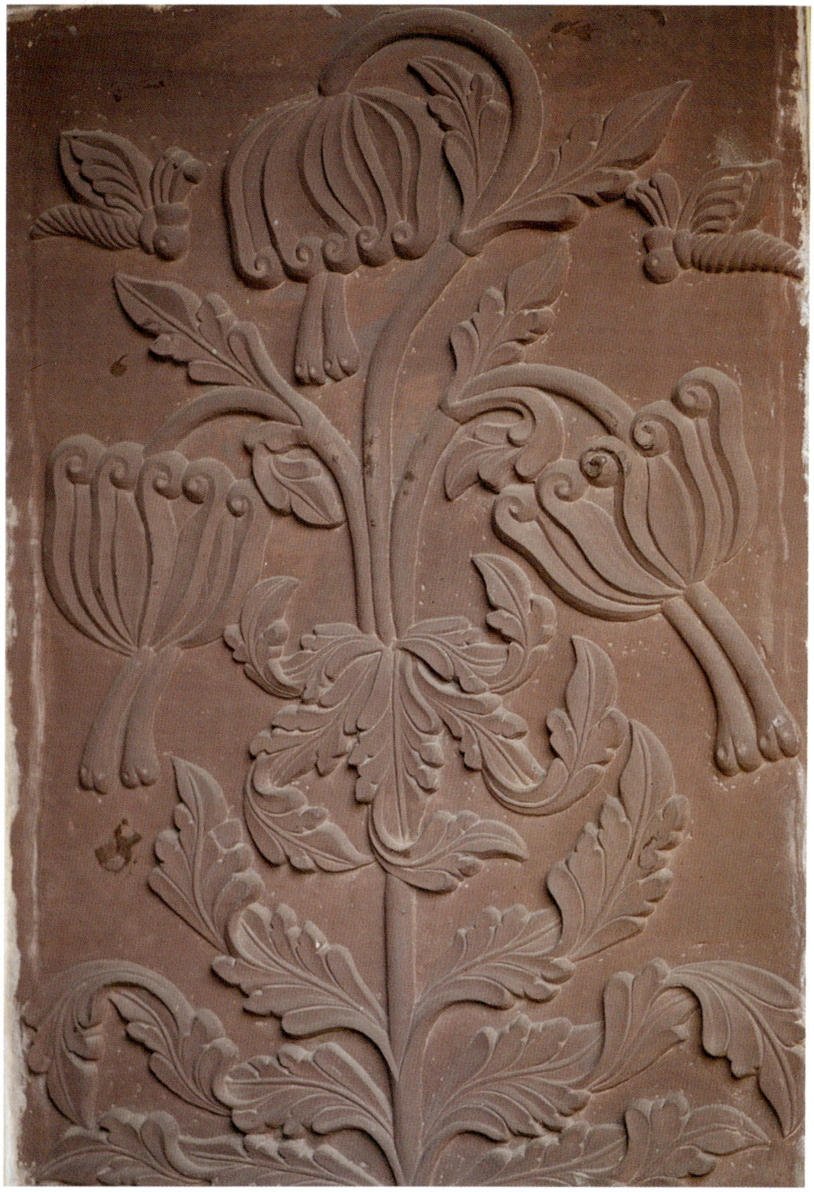

A stone relief from Nana ki Haveli, with traditional floral motifs

Facing page: *Veranda of Rambagh Palace, Jaipur. The queen of Jaipur built this pleasure retreat in 1835. The Maharaja of Jaipur made the palace his royal home in 1925. It was converted into a heritage hotel in 1972*

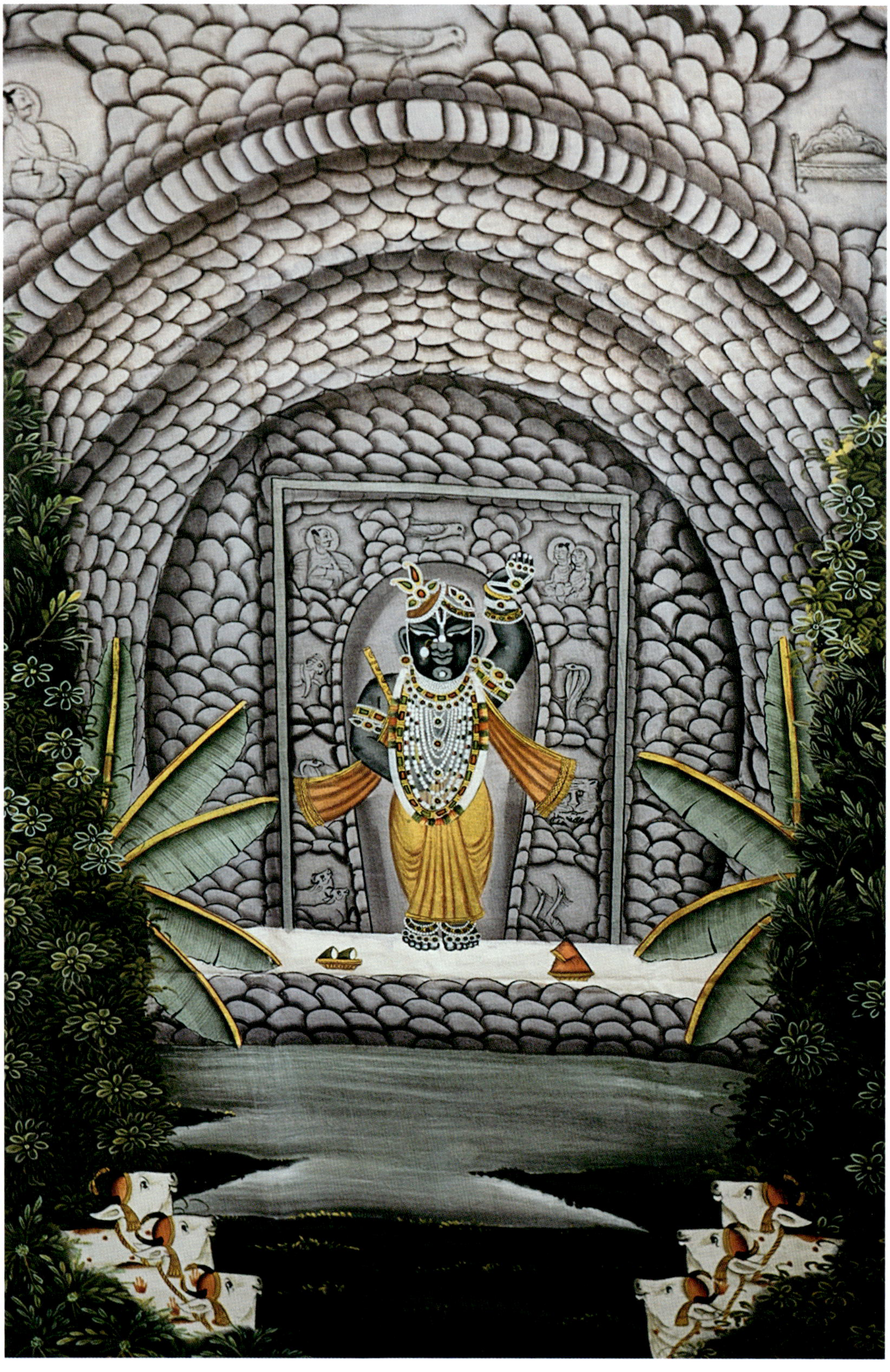

Image of Lord Krishna Shrinathji; pichwai *by Narendra Art, Udaipur. A* pichwai *is a ritual art form—brilliantly coloured painting that often adorns temple walls in Rajasthan. The use of rich and vibrant colours provides* pichwais *a distinctive quality. The themes revolve around Lord Shri Krishna in the form of Shrinathji. Udaipur and Nathdwara are famous for their* pichwai *paintings*

A quilt is a bedcover made by firmly stitching together two layers of cloth or patchwork with a soft and warm substance, such as wool or cotton, between them. Quilting is the act of stitching or process of making a quilt. The quilting bee is a social gathering of the women of a community for working on quilts. The original purpose behind a quilting bee was to enlist the help of several people in order to get the quilt finished much faster.

While working with the Jaipur quilt, I often got the opportunity to look beyond and extend my vista to textiles. A Krishna devotee who was the owner of a shop selling miniature paintings invited me to accompany him and his son to an ancient Krishna temple in Nathdwara, some 40 km outside Udaipur to see a famous statue of child Krishna sleeping under a quilt. We started our journey around three o'clock in the morning on 1 January, 2008. It was quite terrifying as I was swept into a mass of devotees inside the temple but I realised I could not go back any more. I had to proceed with the others and finally pass the altar. Since Krishna is treated like a human, he is bathed regularly, dressed in rich clothes and diamond jewellery during the day, and at night put to sleep under a quilt.

I was happy to have seen this site once I had survived the rush. It took a few hours of waiting barefoot in the temple on cold stone floors and I had probably turned into an icicle! It felt wonderful afterwards to have started the new year with a visit to the temple, and the hot ginger tea that we bought outside the temple tasted divine.

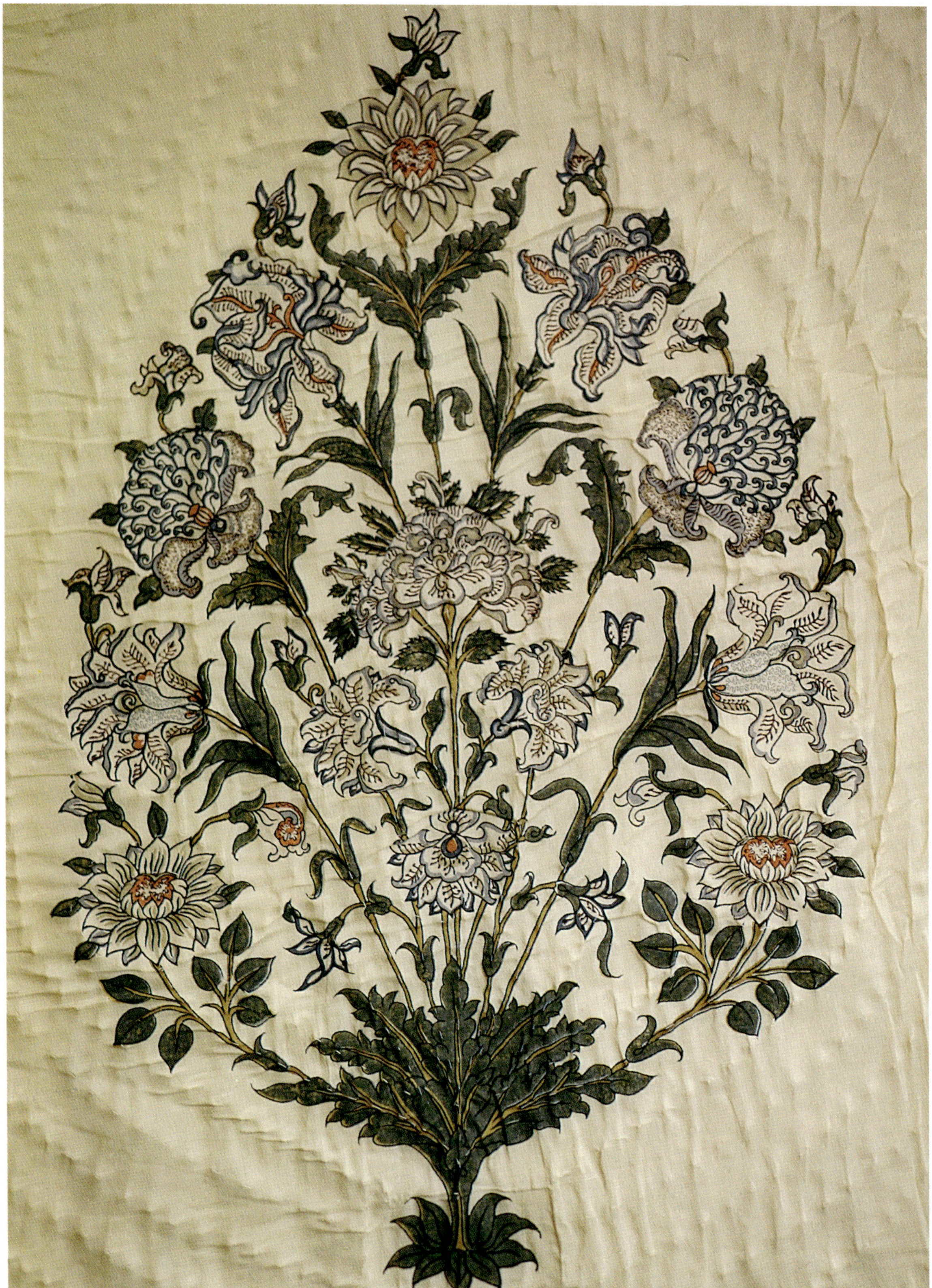

I asked Chandramani Singh, the textile expert in Jaipur, about how much people knew of the history of Jaipur quilts. 'Not much,' she said. Later she helped me to source the available information. The Maharaja Sawai Man Singh II Museum's catalogue, which she had written, also provided me with relevant facts

Of quilts and quilting

The technique of quilting is older than the form in which the quilt is used today. In tune with the popular saying, 'Necessity is the mother of all invention,' the quilt's place of origin must have been a cotton-growing region, where warm clothes would be needed as protection from cold. In India, quilting has been in vogue from ancient times as there are frequent references to the *dagala*, a quilted upper garment, in Indian literature. Surdas, a medieval saint poet, who sang in praise of Krishna, a celebrated Hindu deity, often refers to it. By the seventeenth century a community known as *dhuniya* (carder) had already established itself as a professional group in Indian society.

Michel Biehn writes in his introduction to Kathryn Berenson's book, *Boutis de Provence*, that quilting was one of civilisation's streams that started somewhere in China a long time ago and passed through India and Persia to arrive in the south of Europe and in the New World. It stopped for a while in Provence, France, before it travelled further north again.

Facing page: *'Jaipur Bouquet' with chrysanthemums, lilies, roses and dahlias. Block print by Brigitte Singh*

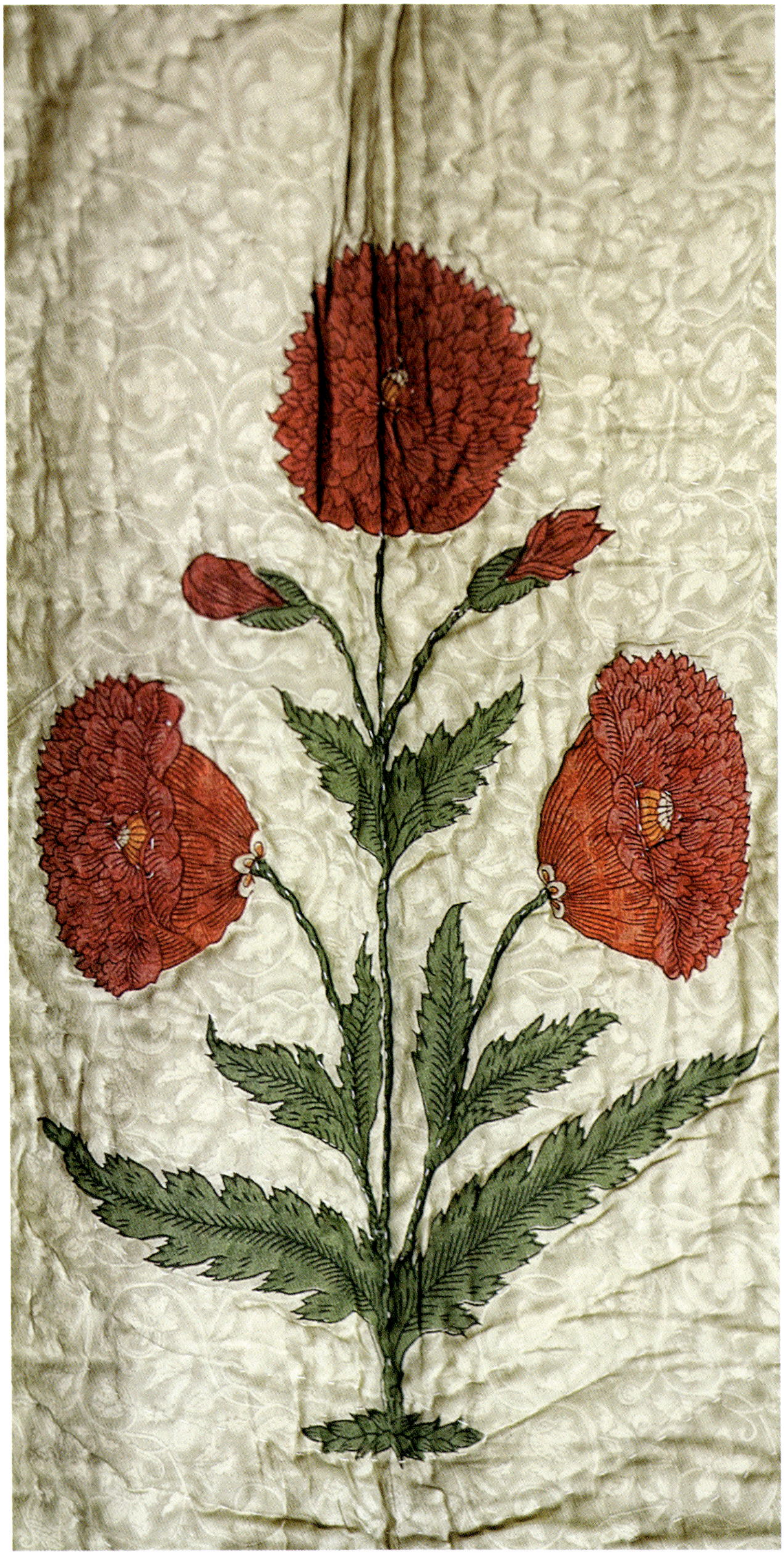

In her essay 'Quilts, the Great American Art', Patricia Mainardi says that the origin of quilting can be traced to Syria, Egypt, India and China. The quilting tradition came to America with the first lot of immigrant women who often copied English embroidery patterns.

However the technique of quilting was already known in Italy and France in the Middle Ages. The Victoria and Albert Museum in London has an extraordinary Sicilian stuffed-work quilt, dating back to around 1395. It is decorated with scenes from the life of the legendary Tristan.

According to Judy Wentworth of The Antique Textile Company and the author of *Quilts*, London's British Museum has a small ivory figure of a king, dating back to around 3400 BC, whose robe has carvings resembling a diamond-quilted pattern. Pieced silk patchwork used as votives has been found in India datable from the sixth to the ninth centuries AD.

Quilting in ancient India

Ample evidence of the ancient textiles of India are drawn from the various sculptures belonging to the Gupta Age (end of the third century AD to the middle of the fifth century AD) as well as from ancient murals, as in the Ajanta caves of the first and the second centuries

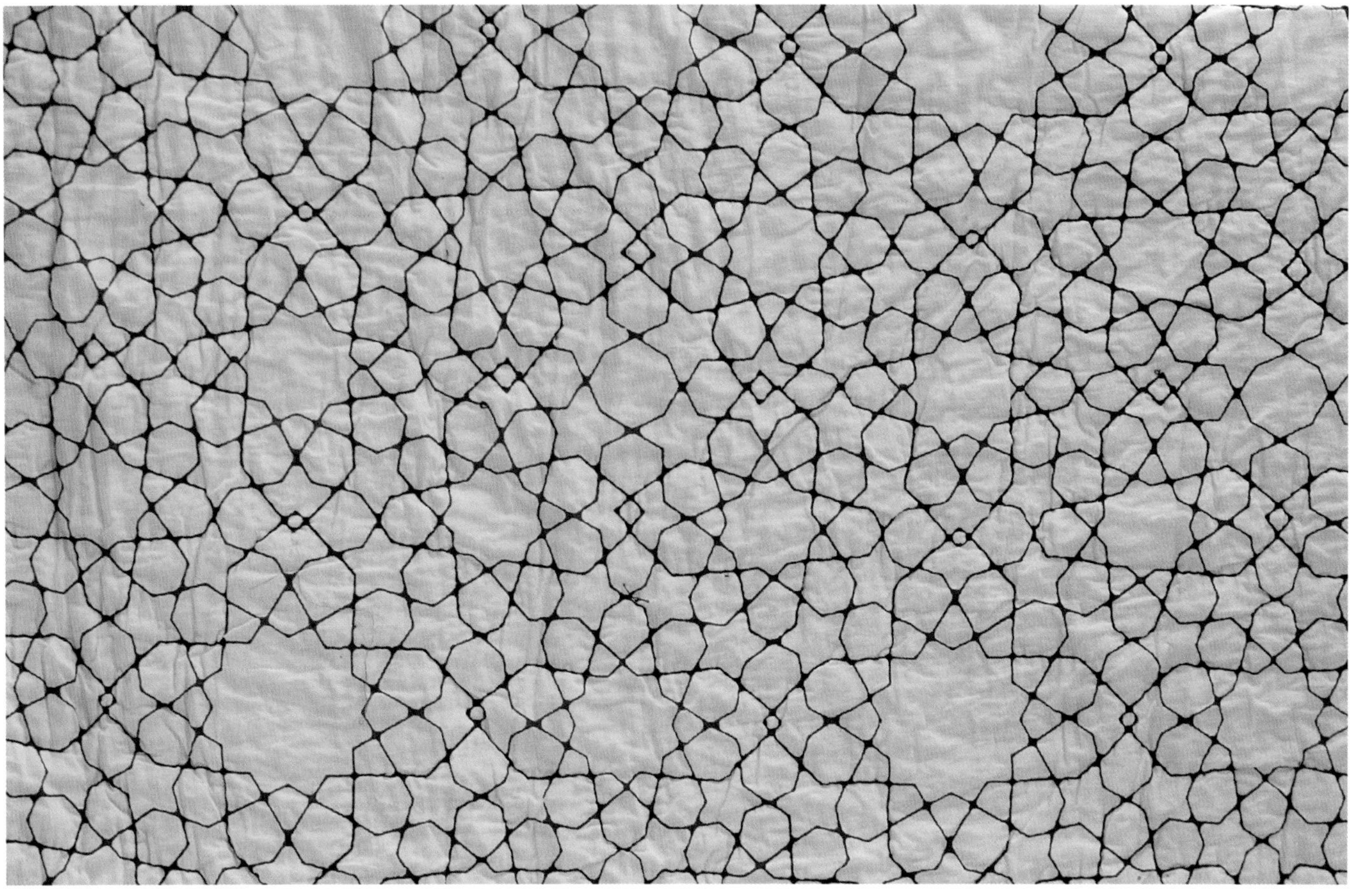

Stylish contemporary jalli *design on quilt created by contemporary designers of Jaipur*

Facing page: *The red Mughal poppy motif on an off-white background lends a rich look to the fabric. From Brigitte Singh's collection*

AD. There are some Hindu examples of stitched garments, primarily worn by the warrior class. Many depictions portray a tunic–short-sleeved and about knee-length–which appears to be quilted in a vertical striped pattern (pre-seventh century AD).

The origin of quilting in India can also be connected to Vishnuism's (the path of thought or belief followed by the Vaishnava sect—worshippers of Lord Vishnu) strict vegetarian rules, which developed in the beginning of the sixteenth century. Chandramani Singh explains that during this time the use of leather and wool was banned by certain religious sects in India preaching non-violence and strict vegetarianism. To protect themselves from the cold, people started quilting clothes, covers for animals, work clothes and bedcovers. They also quilted curtains, floor-spreads and blinds either to preserve the heat or to keep the heat out, depending on the season.

Quilted garments, curtains and quilts are known as *razai* in India. Quilts made of cashmere wool or expensive brocade were used by rich households. As most textiles

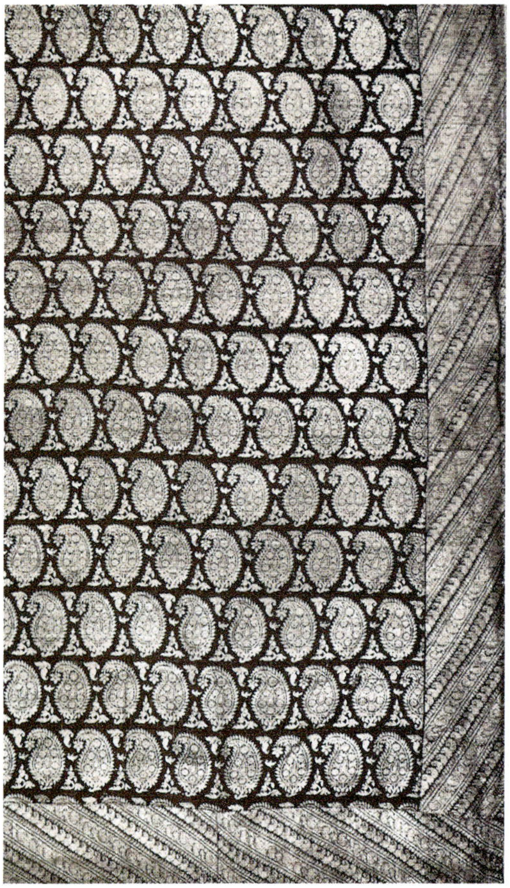 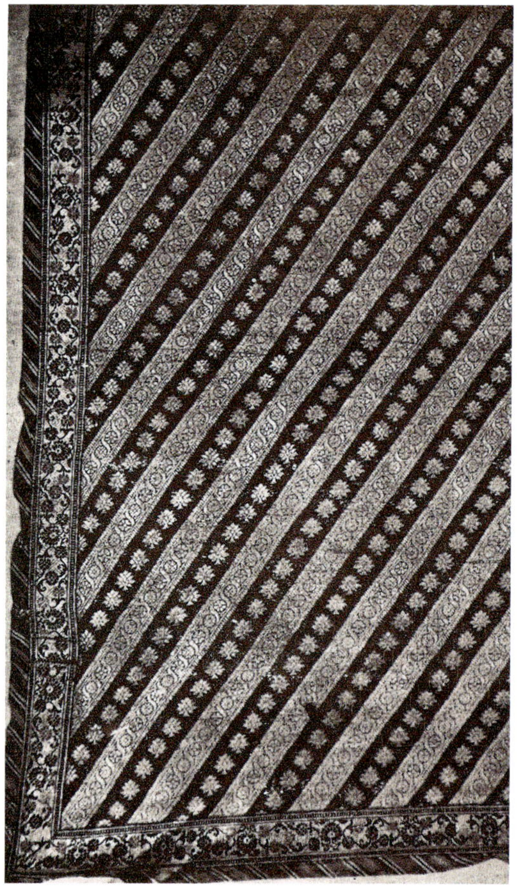

Quilts in Benaras brocade, made in Jaipur, circa 1882 (left) and circa 1850 (right)

Facing page: *Occidental interpretations of exotic motifs. Around 1792, the famous French textile manufacturer du Jouy sent designs with occidental floral motifs to India to lend a more exotic touch to them. The motif outline was inspired by fish scales*

are delicate material and they disintegrate easily, quilts made of cotton and sheer fabric like batiste were easily destroyed.

However the Maharaja Sawai Man Singh II Museum in Jaipur, has a very well-preserved and well-documented collection of quilts. The museum's collection owns a quilt from the later part of the seventeenth century, which was probably created in Amber. Two other quilts dating back to the end of the eighteenth century had been created in Jaipur from rich Benarasi brocade. A number of *sujani*s–bedspreads made of old and used cloth–are an interesting part of the collection. *Sujani*s were used in every household. To make one, four or five layers of saris or dhotis were stitched together, sometimes with new material on the top and decorative motifs were embroidered on it.

The east to west journey

An extract from *Dictionary of Needlework* by Caulfield and Saward (1885) reads: 'The Indian style of quilting was brought to Europe by the Portuguese and spread over the continent. French quilting was

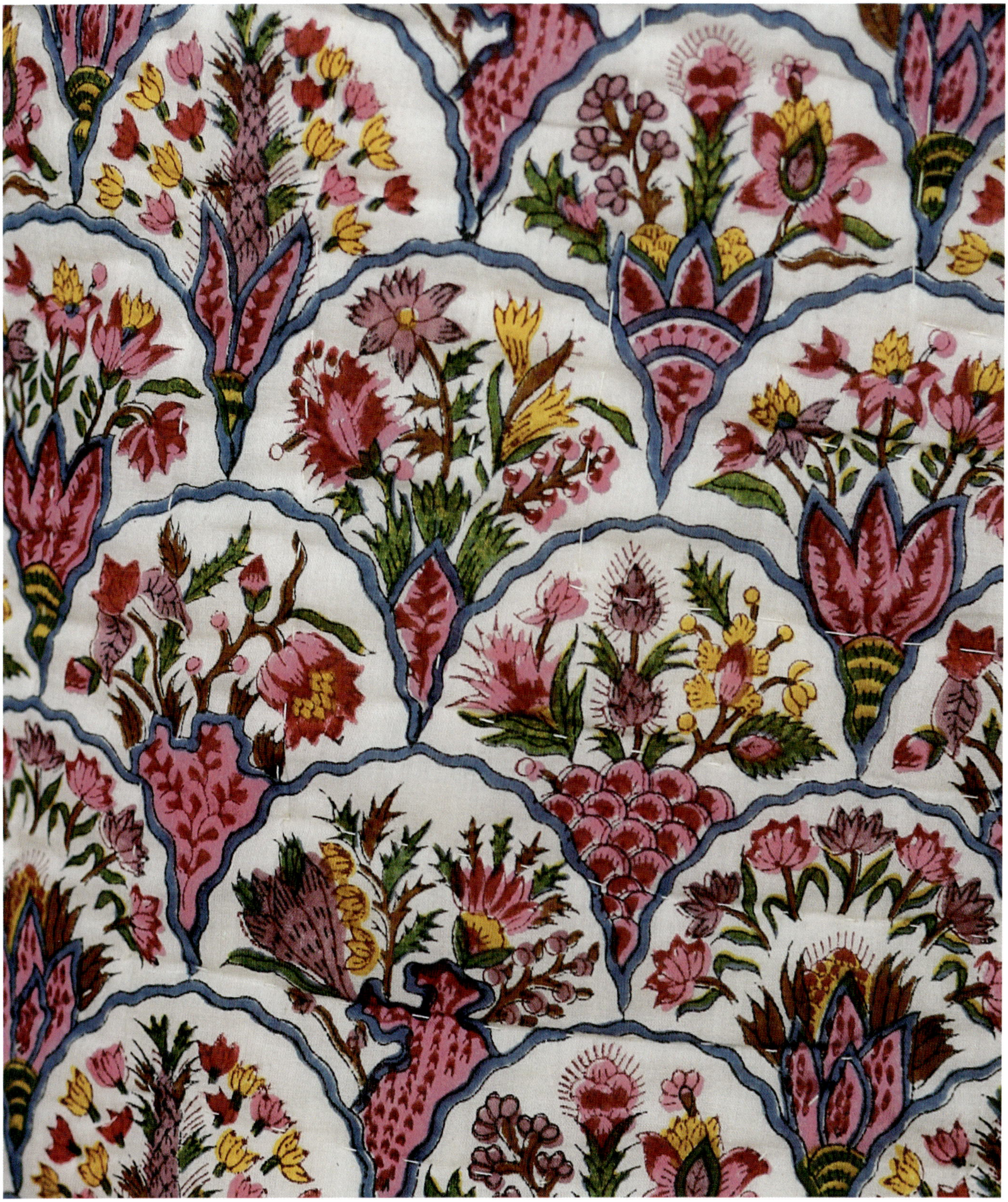

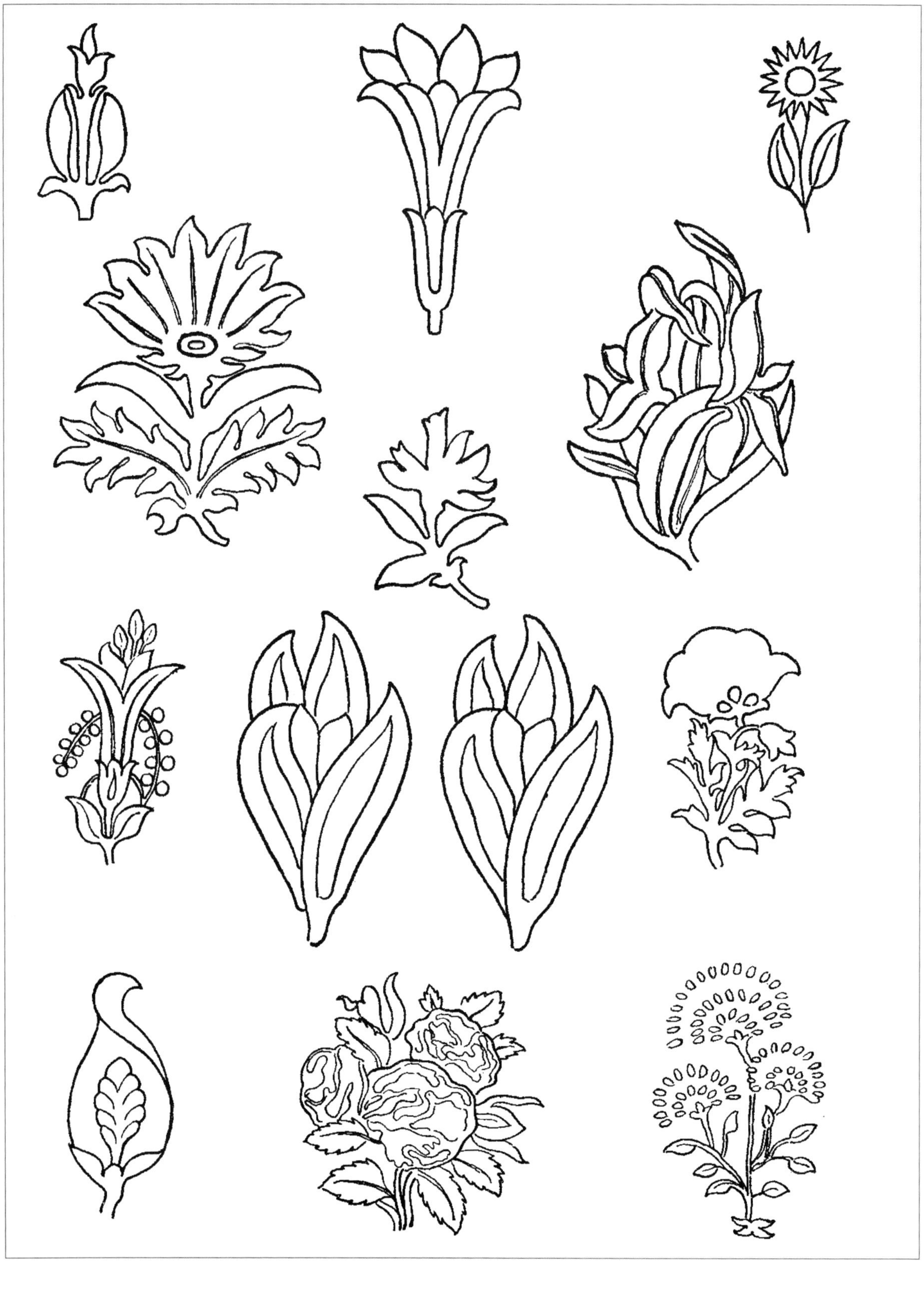

probably a European imitation.' (The Indian quilting advertised in London shops during the eighteenth century was probably a pale imitation of much of the earlier work).

Provence, in the south of France, was very famous for its quilts and was actually flourishing, thanks to quilting as a tradition which was particularly popular during the seventeenth and eighteenth centuries. The first information about quilted textiles for sale can be found in the fifteenth century, in the *Histoire du commerce de Marseille (The History of Commerce of Marseille)*.

Printed cotton, called Indiennes and plain weave, added a special charm to the Provencal quilted garments and quilts. It was imported from India and was popular in France since the sixteenth century.

Indiennes came mainly from Gujarat in the north-west of India. Gujarat manufactured printed and painted cloth called Chintz, Chittes or Indiennes from very early times. Much of this cloth was destined for export. English and Dutch companies mainly brought the first printed cloth to Europe. Indiennes were enormously popular in Europe, but they were also the most expensive ones.

Quilting in Europe

With the increase in the general availability of materials, much needlework was executed. The sewing workshops of Marseille employed thousands of dressmakers and embroiderers to manufacture sophisticated and beautiful quilts, called *broderie de l'interieur* in Provence. The quilting methods were

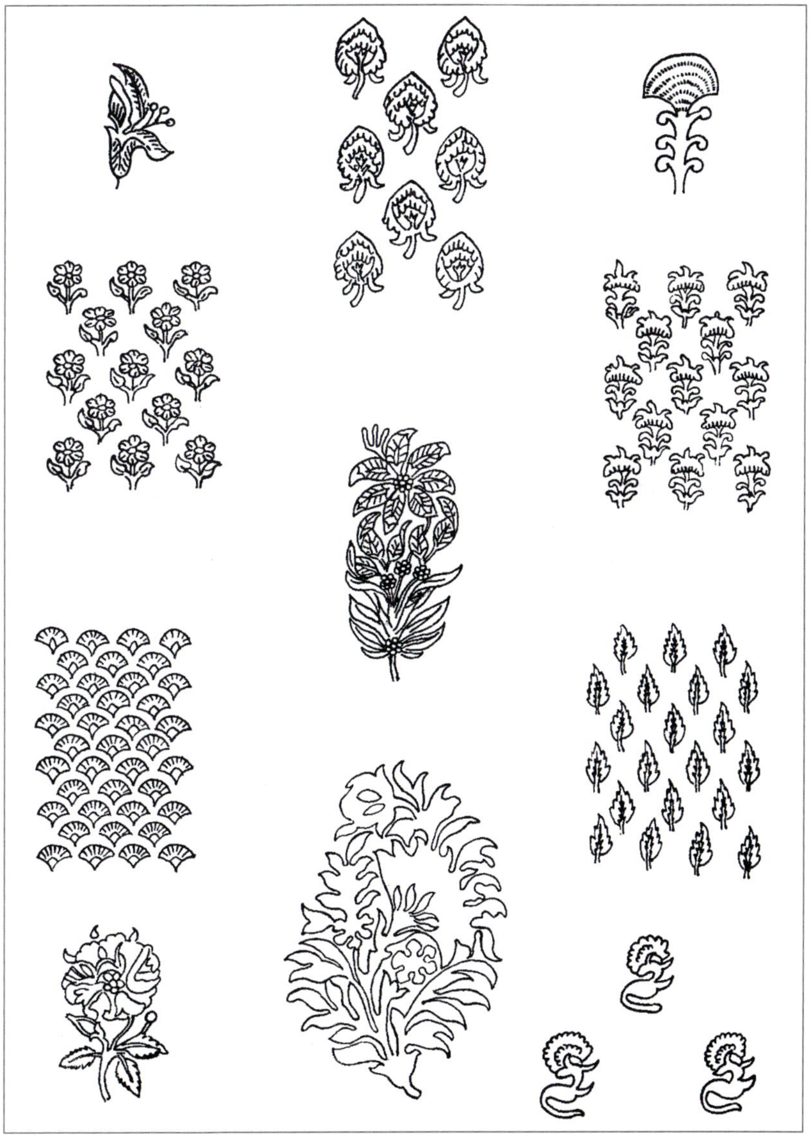

Facing page and below: *Sanganeri pattern charts of the eighteenth and nineteenth centuries, respectively. These old prints were discovered during a study visit to Sanganer*

Courtesy: Maharaja Sawai Man Singh II Museum Trust, the City Palace, Jaipur

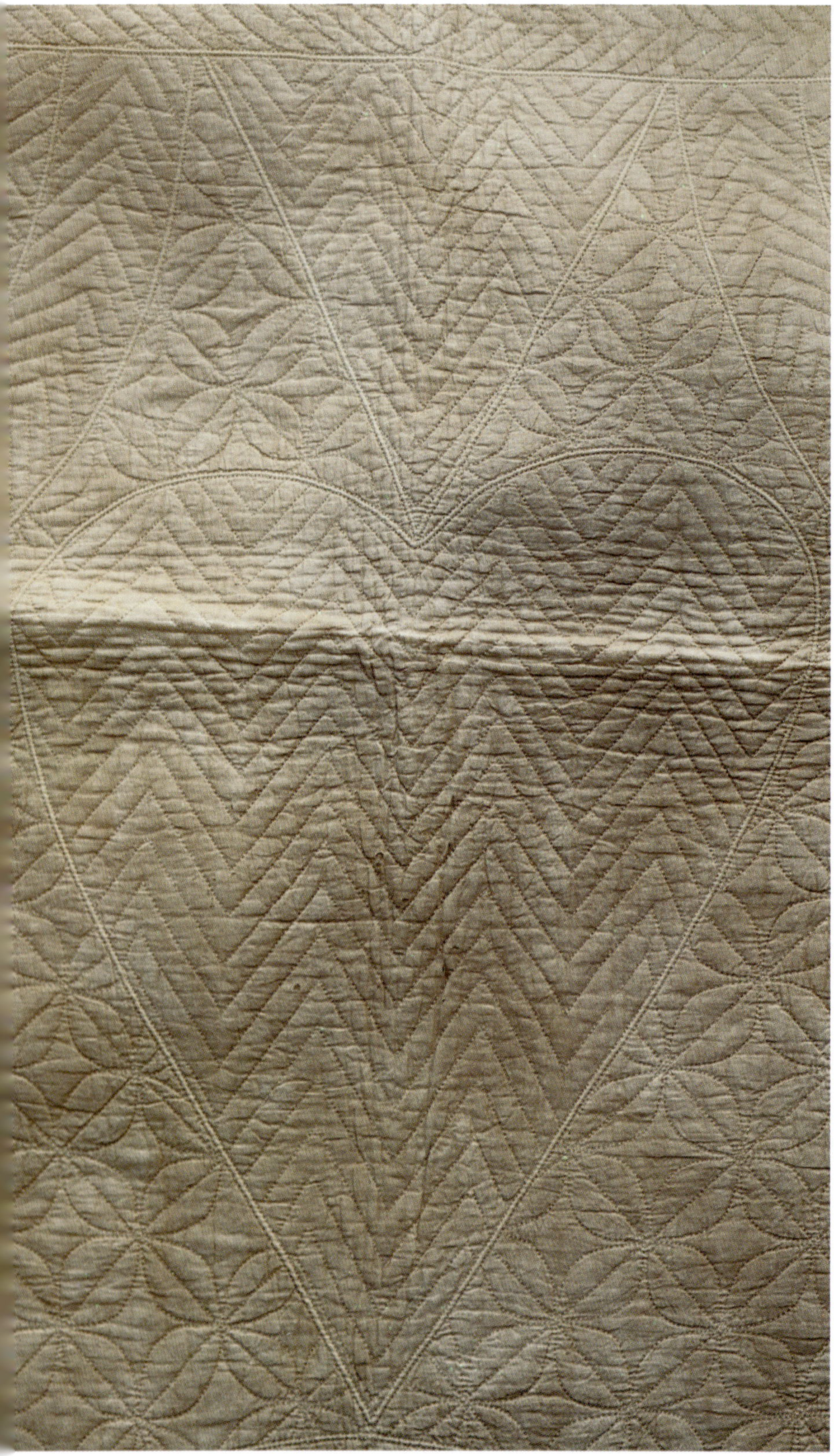

called *boutis* or *trapunto* in Italian, cord-quilting or stuffed-work, which are actually variations of quilting, using different techniques. Quilting was especially popular in the eighteenth century for garments and bed quilts. Plain quilting relies for its effect upon the play of light over its surface. Stuffing some part of the design tightly, produces a patterned surface in high relief. In Provence we find *broderie de Marseille*, quilted with white thread on white material like batiste or muslin. They were used as covers and also as *couvre-lit de marriage*—made especially for the bride's trousseau.

In 1686, the import of Indiennes from India was prohibited as a fall-out of protectionist policies and the ban was lifted only as late as 1759. After the French Revolution, not many luxurious or artistic materials survived in France, and it was difficult to find new material. Therefore, old quilts were renovated or pieces of old and ruined textiles were used for the manufacture of new quilts. Availability of materials has always dictated the kind of stuffing for a quilt. The Provencal quilting was usually stuffed with cotton. Wool was used in Wales and England. Quilted patterns ranged from varieties of flowers, circles, fruits, chains, monograms, animal

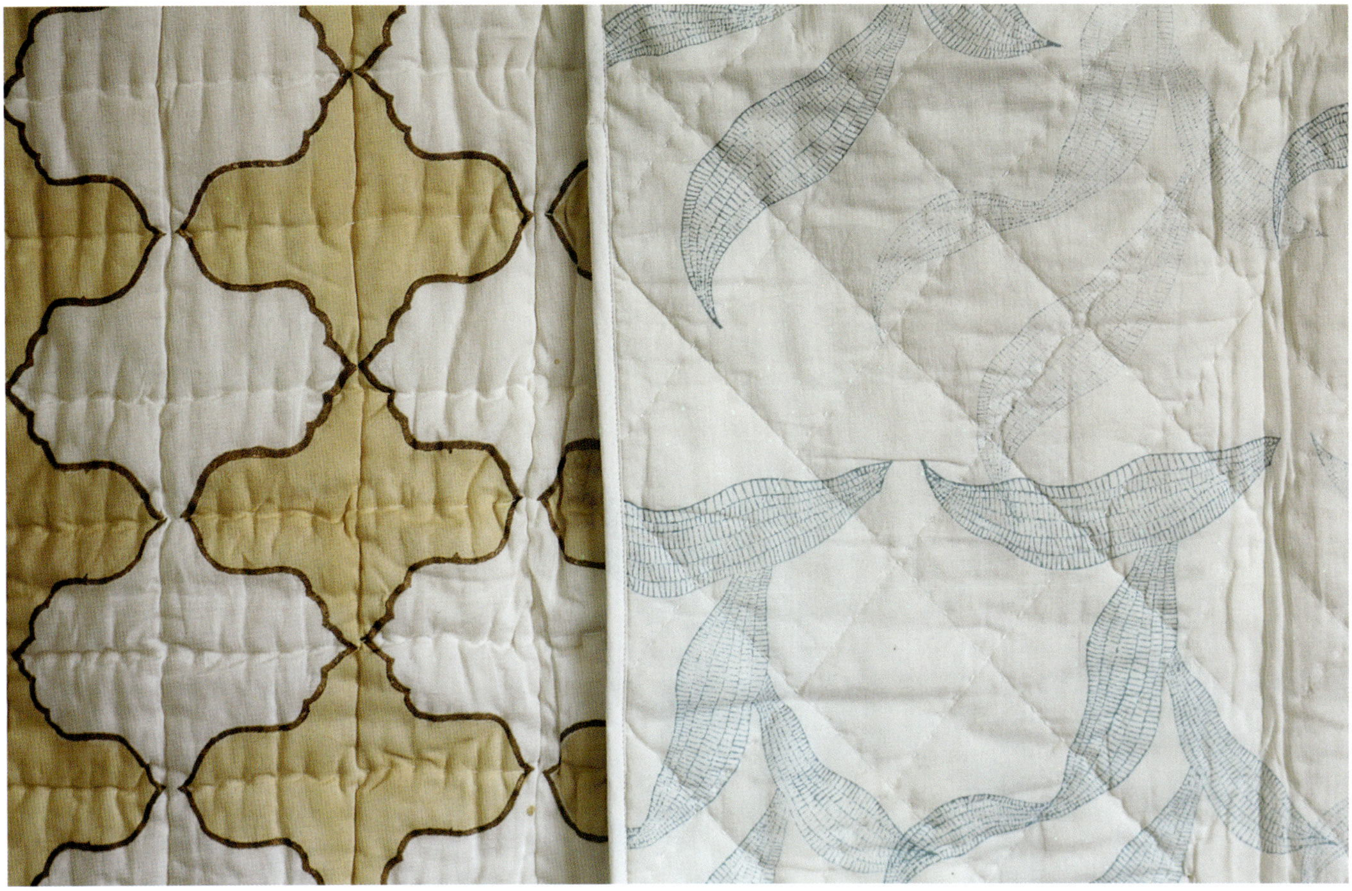

motifs, to even architectural motifs. Wadded quilting makes a more flexible quilt. The Provencal quilts were heavily padded. In North America during the ninteenth and twentieth centuries, patchwork and wadded quilts were popular. The patchwork quilts made by the Amish are famous and their patterns and colour palette are much-admired. Judy Wentworth writes in her book *Quilts*: 'The North of England, as well as Wales, has always been well known for its quilted patterns. Monochrome quilts and striped quilts which used broad vertical bands of material, often alternately red and white, have been highly prized, and famous for almost two hundred years'.

In Europe as in India, many quilts and bed-hangings were made for the great houses and they were often seen as more valuable than the furniture itself. They have been frequently mentioned in wills and inventories over the centuries.

Evolution of quilting

Making quilts is not what women do today merely to pass time; traditional skills are now an interesting medium. The

Experiments in geometric designs and colour tones by contemporary quilt and textile designers in Jaipur

Facing page: *Antique quilt work with* paan *motif Courtesy: Subhash Sharma*

research findings of textile researchers and art historians have ample evidence of this trend. We may look at some of the documented evidences, which may help trace the varying socio-cultural nuances that have transformed the face of quilting since the Middle Ages.

In *Women Artists: Recognition and Reappraisal from the Early Middle Ages to the Twentieth Century*, Pedersen and Wilson write: 'In the Middle Ages embroidery and weaving were highly developed and prestigious art forms. The collective workshops where they were executed did not differ much from the painting workshops and there is proof that women shared in the creation…'

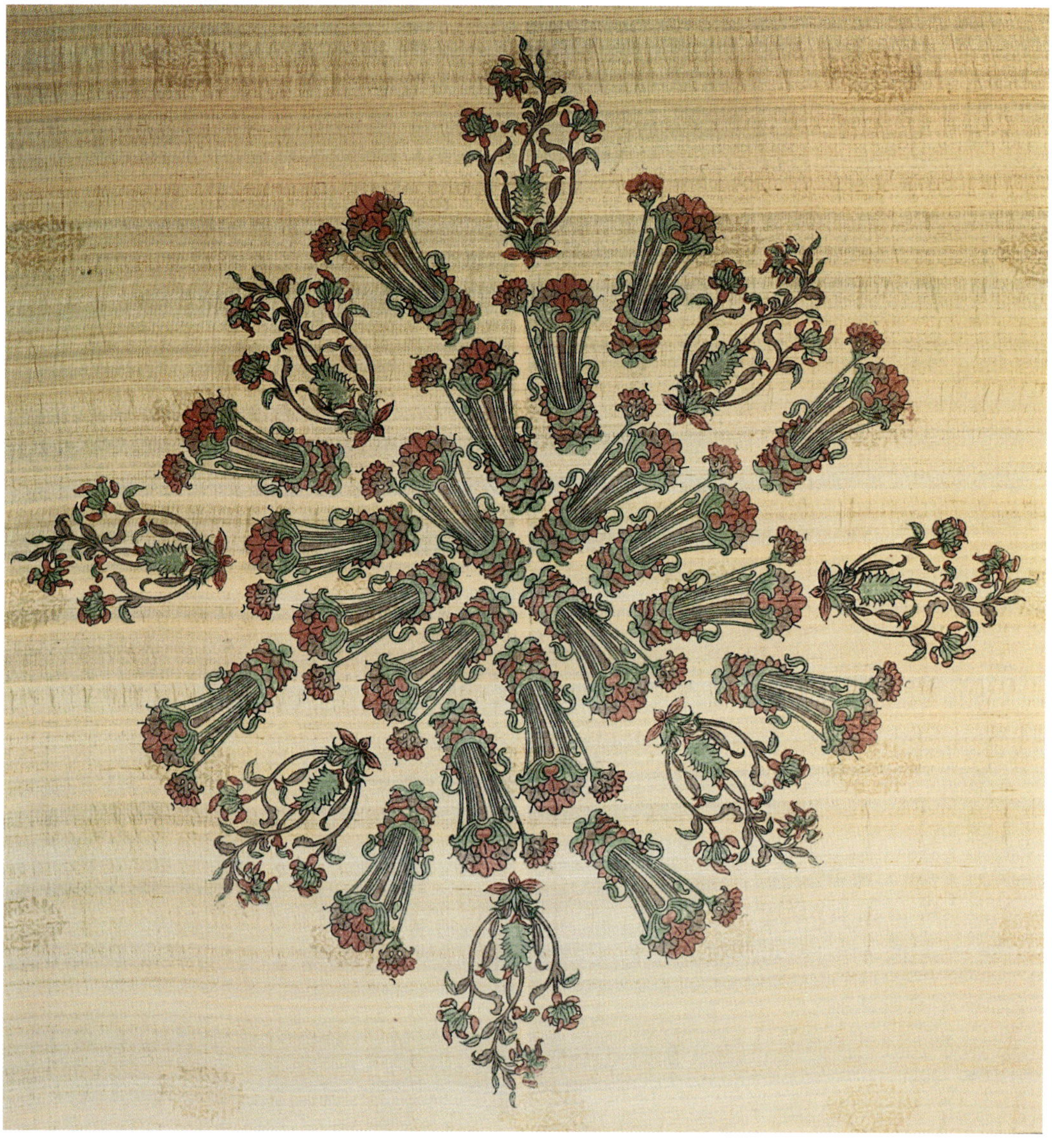

Parker says in *The Subversive Stitch, Embroidery and the Making of the Feminine*: 'The division between art and handicraft came into being during the Renaissance. Workers were divided into the formally trained artist or master, and the untrained amateur. On the other hand women, who were outside the educational system, were of course put in the latter category, with a lower status. When women paint, their work is categorised as homogeneously feminine but it is acknowledged to be art. When women embroider, it is seen not as art, but as the expression of feminity. And, crucially it is categorised as craft'.

Parker goes on to discuss embroidery as an emerging art form and brings to light

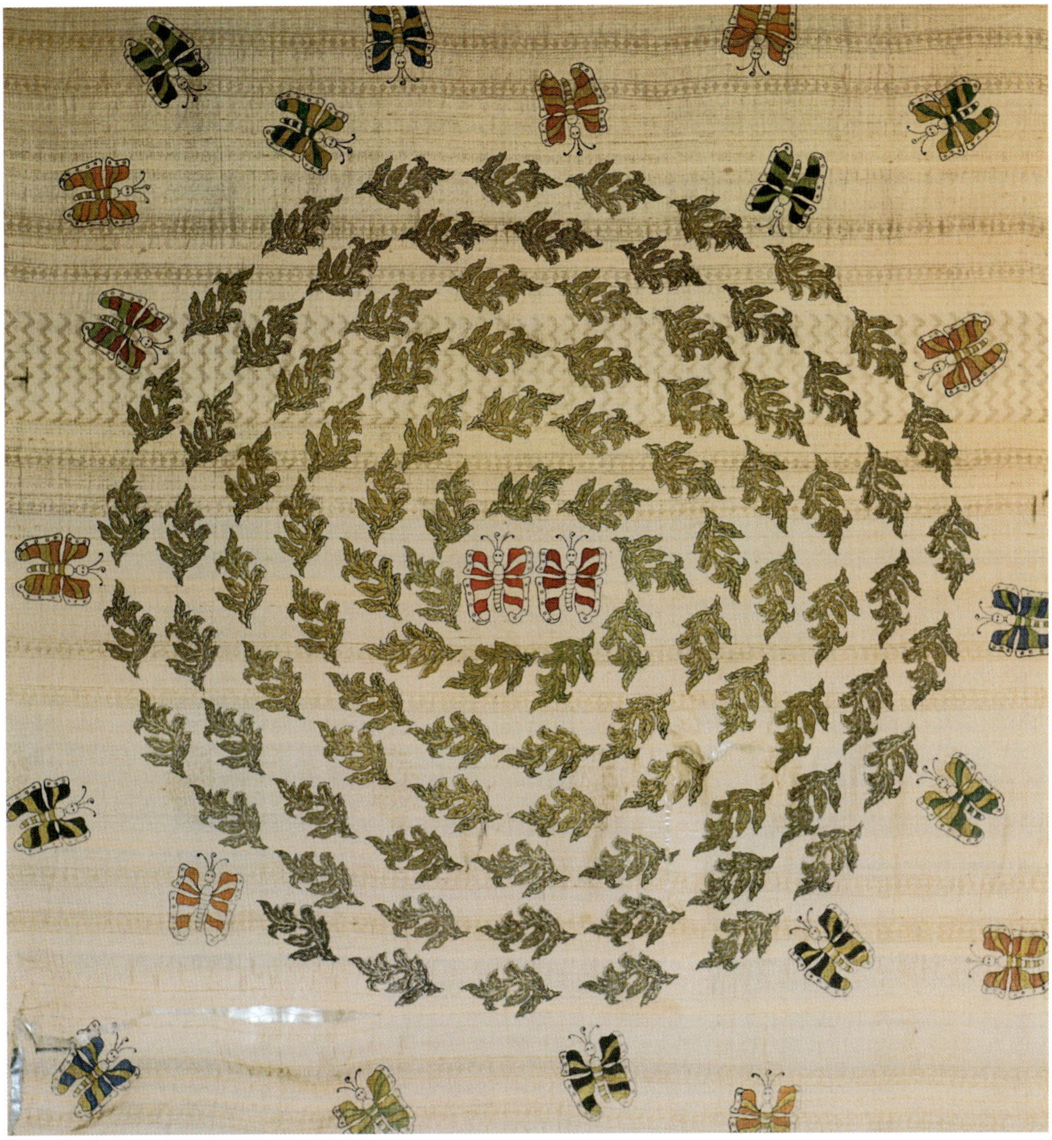

Traditional flower bouquet (facing page); leaf and butterfly motifs. Designs inspired by old Sanganeri prints, which are now used by renowned hand-block printer Kunj Bihari who inherited artworks from his father and grandfather. He received the National Award in 2005

interesting details: 'Embroidery was an important part of the aesthetic education against the mass-produced and machine-manufactured; however it was the designer who was the artist. Twentieth century avant-garde trends, especially dadaism, surrealism and constructivism worked with new techniques. Sophie Tauber and Jean Arp made collage and embroidery, collectively working in what they saw as new material disengaged from tradition. Sonia Terk Delunay's familiarity with needlework and patchwork construction constituted partly the base for her non-figurative colour compositions'.

Gender politics has an important role to play in the determination of quilts as an expression of artistic sensibilities or as a proper art form. Patricia Mainardi, author of *Quilts: The Great American Art*, claims that quilts have been underrated for precisely the same reasons that jazz, the great American music, was also underrated for a long time. Mainardi assesses that because the 'wrong' people were making it, and because these people, for sexist and racist reasons, have not been allowed to represent or define culture, quilt-making was always underrated as an art form. The textile and needlework arts of the world have been especially kept out of the precincts of art history primarily because they have been the handiwork of women. One would have to rewrite art history in order to acknowledge the fact that art is in fact a human impulse and cannot be attributed to a particular gender, race or class.

In India, people started making quilts for personal use and later for the wealthy households and the court. The textile and the design depended on the person who ordered the quilted textile, the occasion and the place. For example, a special pattern sacred to Shiva was designed for the priest of a Shiva temple and another for a follower of Vaishnavism. For the king's court the motifs were based on flowers—rose, jasmine, iris, chrysanthemum, narcissus and marigold.

In the beginning of the twentieth century the quilt industry suffered a decline. Among other reasons was the development and building of textile factories, but in the last few decades quilting has picked up again and we have witnessed an interesting revival. Business houses and textile boutiques have been set up to engage professional quilt-makers in a bid to design, create and market the product as a traditional and exclusive Indian handicraft.

Quilt Art is a group of professional quilt artists from different countries.

It was founded in 1985 and aims to extend the boundaries of quilting as an artistic medium and achieve wider recognition of the quilt as an art form. The group holds regular touring exhibitions.

The Jaipur quilts are generally wadded quilts today and the quilting is not particularly elaborate. The block-printed Mughal patterns and the light textile lend exclusivity to the Jaipur quilts.

Chandramani Singh writes in *Textiles and Costumes from the Maharaja Sawai Man Singh II Museum*: 'Sanganer, a town founded by a Kachhawaha prince Sangaji in the early sixteenth century, developed into an important printing centre and was at its peak in the nineteenth century. It was known for its bright and fast dyes. As far as tradition goes, it is said that it was the king Sawai Jai Singh II who was responsible for giving impetus to the art of printing. He invited artists and craftsmen from different parts of the country to settle in Jaipur.

'The main contributions of Sanganer printers to the Indian printing industry are fast colours and meaningful, well-proportioned motifs designed for *dupatta*s, *odhani*s, dress material, quilts and upholstery. Fine lines, soft curves and refinement are the characteristics of *Sanganeri* cotton prints. Motifs which were localy known as *buti* if small and *buta* if big, were designed after the human figures, fruits, flowers and animals.' These prints, modernised or traditional, stylised or composed in different configurations, are today a characteristic pattern for the textiles of which Jaipur quilts are made.

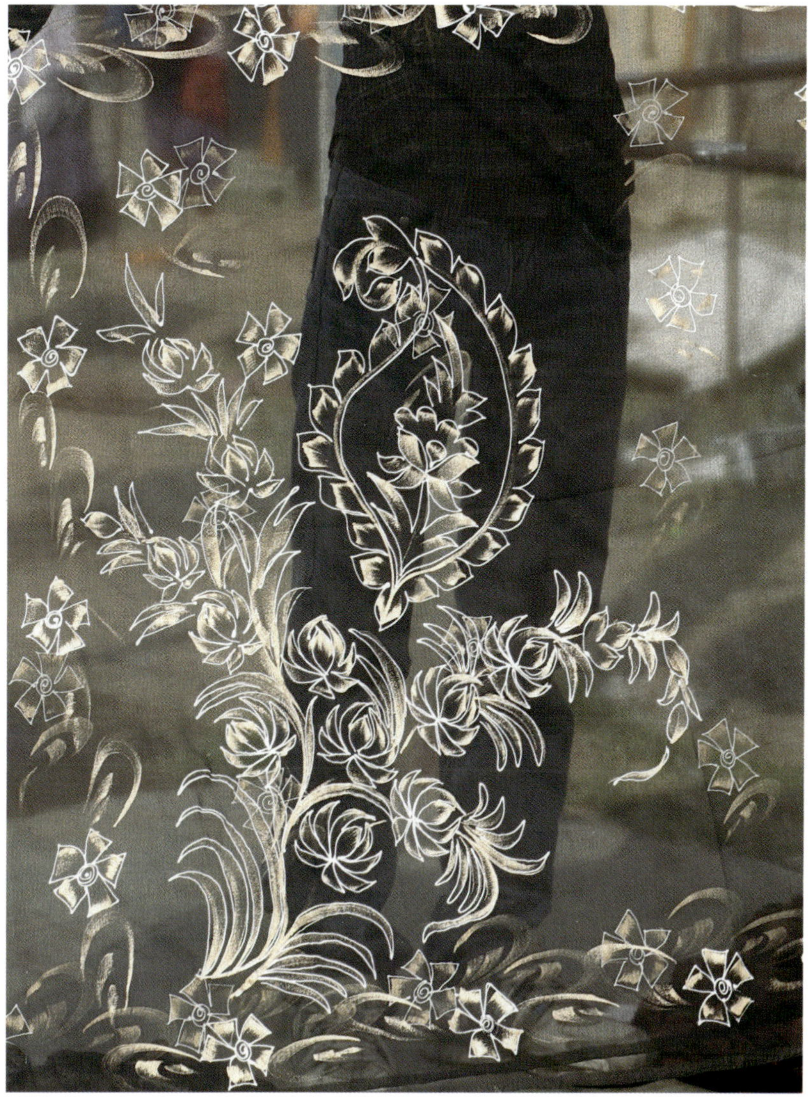

Screen painting using paisley and floral motifs painted directly on silk

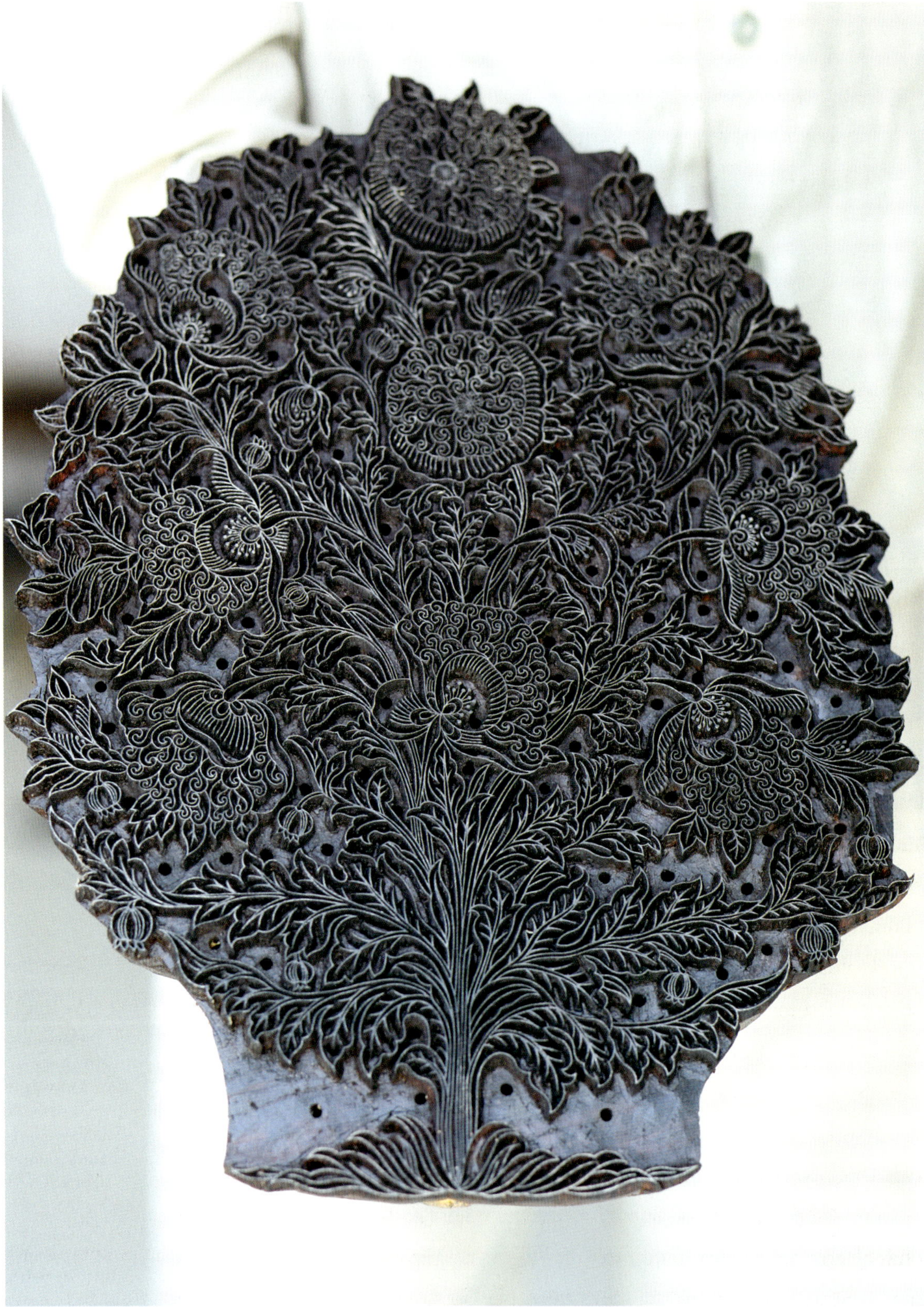

Jaipur is known for its lightweight, warm and durable quilts. The city's skilled carders, printers, dyers and designers are their sole creators. There are many dhuniya *(carder) families, popularly known as* pinjara *in the city*

The origins and the making

The Pink City offers an exciting deal of historical anecdotes, magical moments and objects of beauty and grandeur to artists and art historians, tourists, archaeologists, photographers, shoppers and pleasure-seekers. History, art and the finer elements of life go hand-in-hand with the tradition of royalty and valour here. Shopping too is often an important agenda on a tourist's list of 'must-do's in this city. Among the array of mementos that a tourist buys from Jaipur, the *razai* has always held a special corner in the heart of the serious shopper.

The striking colours and combinations embellished with the traditional Sanganeri prints, bright tie-dyed designs and the marble prints on cotton and velvet come as attractive alternatives to the assembly line of quilts available elsewhere in the Indian market.

Jaipur's Hawa Mahal Bazaar is a hotspot for buying good quilts at reasonable rates as some of the oldest shops line the roads here. However, few tourists have the time or the inclination to know its origins or find out how these beautiful designs and natural colours

Facing page: *Wooden printing block with a beautiful, intricate design used by Brigitte Singh*

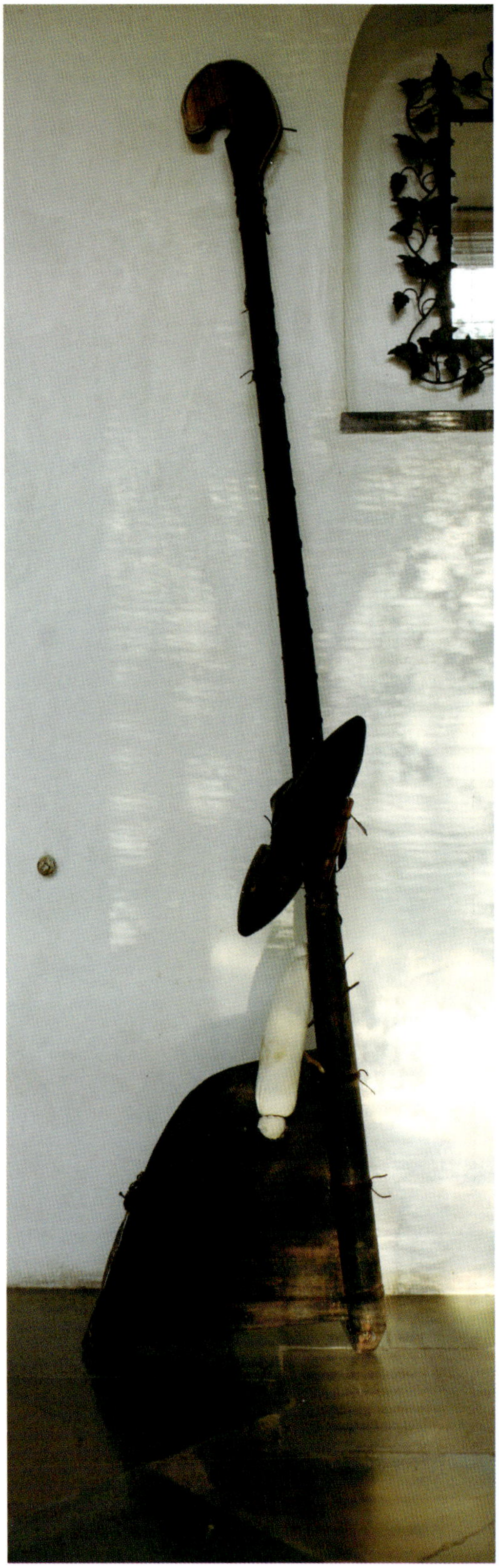

Antique fluffing bow

are created or how in fact, the Jaipur quilt is made.

Nobody is quite sure how or when the Jaipur *razai* first came into existence. However, the reason for having these quilts as warm wraps during winter perhaps lies in the climate and topography of Rajasthan and the traditional way of life of its people. The extreme cold of winter nights and the nomadic *banjara* ways of the Rajasthanis who love to be on the move—seeking new pastures and opportunities of livelihood–have combined to create this warm but all-cotton lightweight quilt.

The Aravalli ranges and the Thar (Great Indian) Desert make the terrain quite inhospitable and the climate rather harsh and cold, especially at night. Winters are particularly bitter and after sundown the mercury plummets suddenly to a freezing low, especially in the deserts. For centuries, soldiers camping out in the cold during a battle, traders on the move and wandering shepherds and *bhopa*s (wandering bards) spent days out in the desert or on the road in camel caravans. They needed the lightweight but warm quilt—a cover to keep the chill out at night without adding much bulk to their saddle bags. The Jaipur *razai* is far from being flimsy however, sometimes handed down the generations and used extensively in winter but easily tucked away in closets in neat piles during the summer months.

From dross to fluff

I went back to Jaipur frequently after my first visit decades ago. As I got acquainted with Jaipur quilts I decided to delve into the folds of history and the artistic tradition of quilt-making and share my first-hand experience of watching a quilt take shape with the reader.

Quilt making involves a long process. A quilt dealer, or a person who wants to have a quilt made, purchases cotton wool from a cotton dealer who buys it from farmers during the flowering season and stores it. Then this wool goes to the carder who with his strong fluffing bow or fluffing machine turns the thickly pressed cotton into a fluffed pile and puts it in a cloth shell or cover. According to some of the oldest quiltmakers, there is hardly anything special in the cotton that they use. Most of them procure good, *desi* (local) cotton wool from Sri Ganganagar just when the fresh crop comes in. The art lies in the carding of the cotton fill before it is stuffed in—separating the cotton fibres and removing all the dross or waste material to retain the finest of

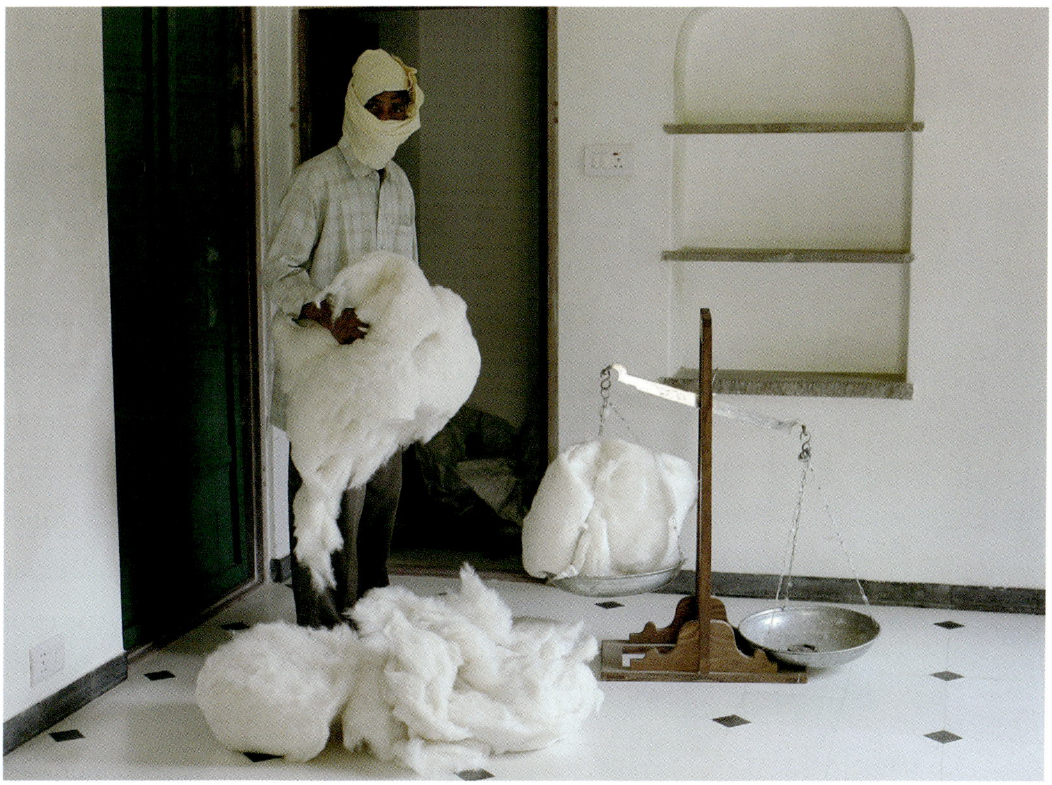

Weighing the cotton

fibres. A good carder can spend a good many days over the carding.

A carding bow is covered on one side with fine teeth. The worker places a ball of cotton on one carder and combs through it with another carder. In the process of carding, a dense cotton ball becomes light and fluffy. For a typical Jaipur *razai*, a worker starts with a kilogram (approximately 2.2 pounds) of cotton, which finally weighs not more than 100g (or 3.5 ounces) after a full week of carding. Makers of these quilts are careful to draw out as much dross and to separate as many of the cotton fibres as possible. The lightest of quilts not weighing more than 50g are sometimes created by repeated carding of the cotton. Light and fluffy, evenly-spread out cotton fill is what makes these quilts warm. Some of the master craftsmen in the Hawa Mahal Bazaar claim that their families have been carders for generations.

The process also involves making the shell of the quilt, which can be cotton, velvet or silk. The price of a quilt is decided by the type of fabric and cotton used, and also the kind of carding and stitching involved.

Evenly layering the cotton fill on the shell in order to maintain its comfort and warmth is an important task. After

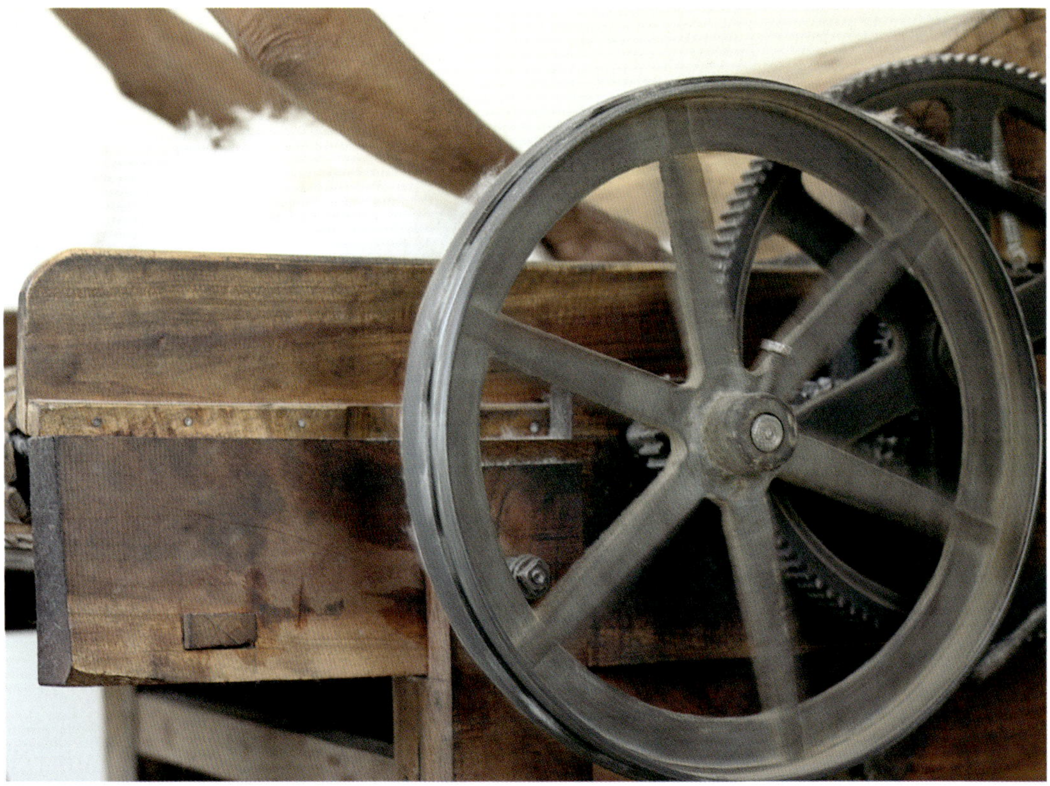

The process of fluffing

Facing page: *Laying out the fluffed cotton wool on the quilt cover*

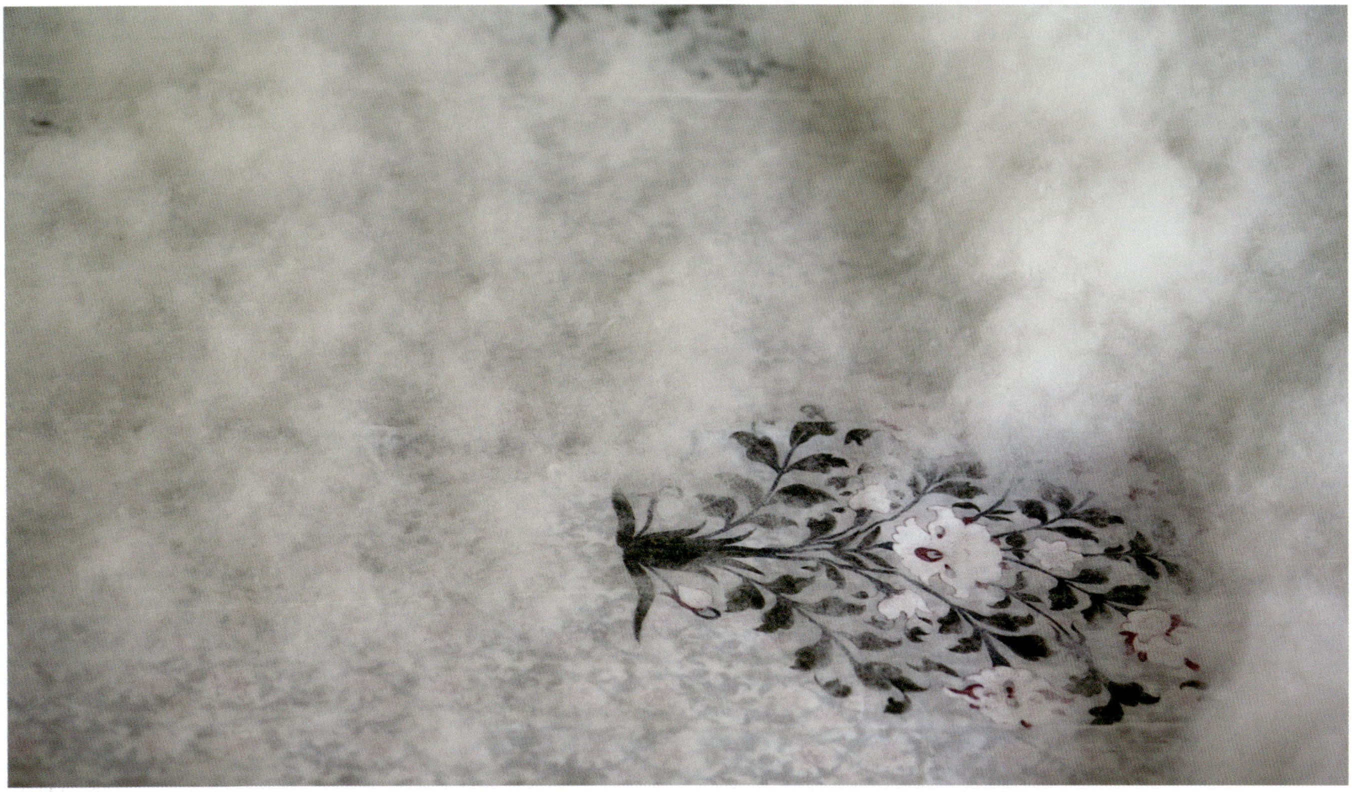

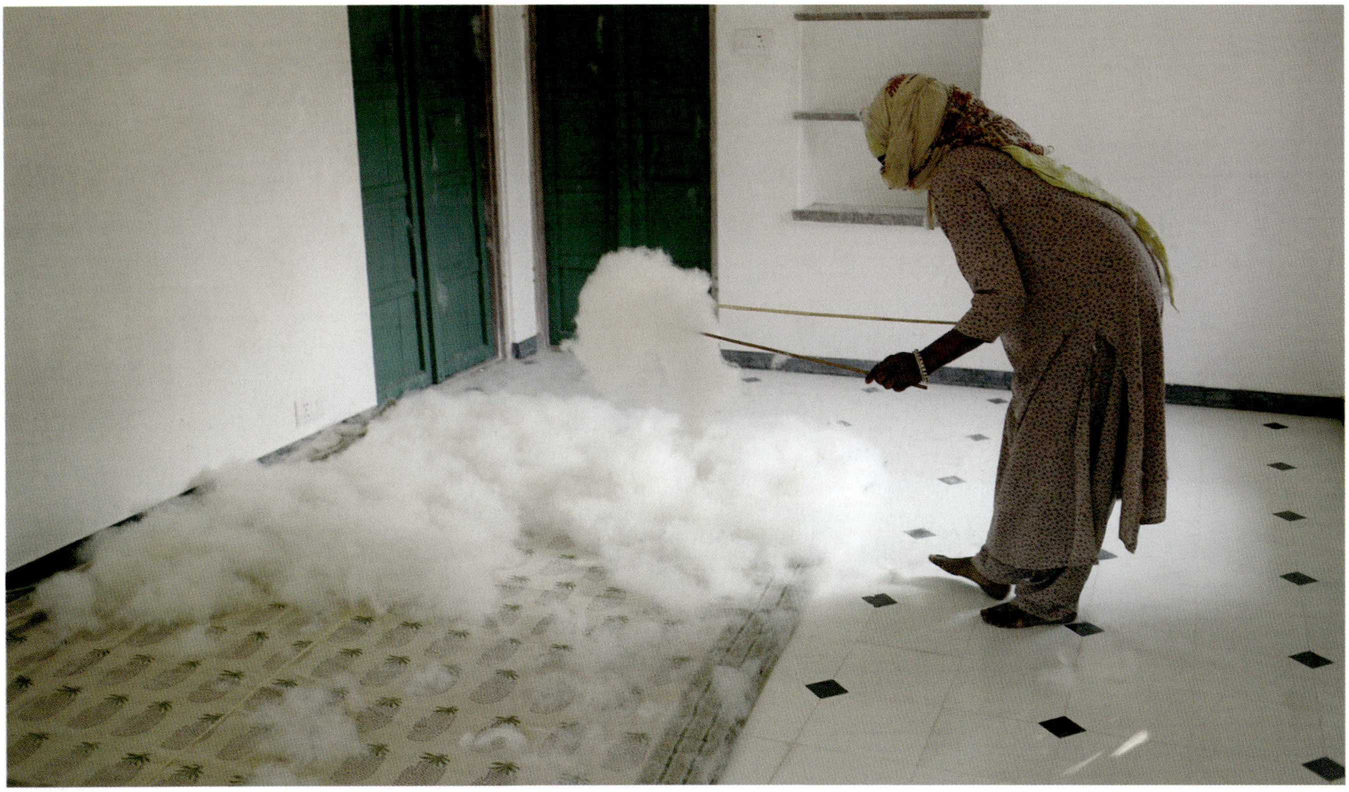

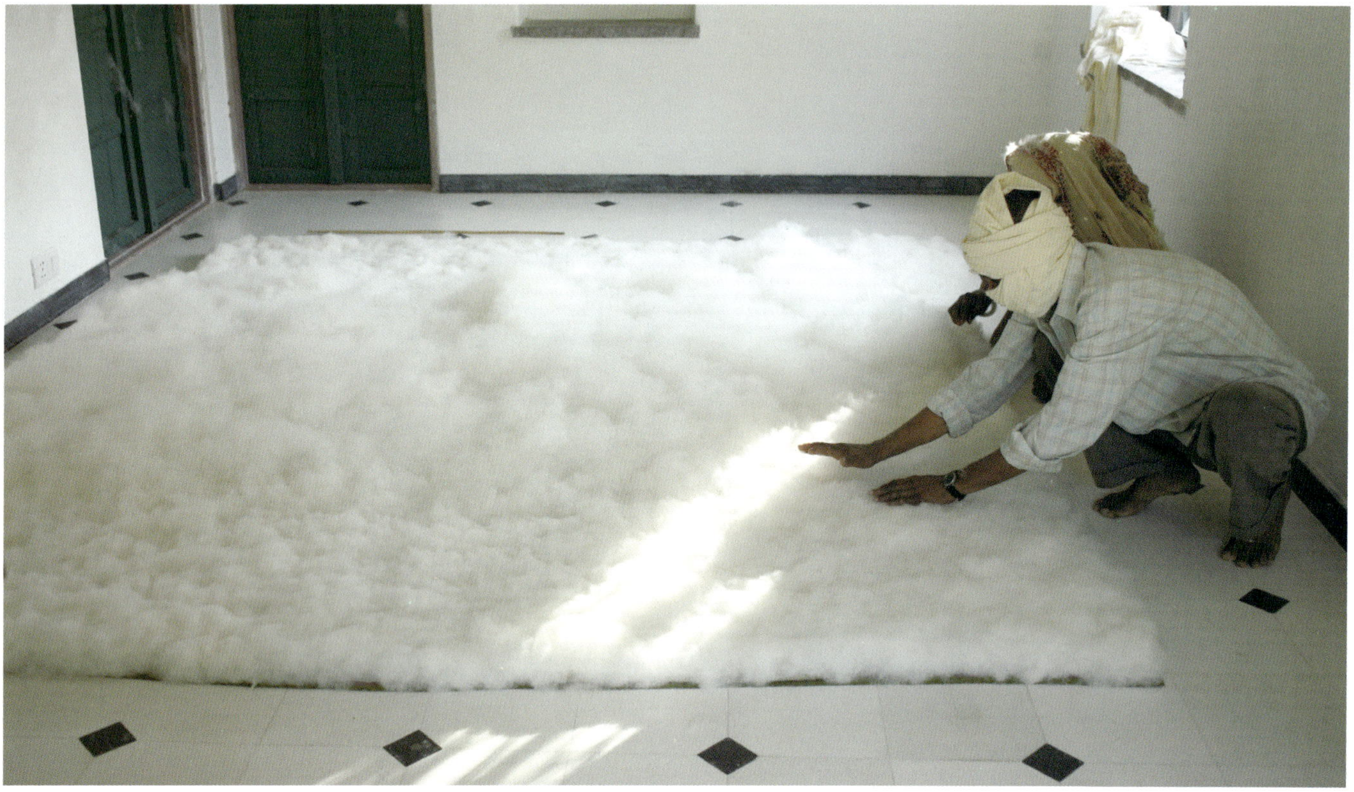

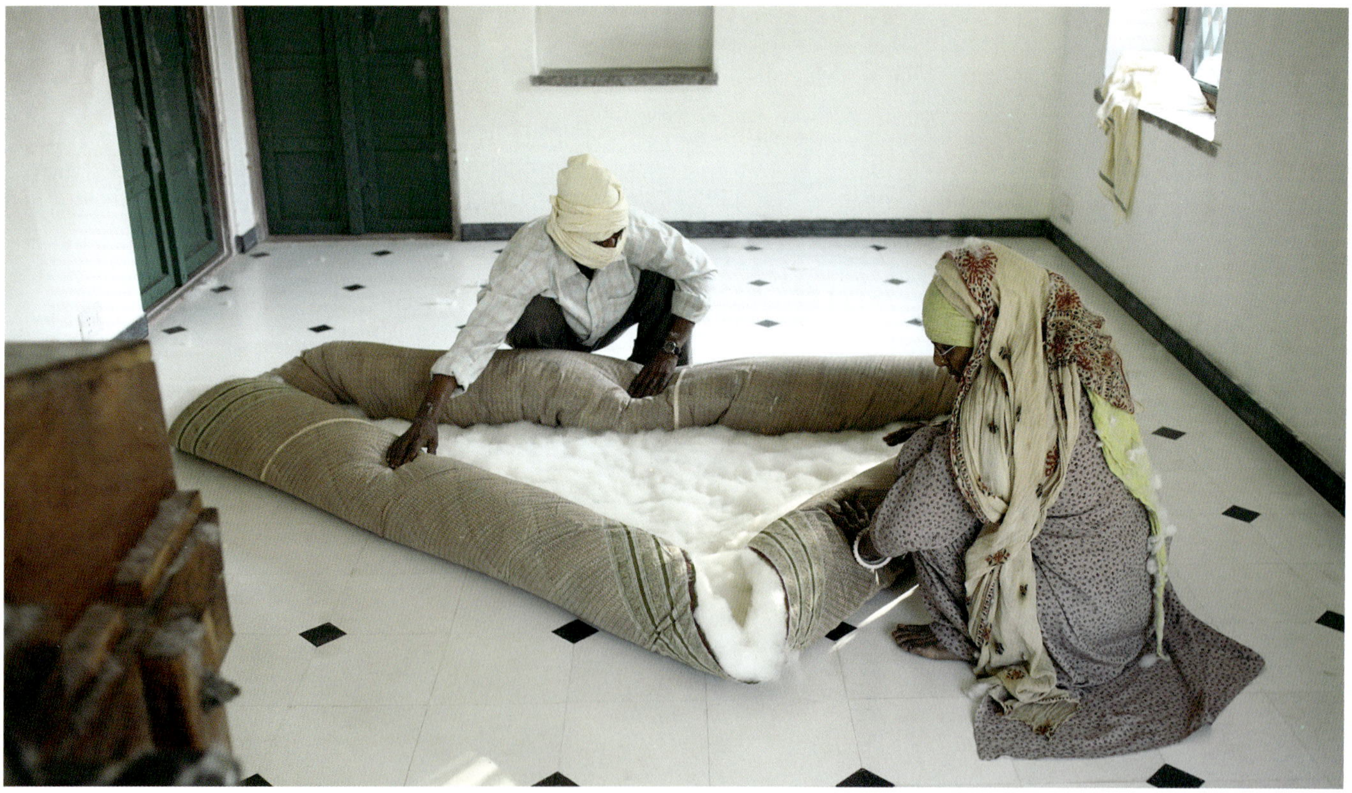

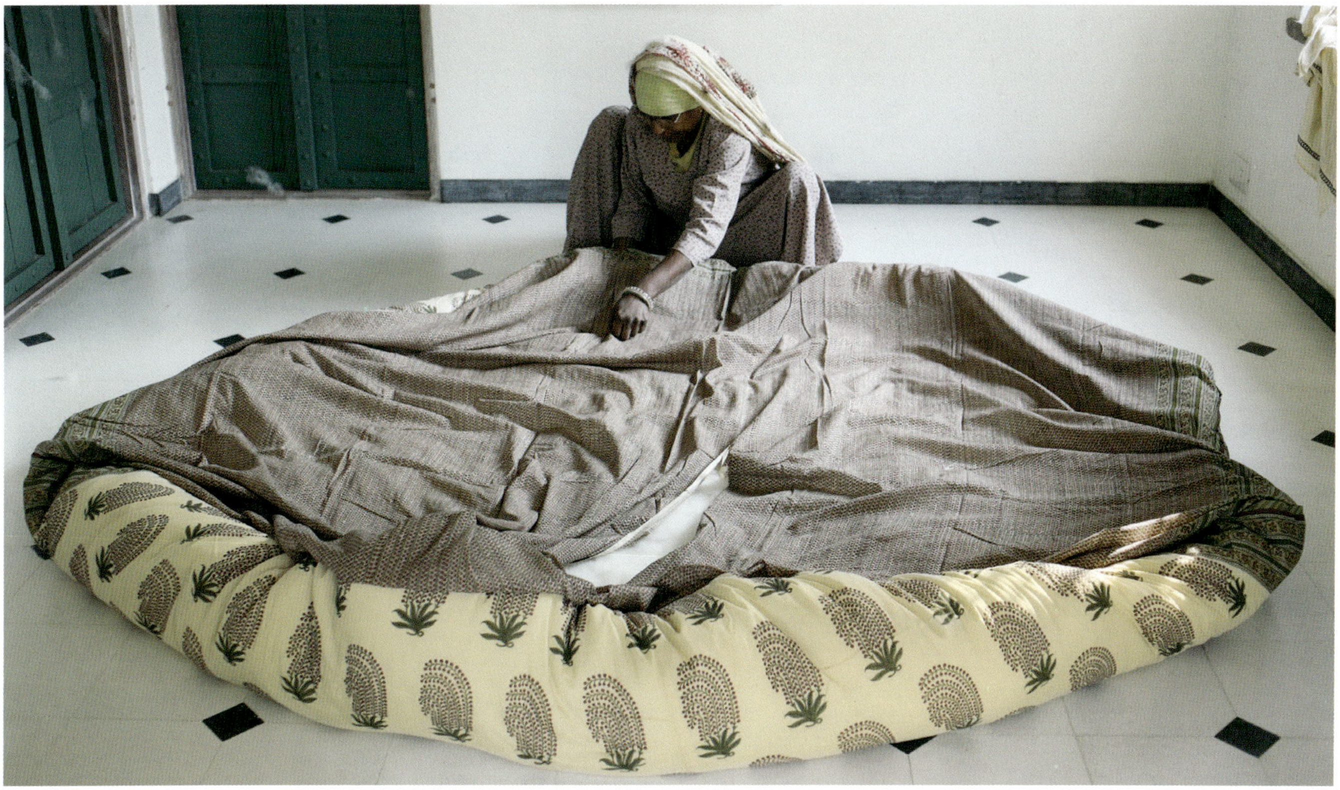

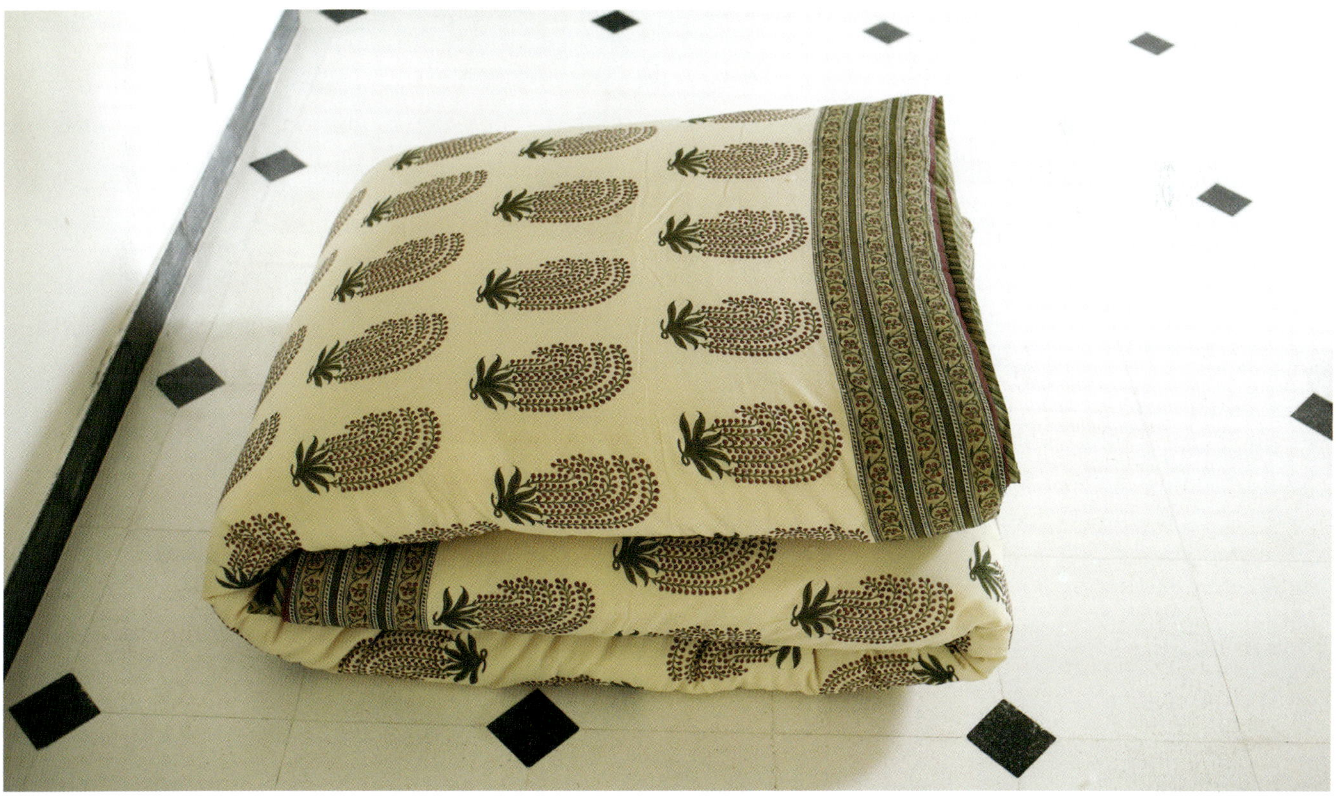

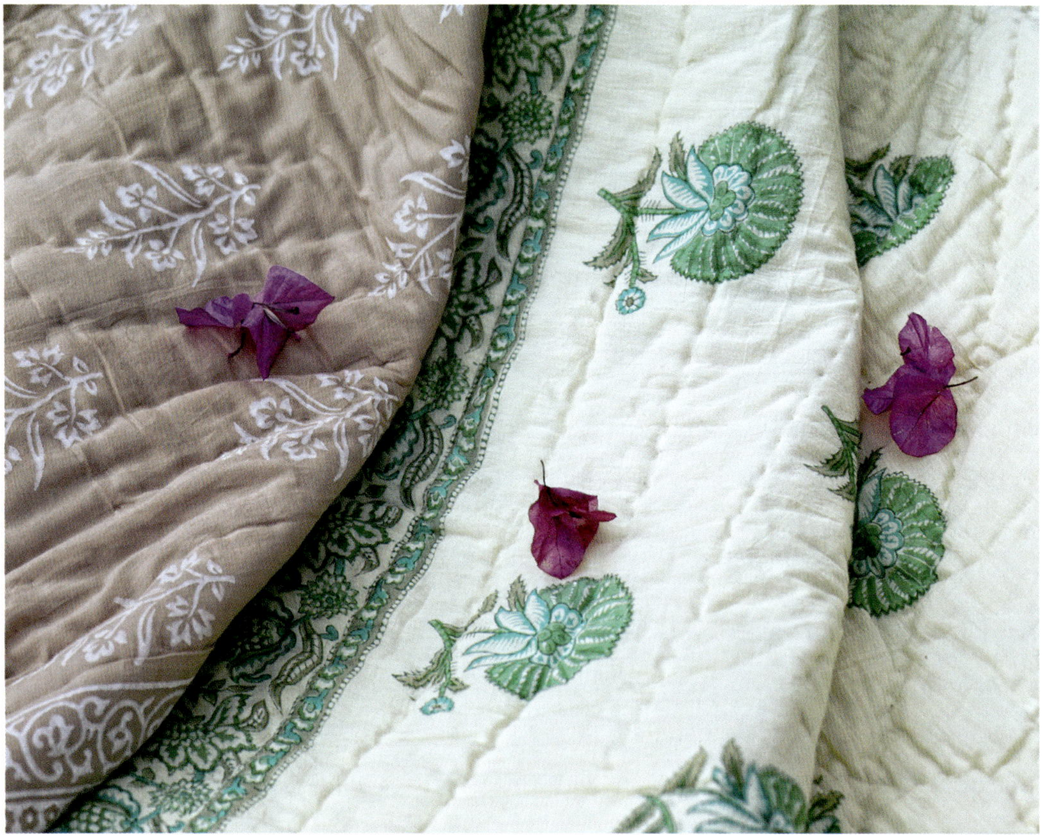

Finished quilts from Kin Fabrics and Soma

Facing page: *Wooden trays containing dyes for printing*

Page 58: *Process of levelling the cotton wool (above); Workers roll up the quilt, turning it outside in, to enclose the cotton wool securely inside*

Page 59: *Stitching and closing up the quilt cover (above); Ready for quilting*

layering the shell with cotton, the quilt is stitched together and quilted. Traditionally, a hand-held needle would be used for stitching the sides. Modern day quilt-makers use a sewing machine instead, which adds to the durability of a quilt. The quilting on the panels themselves is usually still done by a hand-held needle. The stitching on the interior of the quilt surface helps hold the cotton fill in place and adds to the beauty of the quilt.

The cover or the shell for the quilt is made separately by a tailor. There was a time when the quilt covers would only be made from the famous 'Dhake ki mulmul'—a fine cotton fabric manufactured in Dhaka, once a part of India and now the capital of Bangladesh. The fabric now for the Jaipur *razai* is often a lightweight, gauzy cotton fabric with a very smooth surface–the voile–coming mainly from Mumbai. The softness of the voile adds to the snug, cosy nature of the quilt. A standard single quilt uses six metres and a double quilt eleven metres of fabric but there are different sizes and styles of quilts.

After the cotton wool is packed into the shell, it is given to women skilled in the art of threading. This skill is passed down generations. They draw the pattern on the reverse of the cover and thread it in a running stitch, which can be purely functional or decorative and elaborate. *Gol*–concentric circles; *phool*–flowers; *paan*–the betel leaf, and *lahariya*–vertical stripes zigzagging down the face of the quilt are the standard four traditionally popular quilting patterns. Threading is essential, because if it is not done in time, cotton gathers at one place and all the work accomplished earlier is wasted. After threading, the quilt is ready to be used. Two women usually work together on one quilt and between themselves manage roughly two quilts a day, depending on the complexity of the design. The lighter the quilt and the more evenly filled, the warmer and more comfortable it is.

Dyeing and printing

The suburbs of Jaipur excel in the art of hand-block print. Bright and contrasting hues reach a unique and rare elegance when combined, appearing as perfectly coordinated complementary tones.

Sanganer near Jaipur is a leading hand-block printing centre in India. Almost every third home in this small village doubles up as a workshop for resident block makers and printers.

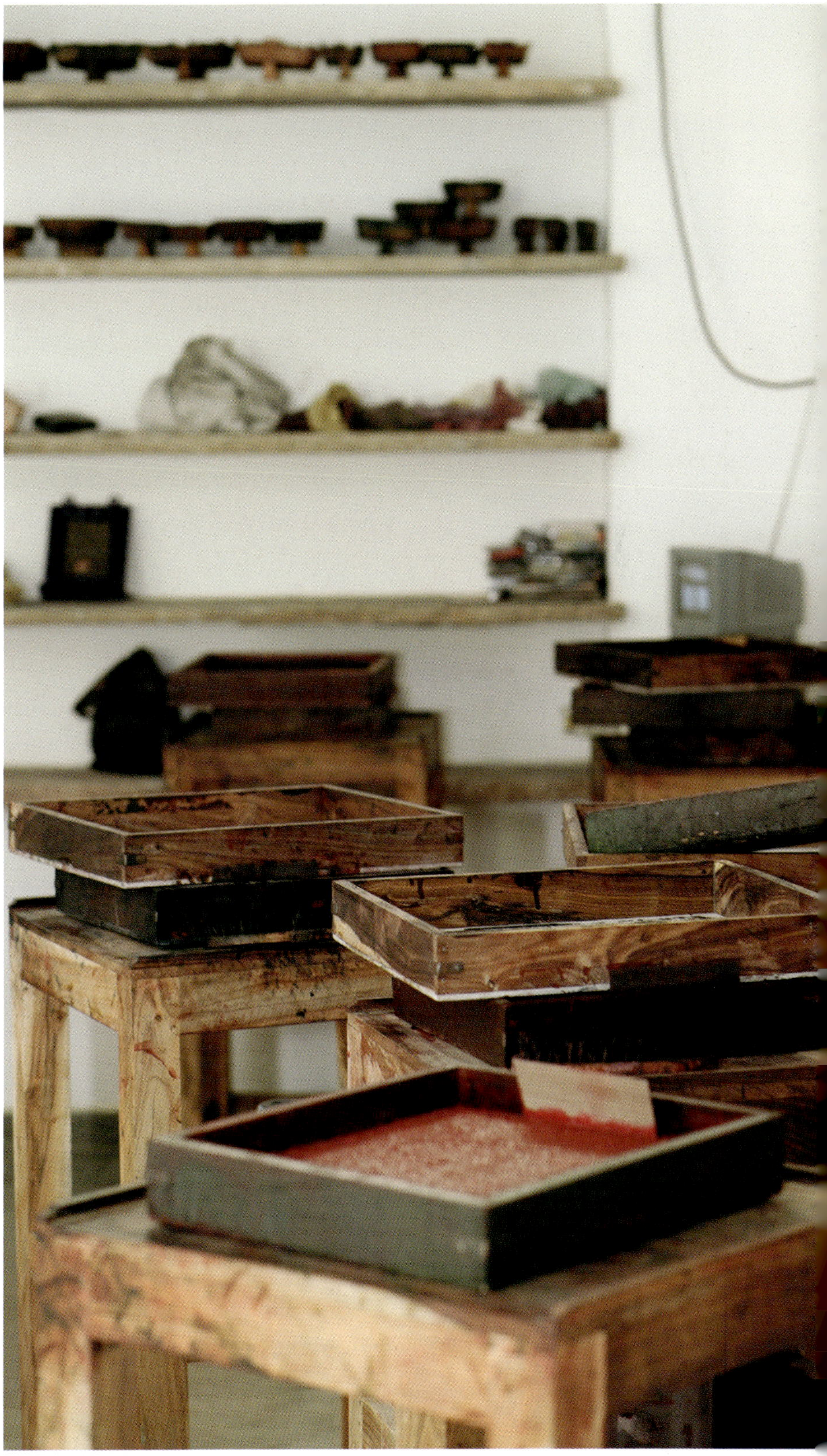

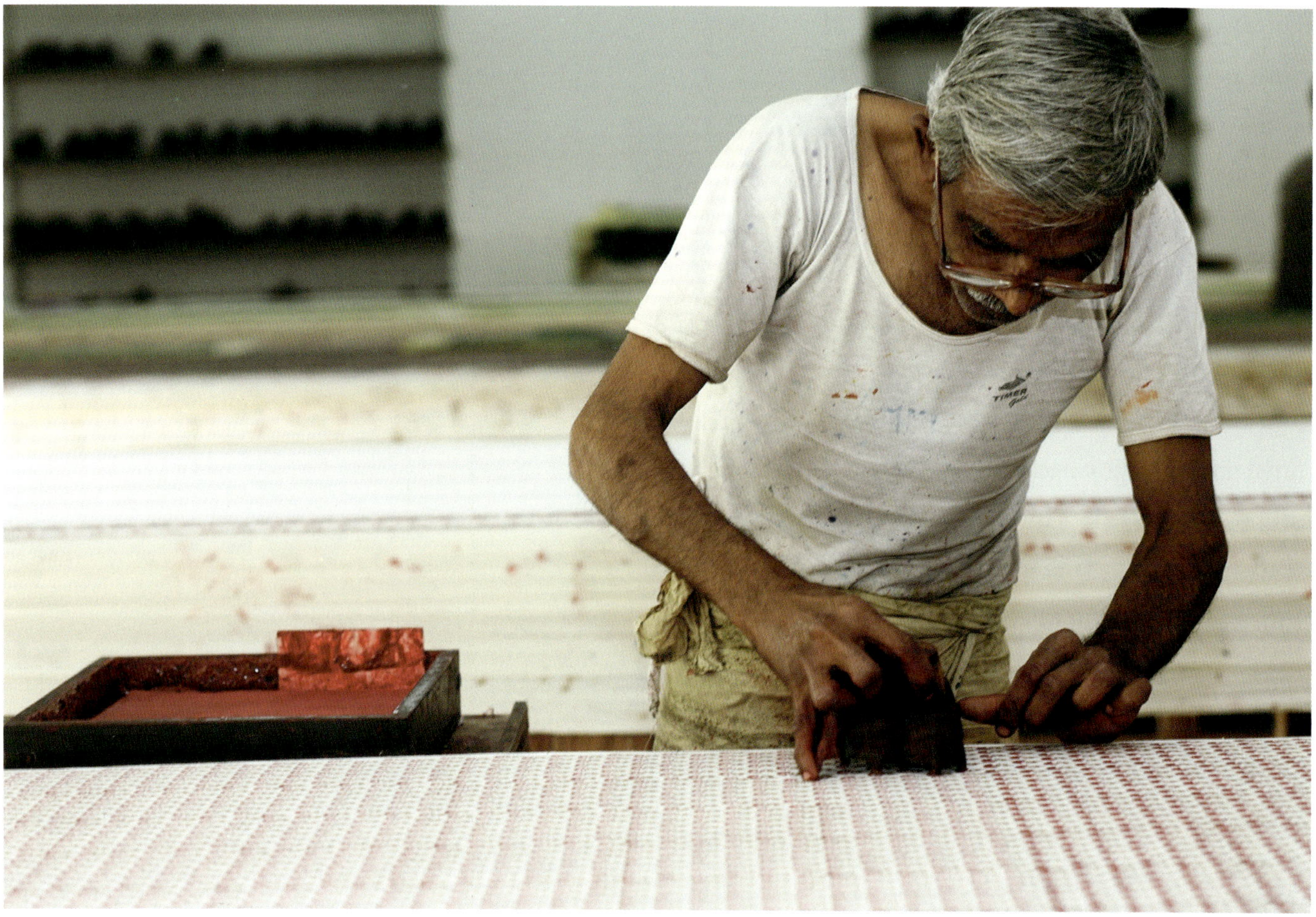

Printing on the fabric. The colour master prepares the dye and makes it ready for use. The print gradually emerges as the colours are applied one by one to the fabric

The whole world is in love with the Sanganeri prints of Rajasthan. Vegetable and mineral dyes are used as a custom. The *khari* or overprinting in gold is also an art which is in vogue here.

Bagru is a town near Jaipur which also excels in block printing. It is known for printing delightful circular designs on bed spreads, quilt covers, table linen and clothes in dark vegetable colours. *Bandhani* or the tie-and-dye art is also very popular in Rajasthan. It is mostly practised in Jaipur. The fabric is tied into small knots using threads and dipped into vats with their array of bright colours. After dyeing, these knotted parts remains uncoloured, creating a mosaic of beautiful designs and patterns.

The antiquity of the Jaipur *razai* can be traced back to about 280 years when a group of *mansuri*s (the cotton mattress and quilt makers) shifted to Jaipur from Amber. Kadar Bux, a young *razai* maker gifted a *razai* or quilt, with only 250g of cotton in it, to Maharaja Madho Singh of Jaipur. The Maharaja was so impressed that he gave Kadar Bux the title of Patel and two shops as gifts, which can still be seen opposite the Sawai Man Singh Hall adjacent to Hawa Mahal. Today, there are several small shops belonging to the descendants of Kadar Bux, carrying on with the rich tradition of *razai* making. As I have said before, the secret and exclusivity of Jaipur quilts lie in the carding (*dhunai*) of the cotton. It is done carefully by hand by carders who excel in extracting the finest of fibres from a mass of freshly-harvested cotton wool so that the quilts remain extra light and emanate special warmth.

Blocks, fluff and colours

I was intrigued by the process of quilt-making in Jaipur, till I had the opportunity to watch the entire process step-by-step and also take pictures from fairly close quarters at Brigitte Singh's atelier.

I had the chance to see as well how the printing blocks were made. There were quite a few intricately carved wooden blocks which were ready for use. I went

Wooden printing blocks on display

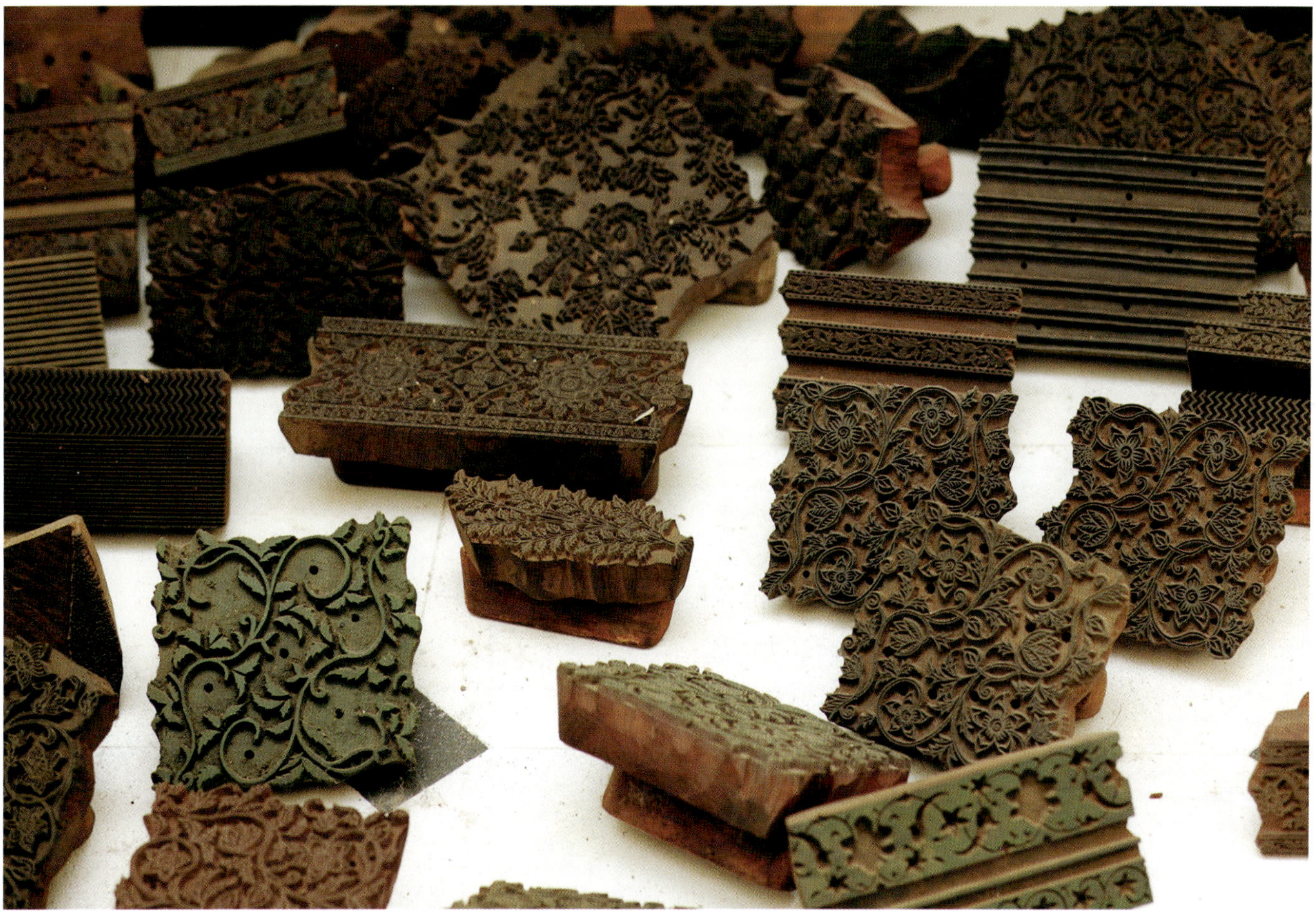

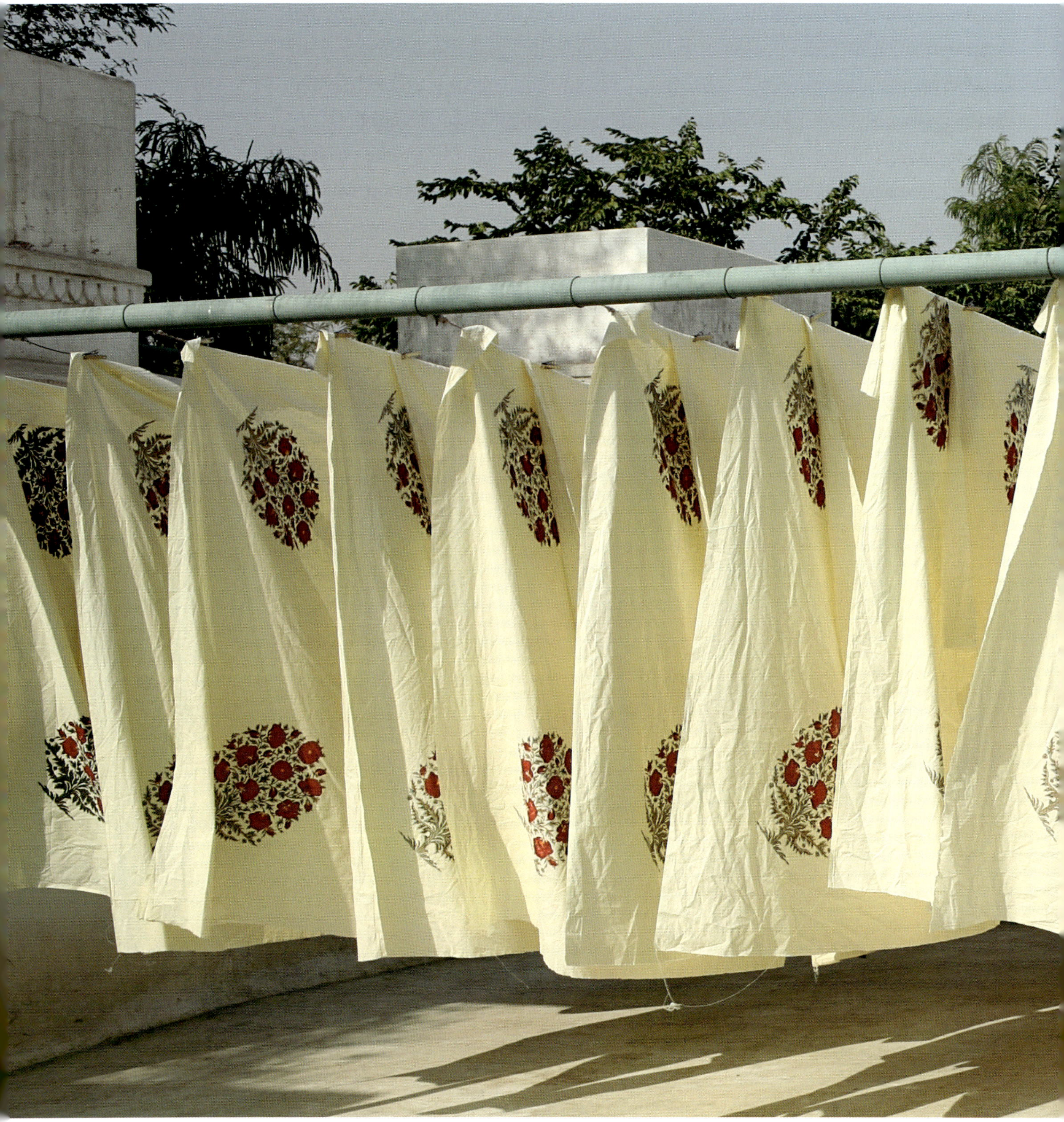

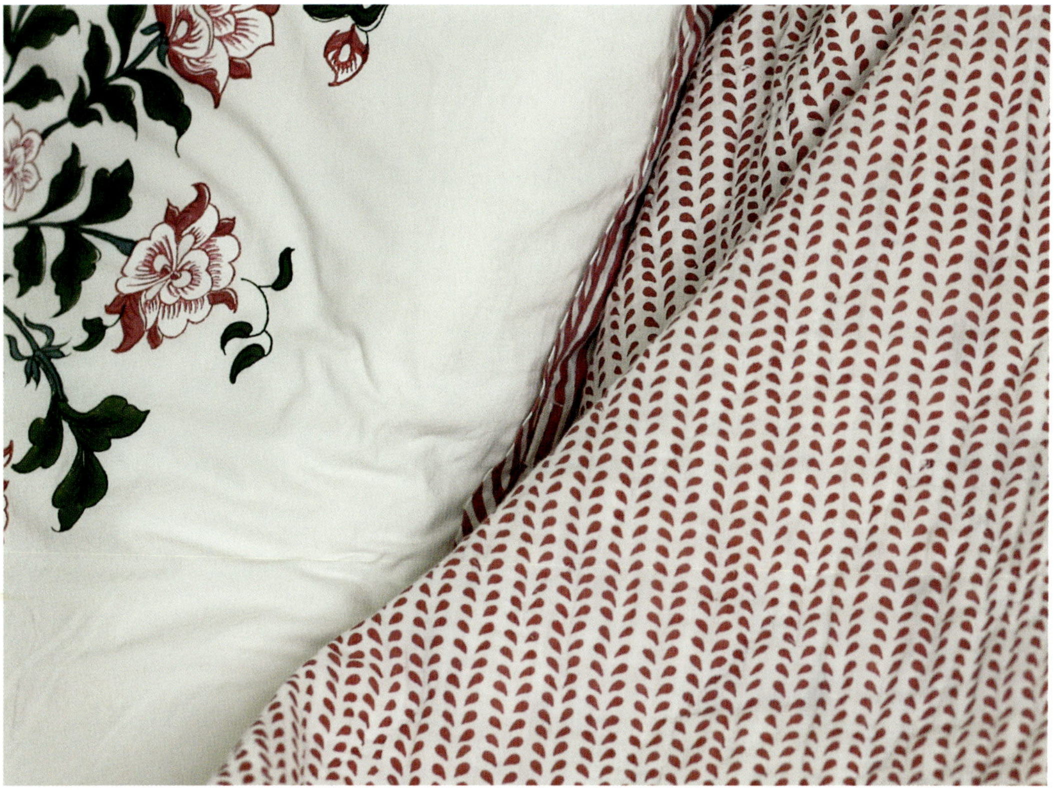

Facing page: *Printed fabric drying in the sun for enhancing and upgrading the brilliance of the colours*

Left: *Printed pillow from Brigitte Singh's collection and leaf print quilt from Rasa*

Below: *Post-modern prints created from traditional* Jaipuri *motifs like the* jalli, *used on quilts made by Rasa*

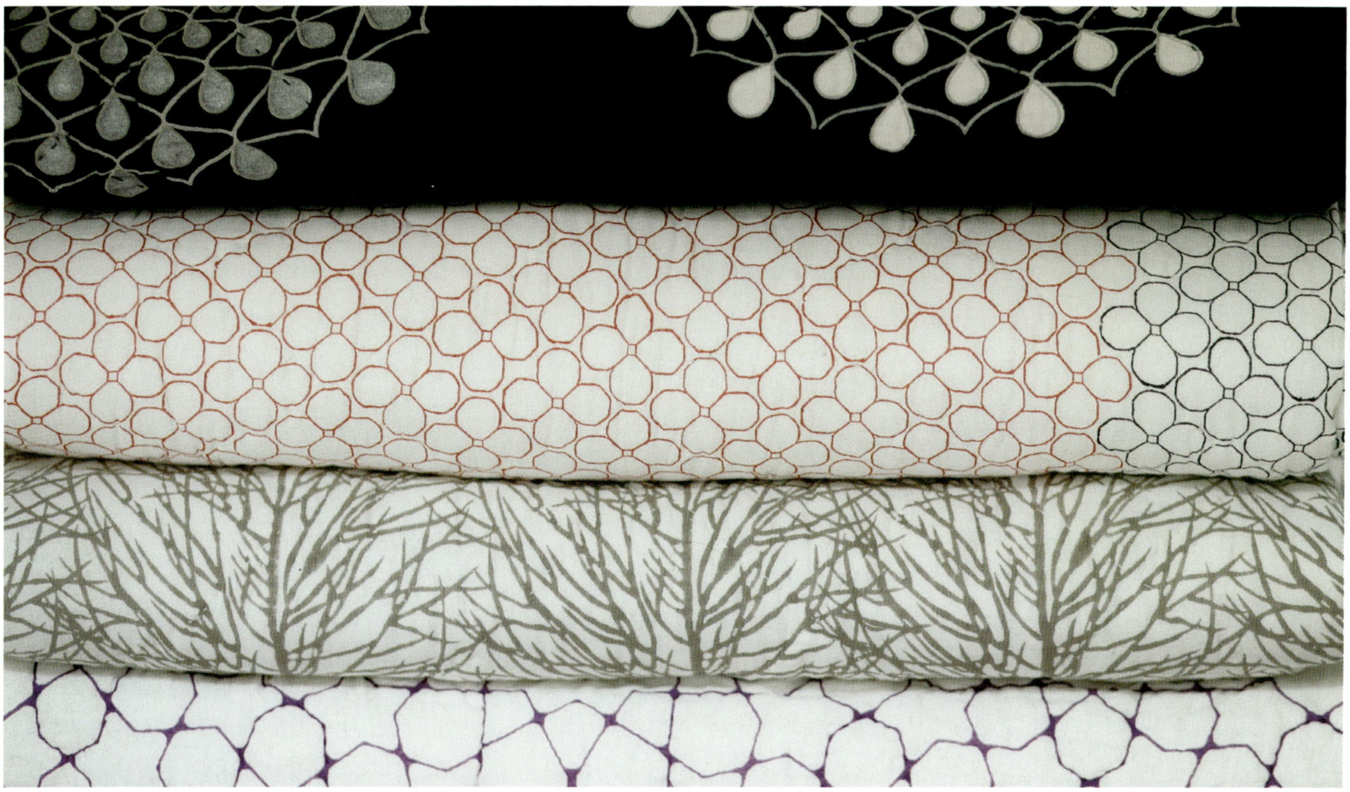

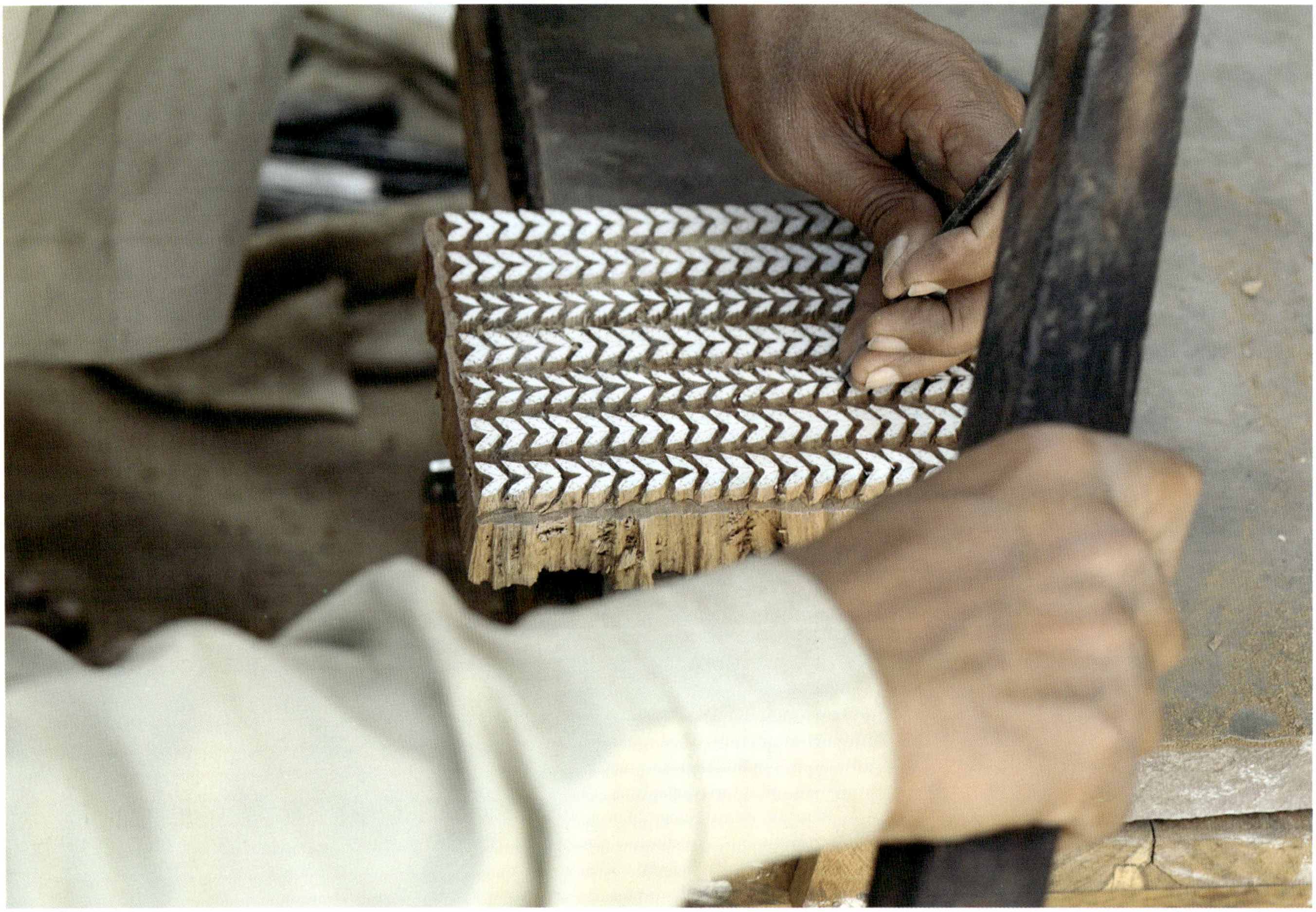

Carving out a printing block. The artist paints the pattern and the original art work is transmitted to the block master who transfers it to a printing block carved out of white-washed teak. The surface of the block is made perfectly plain and smooth. It takes a few weeks to create and finish a contour block

to another unit where the dye was being prepared and the fabric printed. The typical Jaipur quilts are often made of fine mulmul. I saw how the freshly-dyed and printed mulmul fabric was washed and dried in the sun. Finally the dyed sheets of fabric were ready for the tailor to stitch the shell or the cloth cover—a large sack actually, where all the cotton wool would be packed in, to make the stuffing of the quilt.

The next step was watching the cotton wool being weighed. The pressed cotton wool gradually turned into this fluffy, feather-light cloud of cotton. This is done with a bow or a simple machine. The cotton particles fly about freely in the air during this process, so one has to keep one's mouth and nose well covered. After fluffing, portions are fished out on a thin stick and placed on the reverse side of the large cloth sack—the shell.

This is quite a painstaking procedure, needing both time and patience. The worker levels the cotton wool with his hands carefully. The next step is to roll the whole unit together and turn it inside out. Of course it has to be done with utmost care so that the cotton wool is well spread out and does not end up at one end of the shell. Finally the two layers of the shell are stitched together and made ready for quilting. Young girls and women execute the quilting, which is quite an artistic process. I stood watching the women while they sat immersed in quilting in their colourful saris. They made a pretty picture.

When it is not too cold, the girls sit on the veranda facing a nice garden, working quietly. Of course it is routine work for them, eight hours a day, so it is definitely not as pleasant and leisurely a picture as I have painted. But I do feel that to be able to work near their homes in clean and comfortable surroundings, giving vent to their creativity and artistic sensibilities may not be a wholly unpleasant work experience for the women. As Andreé Pouliot of Soma expressed, quilting is a 'harmless' occupation and it permits women to earn some money and contribute to the family income.

Printing of a pattern in green, rust and yellow on fabric from Gitto's collection

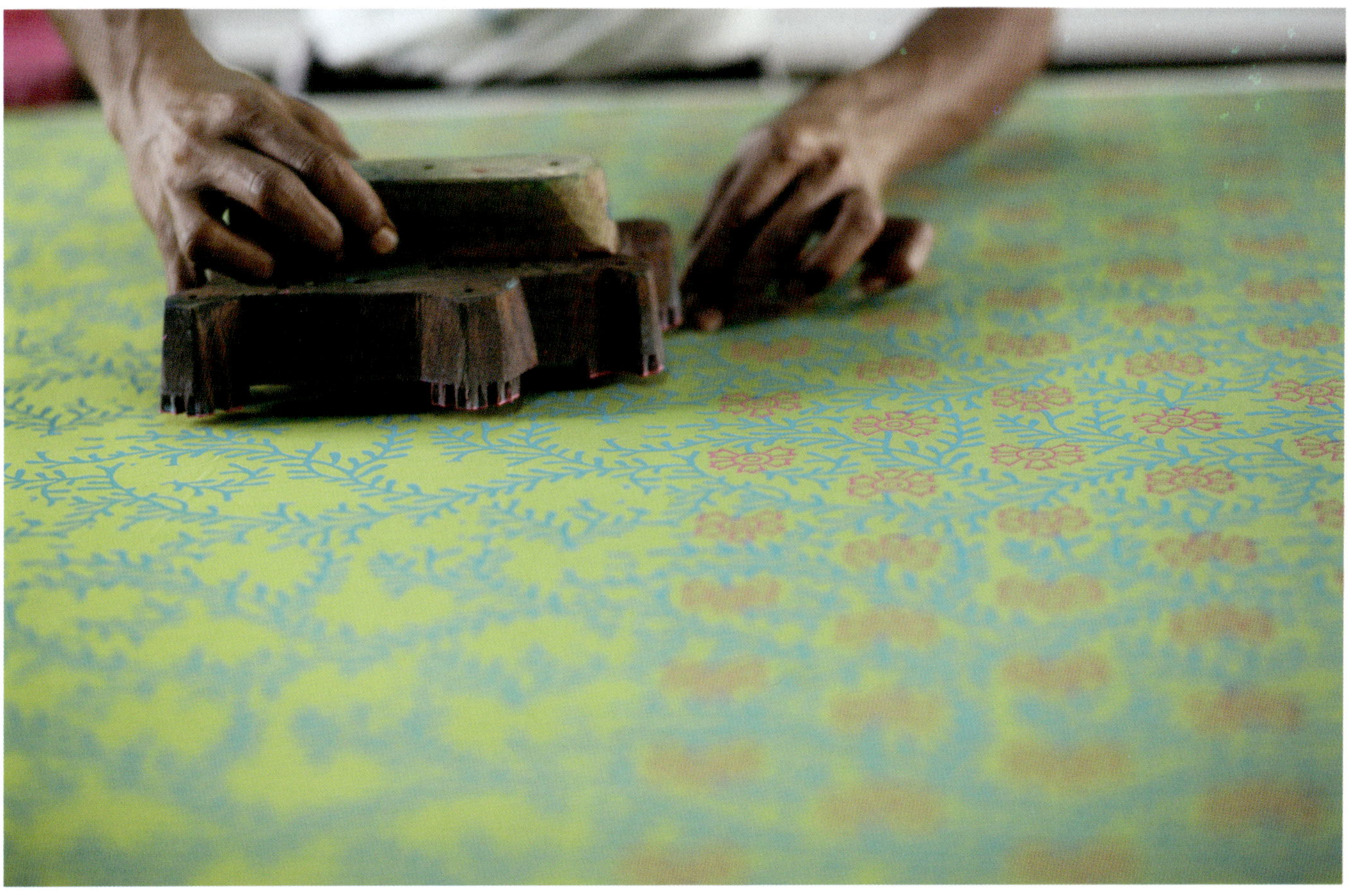

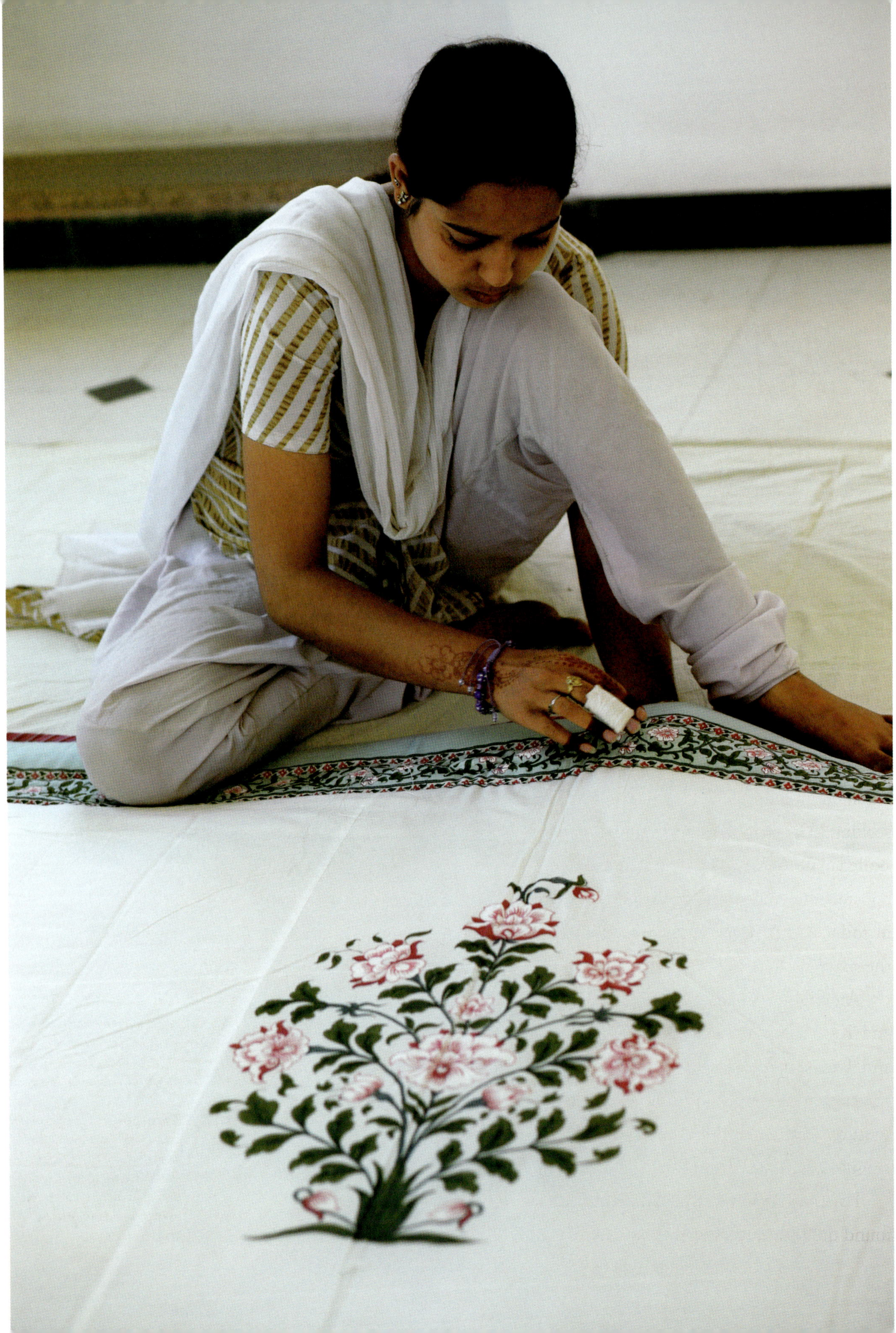

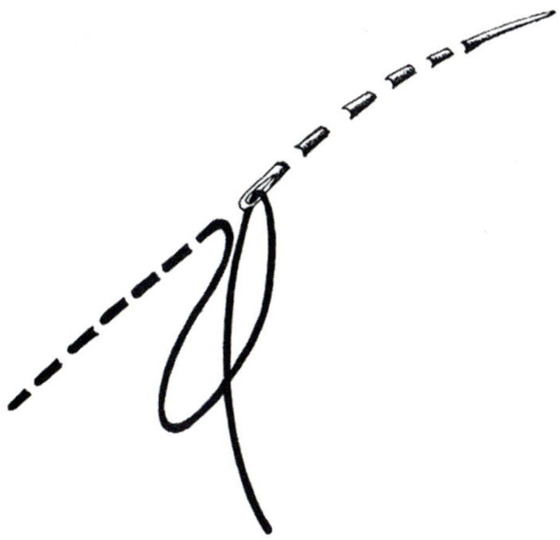

Trade interest

The evolution of the present day Jaipur *razai* was a slow but sure process. It received impetus from customers who gradually expressed an aesthetic interest in quilts and looked upon them as more than mundane items of daily use. Traders started taking a keener interest in enhancing the visual beauty of the quilt, seeking help from designers and women skilled in needlework and stitchcraft. This boosted the trade, and cloth merchants introduced many different varieties of the *razai*.

Among the pioneers were Miya Bajaj and Kadar Bux at Hawa Mahal Bazaar and Lashkari Textiles in Chaura Rasta, all active in the first half of the twentieth century. Later Kin Fabrics, Anokhi, Brigitte Singh and Soma joined in.

I spent a few months in Jaipur and found quilt producers who represented a certain unique style, tradition and quality. I interviewed them and took pictures of their products in order to share the result of my work with the reader.

Some of the questions I asked them were very simple and basic—whether the family was a traditional 'quilt making' family; when and how did all the work start; what type of craftsmen were involved in the production; did they use their own designs or custom-make the quilts… I did not always get detailed replies but they kindly answered most of my queries as well as they were able to.

Artist's impression of a quilting needle and the quilt stitches
Illustration: Danka Jaworska

Facing page: *Young woman engaged in quilting. It has turned out to be a comfortable job option for many women living in and around Jaipur, who can contribute to the household income*

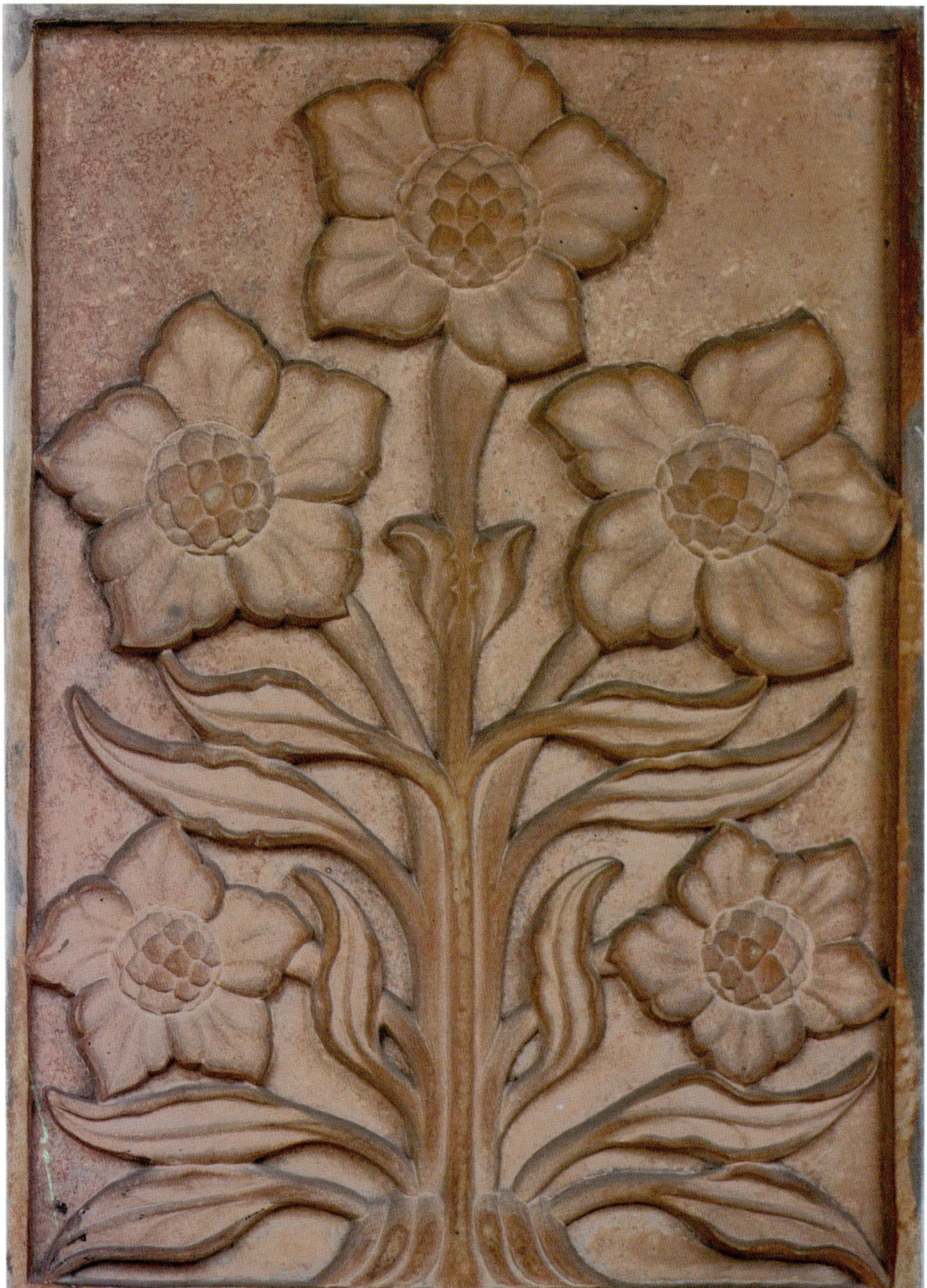

Chandramani Singh told me about the 'old quilt makers', who she said, I ought to meet, as they were the pioneers. I found Lashkari Textiles in Chaura Rasta and Miya Bajaj Razai Emporium in Hawa Mahal Bazaar. In the same bazaar I also located Kadar Bux. Magic Quilts is in Khawas Ji Ka Rasta. Friends Rooi Mattress is lodged in Chandpole Bazaar

Old quilt makers

I took a rickshaw again and went looking for the special *razai* shops in the old part of the city. When one is in a hurry and when the address is complicated it is better to trust a rickshaw driver. They know all the streets, lanes and by-lanes; they know addresses, people and important names and can move fast in spite of the traffic. I found the lanes lined with shops and overflowing with traffic. I spotted cars, cycles, cycle rickshaws, auto rickshaws, camels, even horses decorated for weddings. I watched the ongoing procession. The shops sold quilts and in front of them vendors sold fruits, shoes... almost everything found a place here. It was almost like an MTV show, in reality. I felt energised and alive.

It was not difficult to find the old quilt makers. People have known them for ages. A few questions and gesticulations later, I was in the first shop. All shops are open to the street and you can see the goods that they sell. Of course it all looked very colourful and visually attractive. When a client enters a shop, he is shown dozens of quilts; they are displayed by the shop assistant in a

Facing page: *Stone relief with flower and leaf motif from Nana-ki-Haveli*

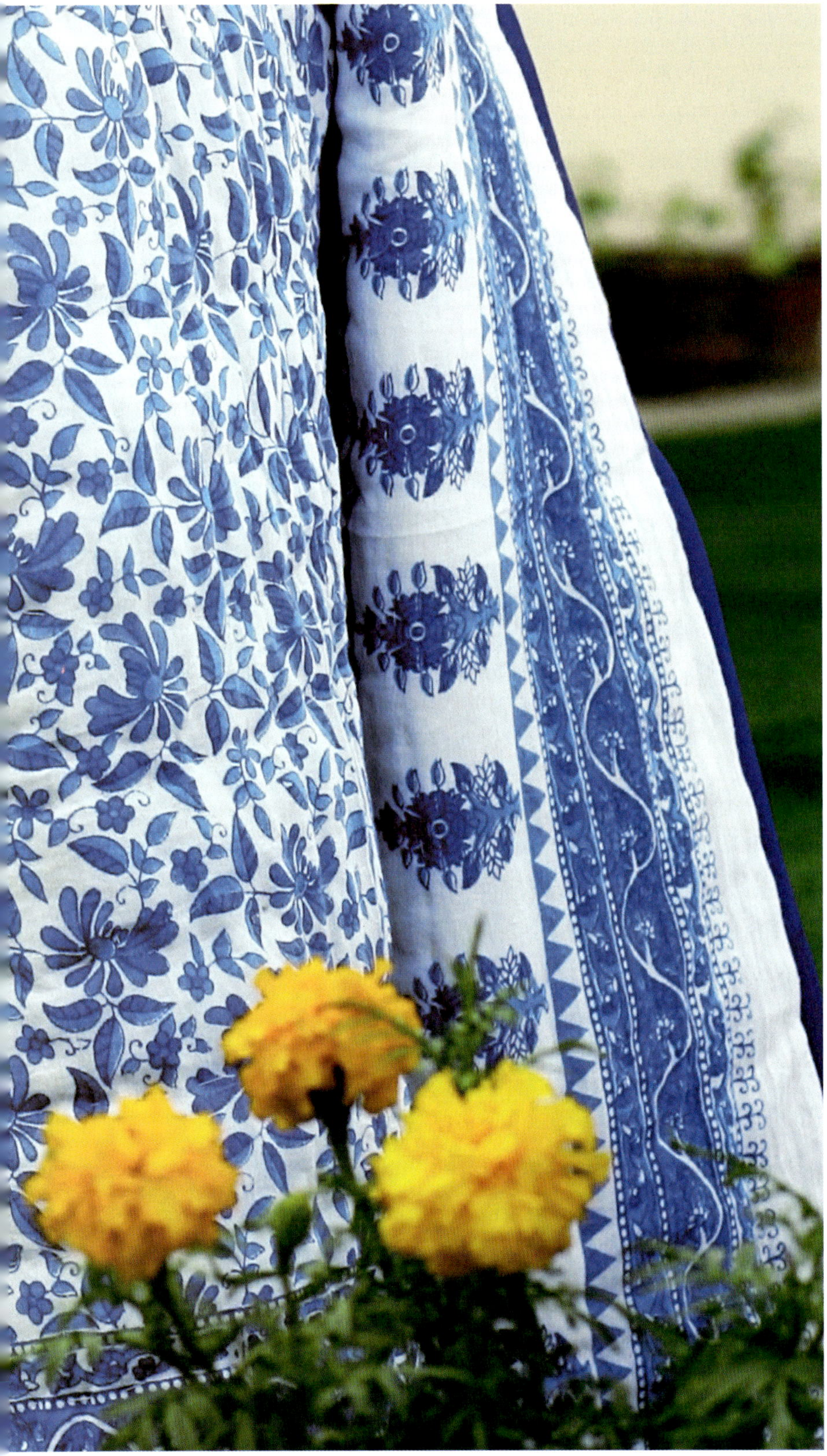

few seconds and then neatly folded back again. You can sit down, take it all in, drink tea and decide later.

I was not sure if the shopkeepers really believed that I was writing a book on Jaipur quilts, but they at least pretended that they did. They were kind enough to talk to me about their business and explain how they came to be in Jaipur. They told me that their entire families were in the "quilt business" and some of them had been around for as long as 250 years! All this sounded quite impressive and unique to me, since in my part of the world I was used to often seeing new shops come up, last a few years and then disappear altogether.

The quilts they manufacture in Jaipur give good value for the price. Mulmul is sometimes block- or machine-printed, but mainly hand-quilted. The patterns are usually traditional—with floral or animal motifs like camels and elephants. Paisley patterns are also quite common. There, for the first time, I saw quilts made of velvet, probably manufactured with the hill stations in mind, although Jaipur can get pretty cold as well, during the winter months, being so close to the desert. It was interesting to meet people who are the descendents of village quilt makers who were brought to Jaipur by the

Maharaja Sawai Jai Singh II more than two centuries ago. They were residents of Amber before they were brought to Jaipur and the origins of all the old quilt-makers are very similar to each other.

One can trace a tradition of working in peace under the shade of communal harmony, with workmen from different communities, castes and religions coming together to create beautiful works of art with utmost care and precision. Together they forged ahead to grapple with fate and turn it around to make success tales of themselves. Stories of grit and struggle merge with those of creativity and vision. But each family has its own and unique story to tell.

These are now mostly family-managed business houses where the new generation has preserved and are practising the old skills well, passed on to them by their ancestors. When these families were brought to Jaipur, they first cooked and slept in their workshops—working, making and selling the quilts by day. Now of course the situation has changed for the better; the quilt makers have made a tidy fortune for themselves and live comfortably in large houses. Some of the leading and pioneering names within the large and expanding hub of Jaipur quilt makers are the Miya Bajaj Razai Emporium, Magic Quilts, Kadar Bux Textiles, Friends Rooi Mattress and Lashkari Textiles.

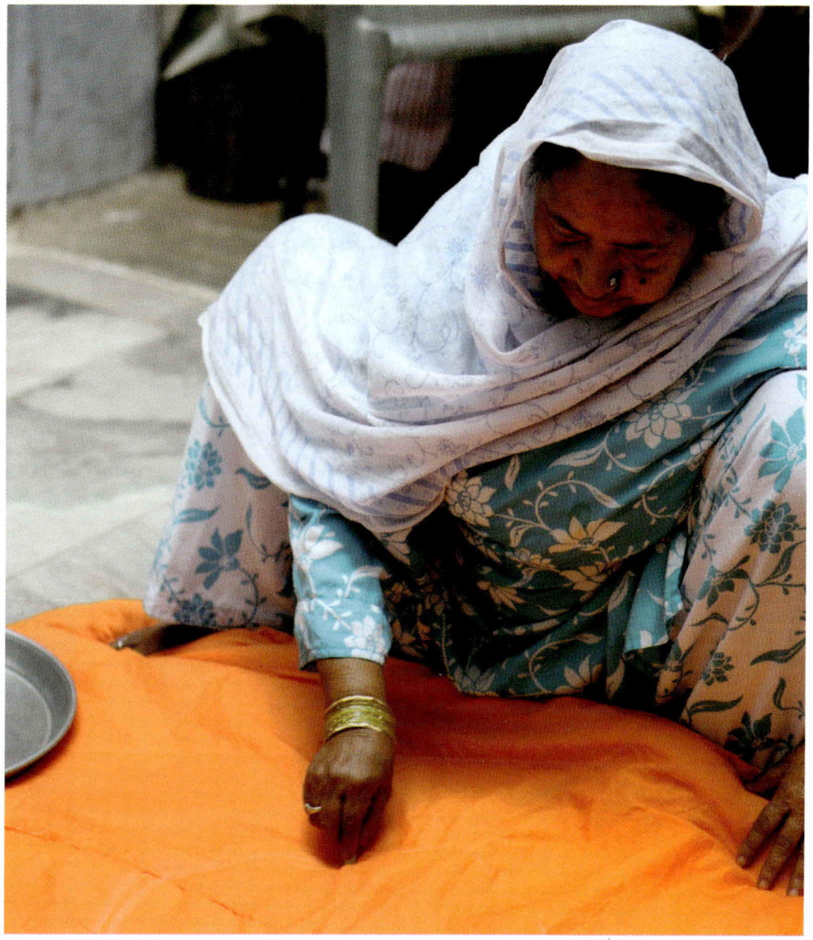

Hazai Babu Khan's wife working on a quilt. Family members of quilt makers in the trade often help out with the processing

Facing page: *A study in blue, this pretty cotton quilt was quilted at Kadar Bux*

Miya Bajaj Razai Emporium

I chose to knock at the Miya Bajaj outlet and discovered nice floral designs in their shop. Coupled with their reasonable prices, the quilts make perfect souvenirs for young tourists to take back home. The family started quilting ninety years ago. Their fabric has always been sourced from townships near Mumbai and

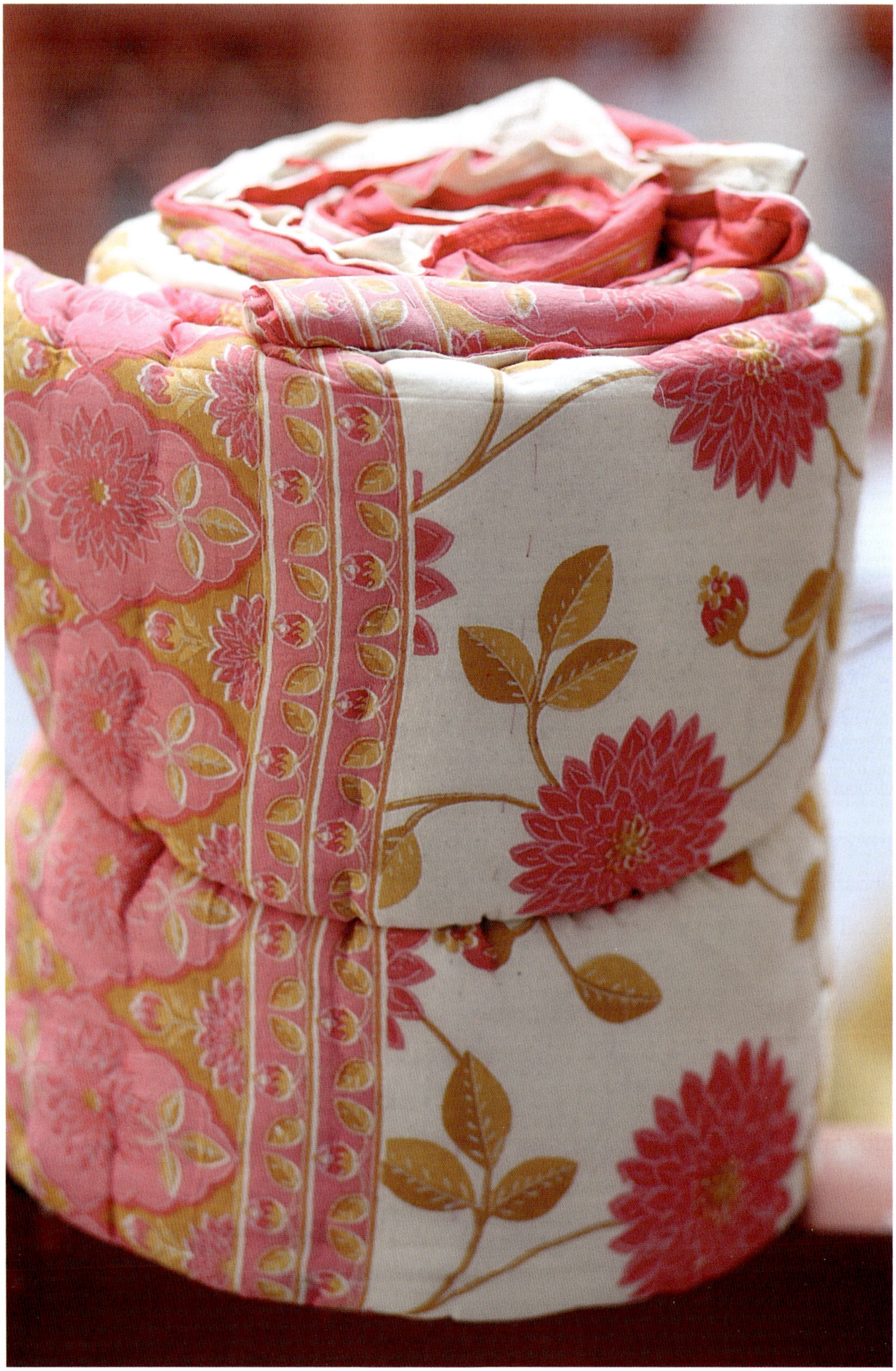

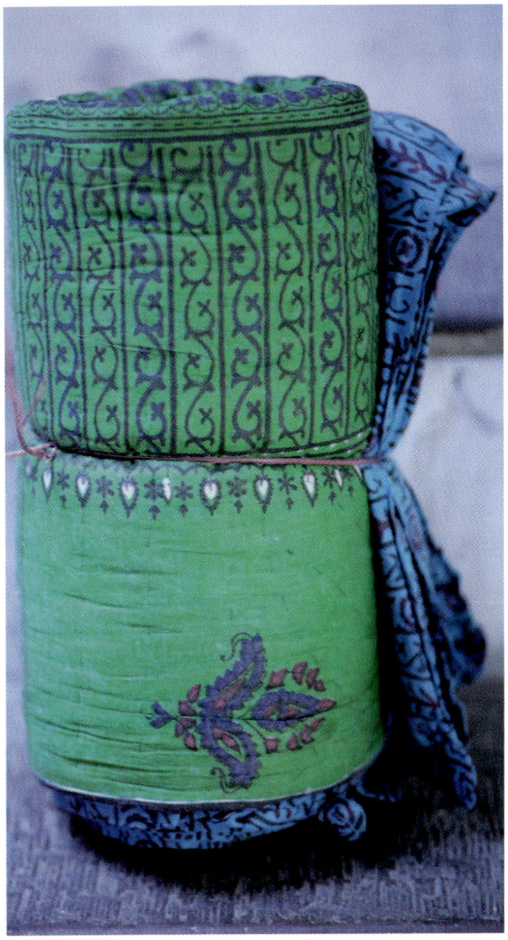

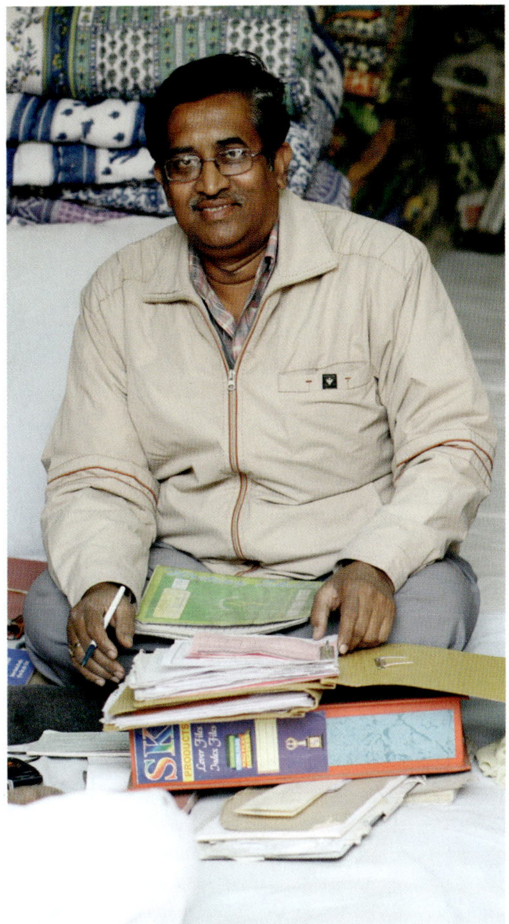

Page 76 and left: *Quilts from Miya Bajaj, ready for the market*

Right: *Manmohan Miya Bajaj, owner of Miya Bajaj Razai Emporium*

Bhiwandi. They have their own printers in Sanganer and the stitching is done by a hired work force of mostly women. They use their own designs, but often cater to customers' personal likes and dislikes and are open to their suggestions. Miya Bajaj makes extra-thick quilts for the hill stations as well. The shop has its list of devoted individual customers which it caters to, besides producing quilts in bulk for the retail trade within India as well as for the export market. The company employs around 100 people from the Mansuri, Dhunya and Binaki communities. The Miya Bajaj family belongs to a close-knit community but an occasional intermarriage with another community is not wholly unheard of.

Magic Quilts

One afternoon I visited Ahmed Manzoor and his family with Kitty Rae, a legendary figure and a highly respected lady amongst quilt makers, designers, retailers and exporters in Jaipur. Rae had spent twenty years with Manzoor's company

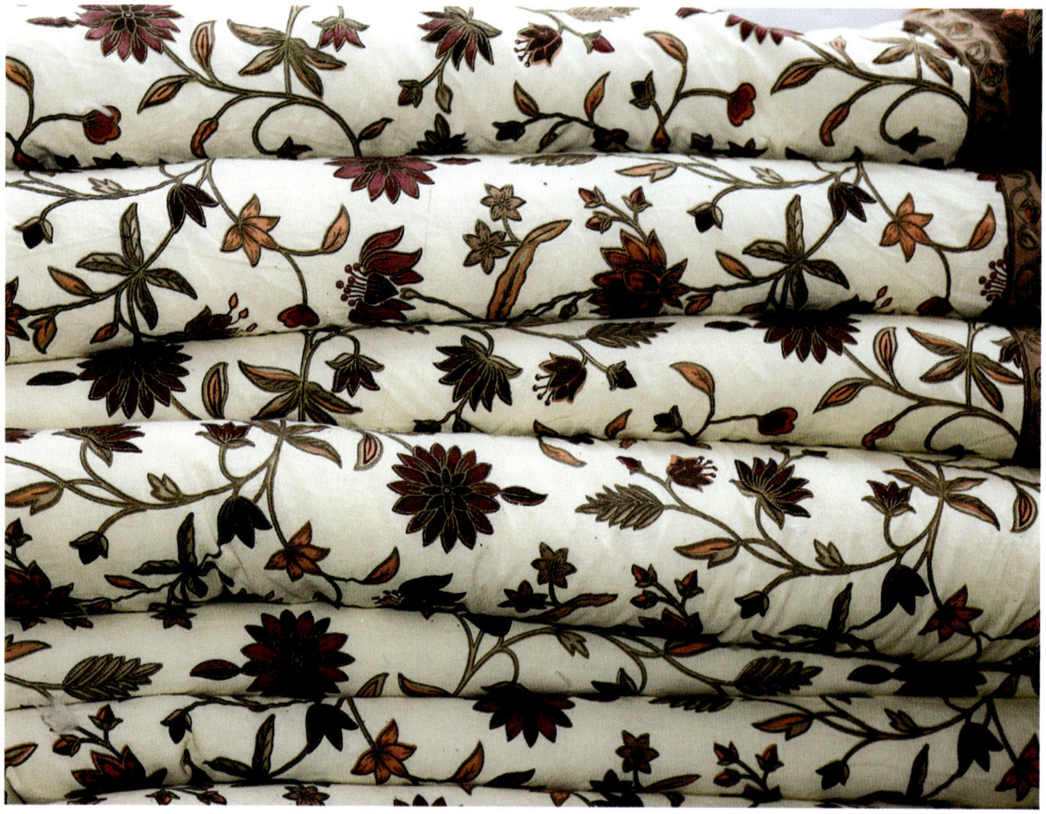

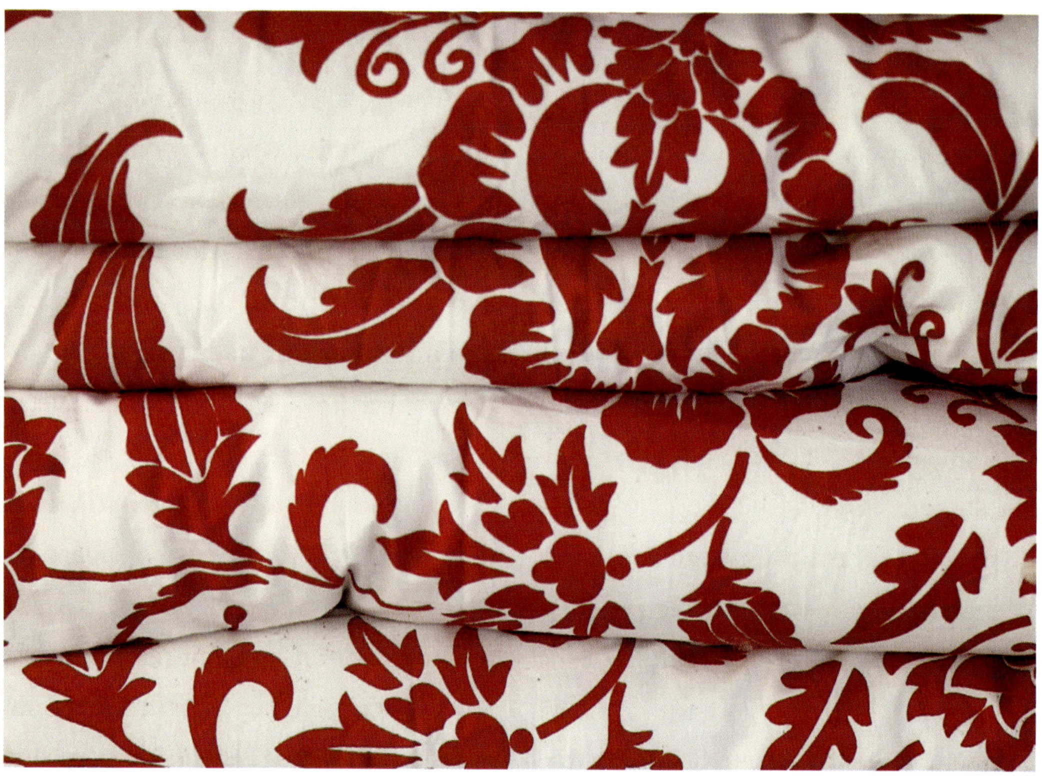

Top: *'Flowers on white'— quilt from Hazai Babu Khan's Magic Quilts*

Bright in red and white, from Magic Quilts

Magic Quilts. After sifting through their quilts and listening to their story of quilt-making, I thought that the name 'Magic Quilts' suited them very well. Indeed, it is a magical story with a fairy tale end.

The family had laid the foundation of their trade amidst humble settings, living–as was the custom–in their small workshop-cum-retail outlets in Hawa Mahal Bazaar. They started business by simply filling the quilts with cotton, moving on at a later stage to take up and control the entire stitching and quilting process. This is how they began their manufacturing units in Jaipur. The family did not have the means to produce in bulk when they launched their business and therefore managed only around twenty quilts per day. Times have changed and the company has clearly evolved through sheer hard work and foresight during the interim years. Today they produce 100-125 quilts daily.

The quilters came to Jaipur from Amber about 200 years ago. Their customers are still mainly individuals–local and neighbourhood residents–who usually require one new quilt every winter. The company also works with two to three exporters. The fabric is usually provided by the customers, the cotton for the filling is Magic Quilts'.

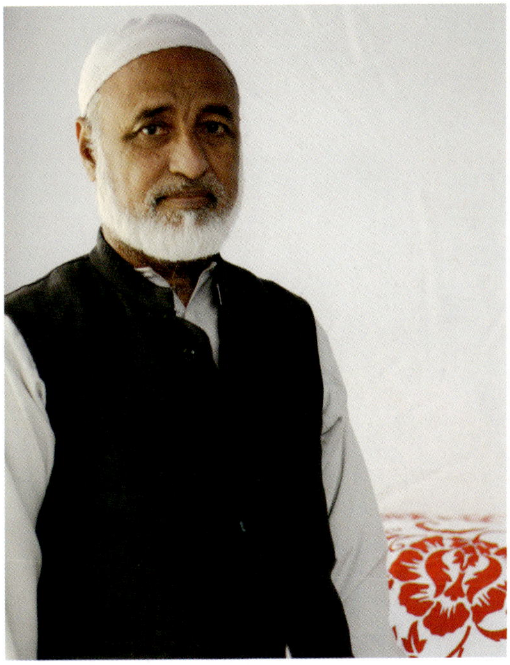

Synthetic material for the cover turns out to be more expensive. Cotton is by far, the preferred fabric of both workmen and customers.

Magic Quilts makes all the varieties—printed, plain, satin and silk quilts. The materials come from Ganganagar, Gulabpura near Bikaner and Madhya Pradesh. Most of the craftsmen belong to the Mansuri community, as do the family members. Family members and distant relatives are also engaged in the manufacture and trade, along with hired personnel. The stitching and quilting is done by women, executed mostly by hand. The company allows other communities to do the stitching but the fluffing of the cotton is handled solely by workmen

Hazai Babu Khan, owner of Magic Quilts

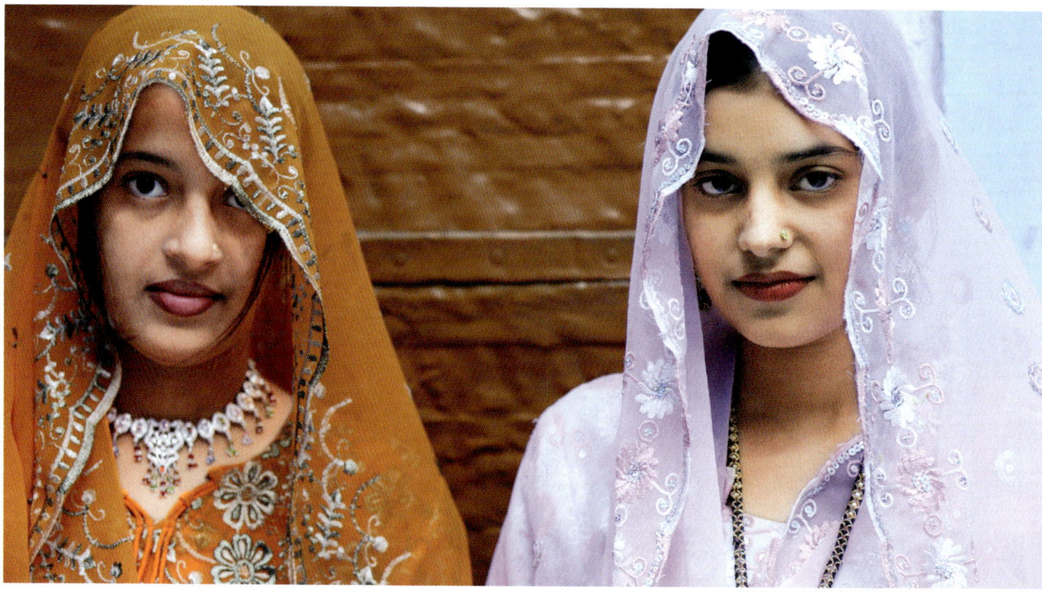

Young women from Hazai Babu Khan's family in traditional embroidered dress, with floral motifs

who are distant relatives or at least from the same community. I was also told that simple fluffing machines are often used now to fluff the cotton wool. I wondered whether the machine fluffing affected their health more than hand fluffing did. It is easier and faster to work with the machine of course, they admitted when I asked them how different the work experience was. However, smaller cotton particles were released during machine fluffing, circulating in the air and causing an increased level of pollution hazard.

There is a good flow of new quilting patterns as customers' suggestions are also taken into account. I was very happy to learn how to transfer a pattern on the sheet of fabric for quilting. Most of the quilting procedure and the pattern to be followed are decided by the quilt-maker but some customers come with a ready pattern for quilting. Transferring the pattern to the fabric sheet is an interesting but simple process. For this, a large sheet of paper is used where the pattern is traced out through perforations. The workers prepare a thin liquid paint by mixing indigo powder with water or sometimes Colgate tooth powder with water. Next, they run a wet sponge or a piece of cloth dipped in the 'paint' along the line of perforations traced out on the paper. The thin paste leaves traces on the fabric, dripping through the perforations, which are then meticulously followed by the embroiderers during the quilting process. After completing the quilting job the fabric is thoroughly washed. Indigo or the white Colgate tooth powder can be easily washed away.

Kadar Bux Textiles

Four ancestral family units of the Kadar Bux quilt makers were brought to Jaipur from Amber by Maharaja Sawai Jai Sing II. They have been working with quilts for the past 250 years. The ancestors lived and worked in their shops when they started business in Jaipur but the present family members live in four different houses. The old shops in Jaipur still exist but stand renovated, altered and enlarged. The whole family is employed in the company. Young daughters, wives and younger brothers quilt at home. The fluffing is done by younger men in the family with a bow and a machine.

Legend goes that one of the ancestors, Madha Singh gifted the Maharaja of Jaipur a quilt that weighed only 250 grams. The pleased king gifted the family three shops in the Hawa Mahal Bazaar—numbers nine, ten, and eleven. A family member Abdul Rahim, improved upon the quilt and made a truly lightweight product weighing only 200 grams, which he in his turn, gifted to Jawaharlal Nehru the first prime minister of independent India. The father of the present owner of Kadar Bux Textiles once made a quilt which weighed an incredible 50 grams and gifted the same to the then Prime Minister of India, Morarji Desai.

Rows of cotton quilts in some of the most popular motifs and colour tones, displayed at the Kadar Bux Textiles shop

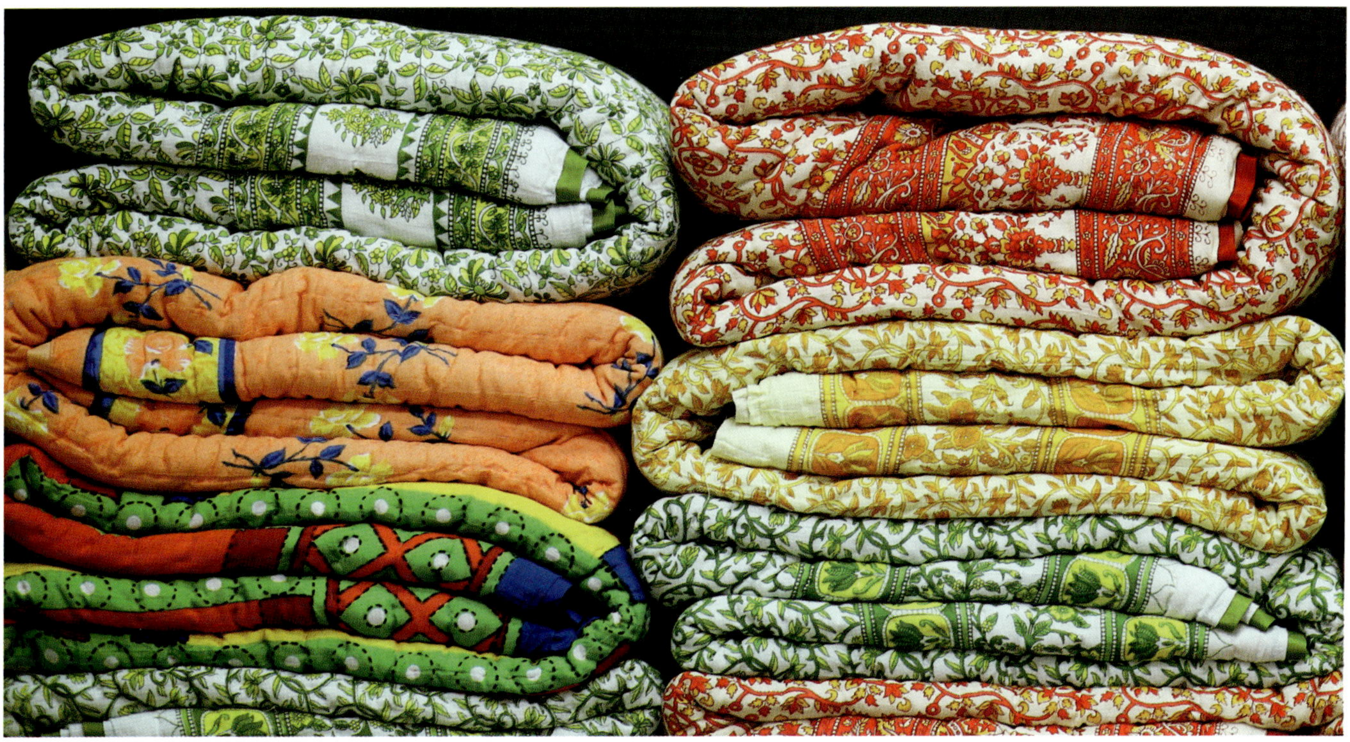

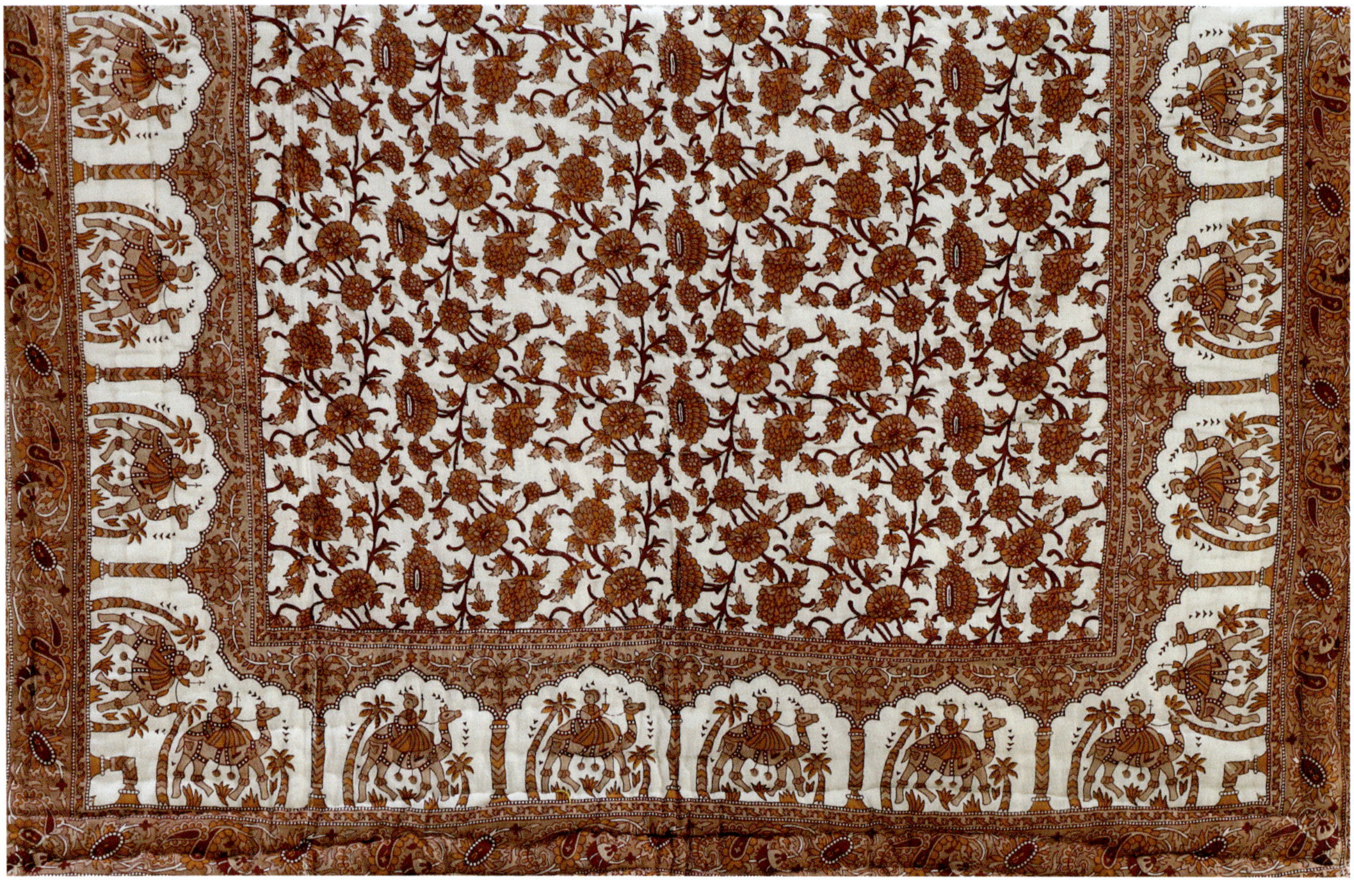

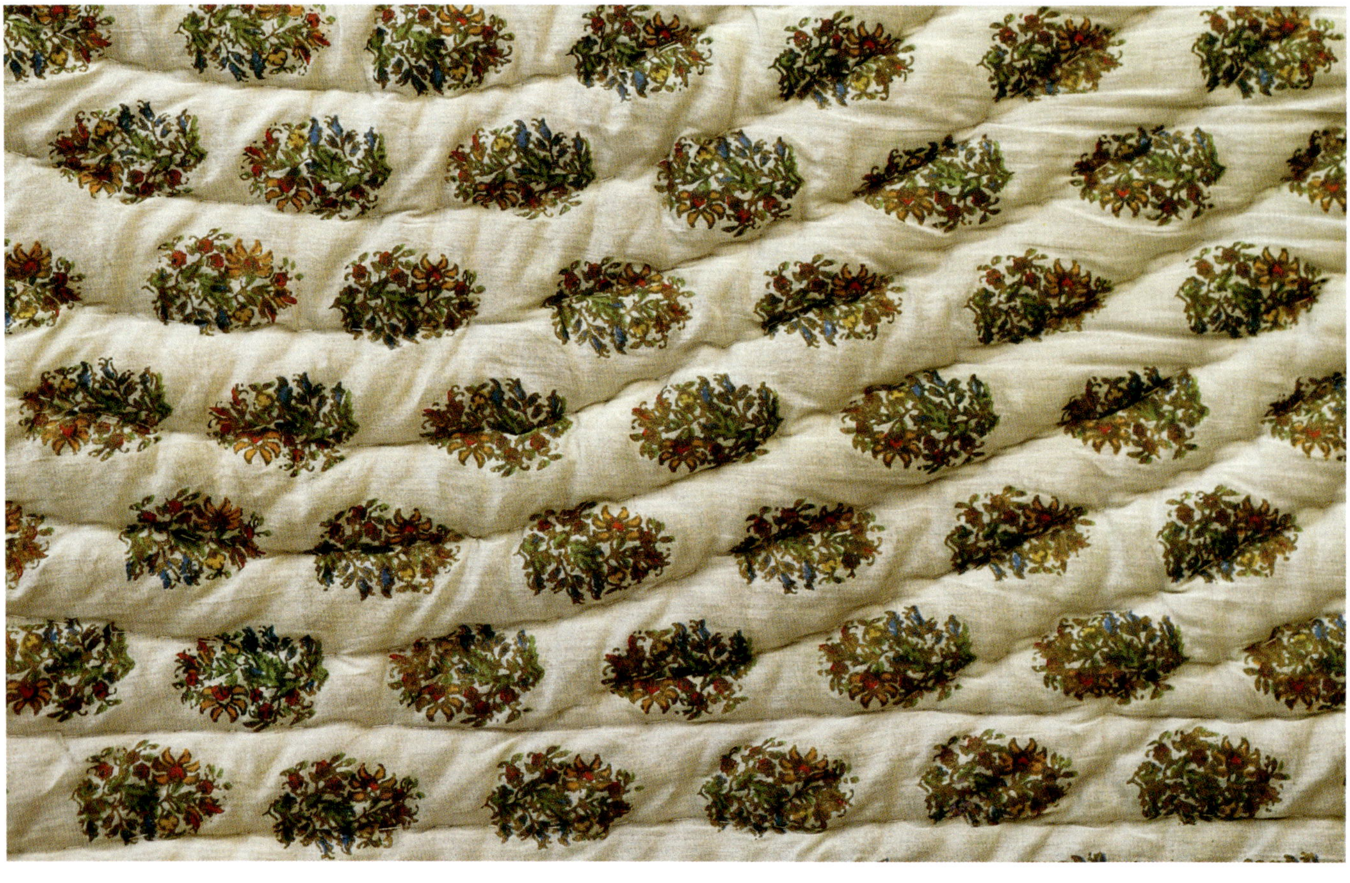

Kadar Bux is a famous brand in the city of Jaipur and has a big band of loyal customers. The printing job at Kadar Bux is executed in Sanganer and the vegetable dye printing is done in Bagaru. The motifs which are used most often by the company are traditional Mughal and Sanganer prints.

There are approximately sixty-seventy people employed with Kadar Bux Textiles. The company experiments with a variety of motifs, colours and fabrics besides making the typical soft cotton vegetable dyed quilts with the Sanganeri prints.

The new quilts are indeed very colourful and novel but the 'real' *razai*, as I am told by the present head of the company Abdul Hakim, 'is made only of cotton' and I too, prefer the old and traditional ones, which come in typical shades, patterns and fabric. These hang outside, displaying their traditional paisley patterns—light gold on white or a combination of some such subdued colours.

Friends Rooi Mattress

The family of Friends Rooi Mattress hails from the village Madhu Rajpora in the

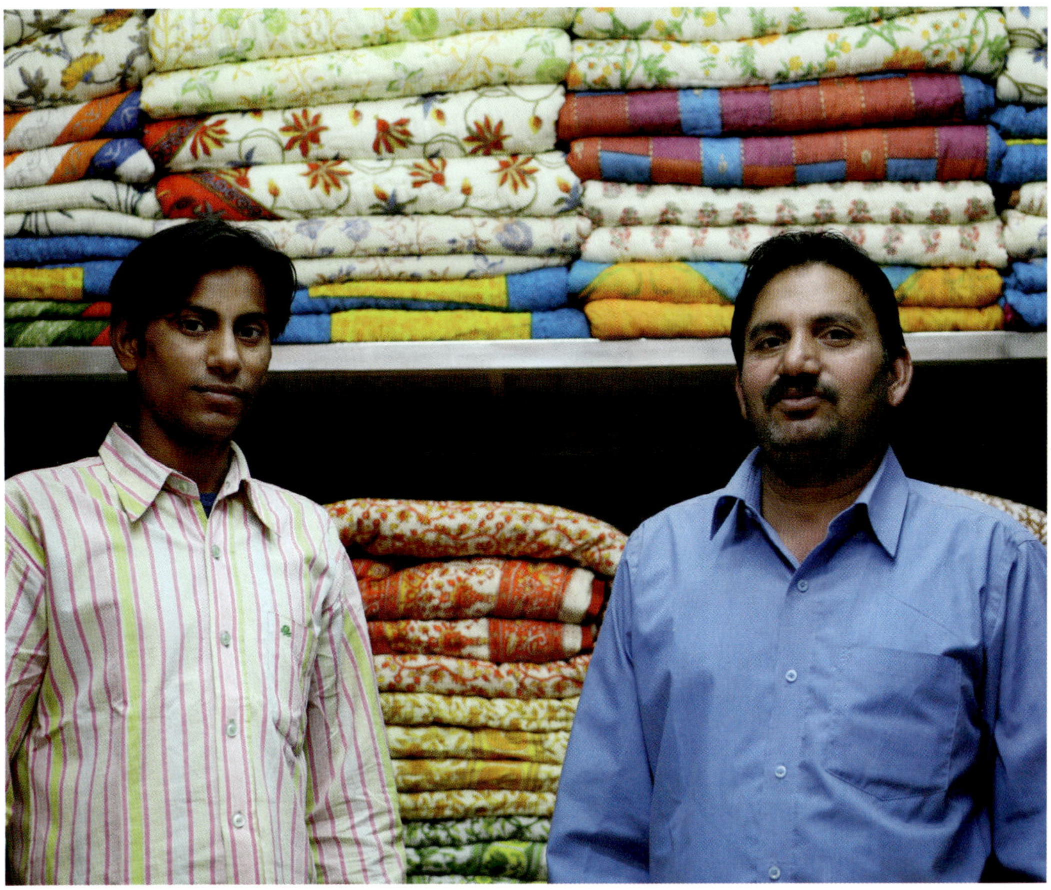

Abdul Hakim, owner of Kadar Bux Textiles (right), with son Abdul Fareed

Facing page top: *Typical Sanganeri print in muted colour tones with camels and flower motifs*

Facing page bottom: *Cotton quilt in soft, subdued hues from Kadar Bux Textiles*

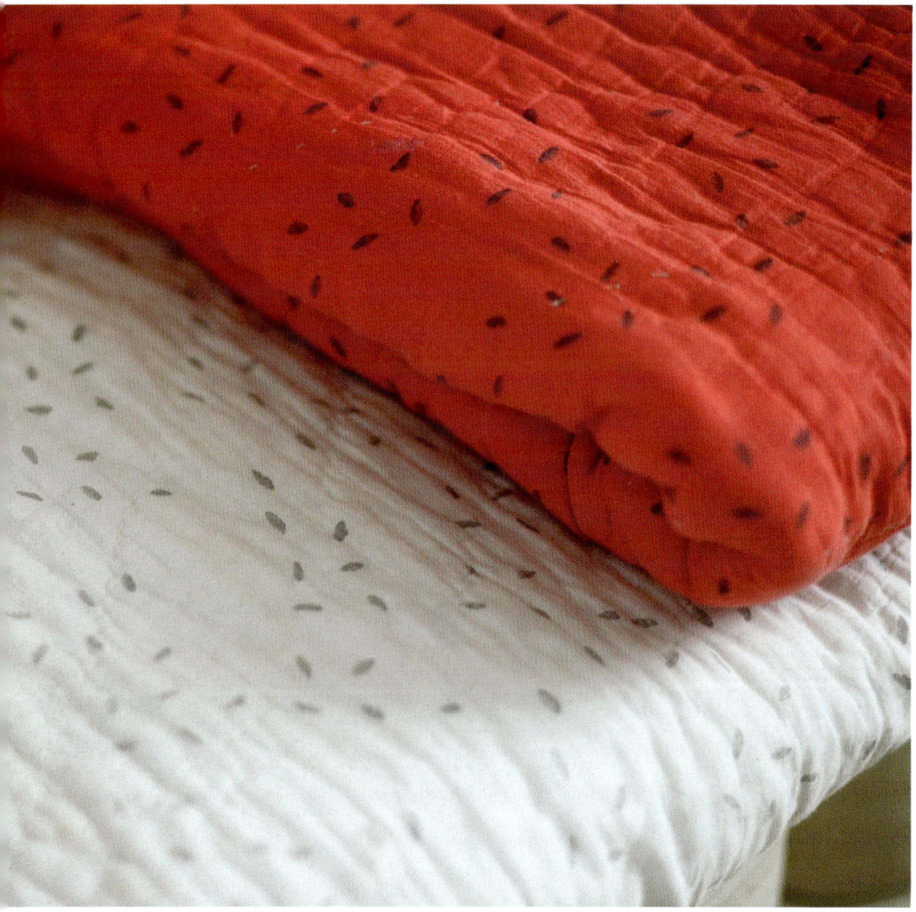

Phagi *tehsil* of Jaipur district, not far from the town of Sanganer. The members of this group of quilt makers marry within the same community and feel that they help improve the inherent skills, the general standard of living and socio-economic background of their community in the process.

The business house has existed for fifteen years, but quilting has been an age-old tradition in the family, having continued for the past 300 years.

Friends Rooi Mattress works for the Indian Government, caters to exhibitions, individual customers and a few select quilt exporters from Jaipur like Soma, Ratan Textiles and Nayika.

The quilting and the quality of the end product are excellent. The fabric comes from the customers, the domestic market, and some of it is designed by the family. Workers come from the Mansuri community. The core family members and close relatives form a part of the managerial staff.

Synthetic material is often used for the cushions designed for Japanese customers, but synthetic is inflammable and cotton is much safer. Their cotton comes from Ganganagar and Gulabpura; the mulmul travels from South India, Mumbai and Ahmedabad.

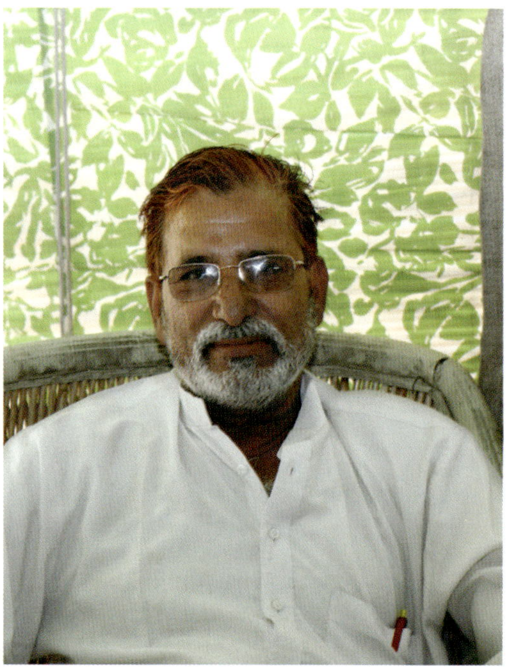

Above and facing page: *The quilts with leafy prints (above) and maroon-on-white (facing page) have been designed by Rasa after the initial fluffing at Friends Rooi Mattress. The white quilt (facing page) wedged in between the printed ones belongs to Friends Rooi Mattress*

Right: *Abdul Gaffur, one of the owners of Friends Rooi Mattress*

Lashkari Textiles

Phoolchand Lashkari, the grandfather of the present generation owners and managers started the company about forty years ago. The family started their trade solely as cloth merchants but later the company evolved and diversified, involving itself in the quilt trade and starting a line of designing and manufacture.

At present there are four sons who take care of different sides of the business. The company owns three shops in Jaipur, which deal in quilts but they do not compete with each other.

The manufacturers belong to the Vaishnava and Marwari community of traders. Lashkari Textiles mainly supplies to the local Indian market through different distributors.

The cotton comes as usual from Mumbai and Bhiwandi, and the velvet which is used for heavier quilts comes from Mumbai and Ahmedabad. Surat in Gujarat supplies the synthetic fabric.

However, synthetic filling is strictly not used. The company uses freelance workers who hail mainly from Sanganer, supplying them with raw materials, motifs and designs.

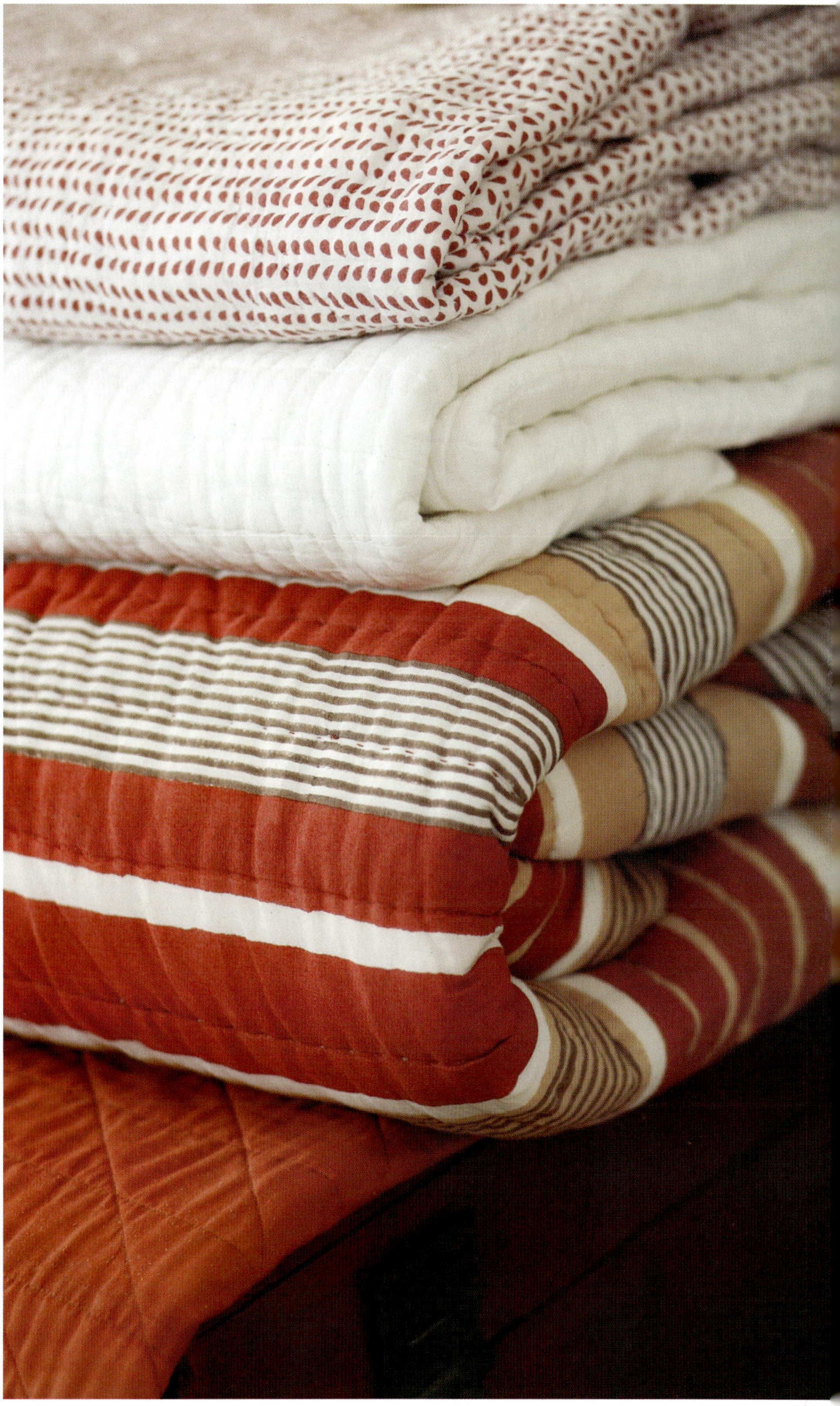

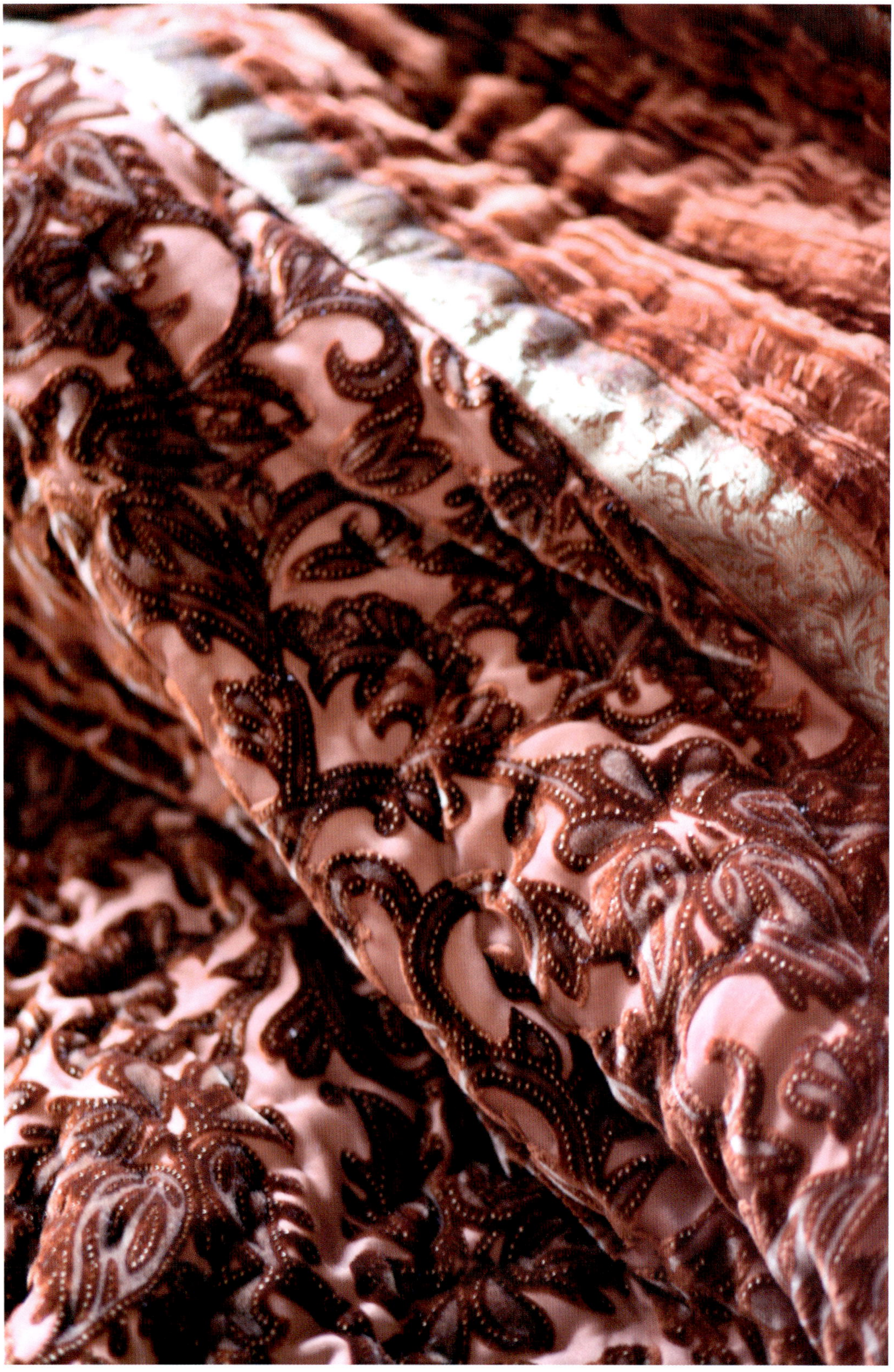

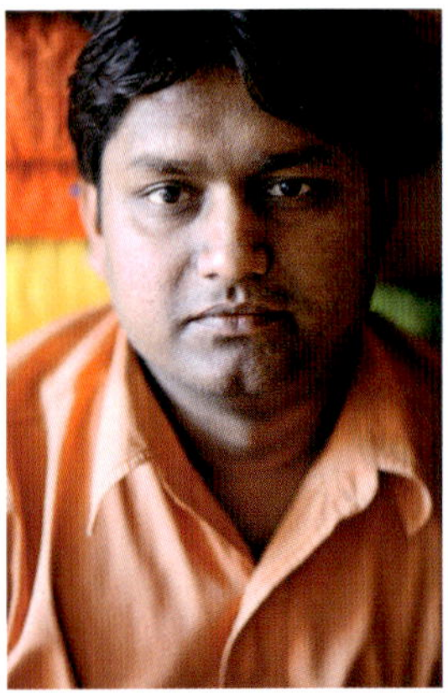

Above: *Manish Lashkari, owner of Lashkari Textiles*

Right: *Luxurious velvet quilt from Lashkari Textiles*

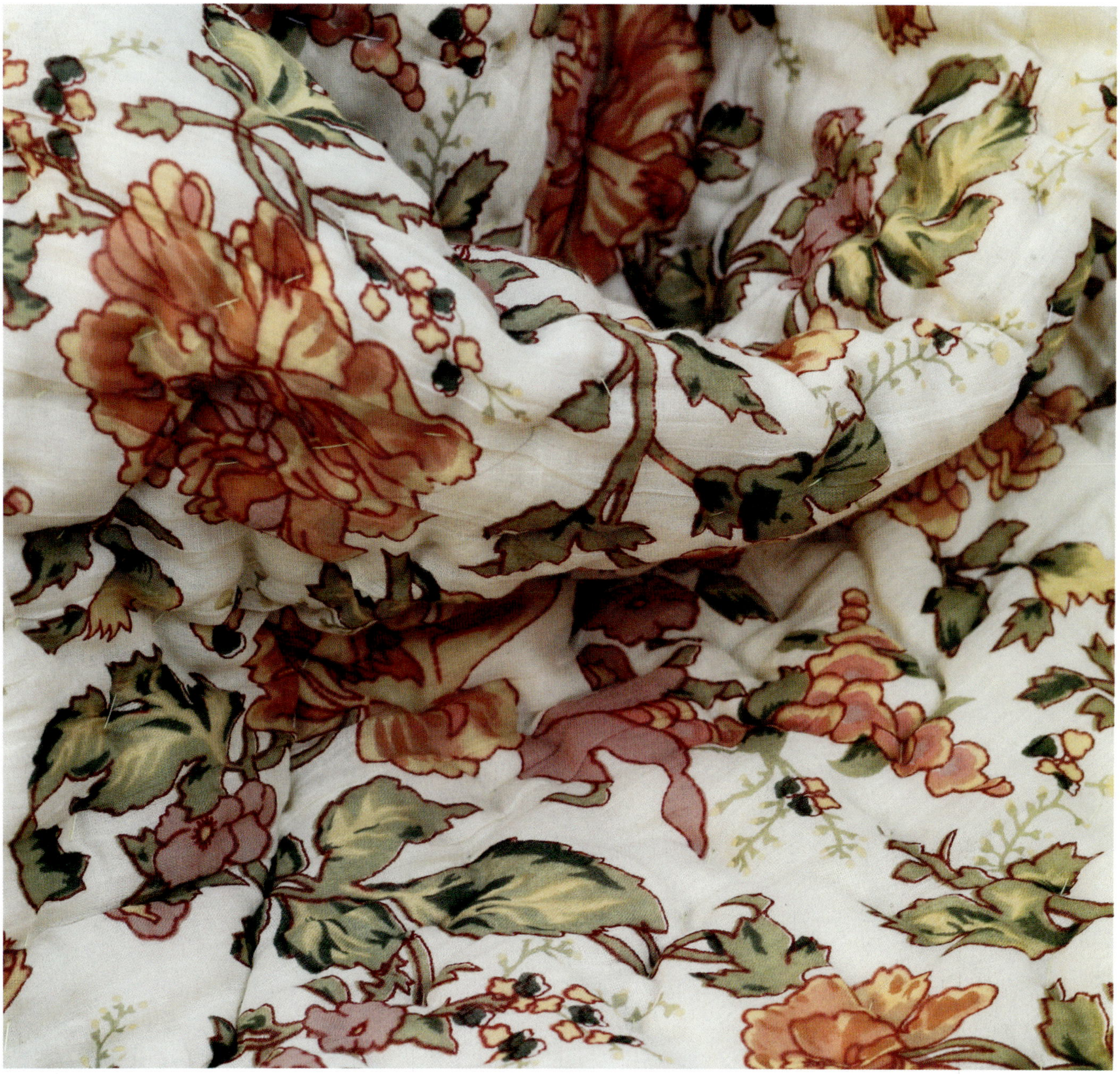

Mix-and-match of muted earthy hues laid out in a soft floral pattern

Some of the designs come from the customers while others are chosen and created by the company. The size of the motifs or the palette of colours used is often the company's choice. The filling and stitching of quilts is handled by separate communities while the printing, dyeing and trading are managed by the family and its community associates.

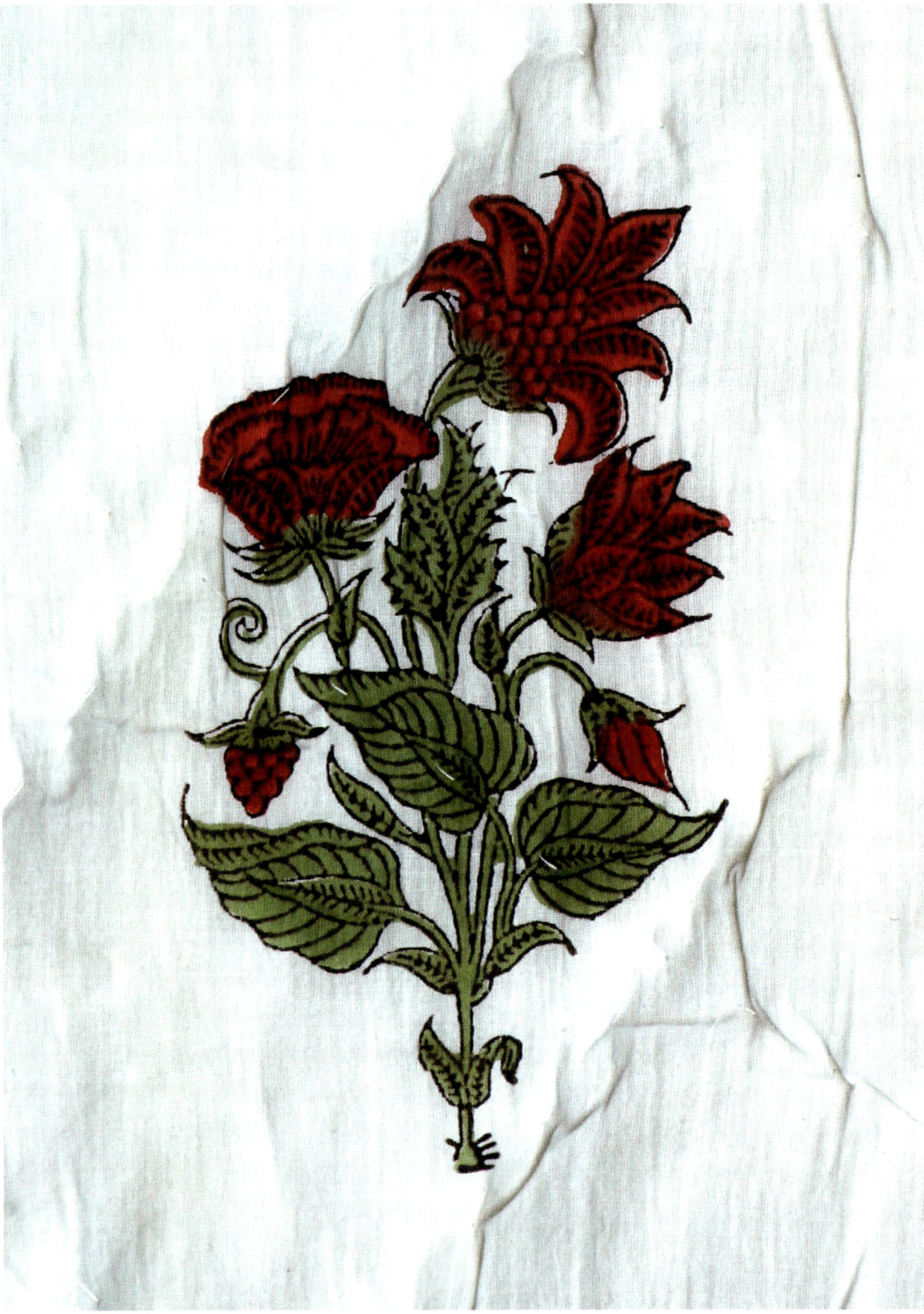

'Legendary' would be the most apt of words describing Kitty Rae. Few have dabbled with new motifs, techniques, printing blocks, fabrics and colours as Rae has. She has also helped lots of people learn the craft

The legendary Kitty Rae

I phoned Kitty Rae, the owner of Kin Fabrics on reaching Jaipur. Her phone number was listed in the German magazine *Architektur & Wohnen* and I had stored it for reference, back in Sweden. I asked Rae if she could meet me and she readily agreed to an appointment. I met a beautiful and stylish woman. She received me in her office–her 'factory'–which is a very simple, long and low building located on the grounds of her property—a large villa, with a nice garden. Kitty Rae keeps her products in her factory and provides work space for her tailors and printers who have worked with her for many years.

Tea and more

Kitty Rae–soft-spoken and composed–observed me calmly. I remember the first tea that I had in her garden, after I arrived in Jaipur on my quest for quilt-makers. It was so fresh, cool and quiet there, although a bustling city throbbed outside with rickshaws, buses and thousands of people jostling to make space and move on.

Later, we met on several occasions. Kitty would often invite me to sit

Facing page: *A Kitty Rae quilt with the flower motif and the quilt texture in highlight*

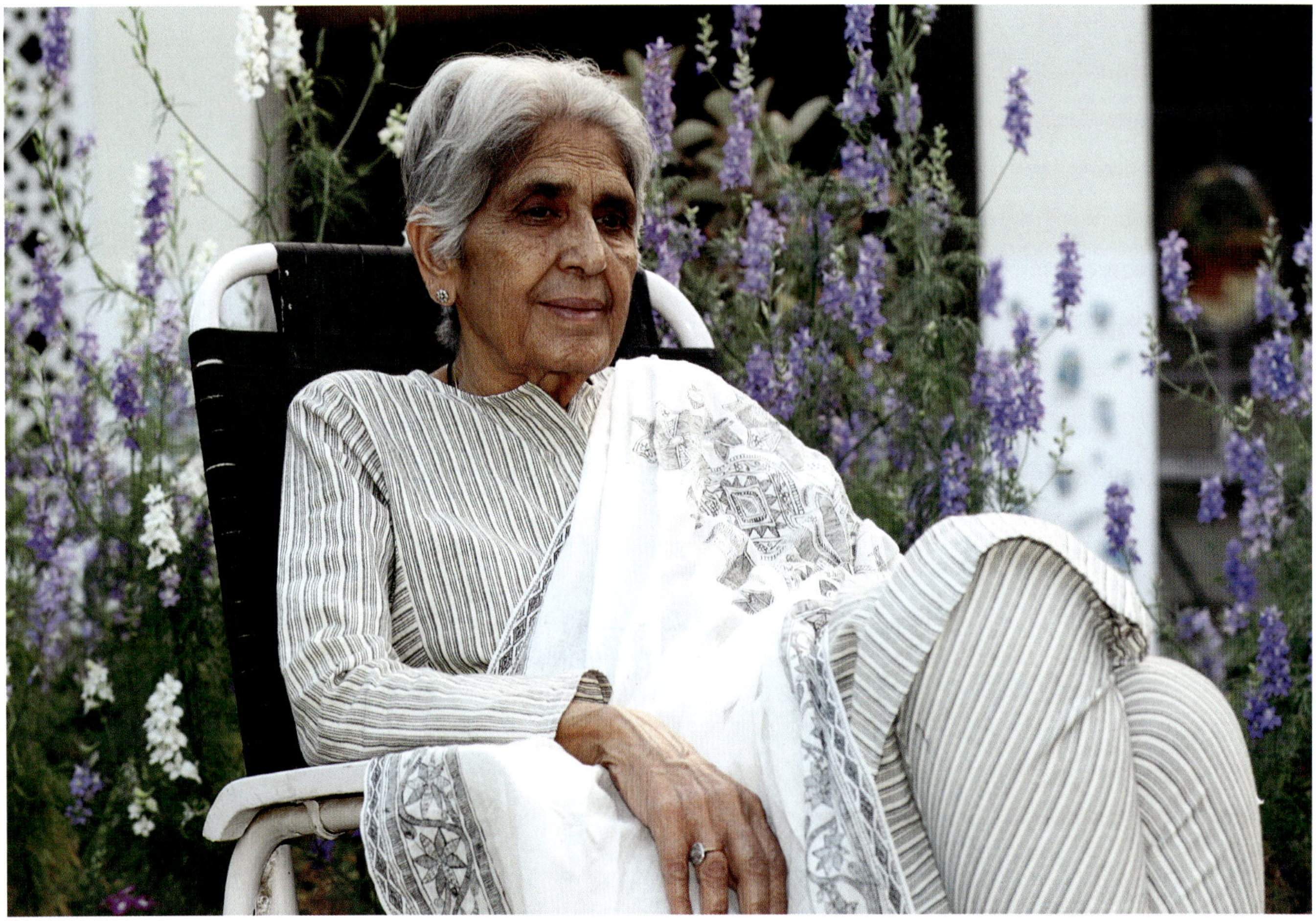

Kitty Rae, founder-owner of Kin Fabrics in her garden

Facing page: *Floral design in a beautiful fresh blue tint*

down and cool off in her garden and as I happily accepted the offer, I would discover yet another interesting pattern on the cushions on her chairs. Once I was reminded of Scandinavian styles and motifs while looking at the cushions—which had an artistic and original pattern created by Kitty. She once told me that she sometimes woke up at night with a novel idea for a new design and wanted to run to the factory to execute it right away. The shelves in her showroom are like a treasure trove. You always come across old customers browsing through her materials, in search of the last and left-over waistcoast or jacket, a shawl, sarong, cushion cover or even a 'cut-piece' of designer fabric.

Pioneer at heart

Jaipur has for centuries been the centre for quilt-making of course, but it was Kitty Rae who started the commercial production of designer quilts in 1963, when she launched a printing unit in her house. She revived the old tradition of block printing, in which the designs and motifs are printed individually by hand with the help of wooden blocks, using a separate colour or tone if required, for each different unit of the design. Block masters and colour masters came from Jaipur and Sanganer–the main printing centre nearby–and Farrukhabad. In Jaipur, Kitty found skilled people to fluff the cotton and make the quilts. She in her turn helped people learn her craft and its unique attributes.

Kitty confided to me that the beginnings were rather primitive and bucolic. She had long wooden tables made for the main printing job. The printed material was washed and later dried in the sun, laid out on sand, outside the showroom. Apparently the sunlight enhanced the brilliance of the colours. However primitive and basic her enterprise might have been, she printed the most exquisite saris from the very beginning. The Maharani of Jaipur–the late Gayatri Devi who was one of the most beautiful women in the world–was Kitty's customer as were other VIPs and some select retail outlets in other metropolitan cities.

Kitty would sometimes print only four saris with the same design and colour combination and send one

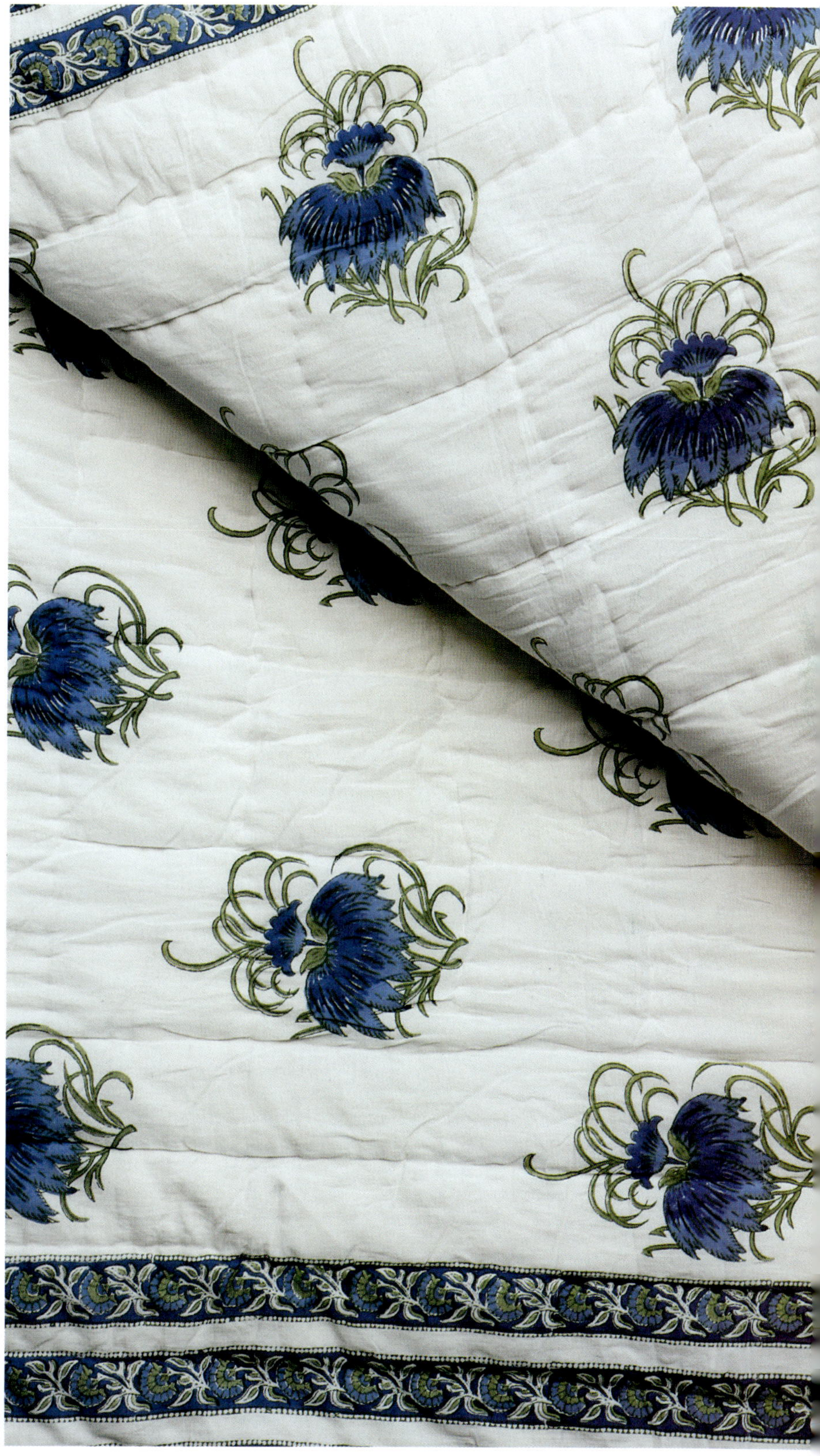

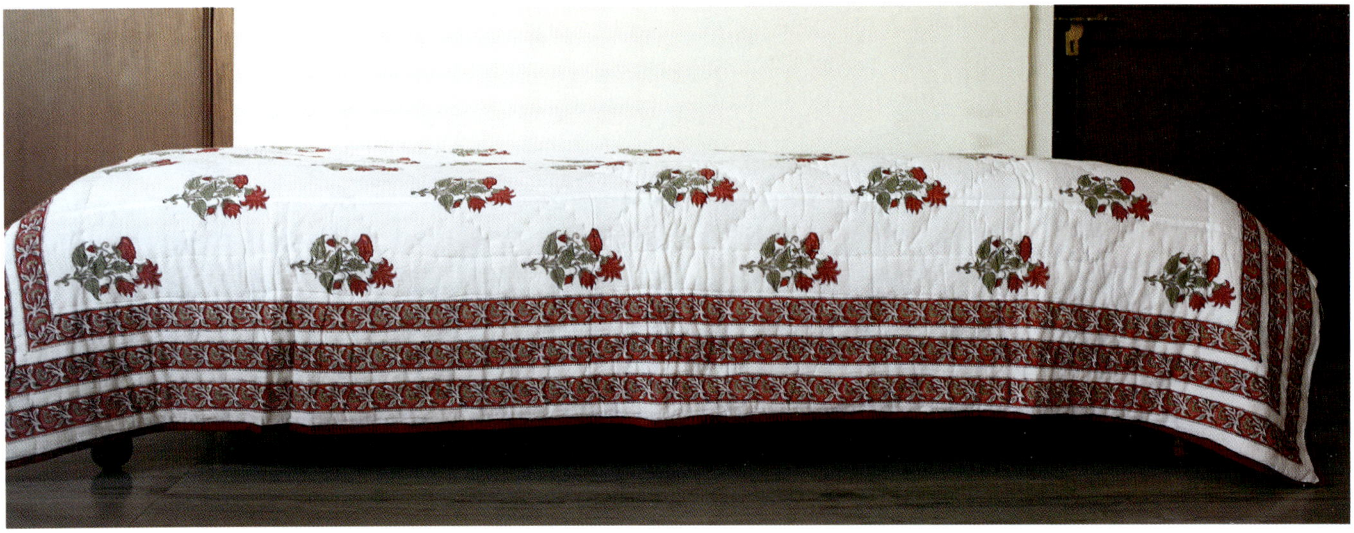

Kitty's quilt spread out on one of the beds in Nana ki Haveli, an old mansion converted into a guest house in Jaipur

piece to Mumbai, two to Delhi and retain one for the market in Jaipur. Such a distribution system contributed in making some of her outstanding creations exclusive and the most sought-after products.

Road to perfection

Having gained confidence from her initial ventures she moved on and decided to make quilts, which she had admired in wealthy houses where she had spent time as a guest. It was almost the same story as her experience with saris. The quilts that Kitty made were exquisite and they became very popular with her customers. A beautiful new quilt every winter turned out to be extra delicate, fluffy, light and very warm when used for the first time. The thin and soft cotton fabric called mulmul and the light stuffing of cotton wool make Jaipur quilts warm but well-ventilated as the fine fabric allows the passage of air and prevents the body from perspiring.

Kitty has personally trained some of her printers and can detect the style of individual printers from what she calls the 'temperament' of the prints used on a piece of fabric. She uses her own designs and does not wish to join the competitive race with other producers in and around the city. 'I would like to keep doing my own thing,' she says. There are no immediate retirement plans as Kitty draws life's sustenance from her work and work space. Passionate about the creative and highly productive environment and the people giving expression to her ideas, she does not believe in life without work and expresses a great attachment with and concern for her workers. Closing down business would automatically lead to clogging the only source of income for many of her workers and associates. 'I must think about my workers too; some are old, where would they go?', she says.

The products are sold from Kitty's showroom and they are often designed to suit customers' specific orders. She now mainly caters to export orders. There is a simple stock room where you can sit and rummage through stockpiles to pull out treasures at bargain prices, almost like a lucky draw. Many of the prints date back to the designs Kitty created in the sixties and there are beautiful sarongs and tunics for modest prices.

Kitty Rae comes from a well-to-do family. After graduating from Jaipur University with English literature she

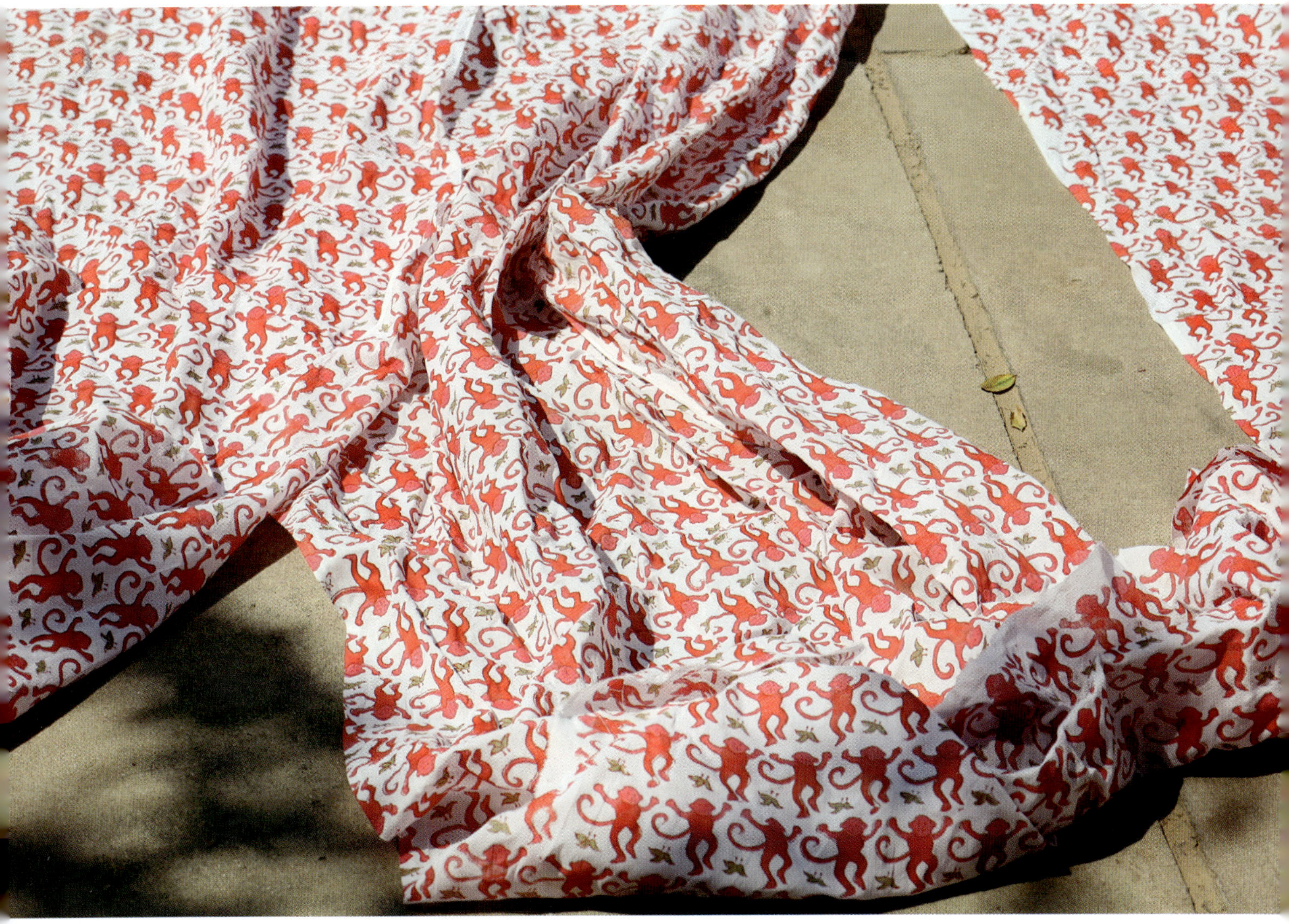

Charming 'monkey' design created for baby quilts, the printed fabric put out to dry in the sun

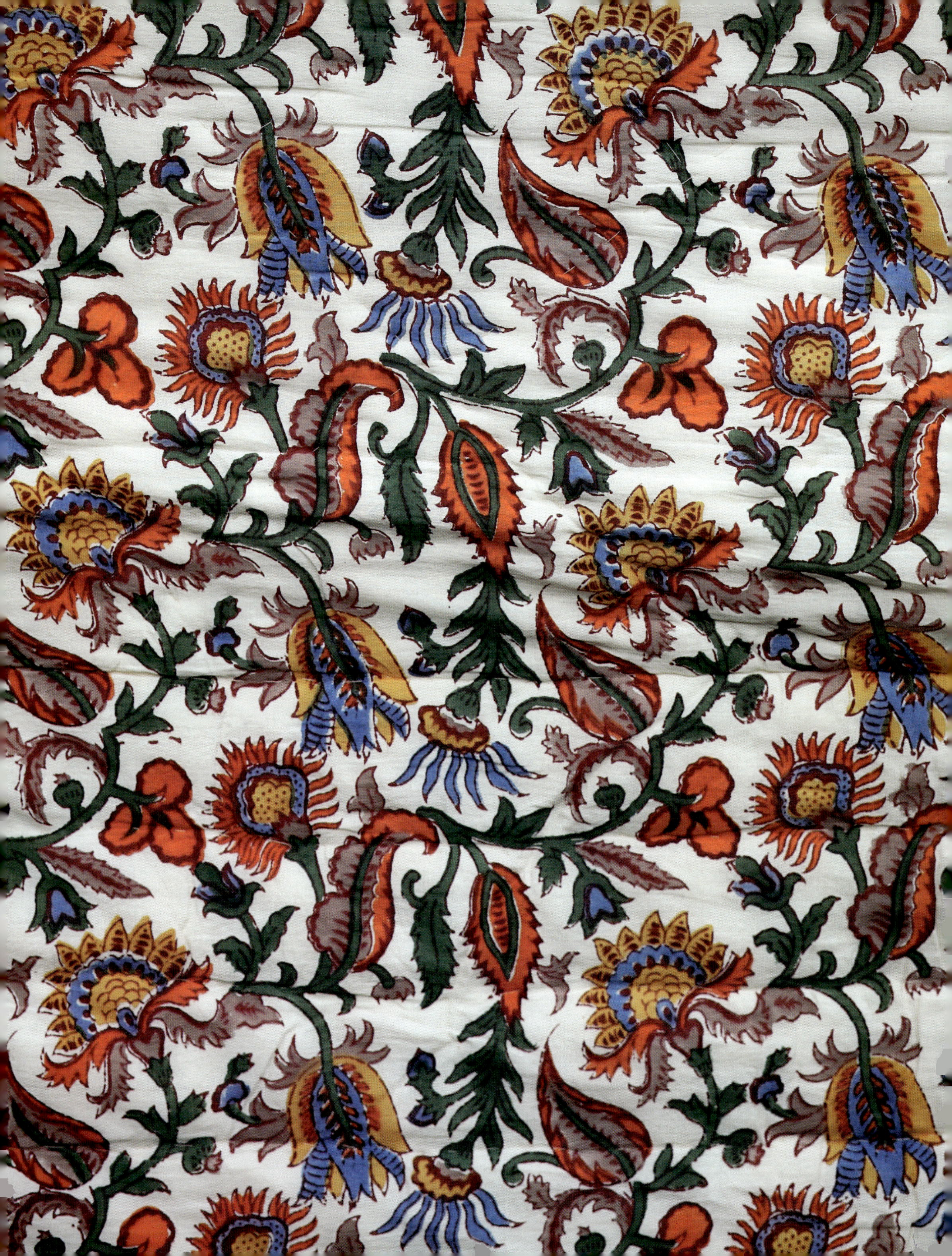

wished to occupy herself with something that she really felt passionate about. She always had artistic inclinations and invested her interest and creative energy into designing fabric prints and later quilts. She has a wonderful inborn sense of colour and tone coordination as well as an inherent flair for and understanding of style.

As a result Kitty Rae's work appears effortless. Although her designs are often colourful and exuberant, they are never extravagant or garish and are always marked by a new and contemporary touch even in their traditionalism.

The friendly artisan

A good part of my research on quilts has been based on first hand information derived from mingling with the people actually involved in the manufacture and design. I would have liked to know more about the people directly involved in quilt making, but predictably enough, language turned out to be a big bar. I did not speak their language and they in turn did not usually speak English. And the 'interpreters' often than not, lacked the patience required to translate the details during a conversation. The Indian craftsmen are very skillful, although they

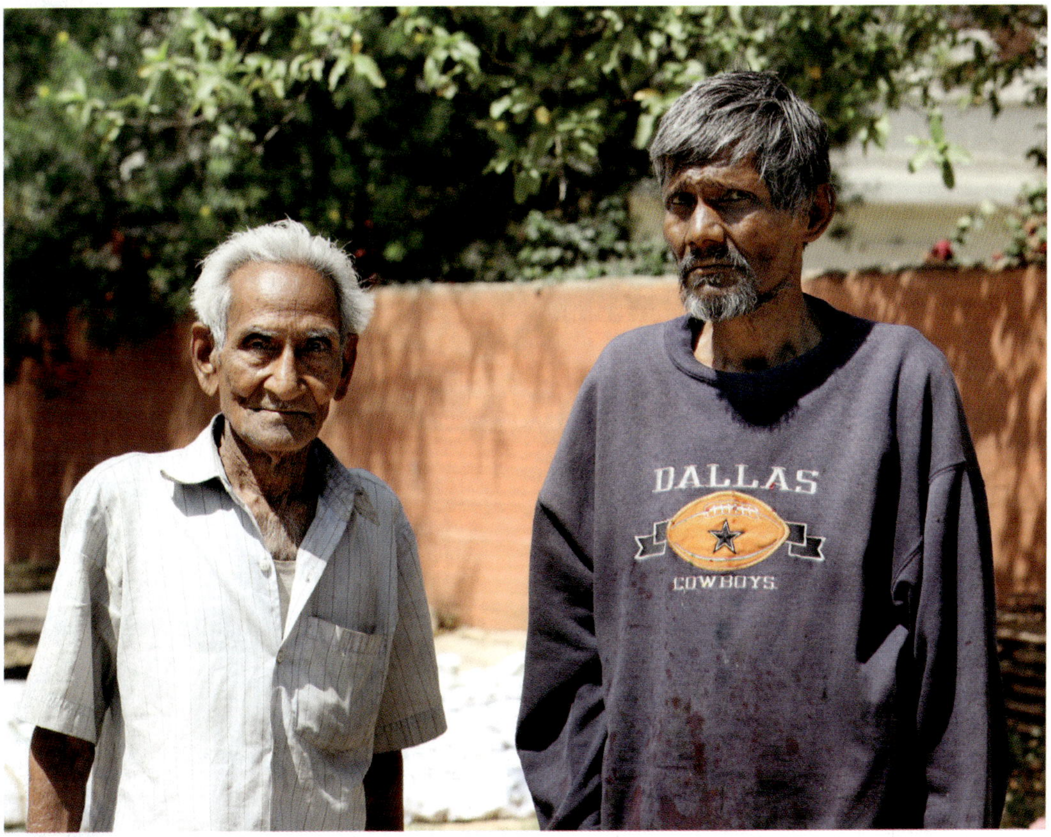

Kitty's old retainers who are the makers of some of the best Jaipur quilts—block master Ezo (left) and colour master Suresh Kumar

Facing page: *Joyful colours displayed in a floral pattern*

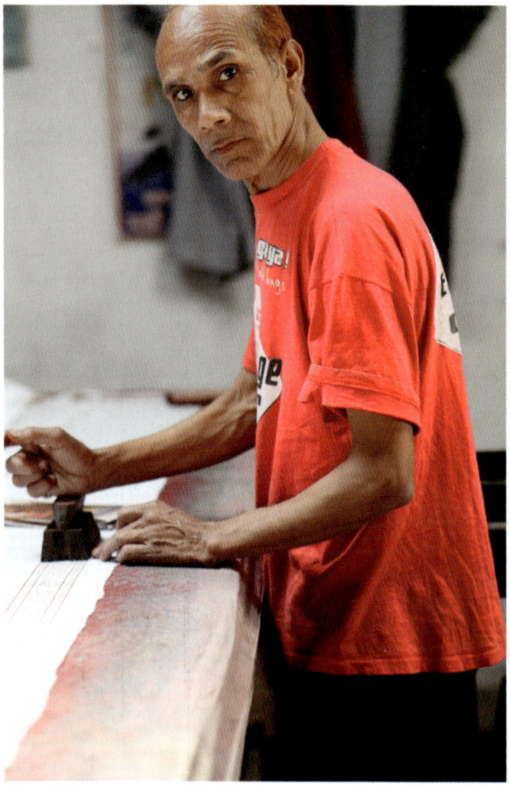

Kitty's old and trusted printer Giran Singh

Right: *An interesting combination of colours and patterns with the geometrical design creating waves across the quilt and the floral motifs restricted to the borders*

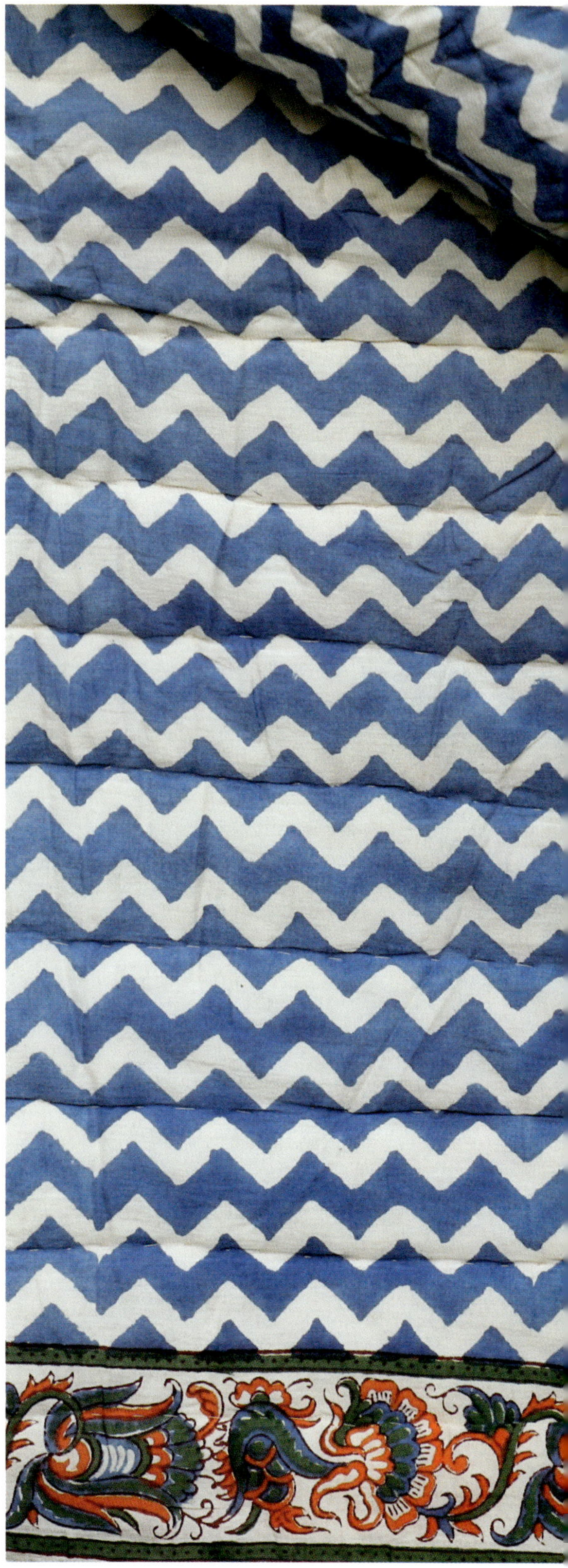

often do not realise their own worth and have difficulty understanding that they, their craft and their lives and family history might be of interest to others. They are not accustomed to articulating their feelings and emotions concerning their work and creativity.

I appreciate their energy, endurance, their easy laughter, their simple ways and their unfailing effort and perseverance to try out new things. They wrack their brains more often over how to achieve something that you ask for, in order to make it work, than professional craftsmen in Europe would. Always in a helpful frame of mind, artists and

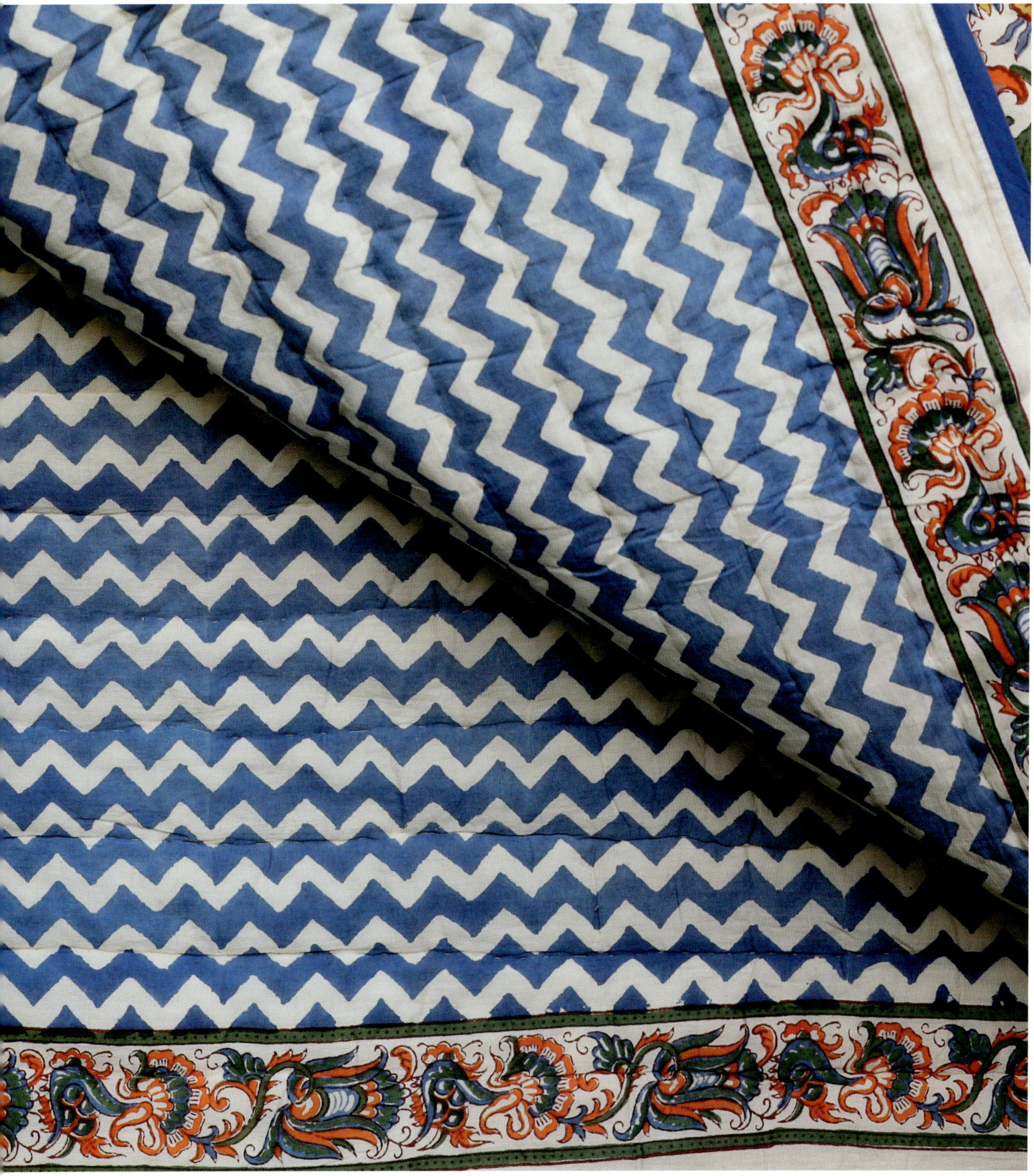

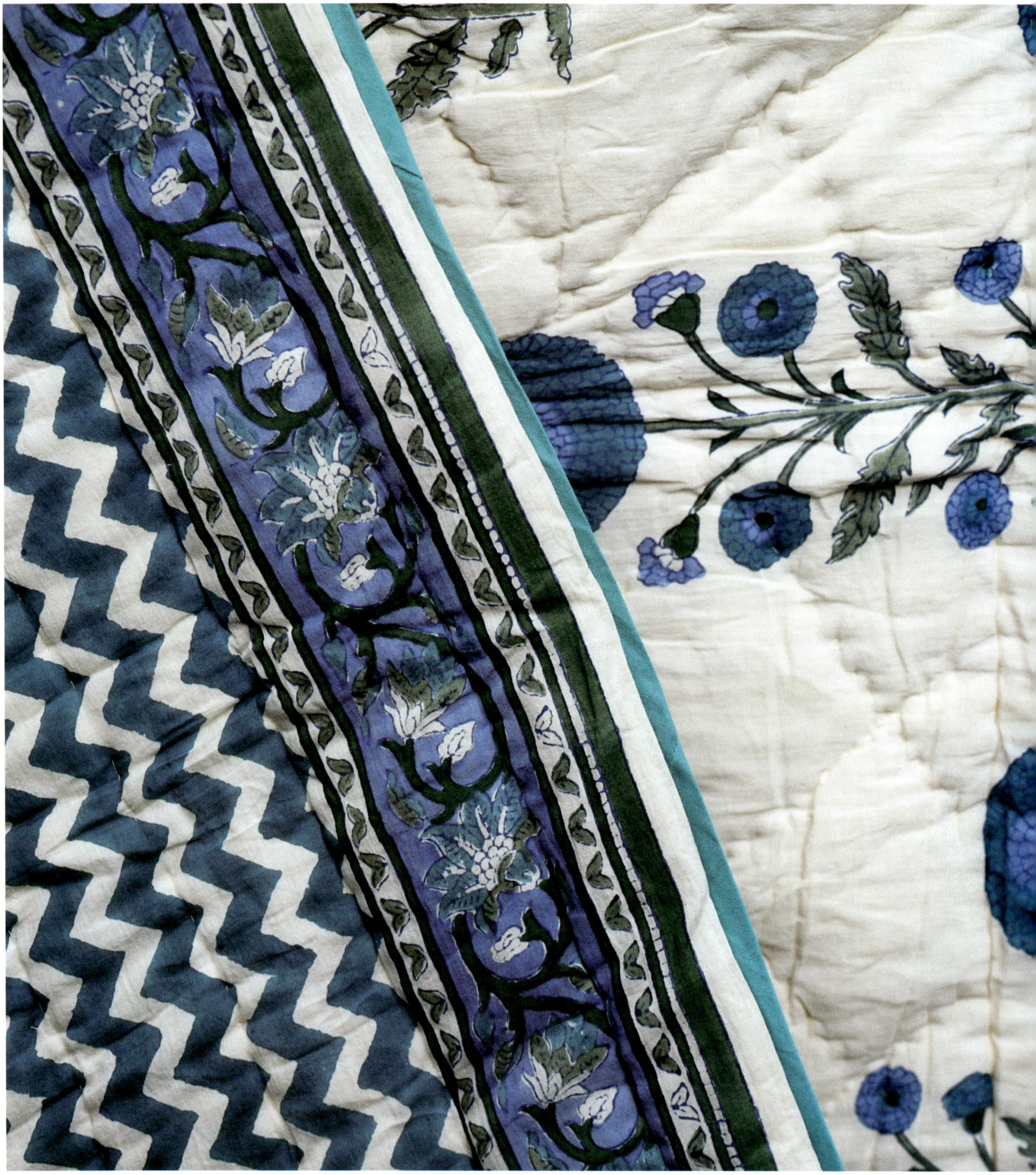

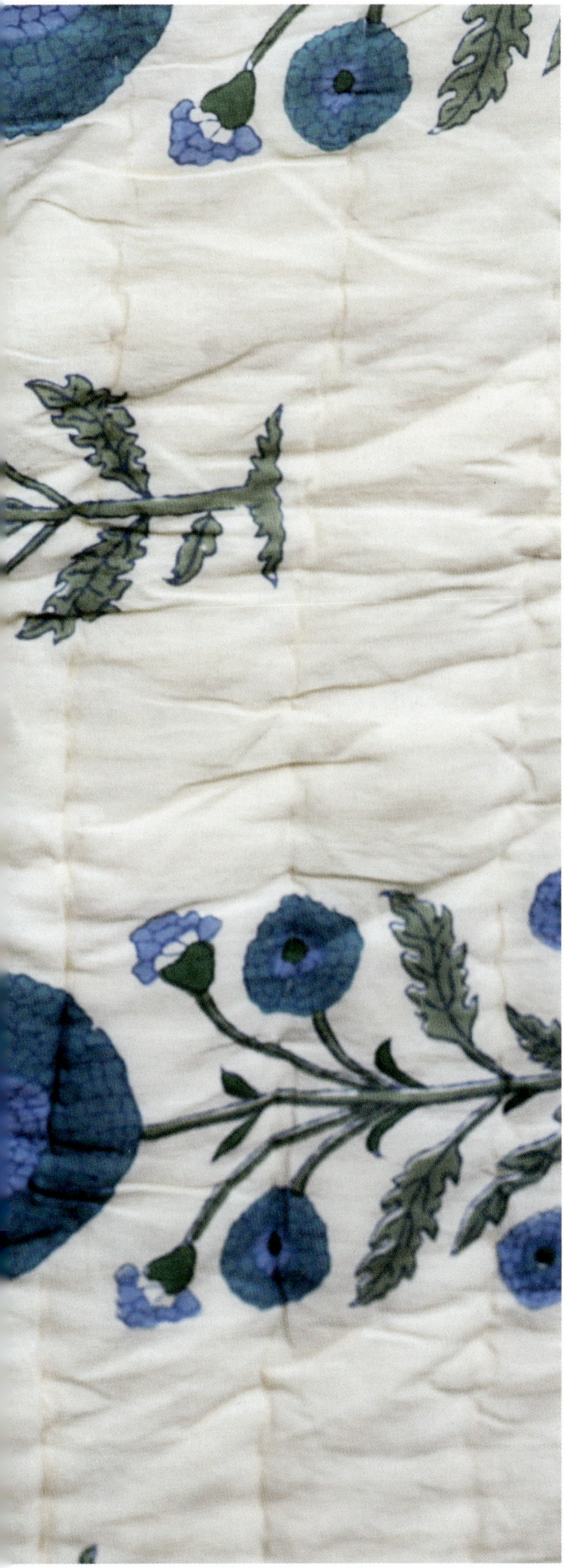

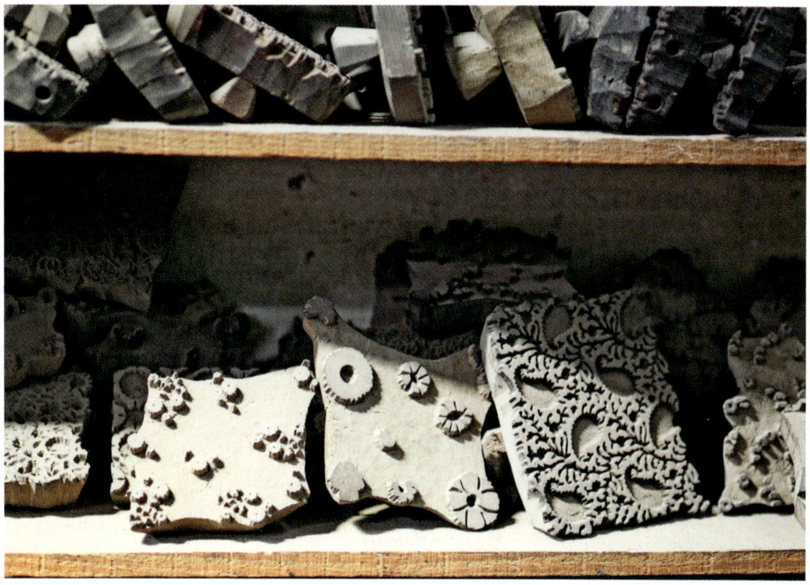

craftspeople in India have often tried their best to achieve something quite impossible and have promised to deliver this impossibility simply because they do not want to disappoint you.

This may not be looked upon as a 'professional' approach in the rest of the world and people may find it difficult to digest the fact that sincere promises and work deadlines often fall apart simply because of the lack of proper resources. But personally, I love the 'customer-friendly' approach and the sincere willingness to dabble in unknown areas. I admire the spirit.

Printing blocks on shelves at the Kin Fabrics workshop

Facing page: *The famous Mughal poppy flower*

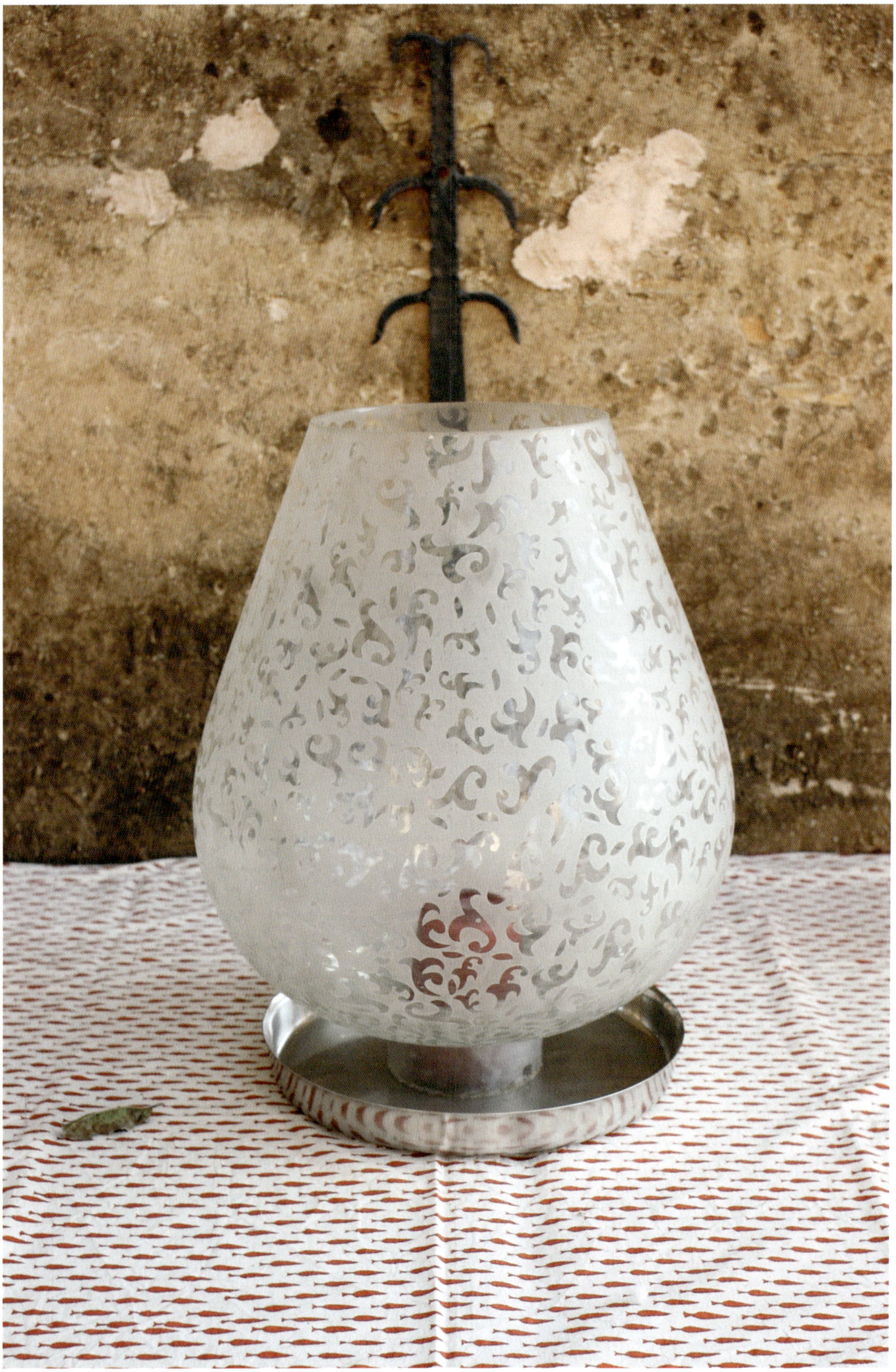

Frosted glass lamp stands on printed cotton table spread in red and white fish print from Soma

In Kitty Rae's factory I had the opportunity to talk to a printer, a colour master and a block master who had worked with her for many years. Giran Singh—a very gifted printer—hails from Jaipur. He started working thirty-five years ago, simply 'because (he) liked this kind of work'. He learned the skills on the job, working in and around Jaipur. Giran Singh prints the motifs and the design patterns that are given to him; he does not create the designs.

The colour master Suresh Kumar comes from Farrukhabad in Uttar Pradesh. He is a self-made colour master. He first worked in Mumbai as a printer for Surekha Dyeing and then in a printing shop for ten years, where he learned how to mix colours. He likes the creativity involved in his work, especially while mixing the colours. According to Kitty, Suresh Kumar is a skillful and talented colour master.

The blockmaster Ezo joined Kitty's workshop after migrating from Fulchand. He worked freelance for different companies. He was eighty years old when I met him and found that he had already worked as a block master for sixty years. He had taught himself the profession. Ezo worked first in Mumbai, later near Delhi and then in Jaipur. I met Ezo and talked to him in March 2007. Sadly Ezo passed away in 2008.

Ezo was a very sweet person and a talented block master. Kitty appreciated his work very much and always tried to find work for him. I asked him how he felt about his work. I expected him to react as an artist would, with some kind of an artistic expression. I was quite wrong as I found out, because Ezo answered calmly and simply said 'It is just another job!' It is amazing how these craftspeople indulge in art, aesthetics and creativity of a very high order every single day of their lives and yet are oblivious of the very fact.

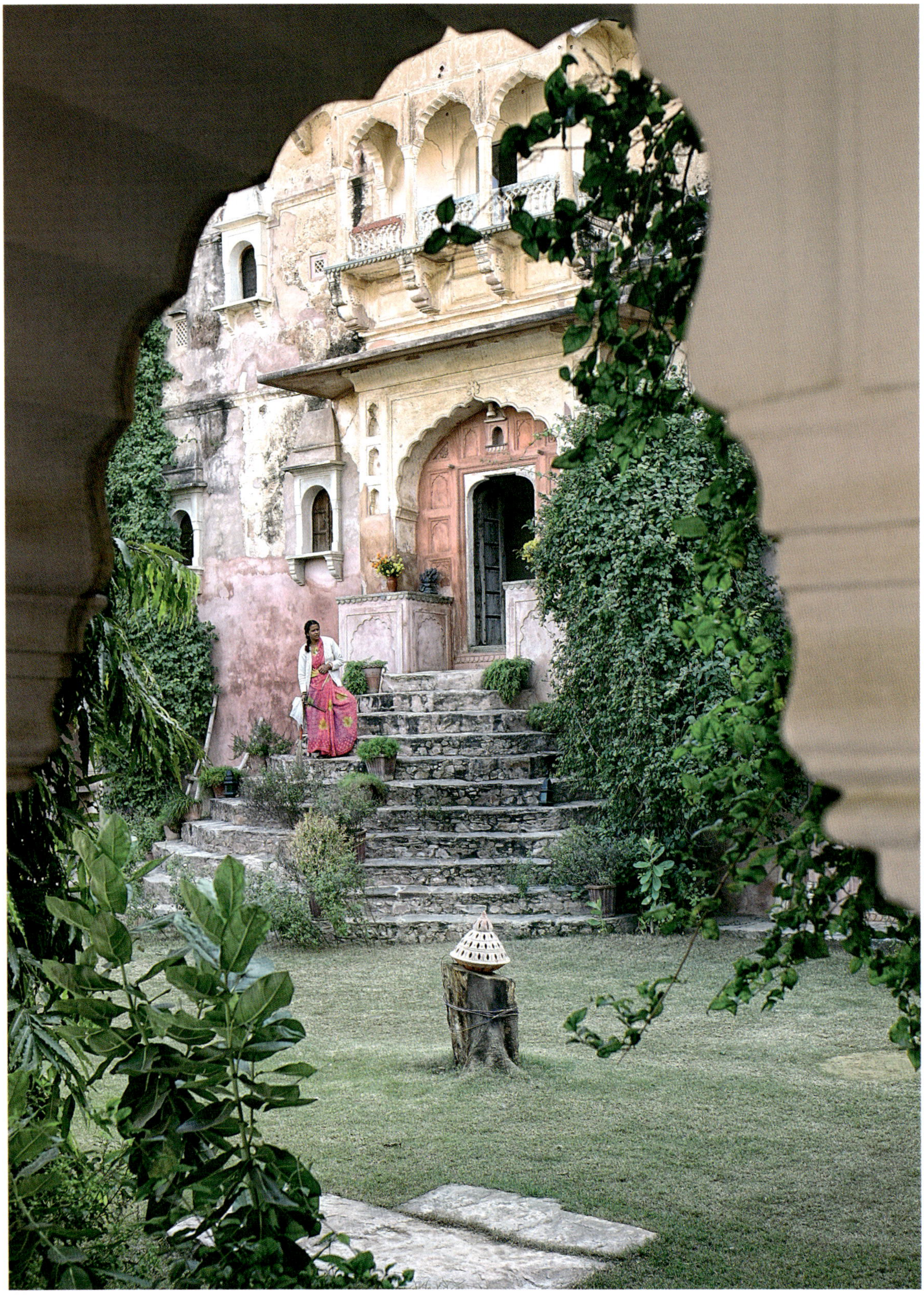

One who visits Jaipur and is on the lookout for good soft furnishings eventually discovers Soma, which has over the years, created a niche for itself. Soma is a maker, retailer and exporter of Jaipur quilts and garments

Soma: Comfort, culture, craft

Soma loomed large on my list of quilt-makers I had planned to meet for writing this book. They have a nice showroom with amiable people to attend to the customers; their products come in a good range of colours and designs; the quality is top grade and the prices are moderate.

There are other important places in Jaipur of course, like Anokhi, which has among other products, also quilts. Anokhi is responsible for the creation of the museum of hand-printing in Amber. If you are in Jaipur you will surely want to visit the elegant Anokhi shop. There are Anokhi retail outlets in all the metropolitan cities in India as it is a very popular brand with more than one branch in some cities. Since a lot has been written about Anokhi already, I have chosen to write about Soma instead, which partly belongs to the same genre.

I phoned the owner of Soma—Radhakrishnan Nair. On asking if we could meet I heard a warm, polite voice on the telephone welcoming me and all my initial feelings of uncertainty were

Facing page: *Entrance to Ninder Mahal, the residence of the owners of Soma. This castle was in ruins before the owners of Soma restored it*

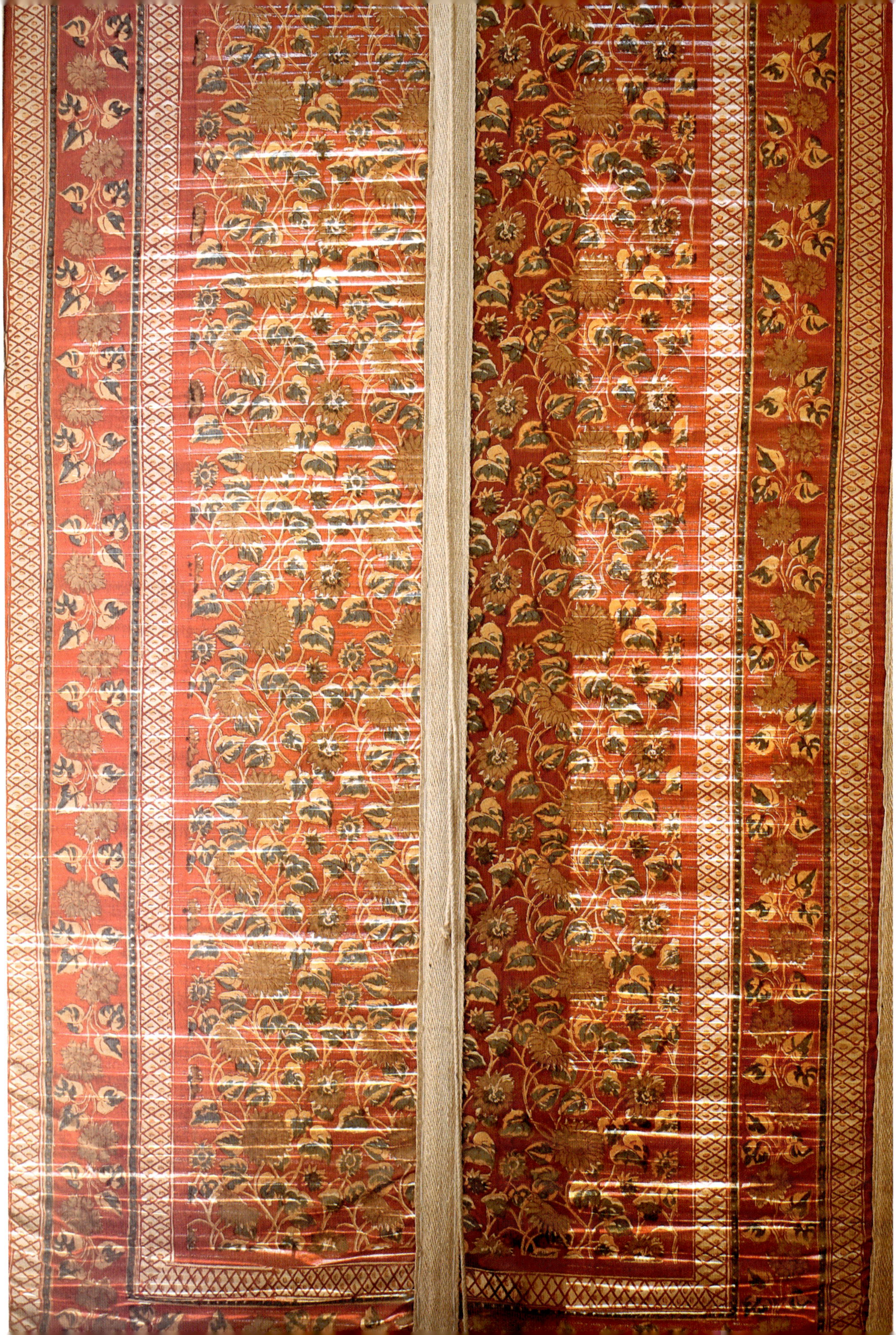

instantly put to rest. I expected an elderly, distinguished and traditional Indian gentleman to receive me courteously but rather formally on my first visit; instead I was pleasantly surprised when a charming and smiling man with contemporary looks and warm gestures opened the gate.

Spiritual stimulations

Radhakrishnan Nair explained to me how he had no background in textiles at the beginning of his working career and how he had to learn from scratch by working closely with various printers, weavers and artisans. Radha, as he is popularly known, also worked for a while with the famous manufacturer-cum-retailer of Rajasthani textiles and prints—Anokhi.

Radha and his wife Andreé, who is Canadian and hails from Ottawa, created their own manufacturing and export company Soma in 1984. Andreé named it Soma, which is a Sanskrit word for an intoxicating drink popular as a spiritual stimulant with ancient Hindu sages of India. It is an extract of the Soma plant and supposed to be a form of 'eternal heavenly nectar'—a life-giving force and the 'Creator of Gods' in Vedic philosophy.

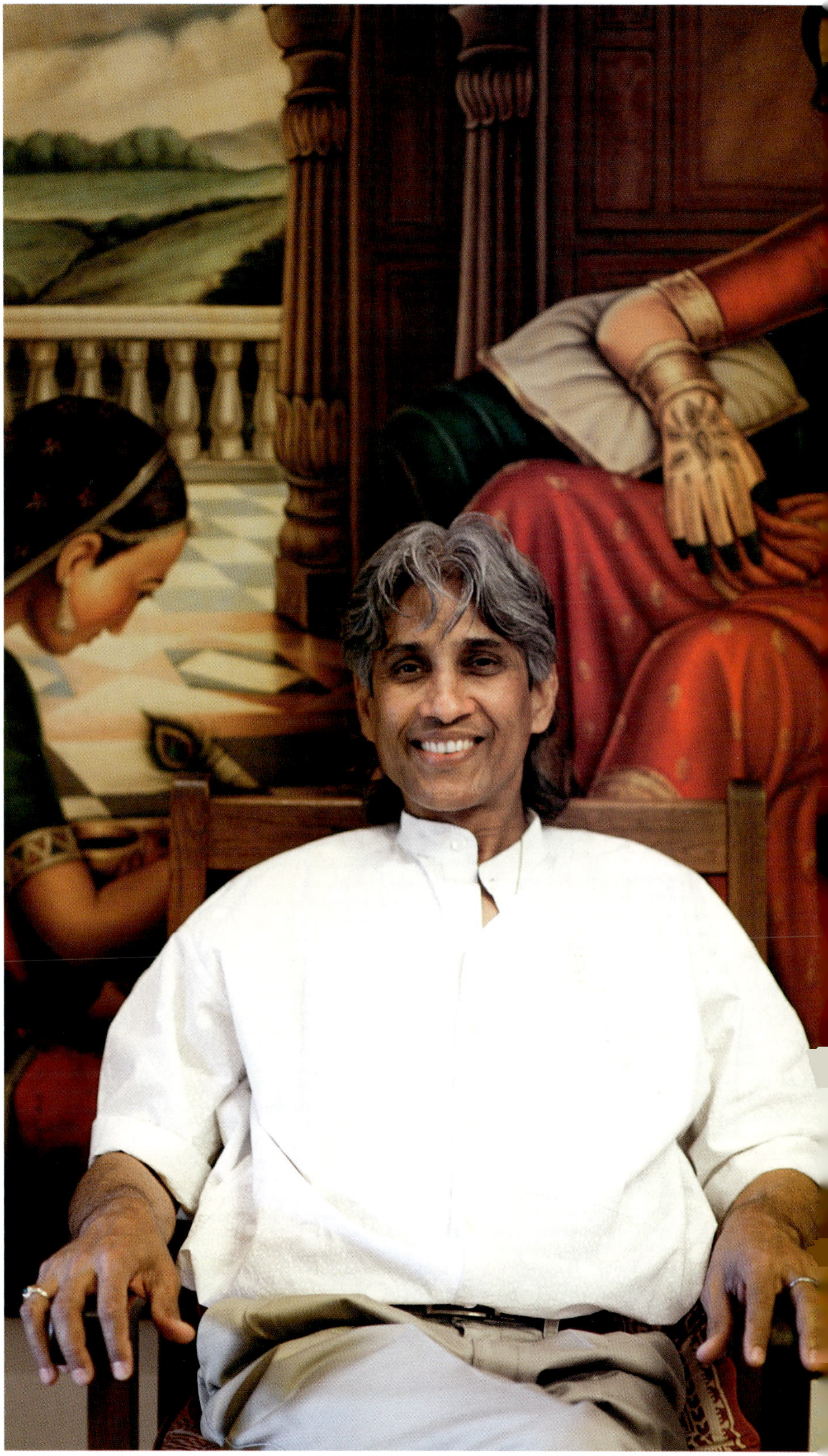

Wide mosaic

Radhakrishnan and Andreé's textile export company Soma decided to adapt its designs to the market's demands and it has succeeded very well. The owners' wish was to keep everything under one roof, which they believed would help them retain the exclusive quality of Soma's products. For eleven years the company concentrated on manufacture and exports. Finally, in 1995 Soma ventured into the domestic market, setting up its first store of the same name in Civil Lines, Jaipur.

Soma is a great believer in natural fibres and uses different fabrics like handwoven linen, silk 'matka' or 'noil' and 'chanderi'. They strictly keep away from synthetic fibres. The patterns are traditional. Some of the fabrics are very bright and colourful, as is typical of the region; others come in delicate pastel shades or even as subtle white-on-white. We see quite a bit of flower patterns,

Page 100: *Quilted blind in bright rust*

Page 101: *Radhakrishnan Nair, owner of Soma*

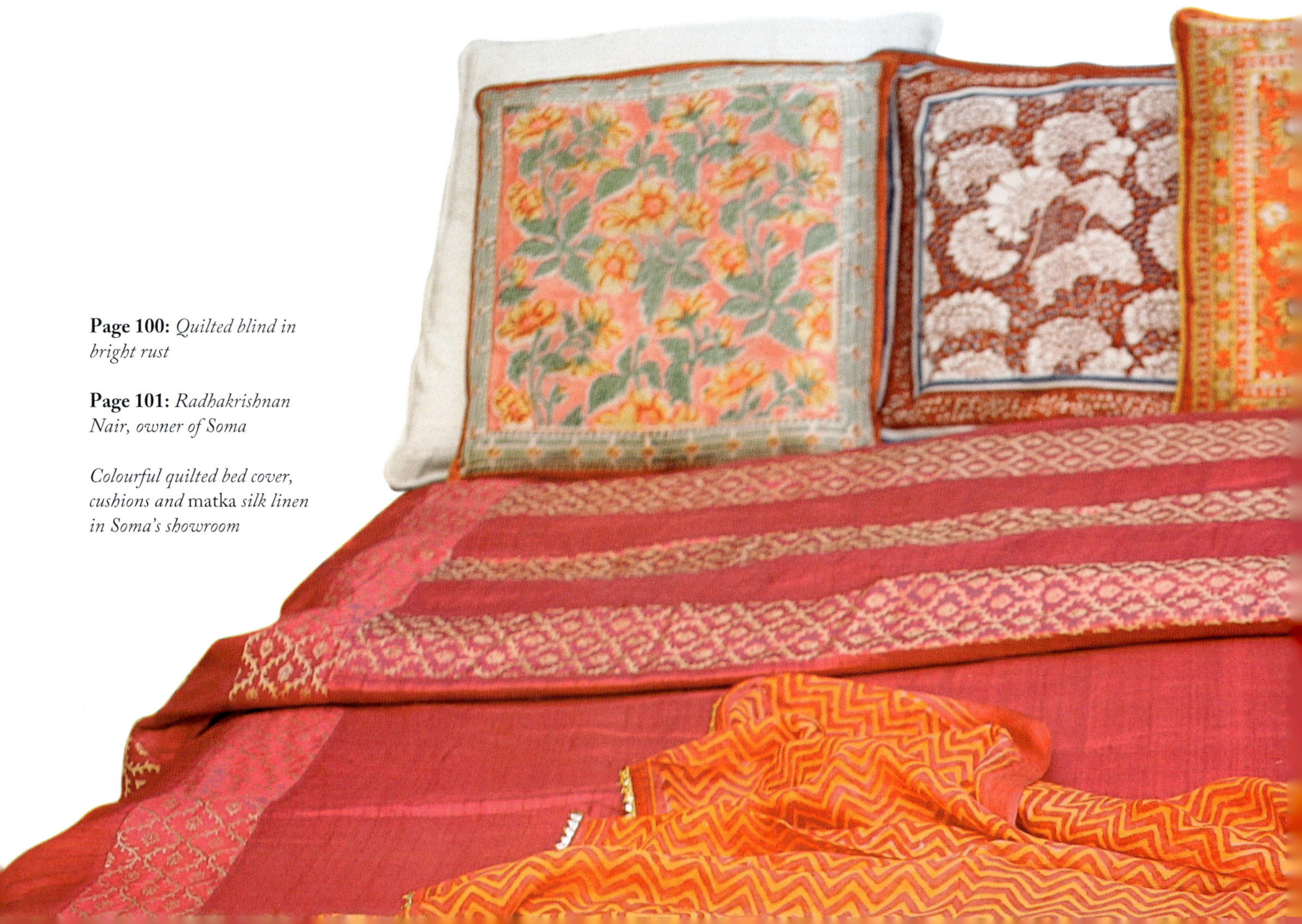

Colourful quilted bed cover, cushions and matka *silk linen in Soma's showroom*

and some stripes and zigzags lending a more contemporary look...in fact there is a wide variety of designs to choose from. Bird and fish motifs are also popular. They do some really fine hand-quilting; the quilts are thin, soft and light and the quality is very good. Apart from the regular quilts, I quite liked some of the gypsy quilts and baby quilts that Soma produces. Their quilts come in different sizes and are as popular with Indians as with foreign tourists.

Trail down the years

Soma has around 700 employees at present, including two large families of quilt makers. Each family has about 30 to 40 members.

It also owns eight printing workshops in Sanganer. But in order to start with the very beginning one should go back considerably in time.

Soma began business on rather modest notes and it was as adventurous and uncertain a beginning as that of any

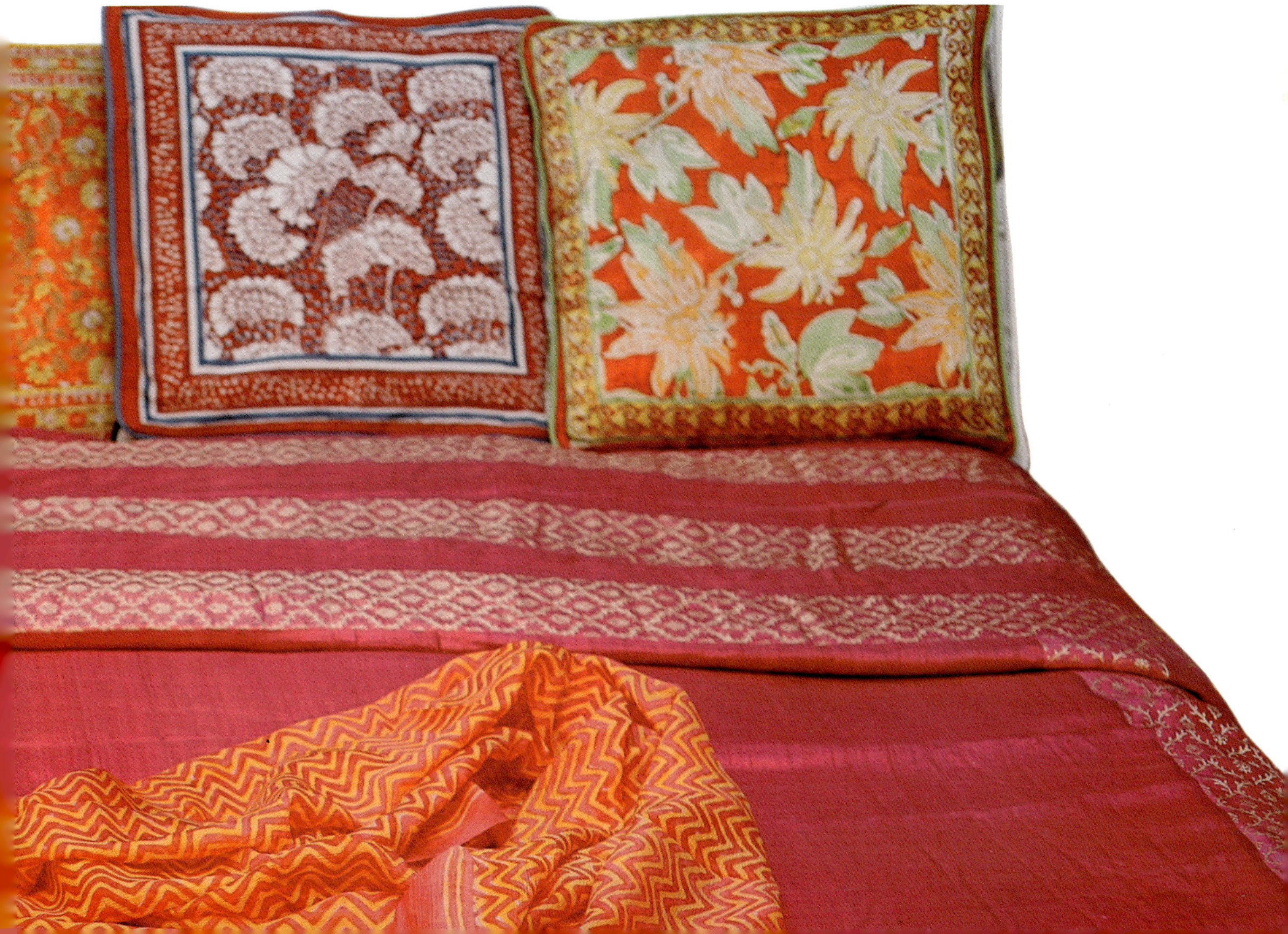

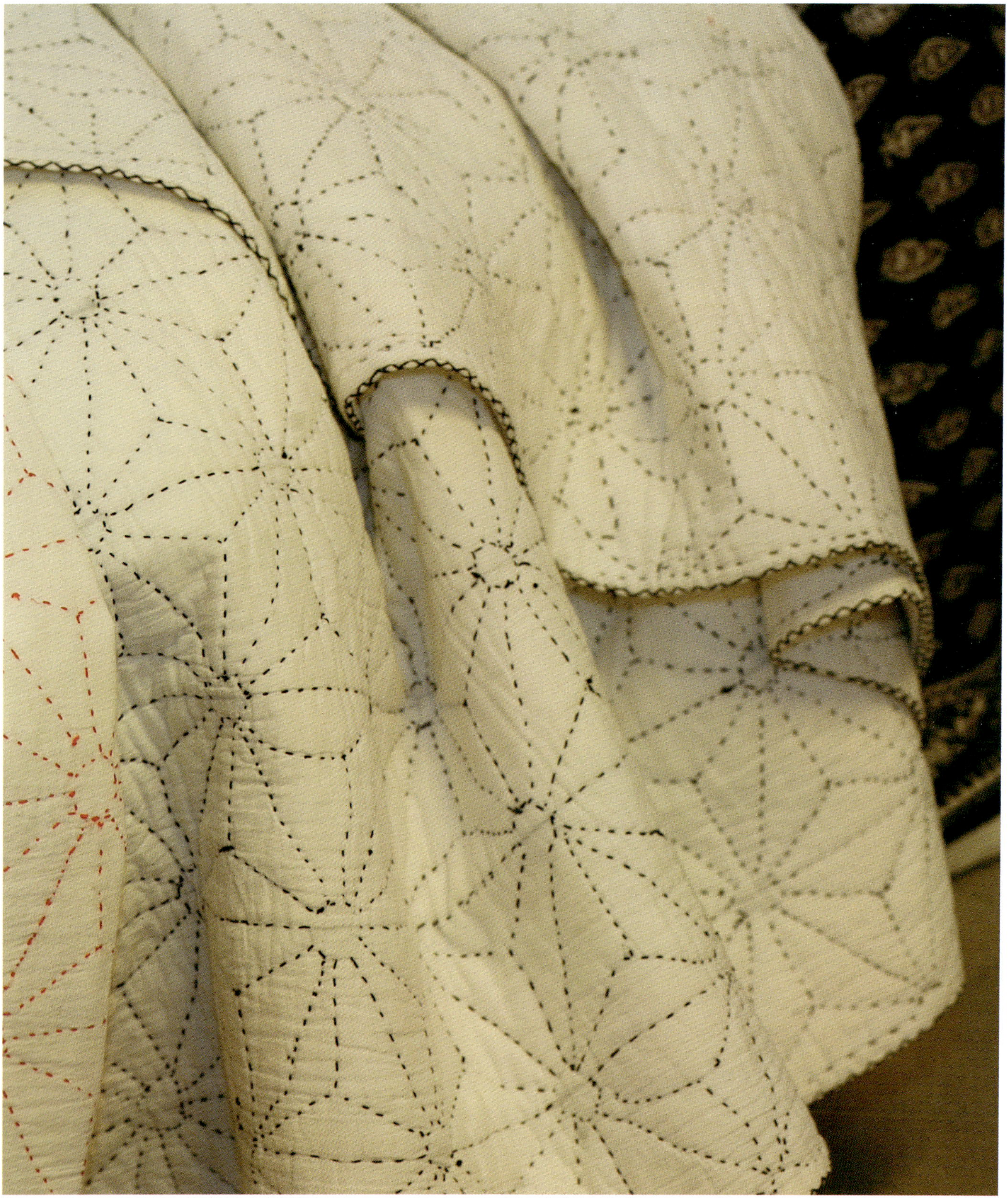

other quilt-maker in Jaipur. The story of the Soma quilt partly began with Andreé's mother, Sarah.

Named the 'grandmother of pleated cotton' and rightfully so, Sarah had a small but successful company with a fashionable, upmarket retail outlet called Sarah's Clothes in Ottawa, which she started in 1967. The Canadian Prime Minister Pierre Trudeau's wife Margaret Trudeau–who was quite a newsmaker herself with her bold fashion statements and personal life–and Queen Juliana of the Netherlands shopped from Sarah's boutique as they were fond of her creations. 'It was indeed a glamorous little boutique!' quips Andreé.

Sarah discovered India and Indian textiles at the Indian Pavilion during the World Fair. There she bought piles of attractive caftans and bedspreads and created out of them her couture pieces. She designed everything herself, even the jewellery.

Sarah stepped out of the world of theatre and ballet into the clothes business. Once she made a stopover in Delhi for a day on her way to Canada from Thailand and as luck would have it, the day changed the course of her life forever.

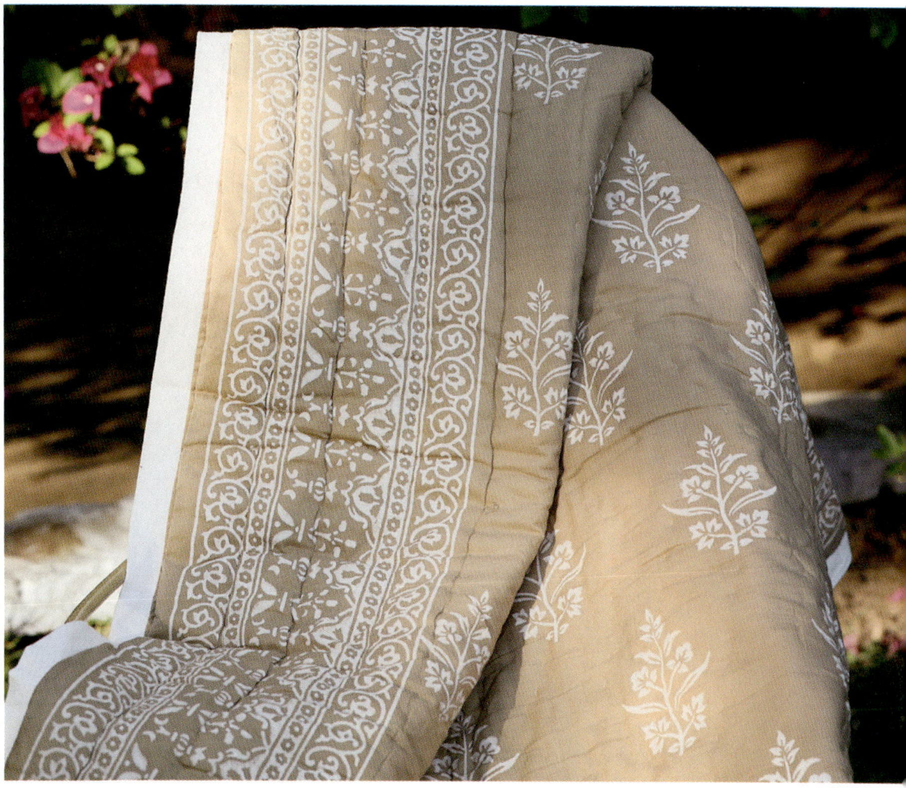

A stylish beige quilt

Facing page: *A gypsy quilt with geometrical floral motifs outlined on an off-white surface*

Travelling in a taxi in Delhi, she spotted the colourful turban of the taxi driver and was attracted by the narrow but neat pleats. She decided to find out how they were done.

The pleating reminded her of the pleated 'broomstick' skirts of native Mexican women and she saw in the turban the seeds of innovation.

The enterprising lady that she was, Sarah now made Delhi her home and workplace, continuing her work with textiles. Textiles and handicrafts were her two greatest passions in life. She sought the help of the 'dhobi'–the local washer and dyer–and experimented with cotton

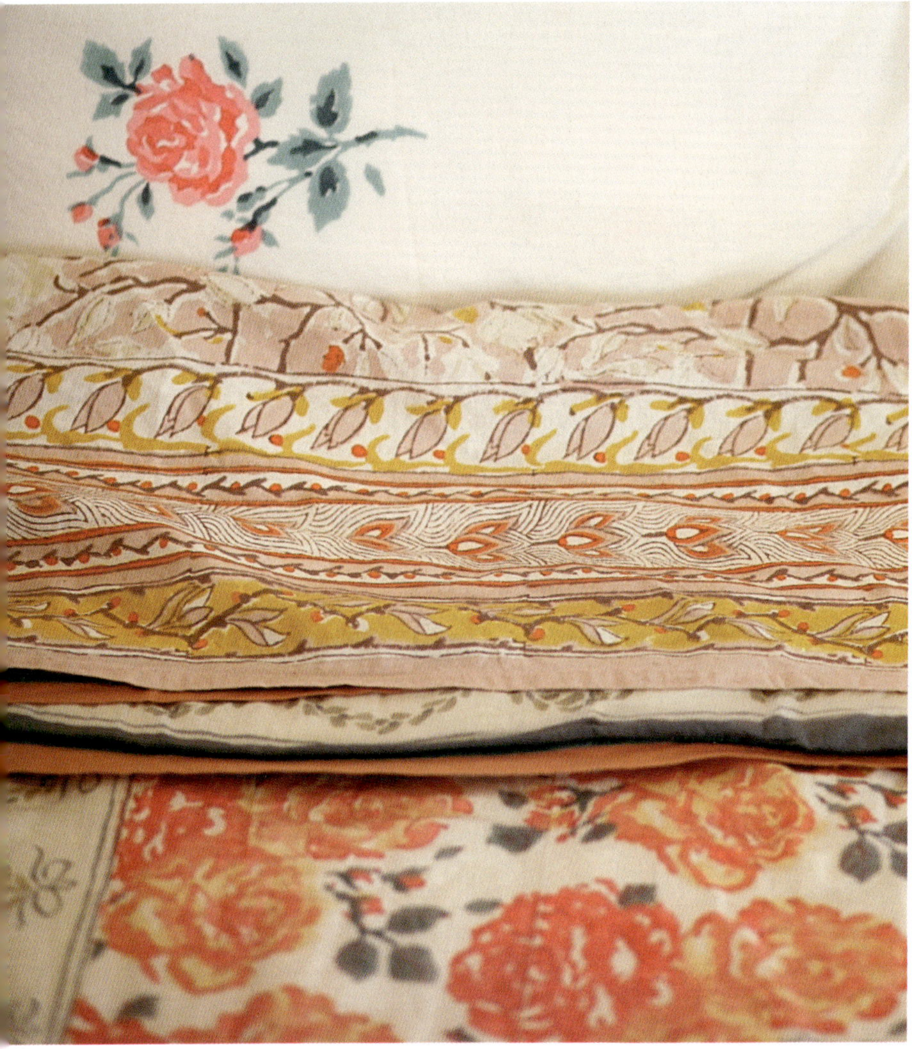

textiles, creating the pleated cotton skirt. The year was 1975. Sarah worked in India and Canada simultaneously. A few years later, her other daughter Madeleine formally joined the company and sister Andreé travelled to India, curious to see what her mother was doing and with the seeds of a wish to probably assist her in her work, if required. Here comes the sequence to the original Soma story.

Andreé was somewhat well prepared for the new task in her life. She had received basic training in art already as an eight-year old and had later attended a commercial art school. After graduating from the art school she took advanced courses in fashion drawing and designing in Ottawa, Canada. Andreé, like her mother, had a great passion for textiles, block-printing and handicraft. She found India to be a perfect place to learn hands-

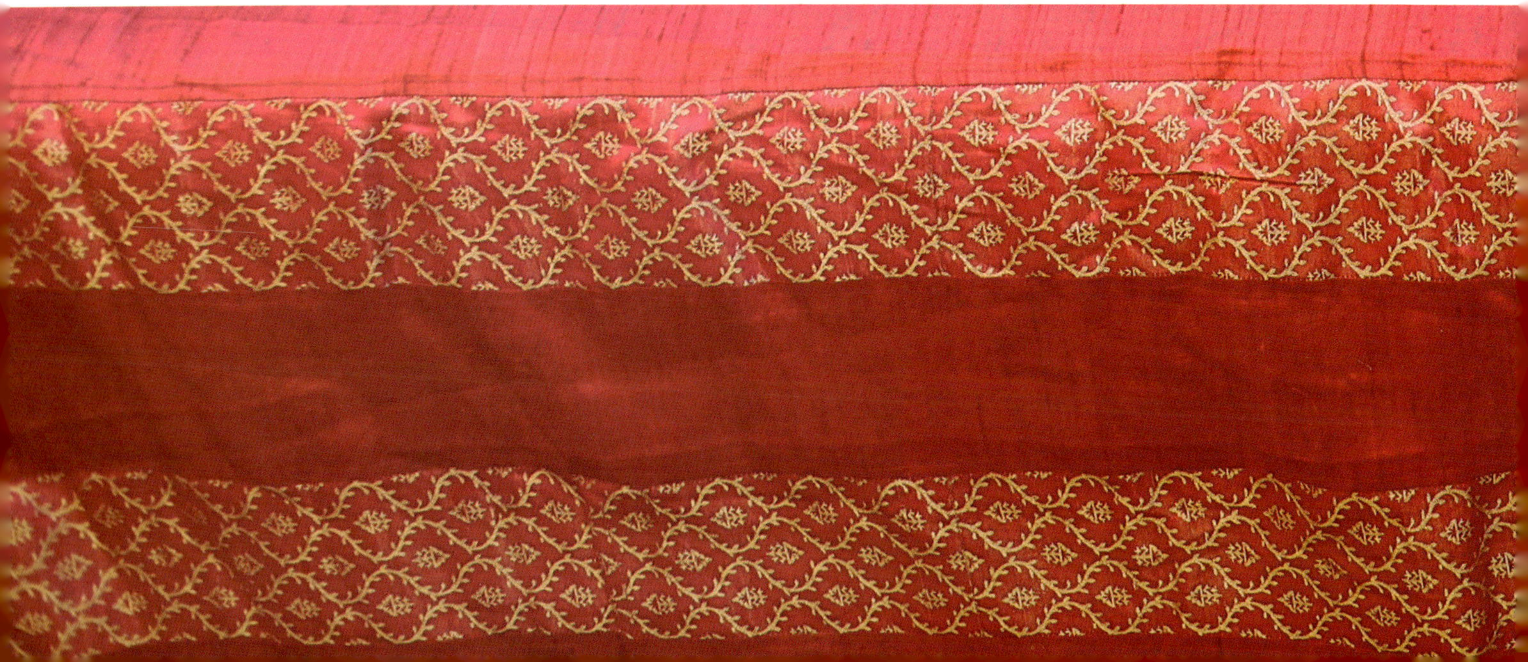

on about craft in real life. Andreé's first job was as a dyer. Subsequently she learned embroidery, mirror work, and the simple art of making tassels. As her great interest lay in handicrafts, she planned and executed an extensive research about Indian handicrafts in 1979, travelling across the length and breadth of the country. This is her pet project but it is still waiting to be completed one day.

Rapid growth

Andreé and her mother worked with Anokhi where she met her future husband Radha. They started a home furnishings company together, which grew to the Soma we know today. The goal was to coordinate patterns, find specially woven cotton of top quality and fine ink for printing. There was also the need to interpret the Indian designs and

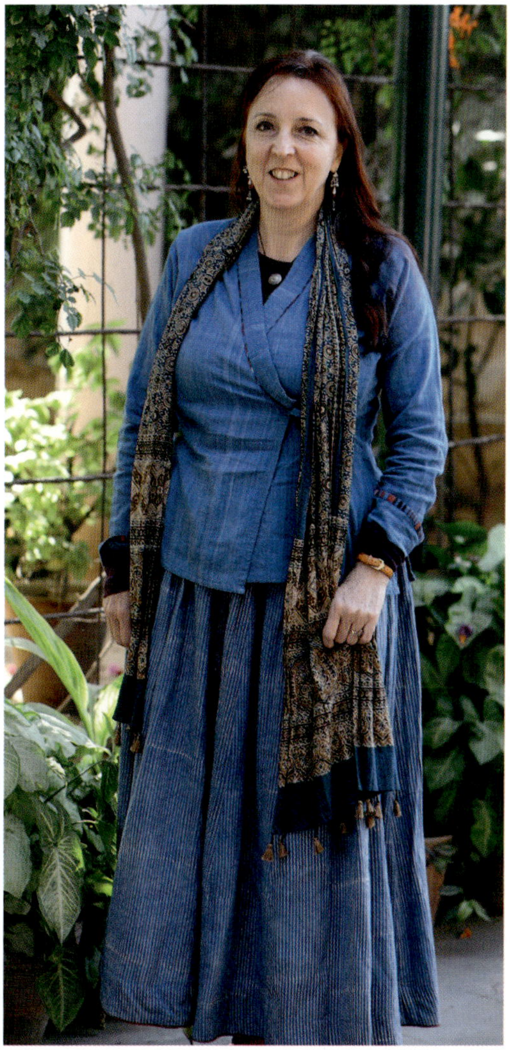

Andreé Pouliot, Radhakrishnan's wife and business partner. She created the first 600 patterns for Soma before getting professional help in design

Facing page: *A study in roses and leaves on a quilt (above); Close detail of motif and of colours melting into each other along the border of a* matka *silk quilt (strip below)*

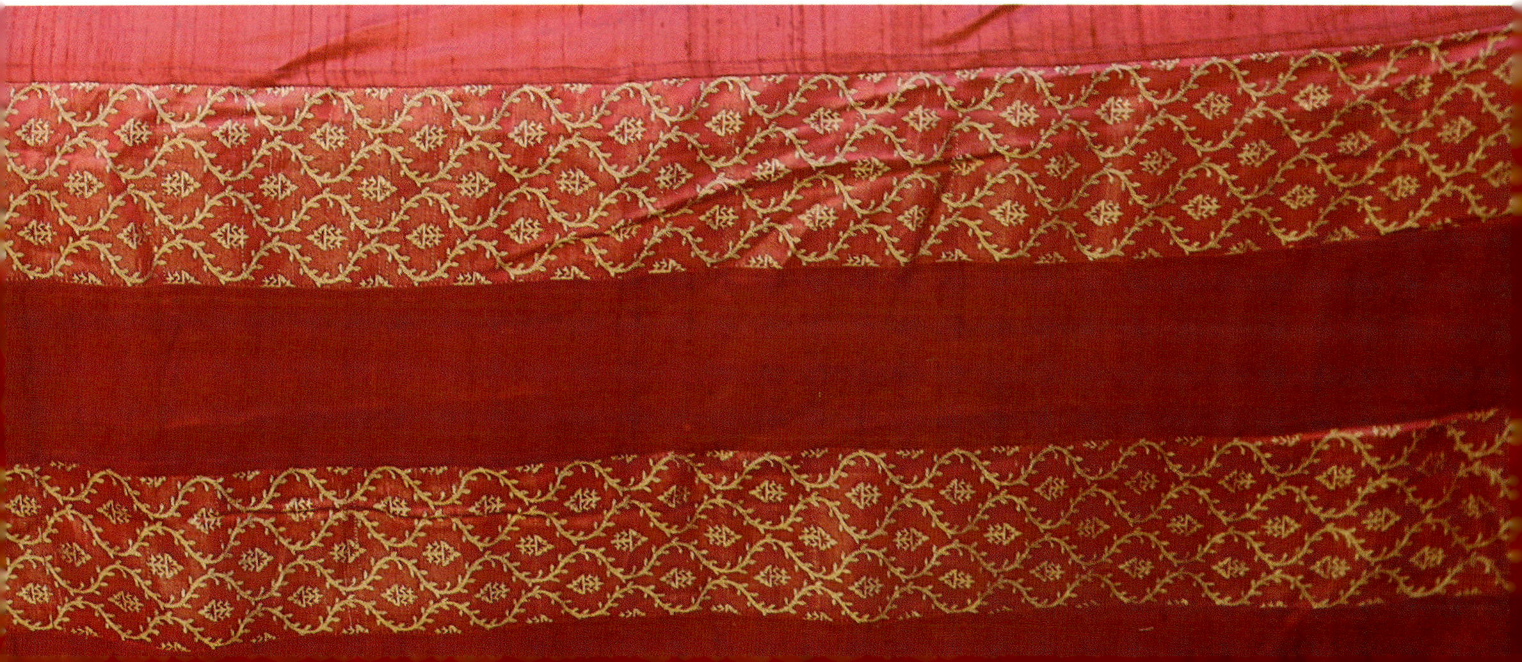

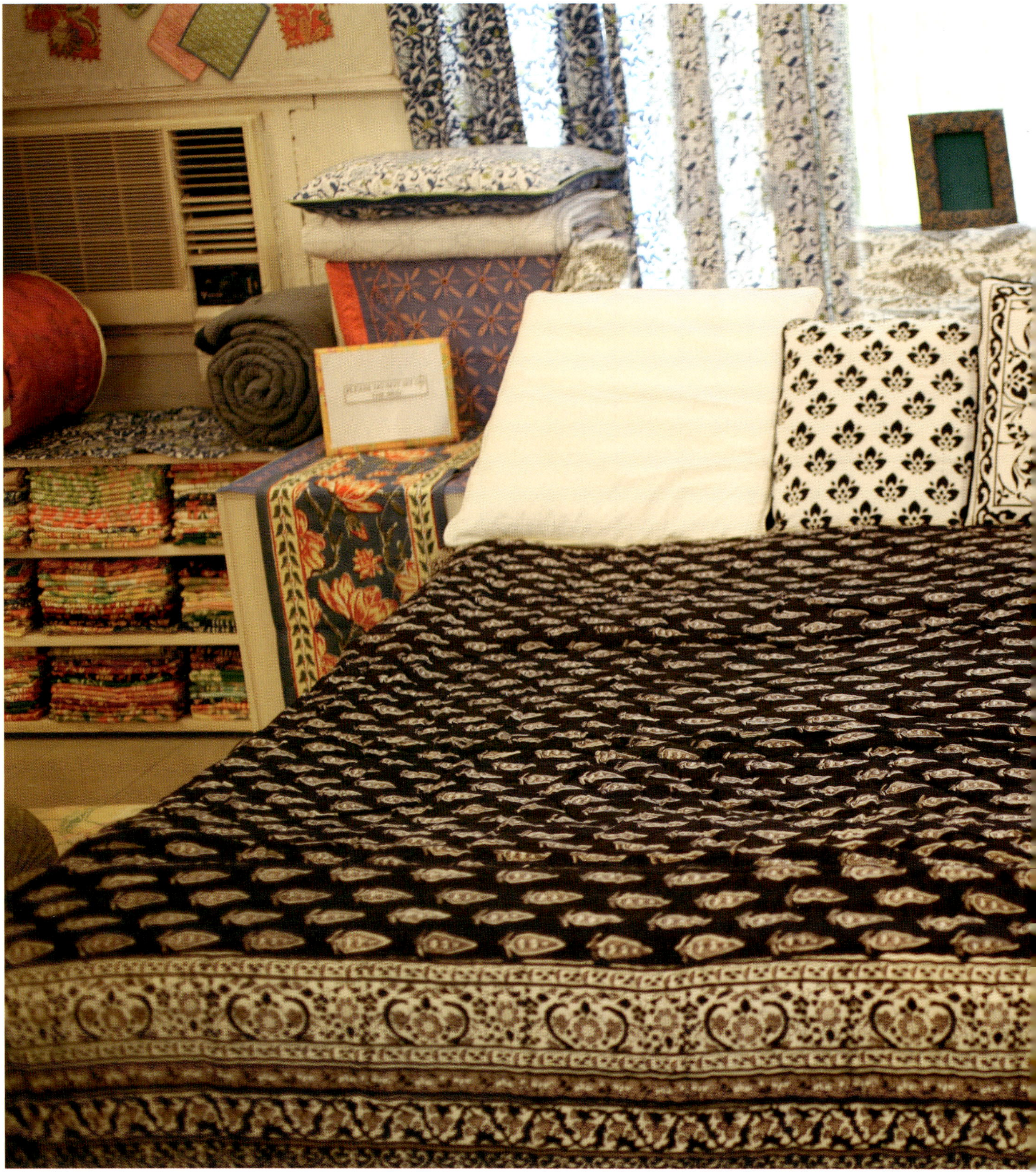

adapt them to western tastes and colour concepts. According to Andreé she just jumped into it. In the beginning, before getting help, she created 600 designs. Some designs were created according to customers' orders—for international linen, furnishings and furniture brands like Pier 1 and Crate & Barrel among others. Crate and Barrel has the popular 'Jaipur bed linens' line, which uses traditional Jaipuri motifs.

There was no looking back. The company flowered and grew rapidly though of course, there were the initial setbacks and some stumbling blocks to cope with. Some of

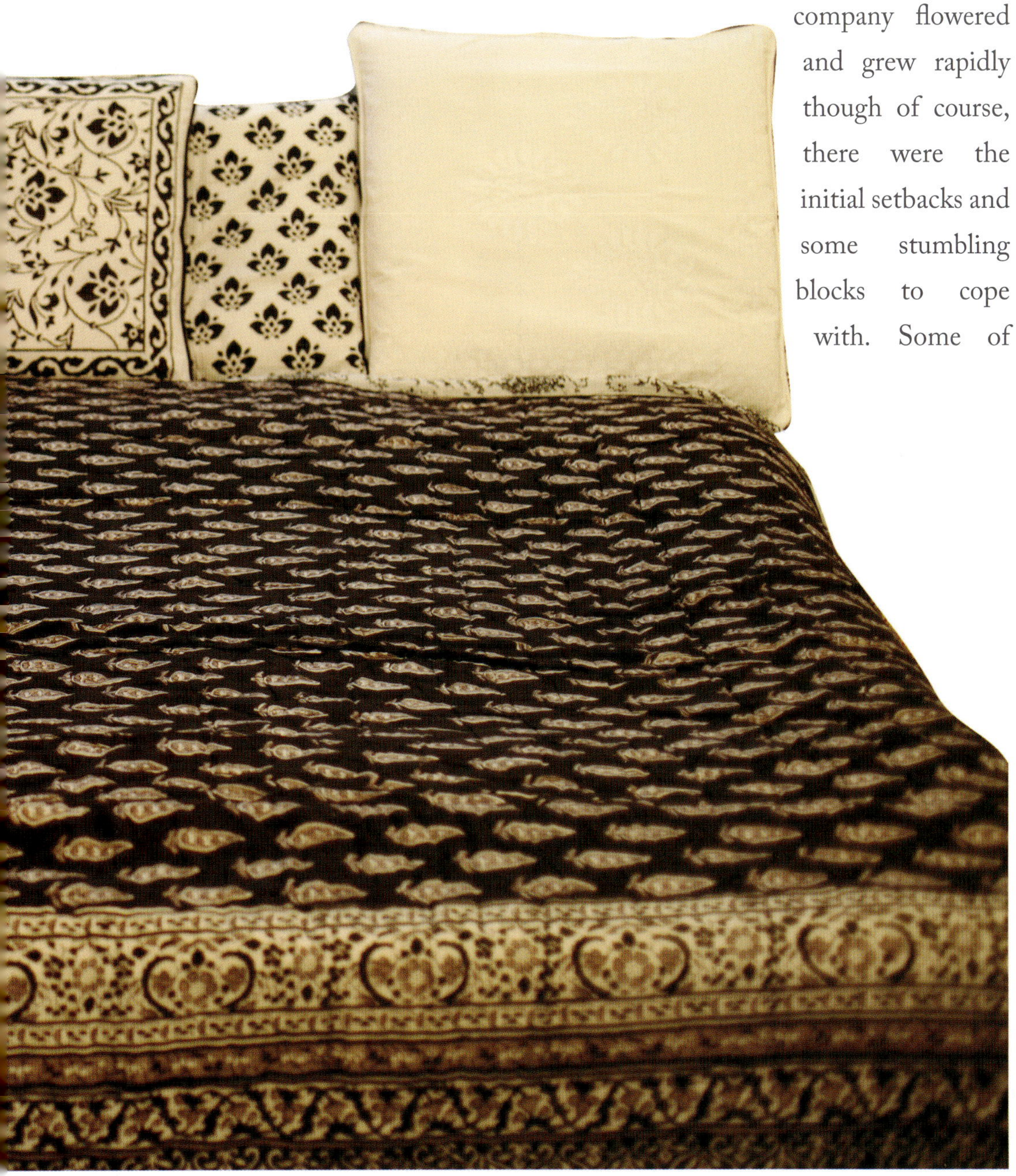

The pea pod motif used on a black surface to create a dramatic effect on a bed cover on display in the Soma shop, with printed cushions propped up against printed curtains and other fabric and bed linen

the oversized printing blocks would come in the way of a printer who would have a difficult time managing work; bad weather often took its toll. Andreé's 'wild' experimentation with prints would often get in the way of traditional printers and their convictions. She experimented with the prints and it was sometimes difficult to convince an old printer to print a well known pattern upside-down. Nonetheless, Soma progressed well.

The subject, regional culture and craft are all important to Andreé. Screen-printing involves quite a different technique and is not as popular as block

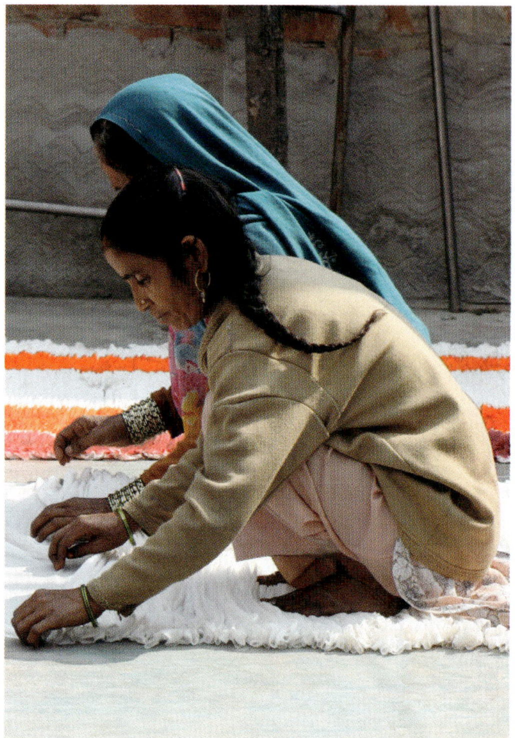

Right: *Traditional printing is carried on in Sanganer where women workers prepare the textile to be painted on. They paint the colour straight on to the material.*

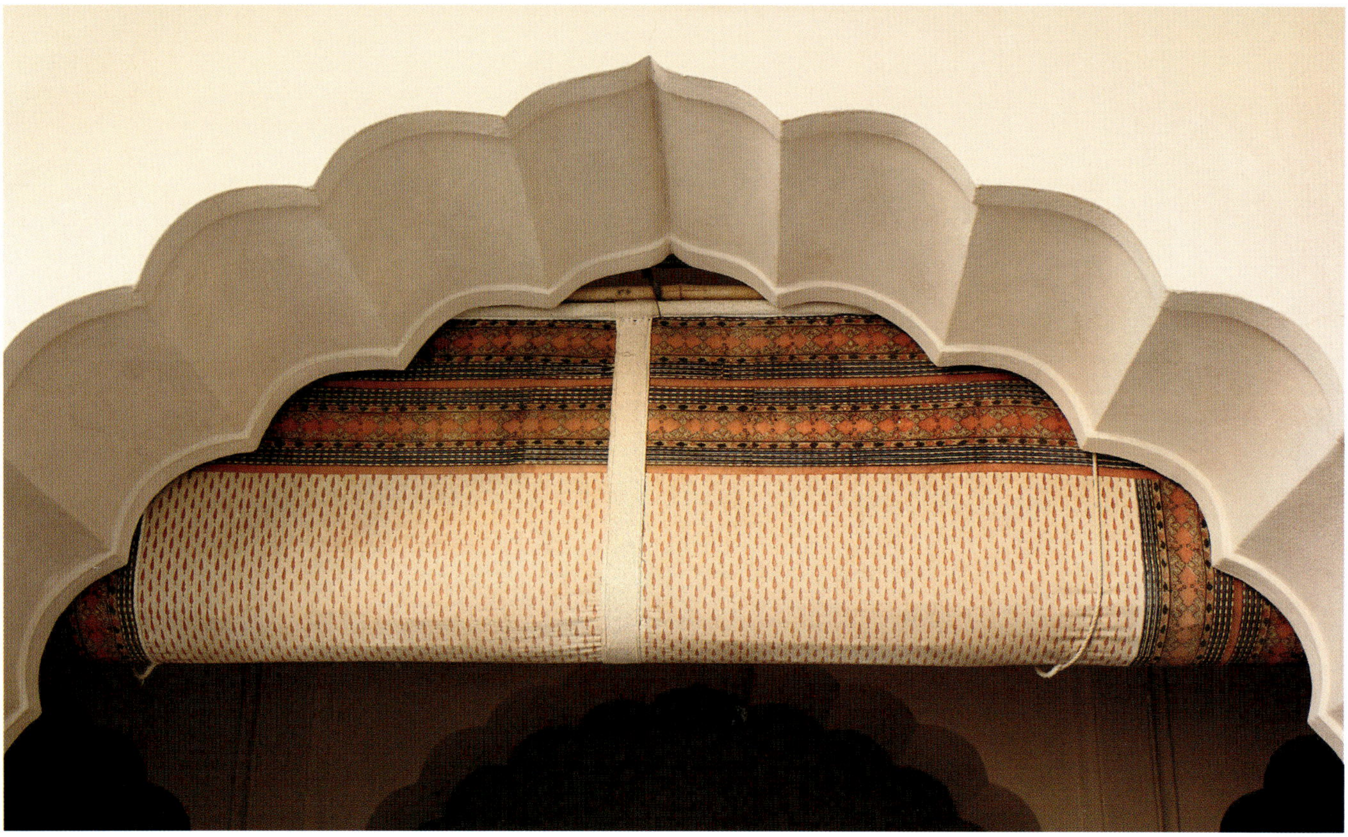

Curved archway at Ninder Mahal with printed screen rolled up to let in light and allow ventilation

printing in Rajasthan. Locals still prefer block-printed textiles and *razai*s to everything else. It is all in the mind of the users, a matter of regional culture and the comfort factor associated with the traditional block-printed *razai*, feels Andreé. She has heard people discuss the soft warmth created under a traditional *razai* in severe winter. Happy, snug and cosy under a quilt 'you don't like to come out!' they chorus. And there is nothing quite like the Jaipur *razai* to beat the desert cold. This seems to be the common consensus among Andreé's local customers.

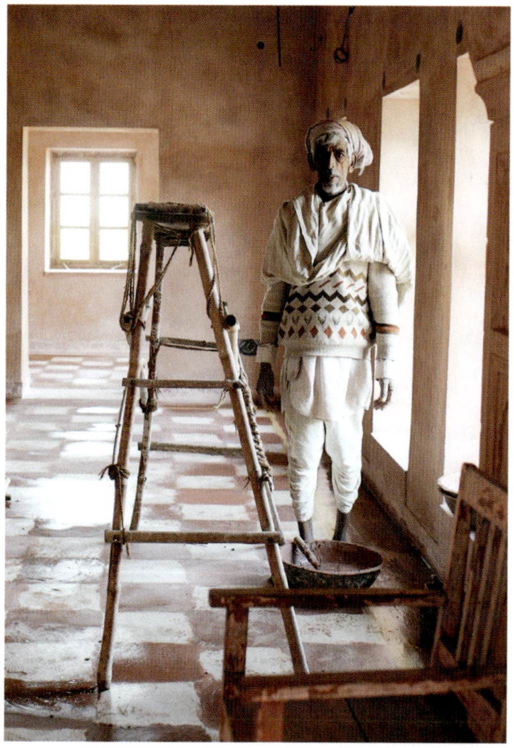

Left: *Restoration in progress at Ninder Mahal*

Below: *A restored bedroom in Ninder Mahal where printed quilts are used as bedspreads*

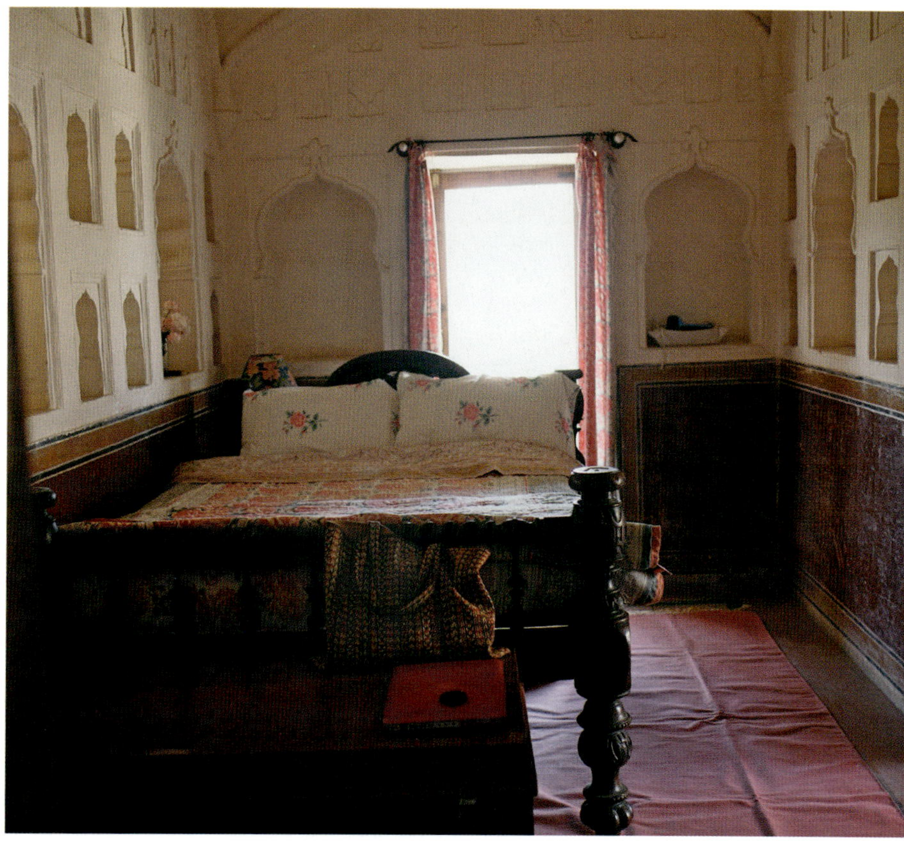

Rustic charm

Quilt-making is a pleasant enough task and entire families can be involved at different stages of the process. The Muslim women population has largely been an unexposed segment, which has traditionally stayed at home, doing household work and raising children. Thanks to quilting, the opportunity to contribute to the family income has given them a new lease of life, and added to their dignity as an earning member of the family. There is also some amount of public exposure and experience in public dealings. Soma's quilts are often quilted in private homes–in villages–in rooms

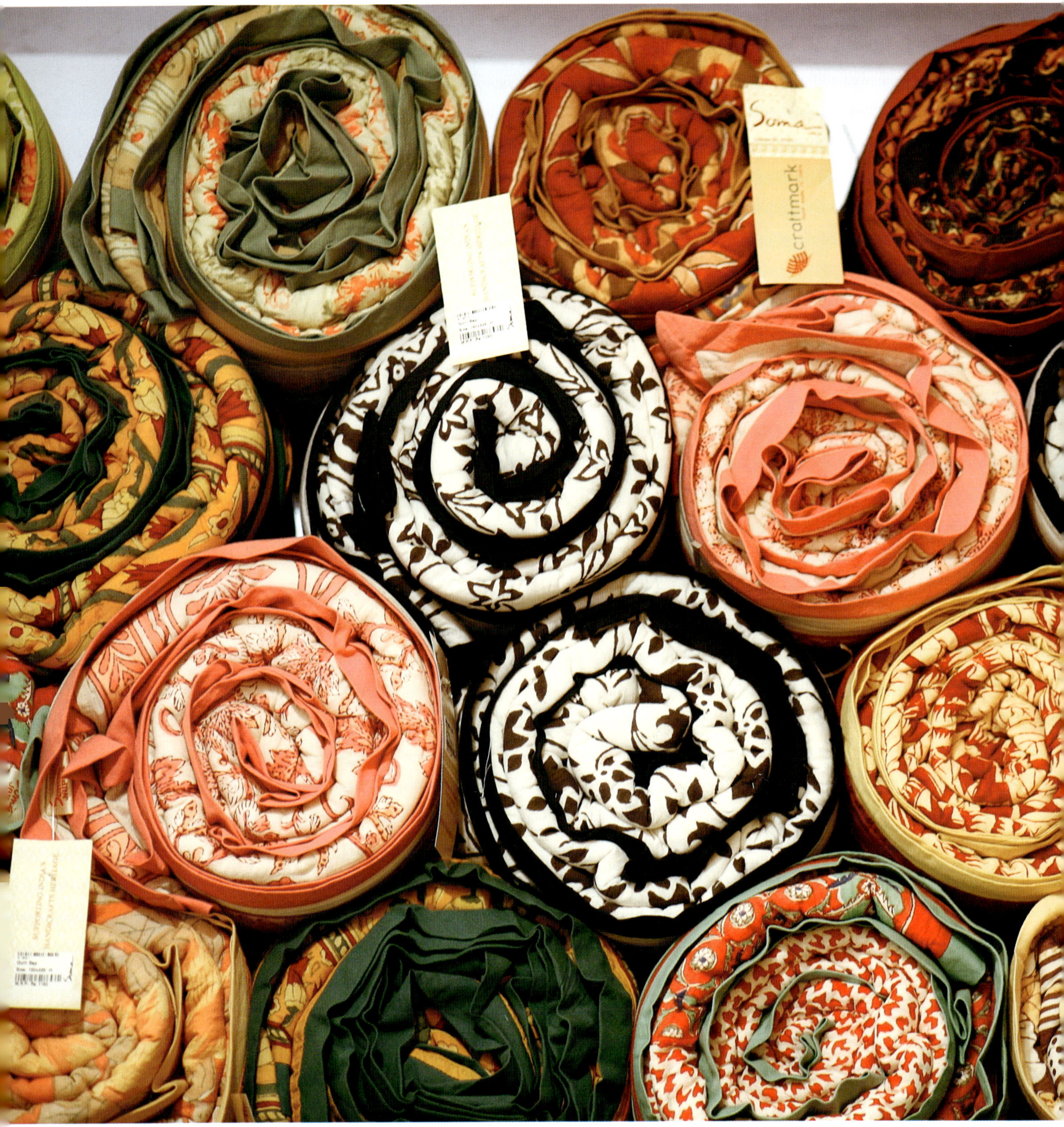
Soma
craftmark

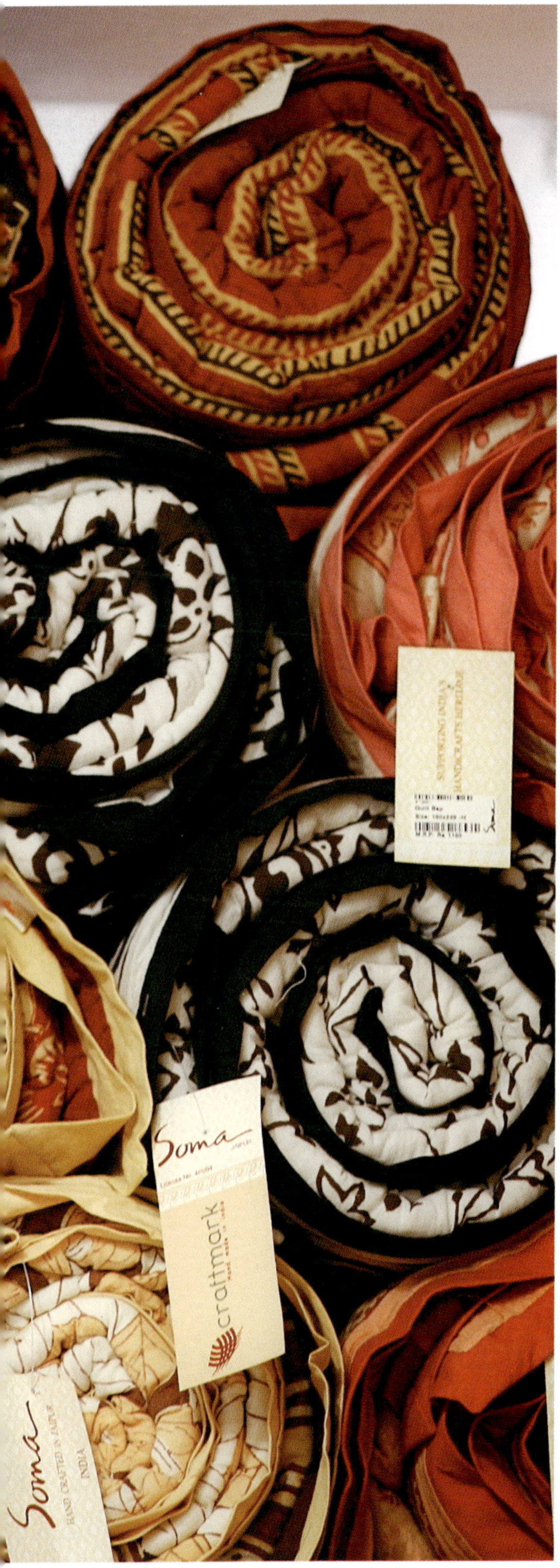

sometimes so small that the worker has to fold the quilt and work on portions due to lack of ample floor space. Andreé's dream is to continue to contribute meaningfully to the industry as a whole.

The owners of Soma too, are far removed from the hustle and bustle of the big city by choice. They prefer living in the country, amidst natural colours and creativity. I travelled to a village outside Jaipur to meet them at Ninder Mahal, an old restored castle which is now their home. They bought Ninder Mahal around twenty years ago but at that point of time it was only a large ruin, which had to be restructured and restored. The restoration of the castle is still in progress. The interiors are decorated largely with Soma textiles, furniture and *razai*s. The décor is unpretentious and everything looks natural, never out of place and in complete harmony with the castle and its environment, the local culture and tradition. The beautiful old and new Soma prints in my bedroom at Ninder Mahal were truly charming and represented ethnic Rajasthan in its truest colours. When I woke up the next day and opened my eyes to the morning sunlight I saw a peacock sitting upright at my window. The tapestry was now complete.

A riot of colours and designs in the neatly rolled Soma quilts

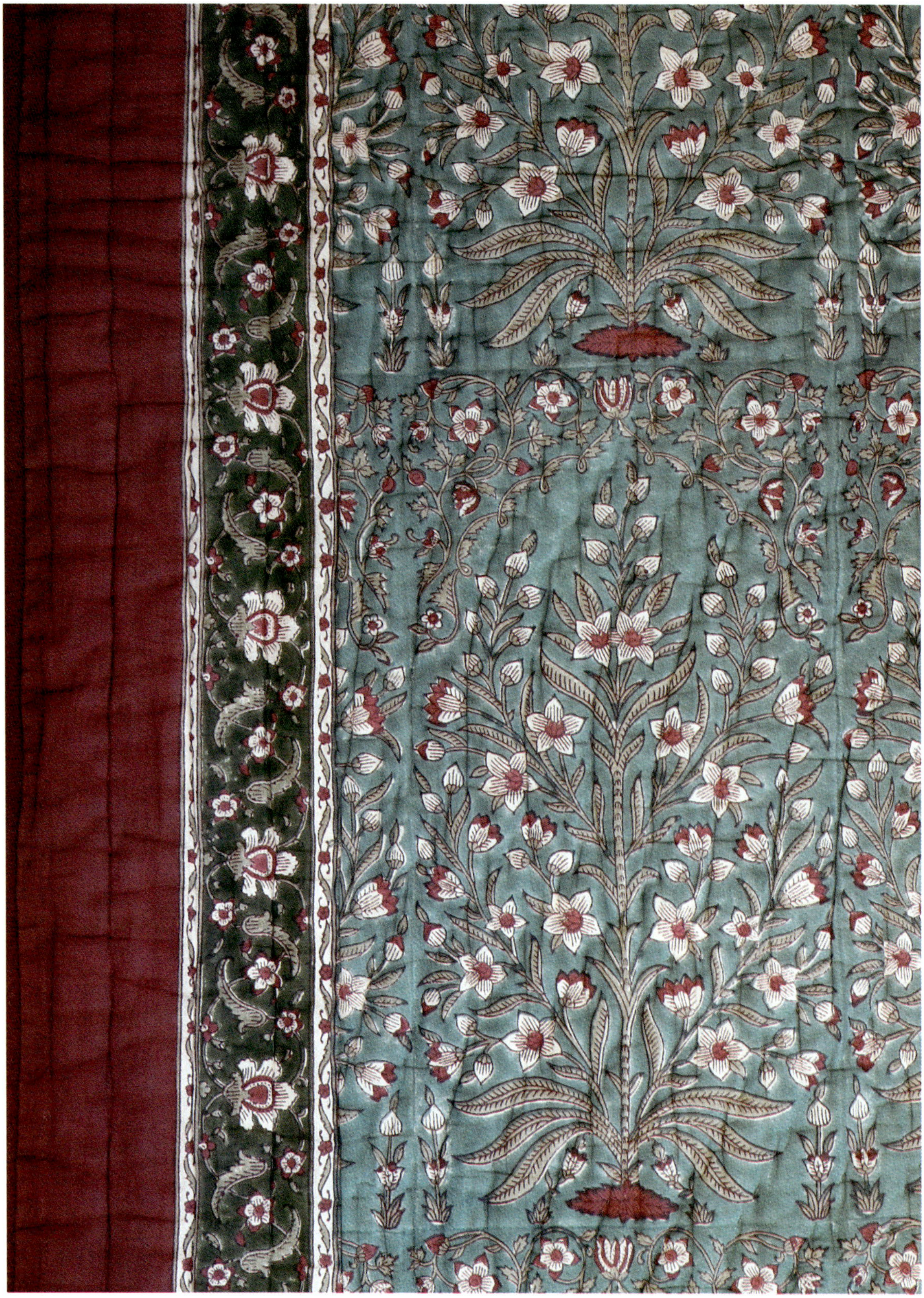

Superb quilts with an abundance of the poppy motif. Graceful embroiderers, a white haveli, *an attractive young woman…*

Mughal garden

Photographs of designer Brigitte Singh and her beautiful quilts published in *Architektur & Wohnen* were perhaps the most powerful of all the visuals on Indian quilting traditions, calling out to me to visit India again.

I knew little about present India the first time I landed in Mumbai in 1980. I did not know then, about the *Lonely Planet* guide book. However, fortunately enough I ended up in nice hotels and special places. I met original travellers who gave me company and were often my guides.

A life track switch

The first time I was in India was when John Lennon died. I was sitting on a beach in Goa and a Swiss girl came by and said, 'John Lennon has been shot'. But somehow it did not quite make sense on the beach in Goa. Now I was in India once again, tracing my way down to innovative manufacturers and retailers of the Jaipur quilt, believing that this 'innocent' and unchartered way of travelling was the best way to be here. Actually everything fell into place fairly smoothly. I found a room at Diggi

Facing page: *A quilt in contrast colours and traditional floral pattern from the collection of Brigitte Singh*

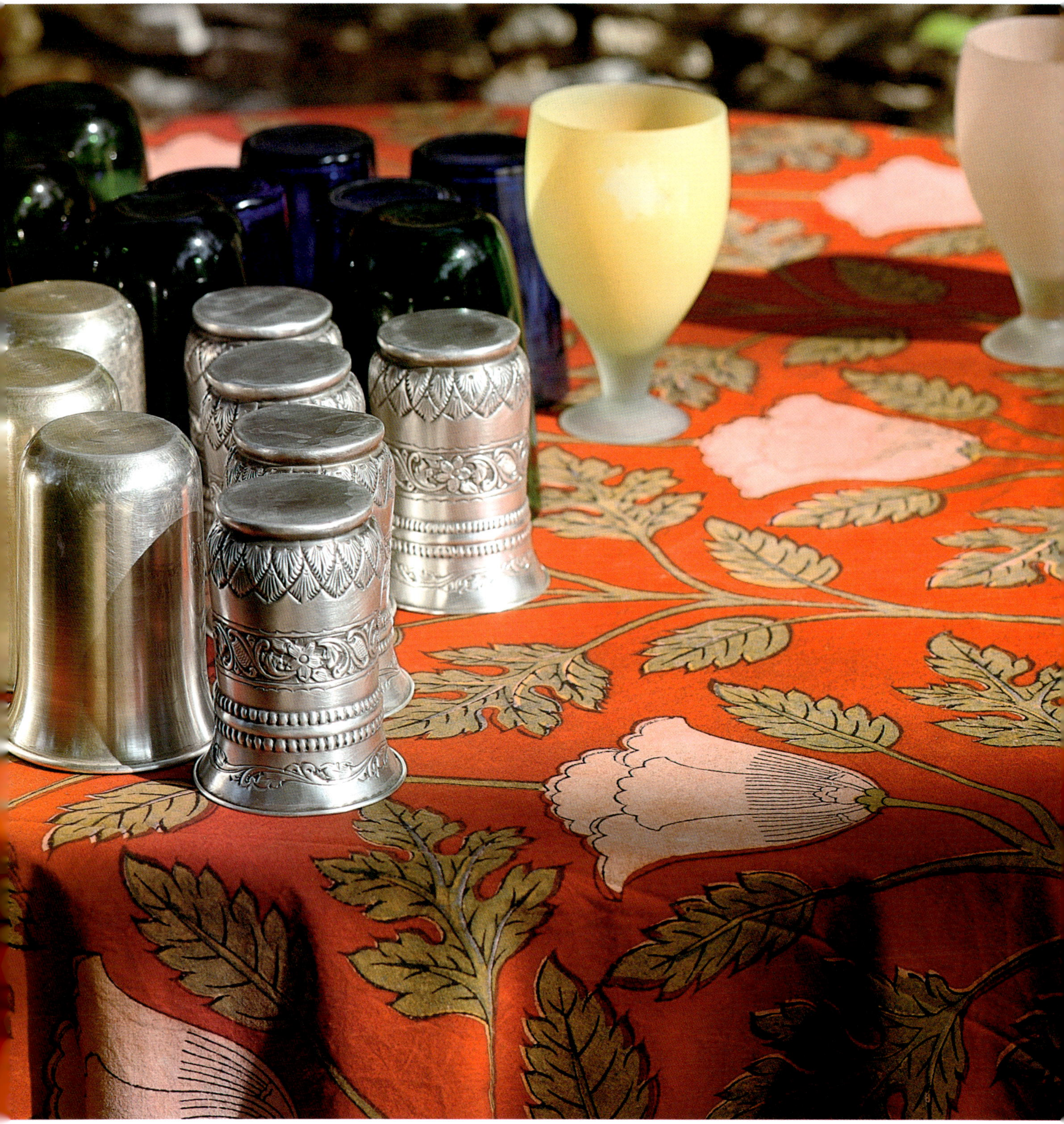

Palace hotel in Jaipur, and I managed to get an appointment with the designer 'from the picture'—Brigitte Singh. This second visit to India changed my life, not through the spiritual influence of gurus, but simply because I felt singularly at ease and at home. I was exposed to new views and crossroads in life and I learned many new things. It was like a changeover, a life track switch of sorts.

Meeting Brigitte Singh

I booked a rickshaw and set off on the road to Amber to meet Brigitte Singh. Some parts of the road are very pretty and I stopped to take photographs at my will, and at rather frequent intervals. My subjects were many and varied. The little palace on the lake, white, orange and fuchsia bougainvillea, the sand-coloured Amber Fort at a majestic elevation, fleeting views of the bright saris of women and painted elephants ambling past, the earthy and exotic smell of Indian spices and the roadside flora added up to make the short journey a rather romantic affair. After crossing Amber we left the road and turned off into a patch of dry land punctuated by delicate thorn bushes and trees.

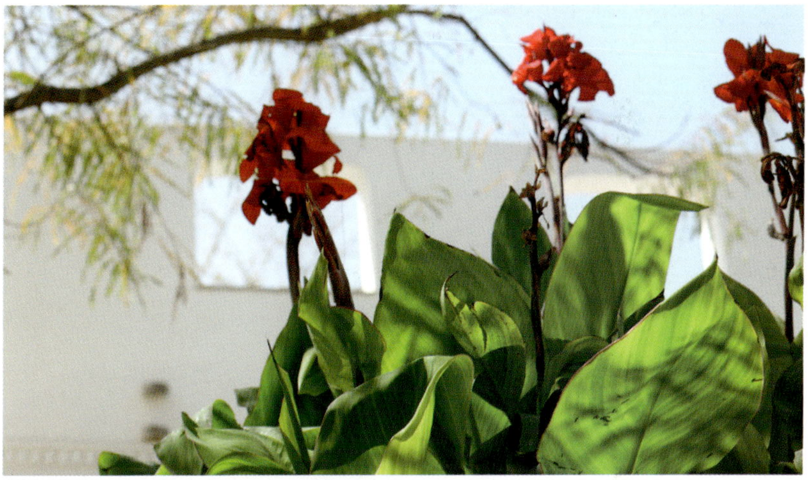

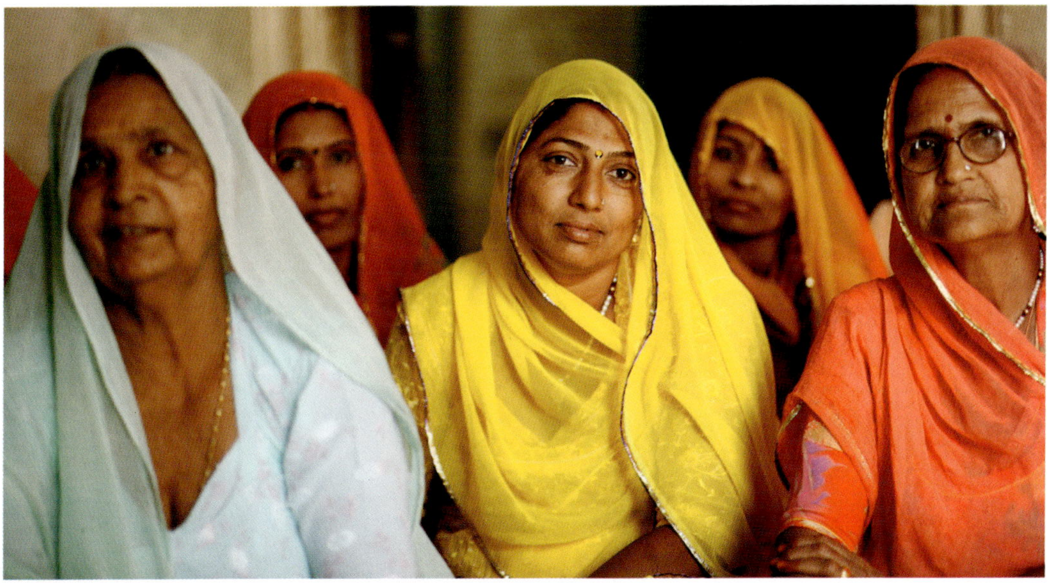

Canna in full bloom in Brigitte Singh's garden

Left: *'Fleeting views of bright saris of women', a common sight on country roads near Jaipur*

Facing page: *Bright printed table linen by Brigitte Singh in her garden, complementing the silver and glass tableware*

Below: *Women working on a quilt in Brigitte Singh's spacious atelier*

Lunch break at Brigitte Singh's workshop, where the women relax in the adjoining garden in cool weather

The rickshaw finally stopped in front of a large green gate, which promptly opened, much to my relief. The path inside led up to a beautiful white haveli. The house was inspired by the grand patrician mansions peppering Rajasthan—built around a patio and an interior court. It was constructed with traditional materials and had a garden full of bright flowers and trees. There was a vegetable garden as well. This haveli is Brigitte Singh's home and a part of it is used as her office and sewing rooms. She has recently added a few buildings where the printing unit is housed and other activities related to the production of soft furnishings and garments are also carried out.

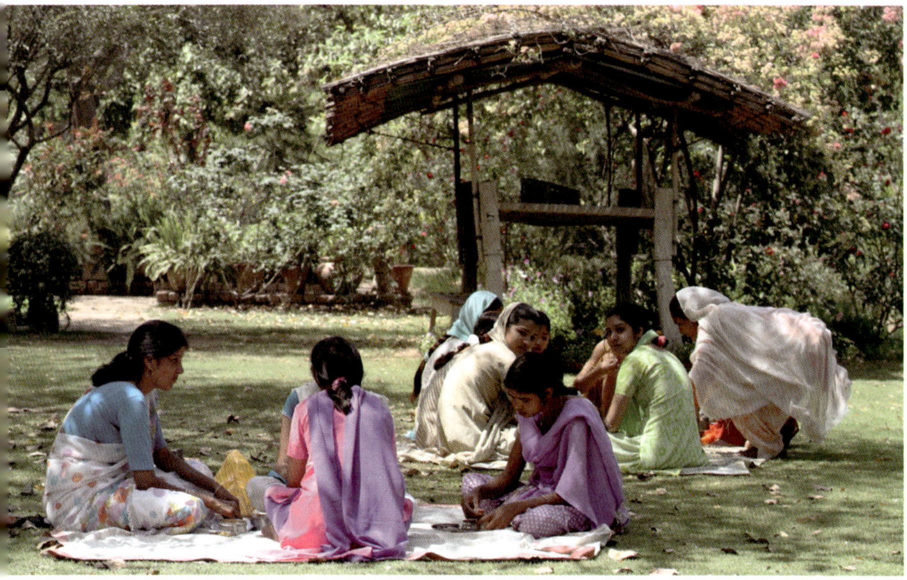

Brigitte's workers come from different communities, religions and castes. Brigitte employs around a hundred families at a time and the workers have often than

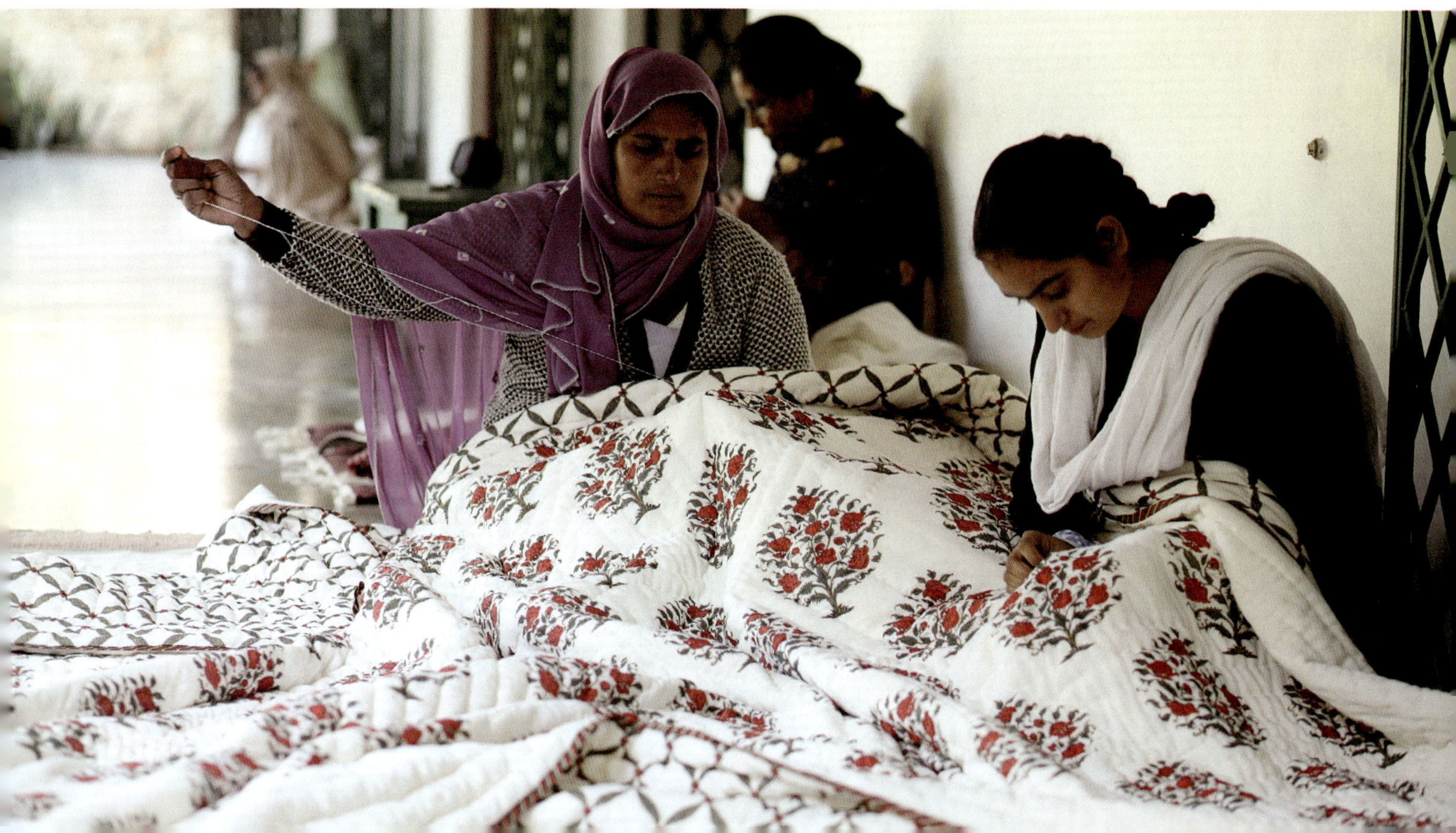

not, been trained by her. They work in peaceful, comfortable and picturesque surroundings and I must admit that at times I was rather envious of their work environment. The working hours are the regular eight–9 am to 5 pm–with a break for lunch.

Time present and time past

Brigitte Singh is French. I learnt about her family and background while I chatted with her informally. She was born in Cholet, in France. Cholet incidentally owes the rise of its prosperity to the settlement of weavers set up by Édouard Colbert, the count of Maulévrier. Brigitte's ancestors came from Catalonia—one of the richest and highly industrialised regions in Spain, and from Alsace—a province in France. One of her ancestors, Charles Schoessler was a miniature painter and draughtsman of the popular and expensive Indiennes fabric in the nineteenth century. Brigitte started her drawing lessons with the painter Joseph Martineau when she was only thirteen years old and continued until she was eighteen. After that she left France and studied Islamic Art at Cairo University and was a student at the Academy of Fine Arts. Later on she returned to France and studied Applied Arts at Ecole des Art Décoratifs in Paris.

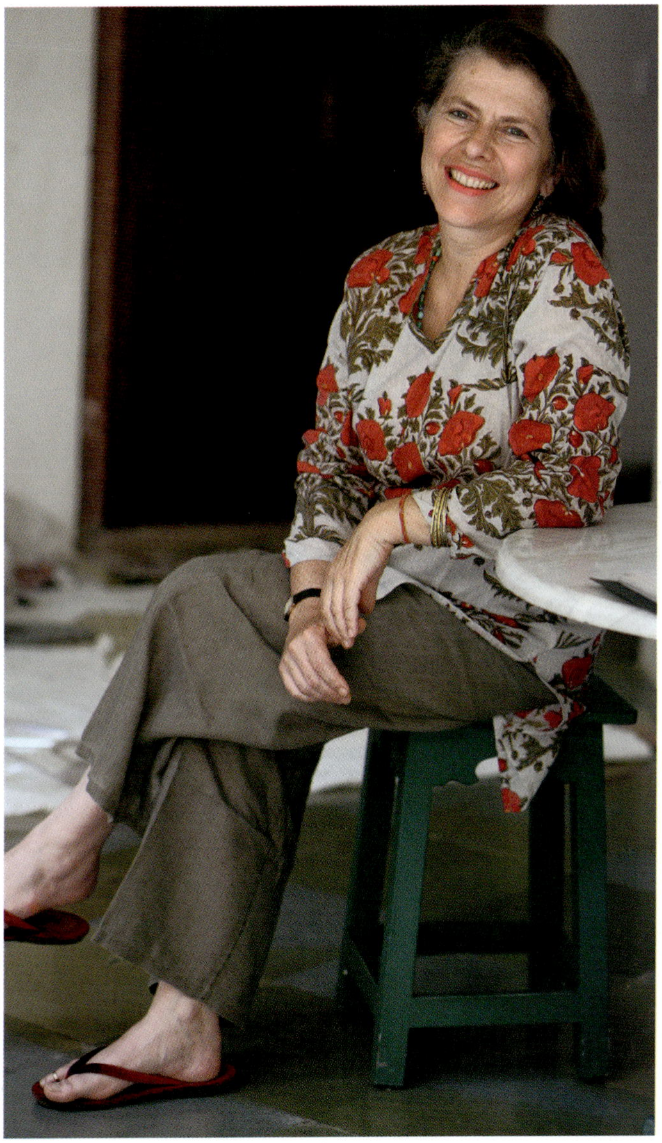

Brigitte Singh in a 'poppy print' quilted top

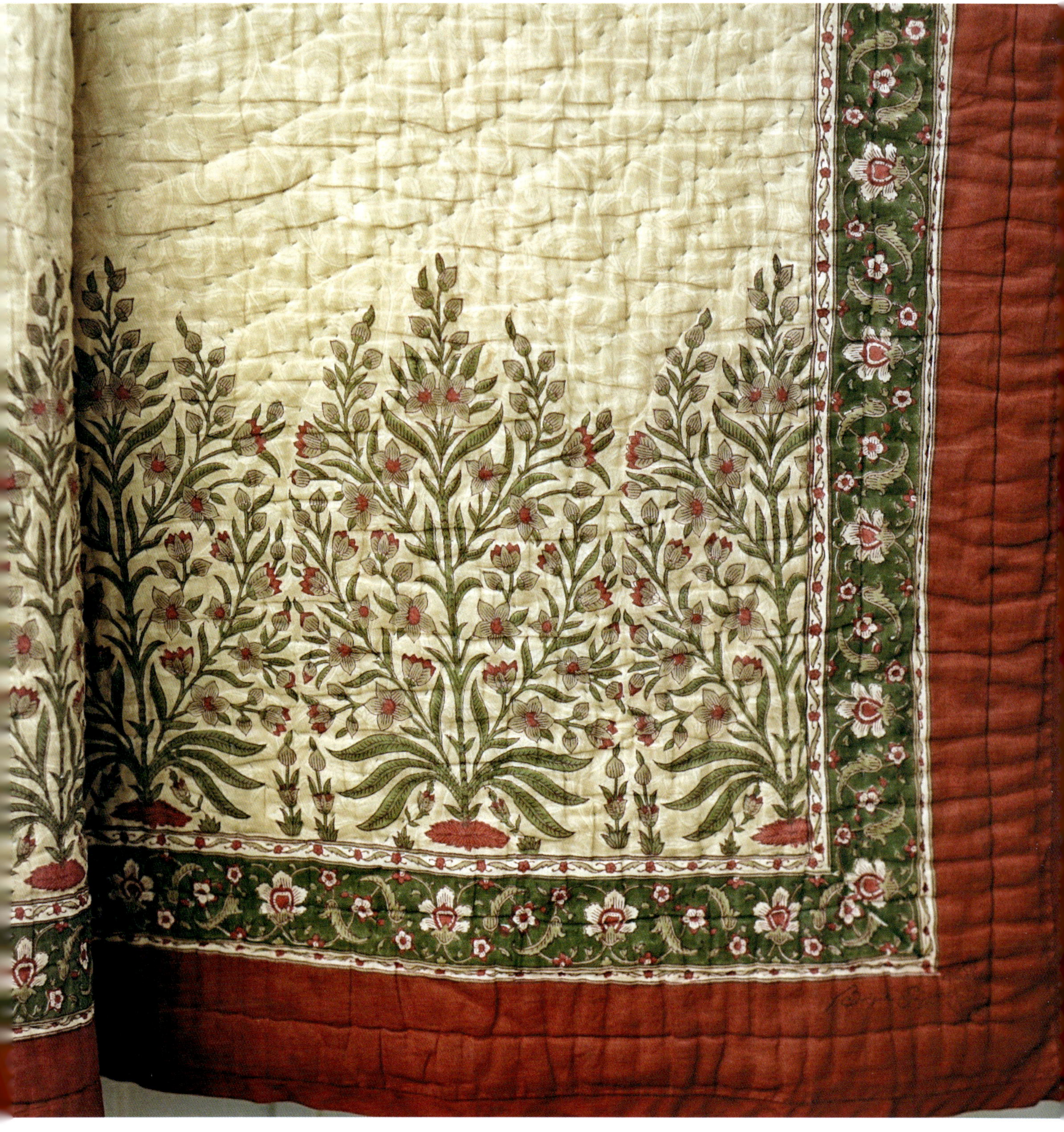

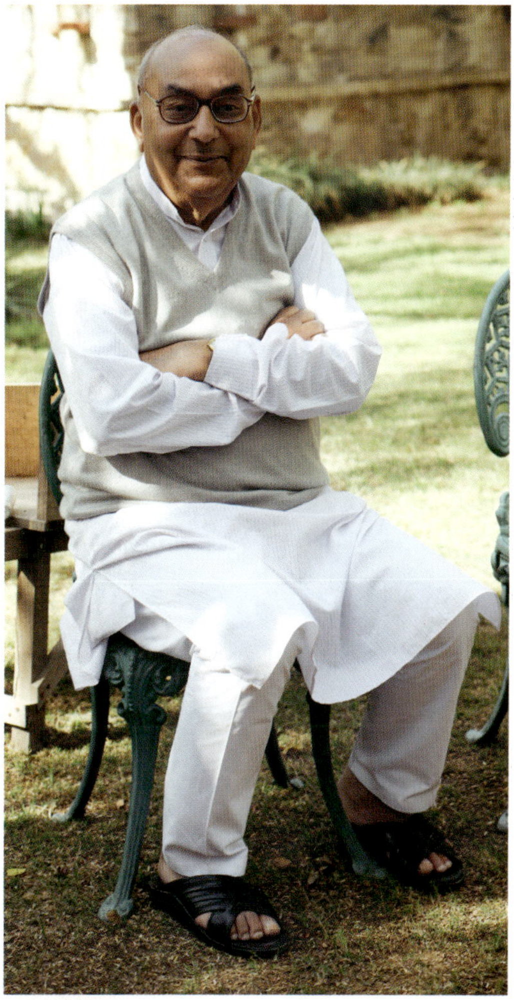

Brigitte had a great admiration for Turkish and Persian miniature art and was fascinated by the composition and finesse of the drawings. Unfortunately the political situation in Iran made it impossible for her to study there. Another option was Rajasthan in India, where miniature art had developed and flourished since the seventeenth century under the patronage of the Mughal maecenas. She received a two-year scholarship to study the technique of miniature paintings in Jaipur and arrived in India in 1980. It was not an easy start of life, education and career for Brigitte in Jaipur but it was during this time that she met her future husband S.V. Singh and his father. Singh was an eminent collector of Rajasthani miniatures. In his studio of miniature paintings, Brigitte met Jagdish Chandra Mahindra who oversaw the work

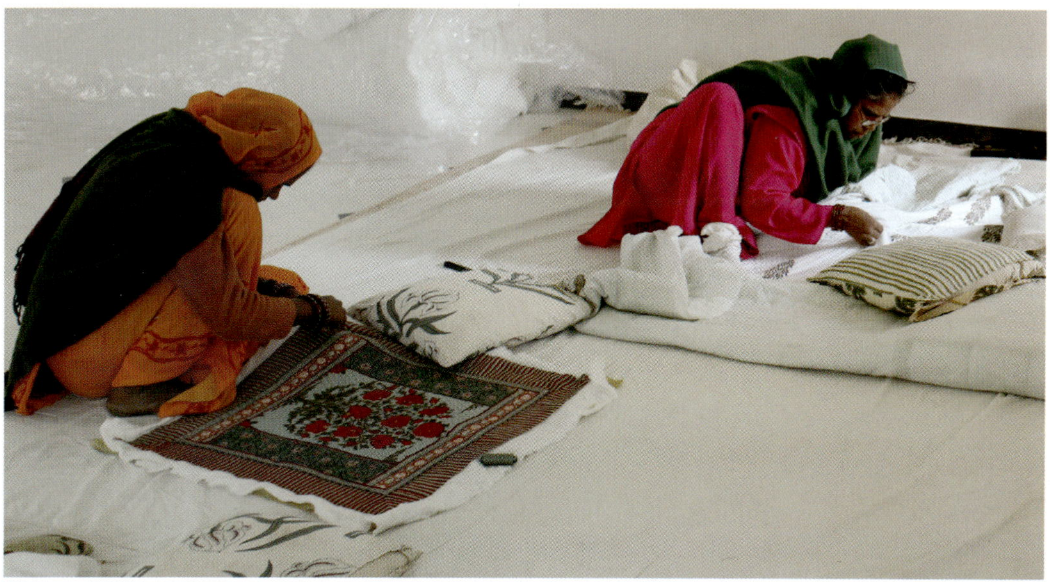

Left: *Quilting in Brigitte Singh's atelier*

Above: *Jagdish Chandra Mahindra, Brigitte Singh's long time manager*

Facing page: *Close front view of quilt by Brigitte Singh in cream and burgundy with details of the stitches*

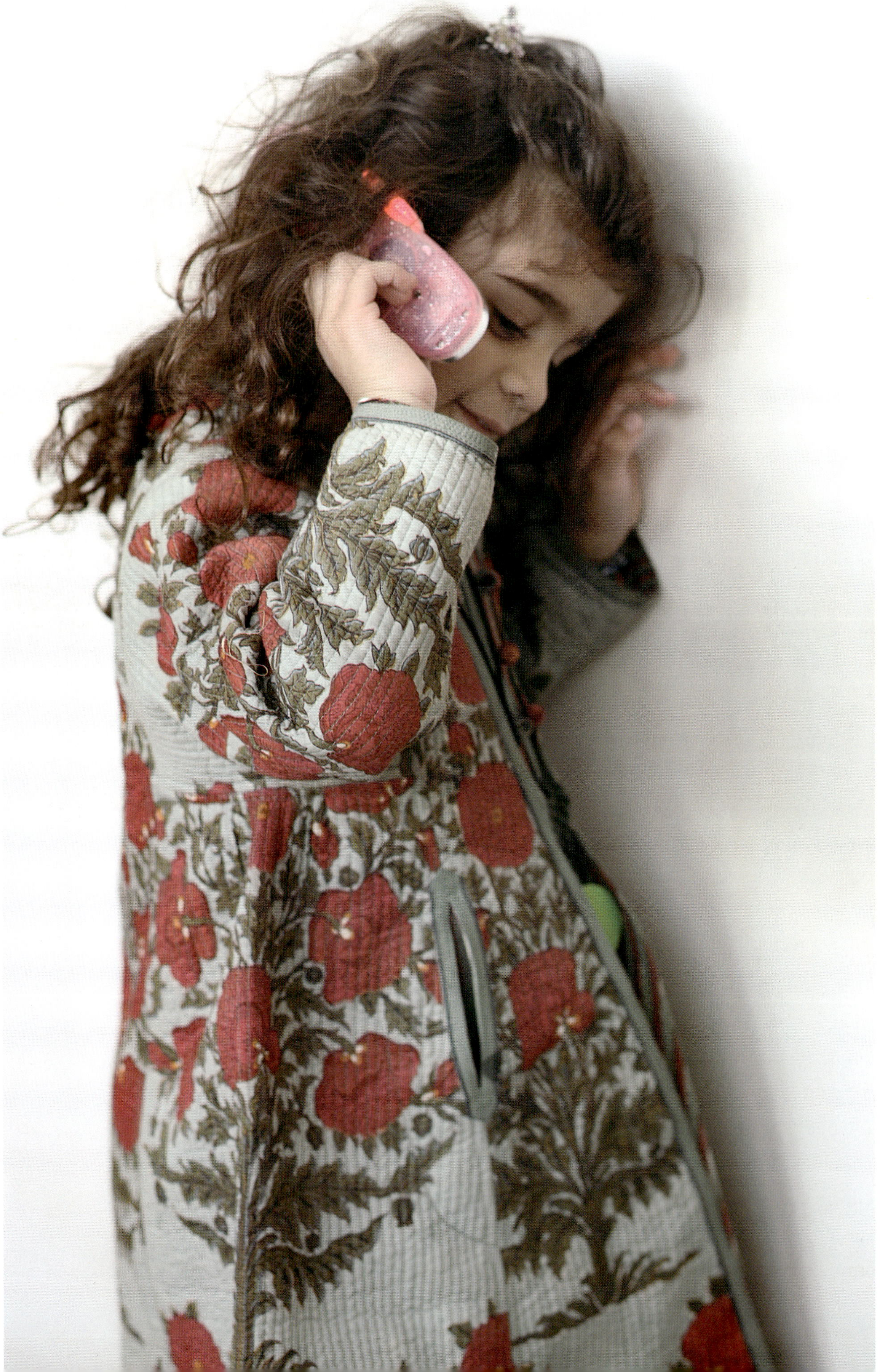

and with whom she still works today. He is now the manager of her company. 'He is my guardian angel', says Brigitte.

Here she also met Vedpal Sharma, an excellent technician and well-known restorer, with whom she did a six-month apprenticeship. After she was married to S.V. Singh, Brigitte took over the studio as manager for the following nine years. During this time she used to visit Sanganer very often on work, and one day she found beautiful and refined pattern samples from the eighteenth century at an old printer's workshop. She asked the old printer if he could make prints of the same quality for her. She placed an order with him to produce a series of scarves, which she took to England. She received her first order with these scarves from Colefax and Fowler, an interior decoration company.

Inspired art

I asked Brigitte Singh, why she started producing quilts and what led her to the industry. She smiled back impishly, explaining that it was not as if the Holy Mary manifested in one of her dreams and ordained her to make quilts. Rather, one thing led to the other. The sight of something new which caught her fancy perhaps, an unexpected lucky connection, a word or a phrase heard in passing… leading on to another road, revealing new possibilities for an exciting future.

The sight of quilts everywhere was inspiring enough. Brigitte created textiles, often lending a fresh interpretation to the existing motifs, adding elements of her own artistic language and favoured colour palette. She changed the graphic vocabulary of printing in Jaipur and Sanganer by reintroducing the Mughal motifs. Brigitte began manufacturing clothes in 1984, first for herself, later for friends, and slowly it evolved into a production process of timeless garments: clothes for children, textiles, quilts and soft furnishings. She uses mainly floral motifs in her designs.

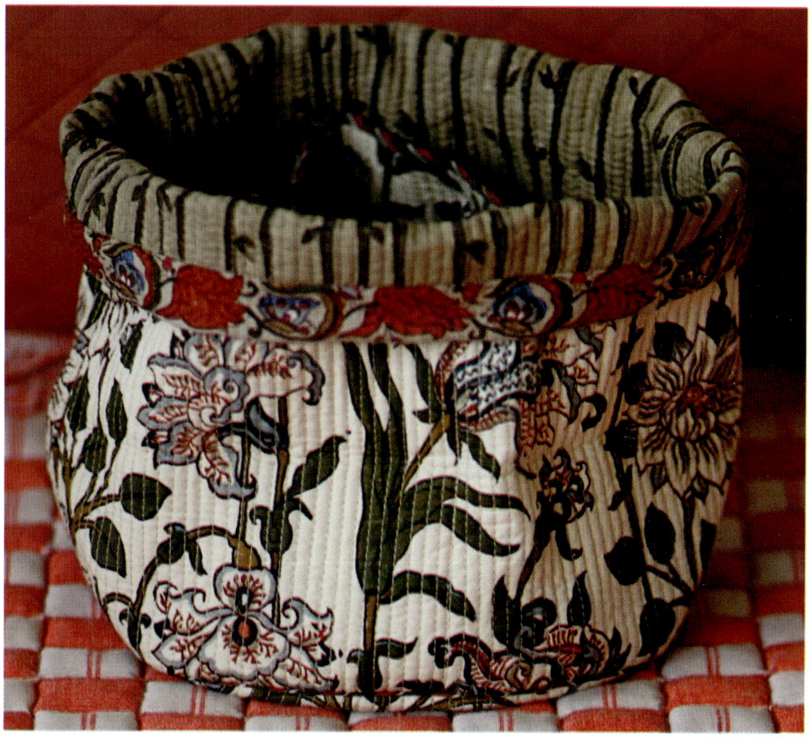

Brigitte Singh, quilted cosmetic bag

Facing page: *Brigitte's daughter Lilah in a quilted robe designed with red flowers*

Below right: *Narrow stripes lend style to quilts*

Block printing in progress

One of the most beloved of Brigitte's motifs is the poppy, a pure perfection, which was created by a draughtsman of the royal court in the middle of the seventeenth century and originated probably from an imperial tent. Another sublime motif is that of the stylised cypress tree. The artist paints the motif with a thin brush and Chinese ink on carbon paper. The original is transmitted to the blockmaster and he transfers it to a printing block chiselled out of whitewashed teak, made perfectly plain beforehand. It takes a few weeks to complete a contour block which is done by fine chisel and wooden mallet. The contour block serves as a standard when cutting other blocks, which are used for printing with colours and are made of softer wood. Before they are used, the sculpted blocks are dipped in a bath of mustard oil to harden the wood and make it easier for the colour to adhere.

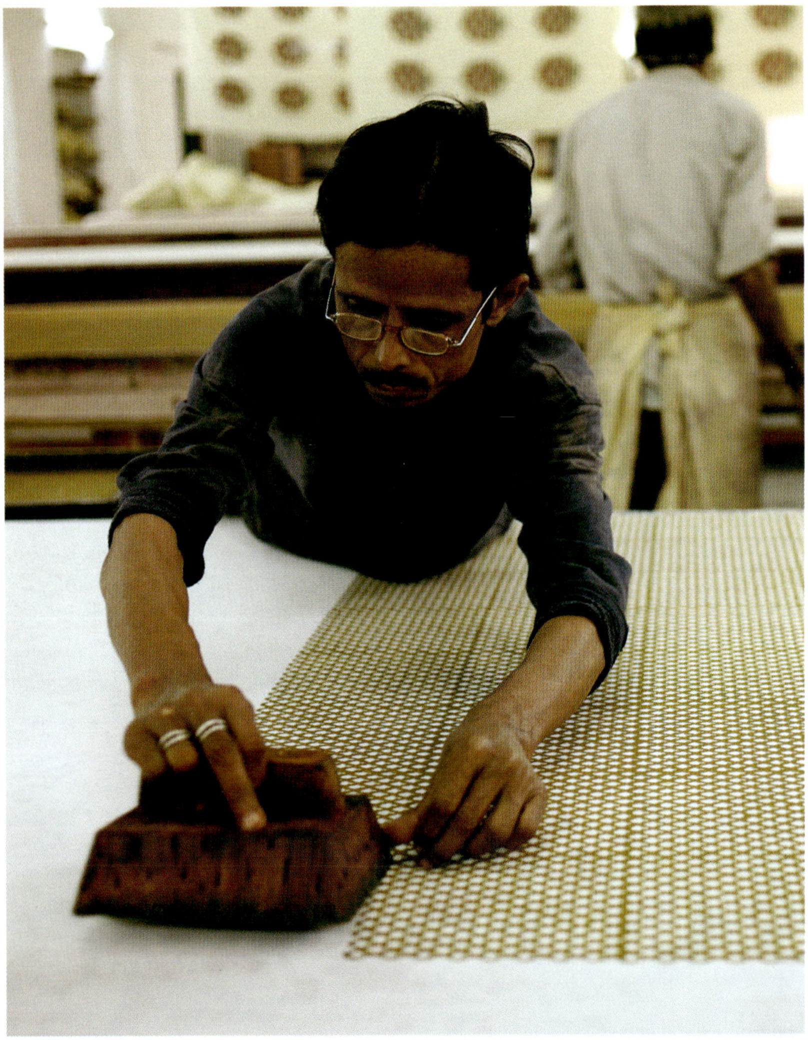

Blend and fuse

The prints emerge step by step on the fabric as the colours are applied one by one. A set of blocks is used up rather quickly; it can be used for 50 to 300

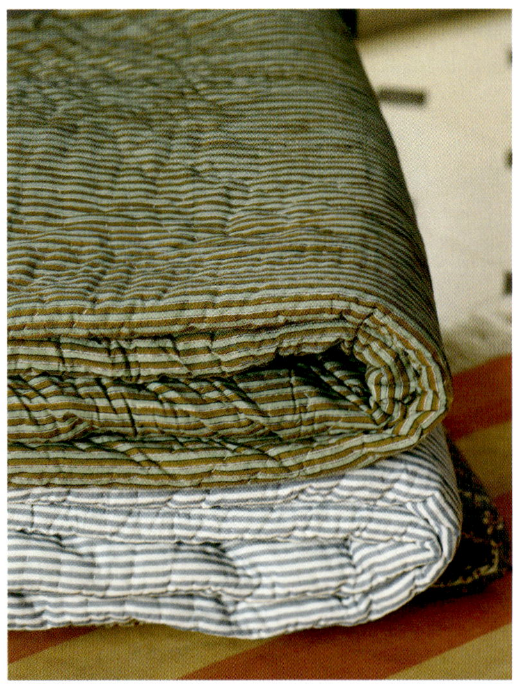

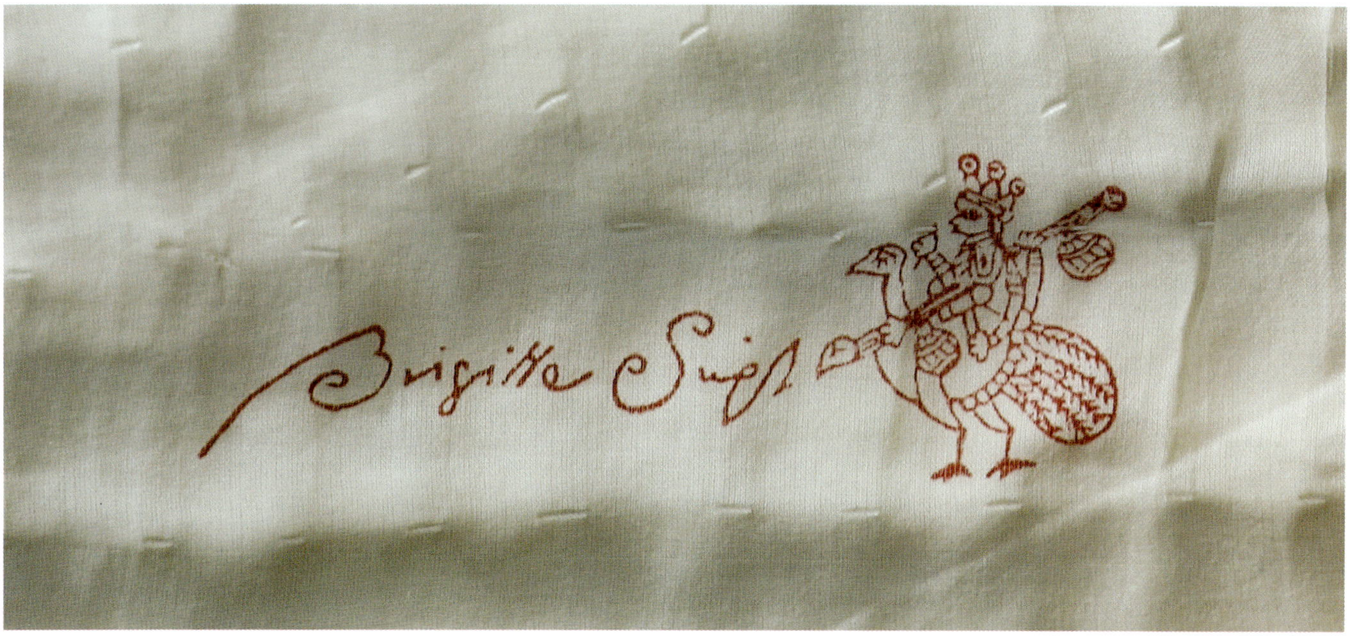

running metres of fabric, depending on its thickness. Many of the blocks are used to reconstruct a motif, correct a background or print a border. Forty five blocks are required for the large hibiscus—a popular motif. Brigitte says that she enjoys choosing the colours and trying them out with the printer. Her quilts are visually striking and attractive. The design is skillfully composed with a mix of different traditional Mughal elements, the colours interacting perfectly with each other and leaving the image well-balanced. Print, quilting and finish are all of a very high standard.

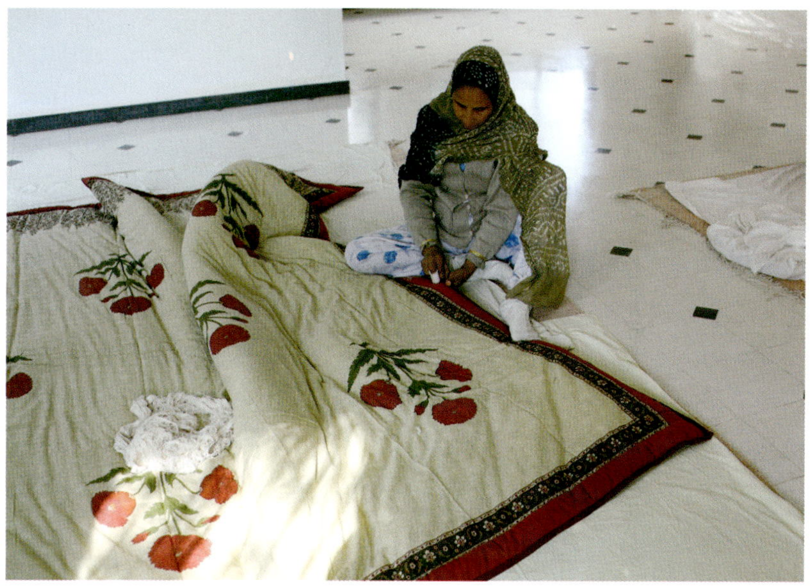

Brigitte's atelier–worker busy at quilting

Above: *Brigitte's signature and logo—the Saraswati emblem. The goddess of knowledge and music, Saraswati rides a peacock in this logo and holds the Indian musical instrument, the veena*

Quilts are articles for everyday use and at the same time they represent a piece of good handicraft or art, with a harmonious blend of traditions and cultures. Brigitte Singh is a connecting link between Indian and French traditions; between the past and the present. It is as if she has brought back to the Indian soil what had previously migrated to France.

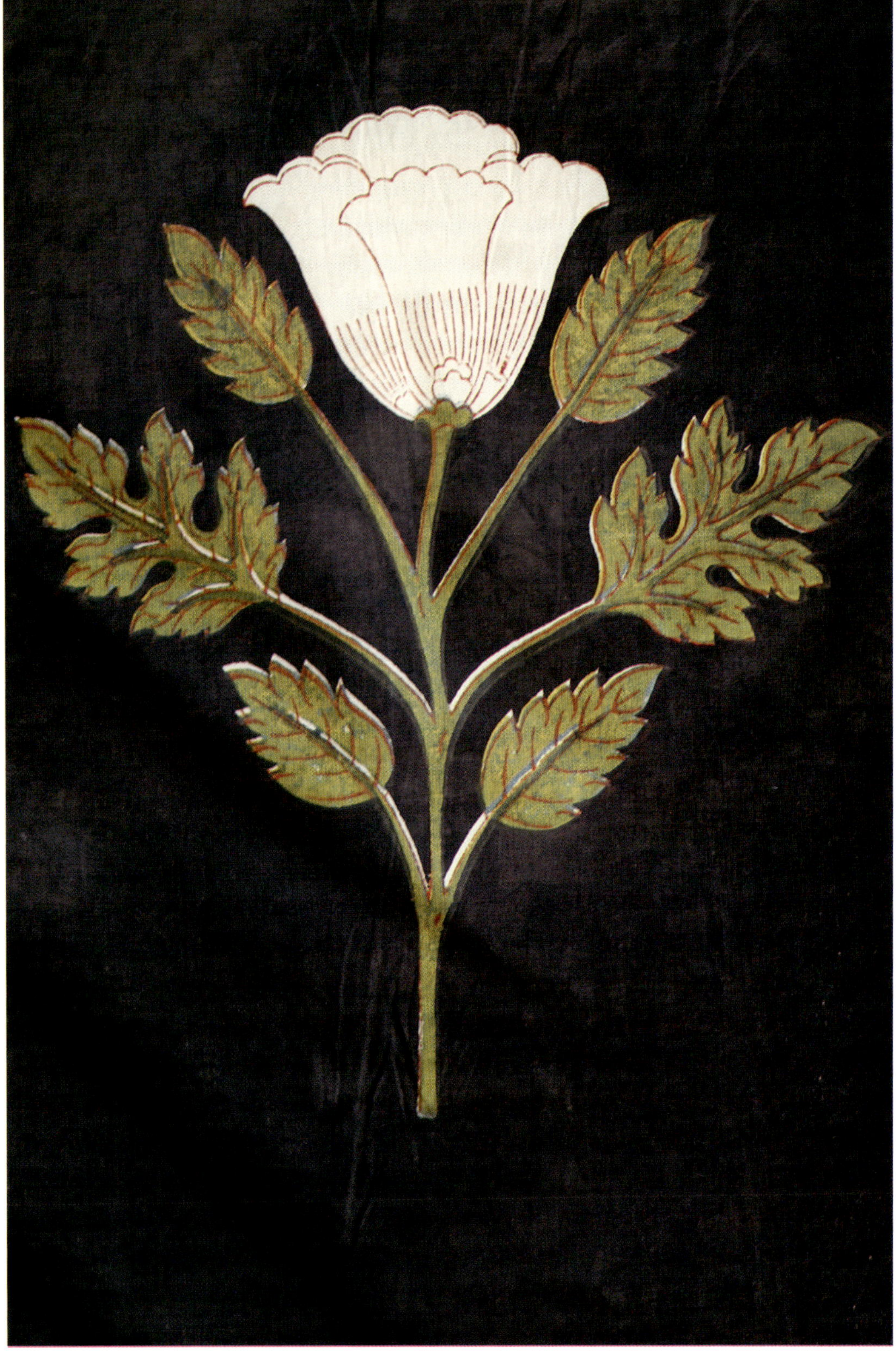

A popular floral motif in off-white, set against a dark background on a cushion cover by Brigitte Singh

A few useful secrets about Jaipur quilts.

I have always noted with amazement that most of the people who buy quilts think about them only as bed covers. They also often choose the king size quilt for a double bed. But there are so many more ways to use a quilt. You know by now, that Jaipur quilts are very light, often thin but adequately warm. You can wash them in a washing machine using a wool programme so that the cotton wool inside the quilt survives the cleaning process. The centrifuge should not be set in violent motion or for too long. To dry the quilt you can hang it out in a drying room or in the garden. It should dry in the shade though, to preserve the colour well.

The quilts are washable; you can use them instead of a duvet even without a protecting sheet. You can buy a single size quilt for that purpose; you just neatly roll up your quilt and your bed is done. In the morning the quilt lies flat on the bed and looks tidy and elegant. You avoid the 'sand dune syndrome', so common with duvets.

You can use the smaller quilts to cover your feet for instance.

In France ladies used the *couvre-pieds*, to cover their feet when they rested in a chaise longue.

When you watch television in a cold room a quilt will keep you warm and comfortable. Since they are made of thin cotton, they do not glide off easily.

I used to take my older quilts to the beach. It is easy to spread your quilt on a sandy beach and be protected from the sand. If you are staying on the cliffs, the quilts are soft and convenient on the hard, rocky surface. An old quilt, with a flower design can be used as a spread (rug) at picnics on which you can sit and place a tray table with coffee and cake. There would also be enough space for children, if it is a family picnic. For a separate children's corner you can choose the Jaipur baby quilts.

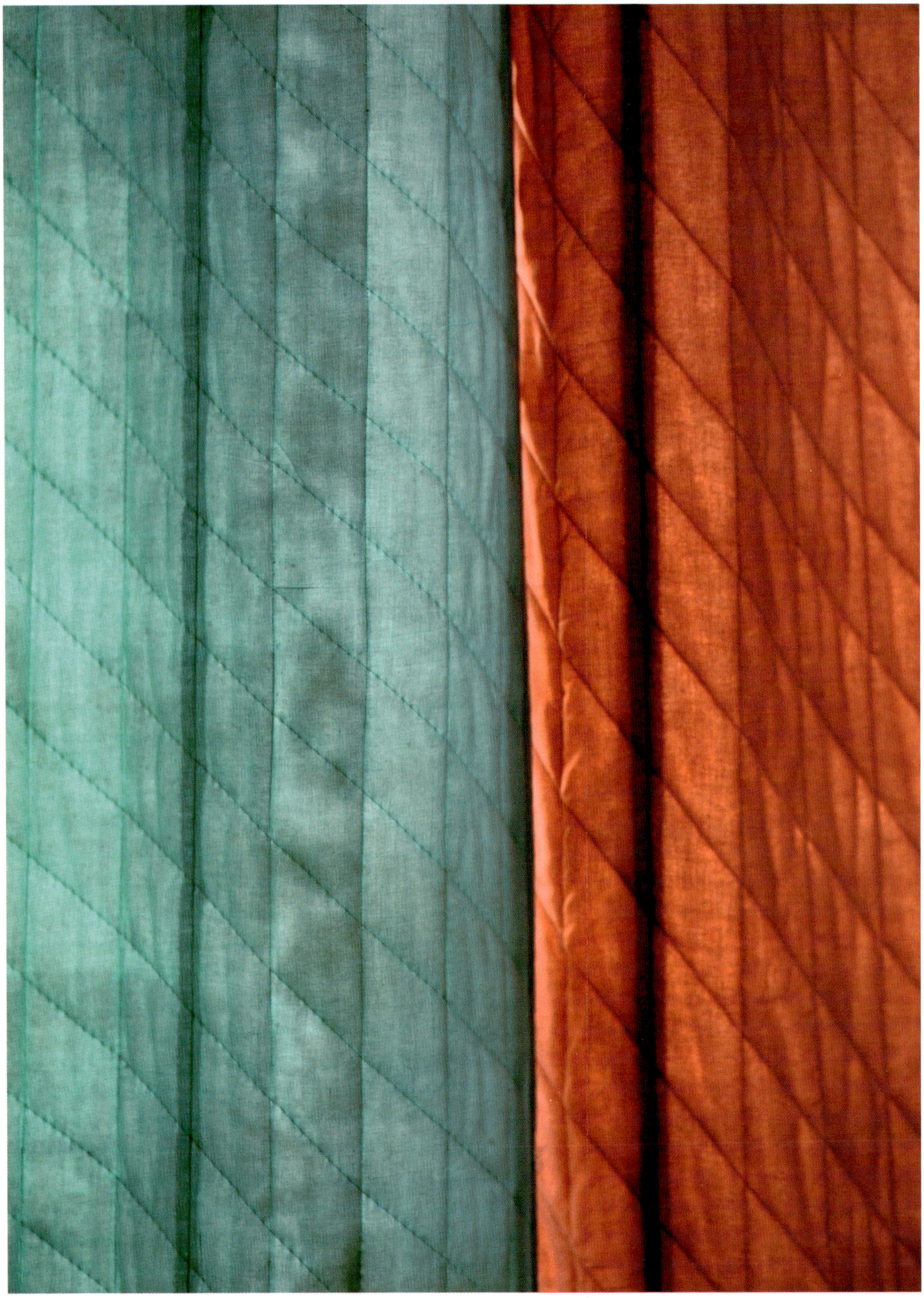

I was introduced to Rasa and its owners the day I accompanied my friend, an aristocrat of style, to pick up some garments from the Rasa showroom. Here, I soon discovered that Rasa's design would suit all sophisticated interiors

Urban charm

Lightness, contemporary looks and good taste are the keys to Rasa's success and popularity among customers in India as well as the global market. Among the many world-famous brands for Jaipuri block-print craft based in the city, Rasa is one of the best boutiques for contemporary block-printed textiles. The young and creative husband-and-wife team of Madhulika and Manish Tibrewal opened this showroom to retail their home furnishings as well as men's and women's fashion collections. They worked hard to create post-modern looks

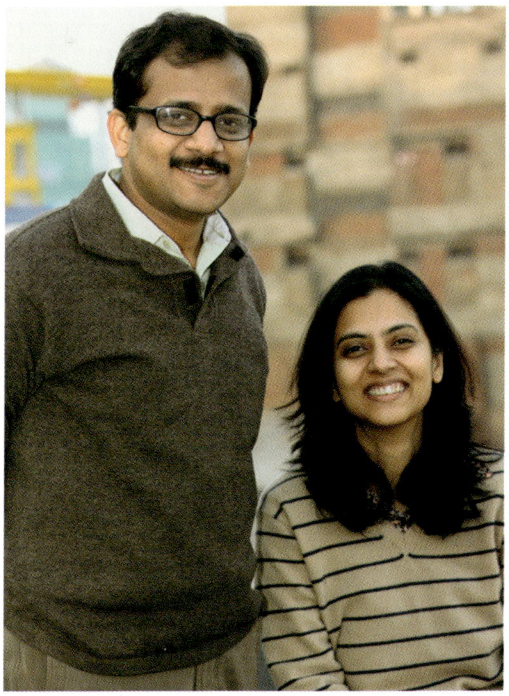

Madhulika Singh and Manish Tibrewal, owners of Rasa

Facing page: *Quilted diamond pattern on cotton, by Rasa*

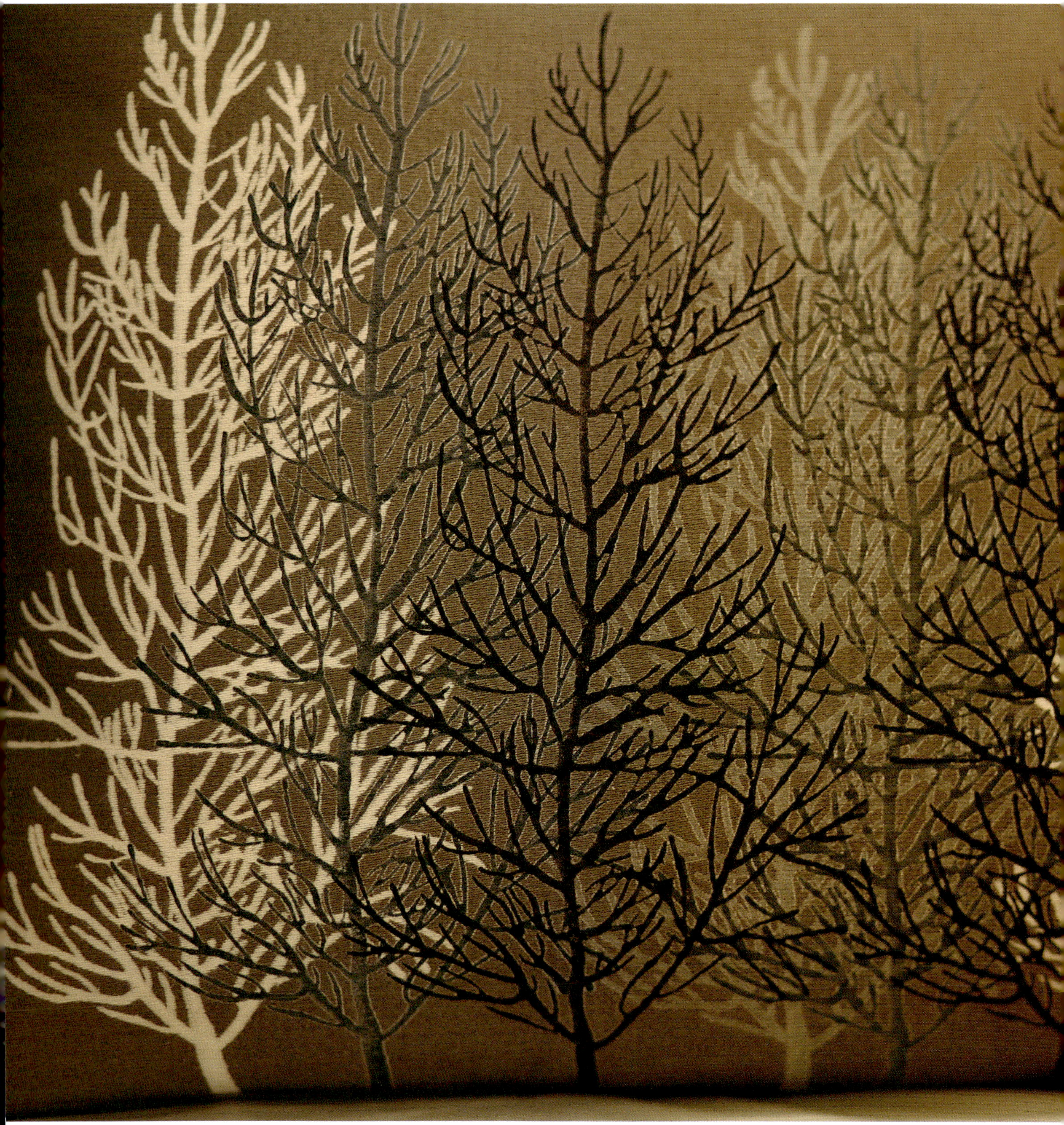

for their quilts and have made a name for themselves in a fairly short span of time.

Youthful vigour

The young designers started with little money and not much experience. What they had in plenty was youthful energy and enthusiasm. Running an independent business house was in itself a daunting task for an inexperienced young couple. As they settled down after setting up home and work in Jaipur, life in this city drew them into quilt making since '(they) saw quilts all around (them)'. They had only one tailor in the beginning and the printing was executed on a 2.5 metre long table. Manish had his own pharmaceutical business, which was his main source of income then. The printing table was somehow squeezed in and positioned in this office.

Making space

The Tibrewals look back at their very first efforts with some fondness and relate the lighter aspects of their daring venture–how their printer stood scratching his head, bemusedly eyeing the tiny office and the restricted space he had for himself and his printing table. To begin with, the table itself was small enough to arouse his apprehension as he had never

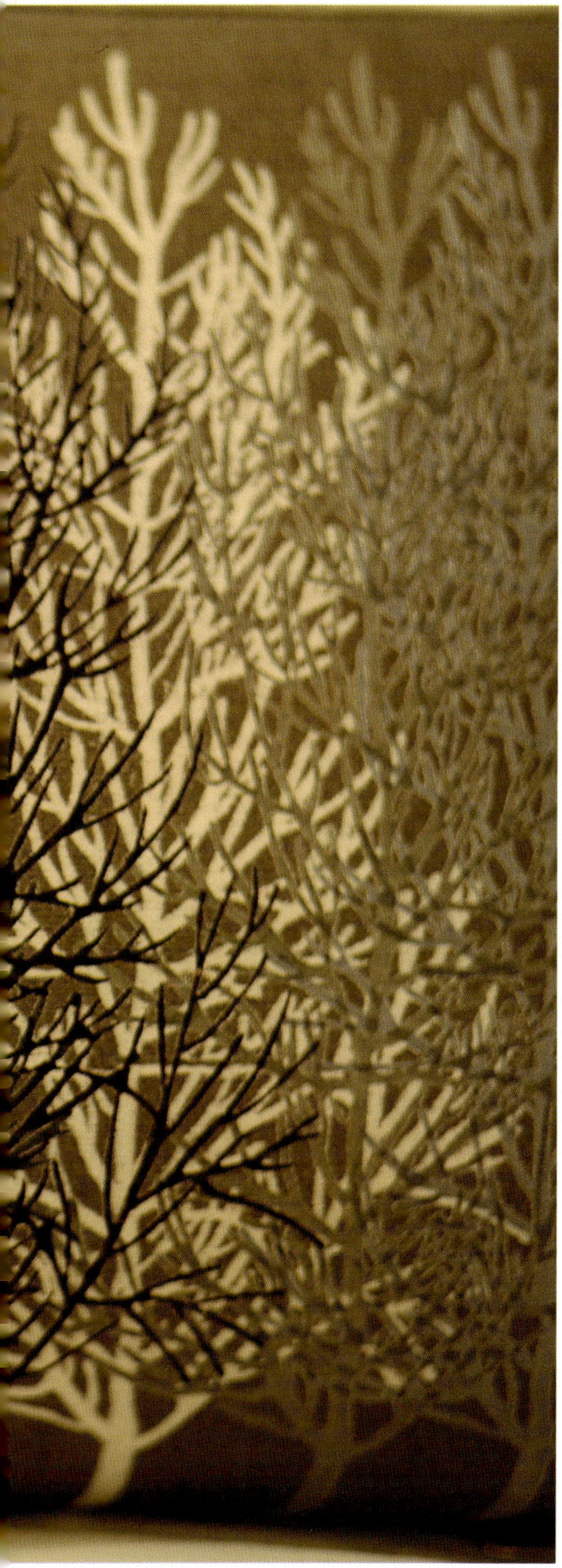

Printed cushion cover with a surreal study of a forest scene in a light and shade composition

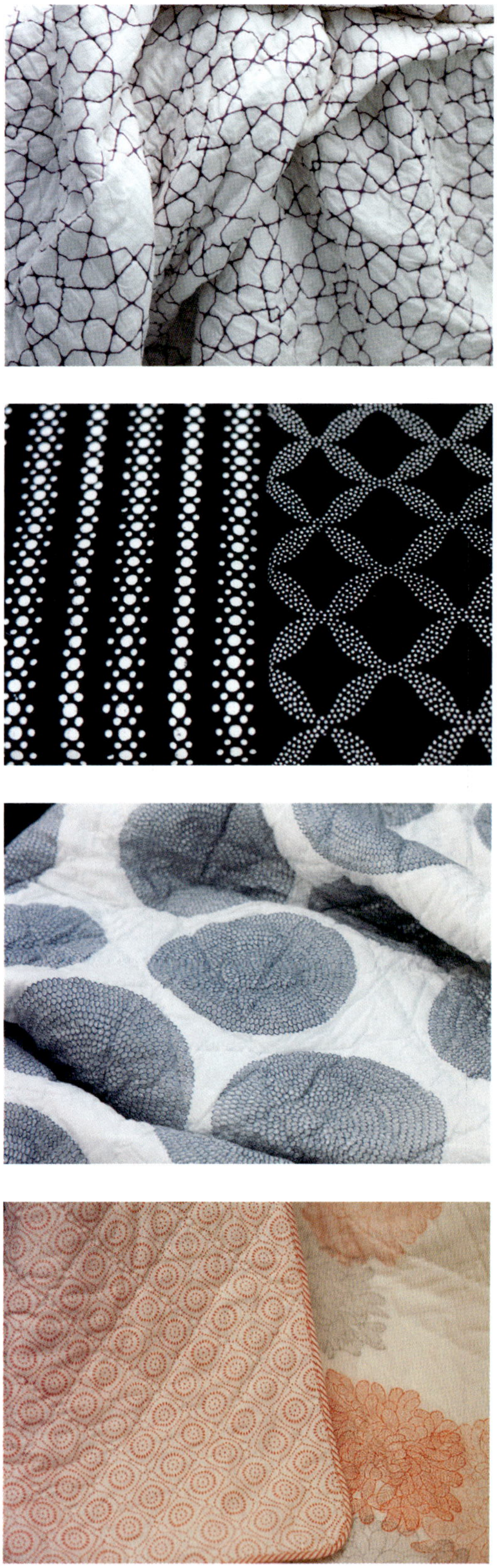

Details of a range of quilt motifs with honeycomb, jalli *and concentric circles used in post-modern concepts*

executed printing jobs on such a small table. Brisk business happened around him all day and professionals in crisp suits and ties rushed past. Madhulika and Manish were the principal decision makers, working at the workshop by day and making printing blocks at night. They worked for hours on a particular shade of colour to get the right tone of grey or beige. Rasa still uses soft and light colours but not necessarily pastels like old rose, sage or olive green, which people in India refer to as the 'English colours'. They did not find anybody to teach them the technique of mixing dyes and nor did they wish to outsource the printing work to printing shops in the city.

But Manish was determined to learn the art. He chose a shop selling dyes in Sanganer and occasionally sat outside asking the customers relevant questions regarding the items they bought, their quality and worth, what they used the glue for, etc. This is how Manish trained himself up to be an experienced 'colourmaster'. The creative couple did not want to use the old and traditional Sanganer motifs or design patterns. They were certainly inspired by them but the young creators wished to do something completely new and original. They had started from scratch and hoped to create

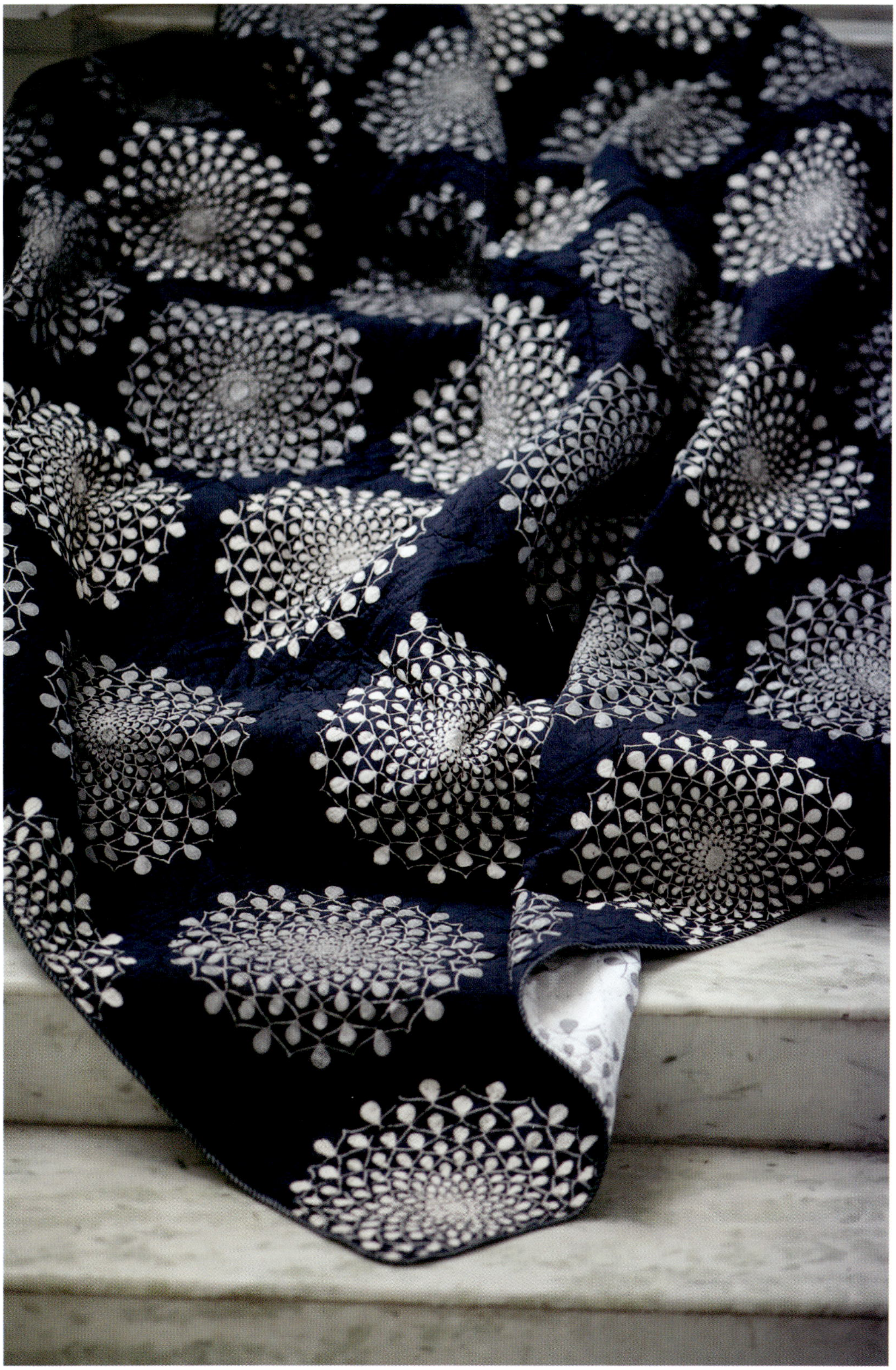

White pattern on midnight blue—the 'Duple Dome' quilt

Page 148-149: *The resplendent peacock design inspired by ancient art, in classical black and white*

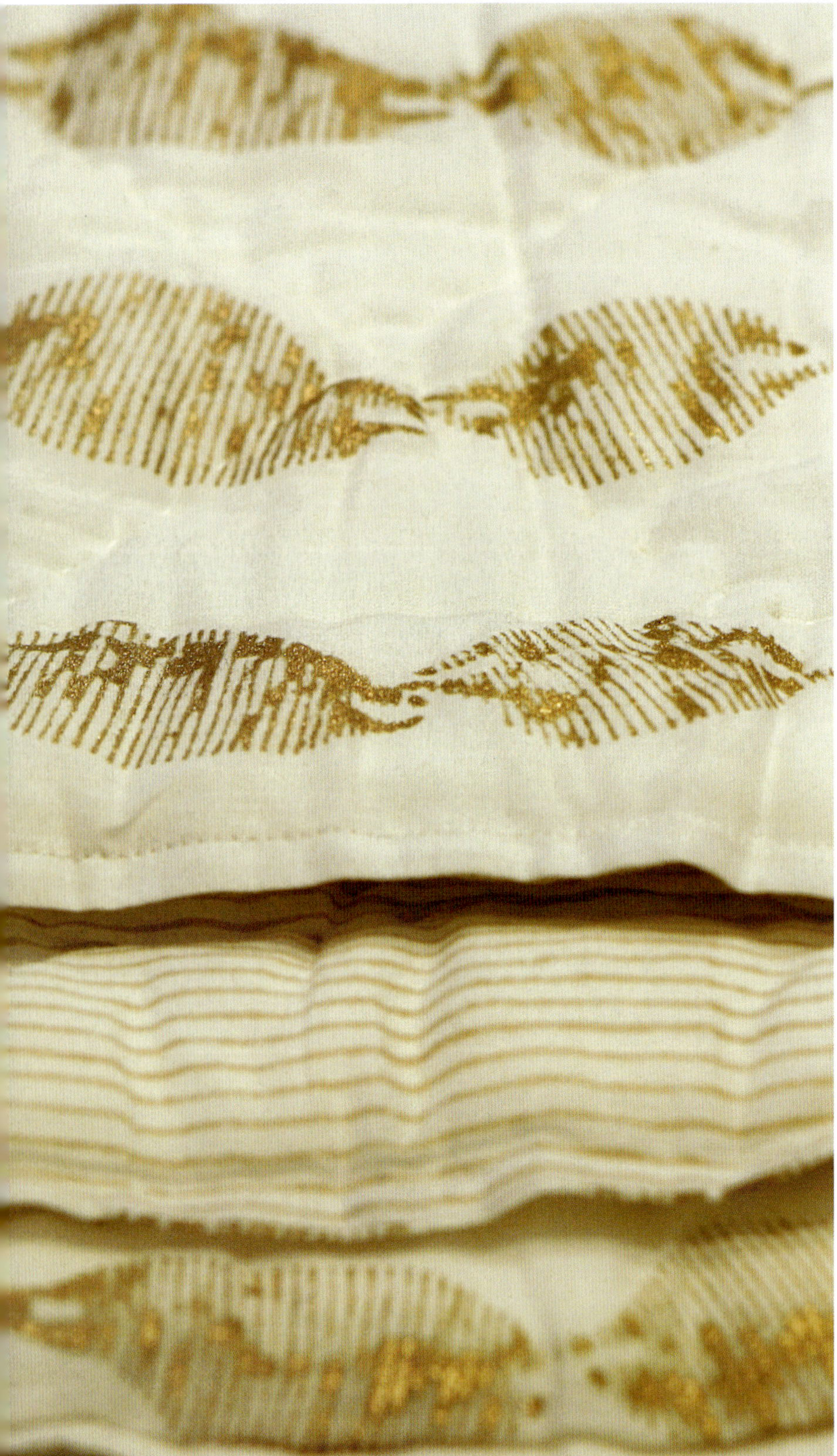

everything afresh—including designs and motifs. Later they did realise that this was not how success would come their way. One had to make occasional compromises. Manish and Madhulika still continue to be innovative in their own way and find creative inspiration in the simplest of objects around them. A passing glimpse of a sari or a certain combination of shades and shapes while driving down Jaipur's roads can be a boost to a sudden burst of creative energy.

Style statement

Controlling a big market for their products was not really a part of Rasa's long term plans, although the company has got excellent response from the market and very good feedback from the customers. They needed a bigger market to keep the company afloat. Madhulika admits that she would like to have more time to herself to work with creative designing. She is now forced to spend too much time controlling the production.

A low-key style is characteristic to Rasa. The colours are subdued, but the creations have character and are sophisticated. The designers have 'cleaned up' and transformed old patterns, making them look contemporary, matching global fashion trends. The uniqueness of

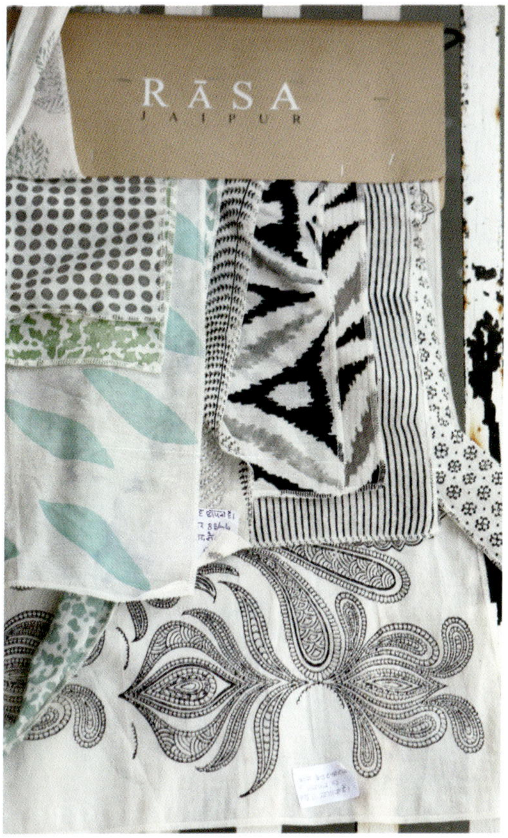

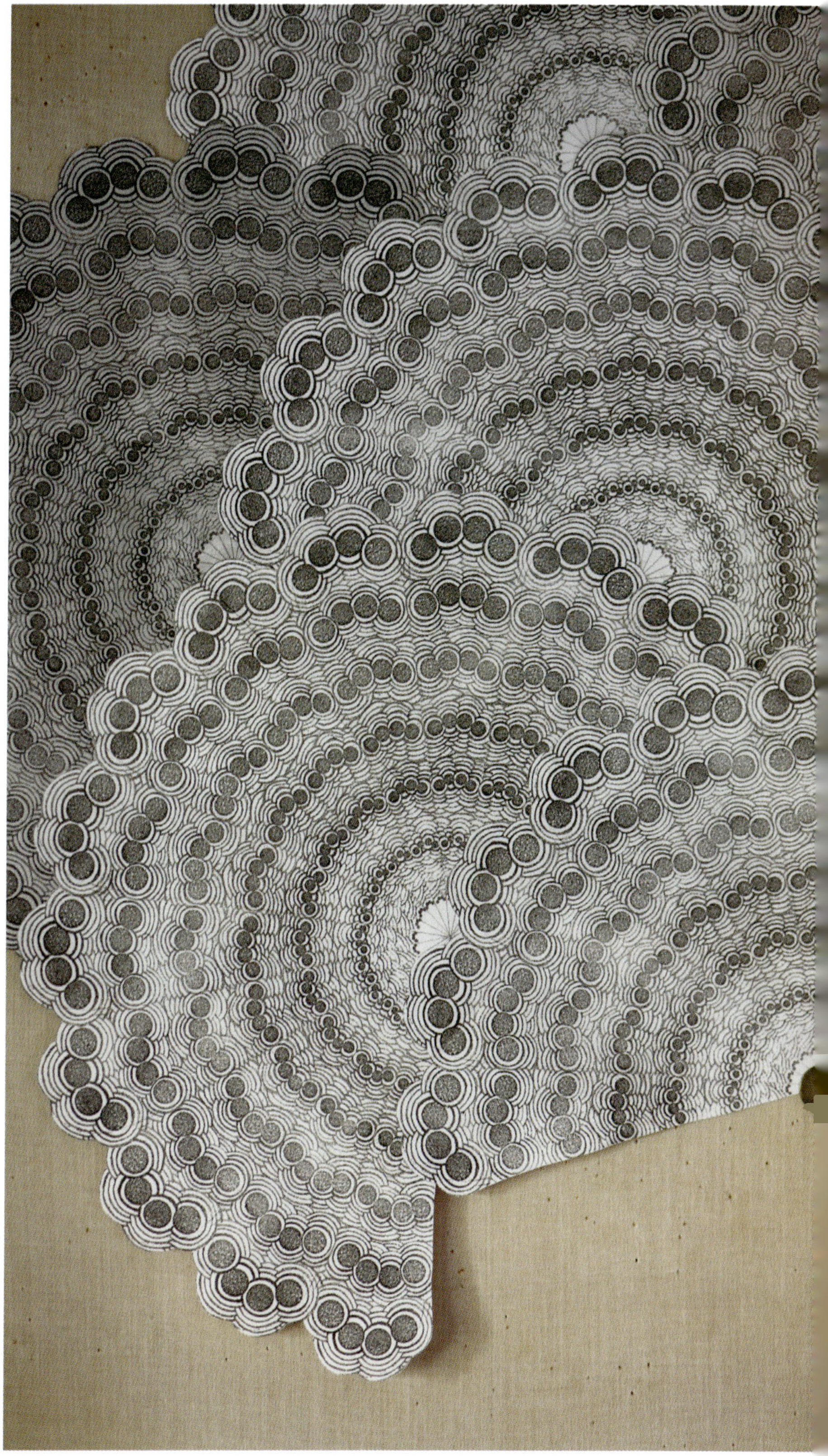

each pattern lies in the subtle traditional twist they carry. The Tibrewals are not much into floral designs, and if they do indulge in florals from time to time, the motifs are highly stylised. Rasa's strength lies in innovative and stylish design, excellent quality of fabrics and well-crafted products. The finish is truly perfect.

Manish and Madhulika consider themselves fortunate to have access to local mills and weavers; they can develop fabrics for themselves and do not need to depend entirely on the off-the-will fabrics available in the market.

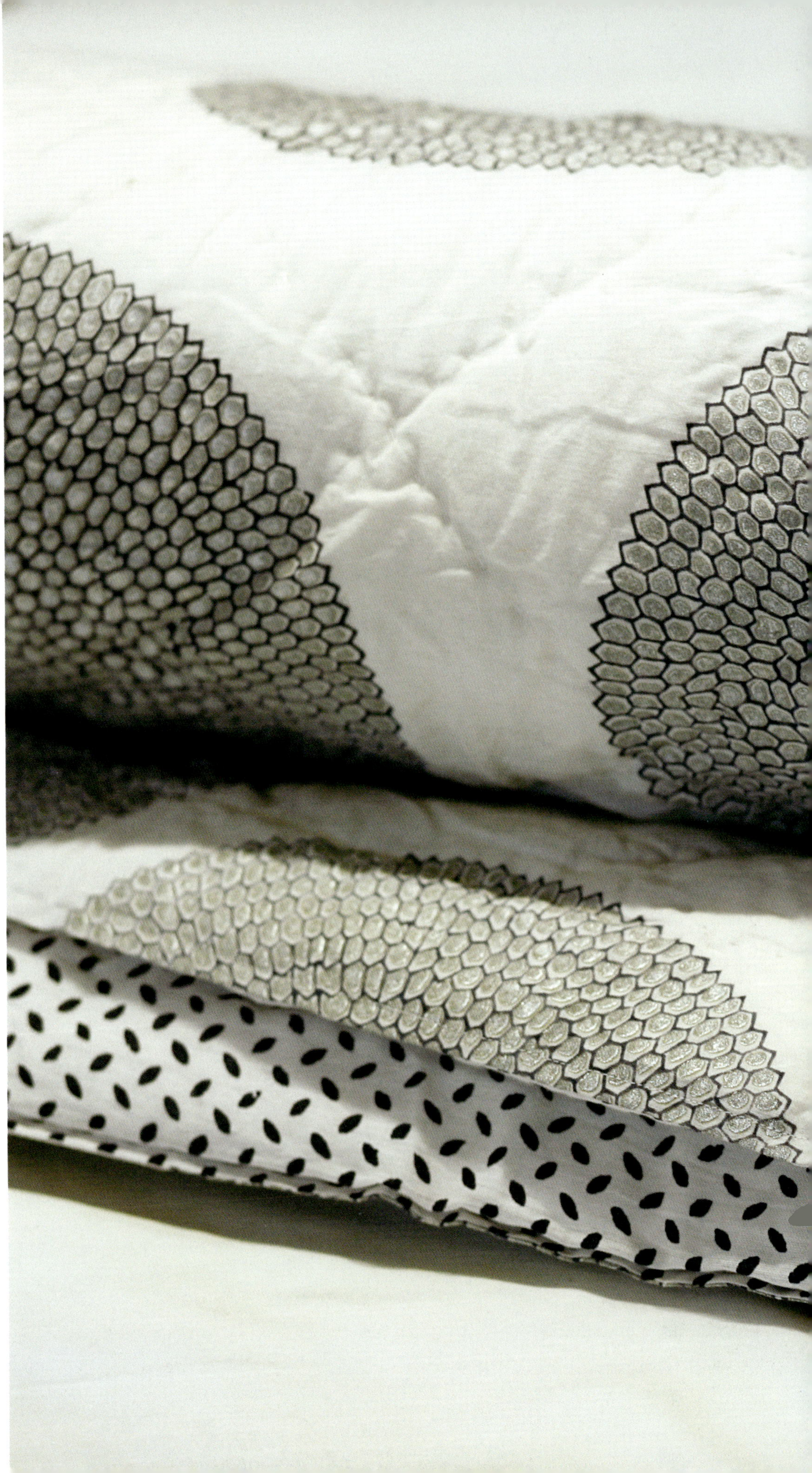

The honeycomb and the leaf in classic black and white

Page 134: *Understated gold on pale cream*

Page 135: *Print samples from Rasa (left); working out new designs with the lotus flower motif (right)*

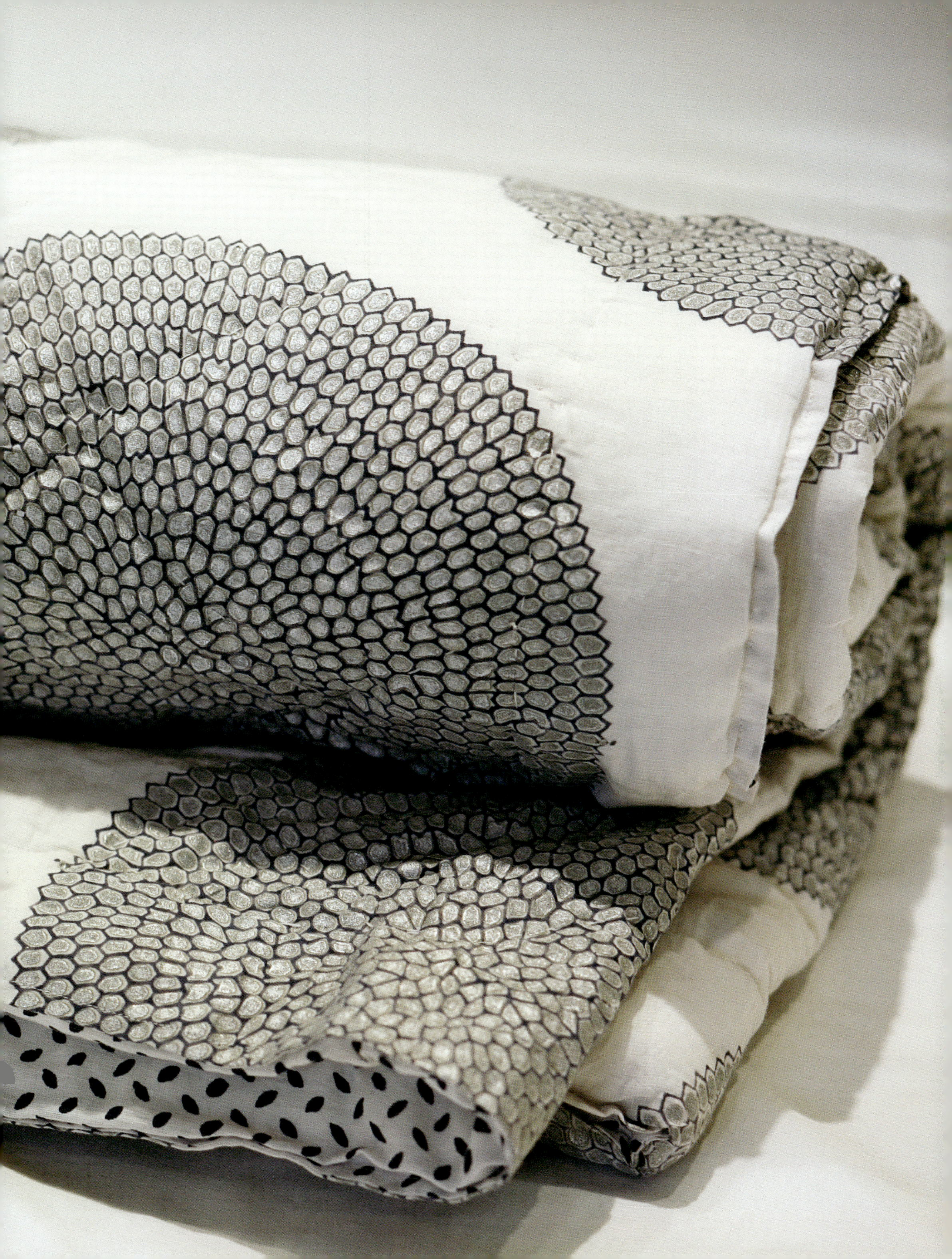

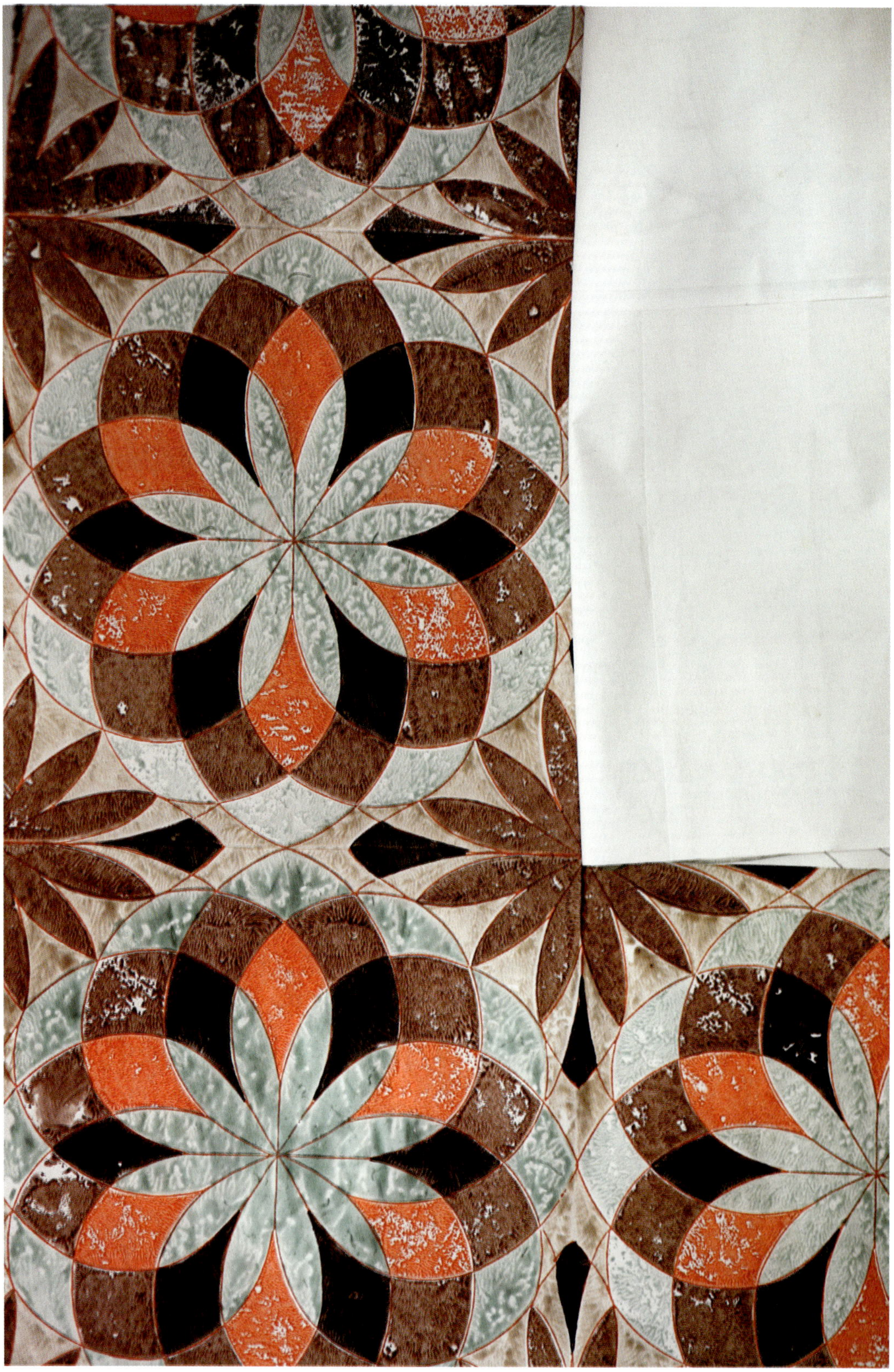

Experiments with the traditional lotus motif and colour combinations

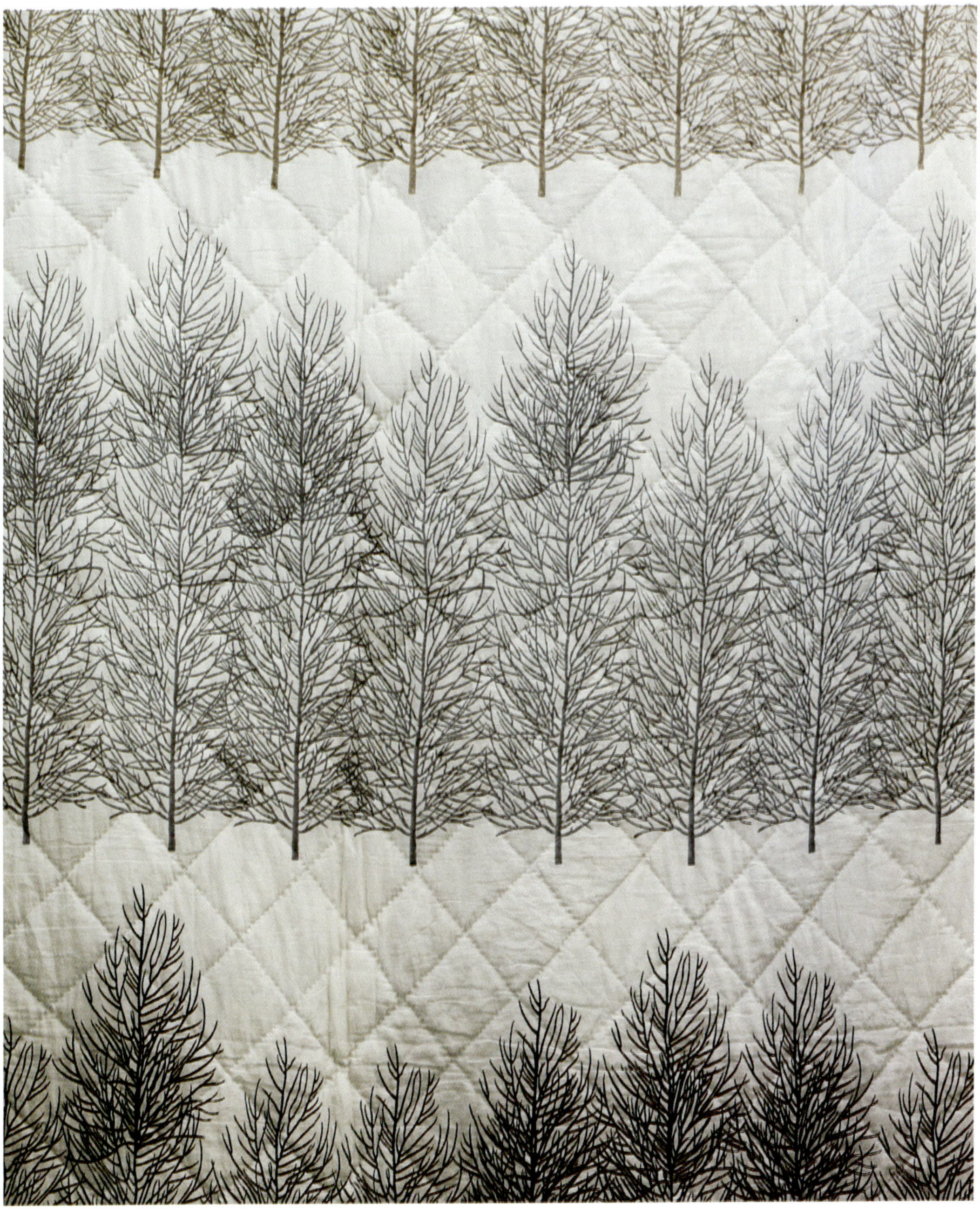

Manish confided in me that Rasa is now venturing into new pastures—working for the environment, using organic, low impact dyes. These are expensive of course, but the Tibrewals are willing to try them, hoping that there is a future in the effort. They feel the need to educate themselves and their staff and upgrade their knowledge constantly in new thoughts, concerns and methods.

This stylish quilt is an artist's impression of Arctic forests in winter

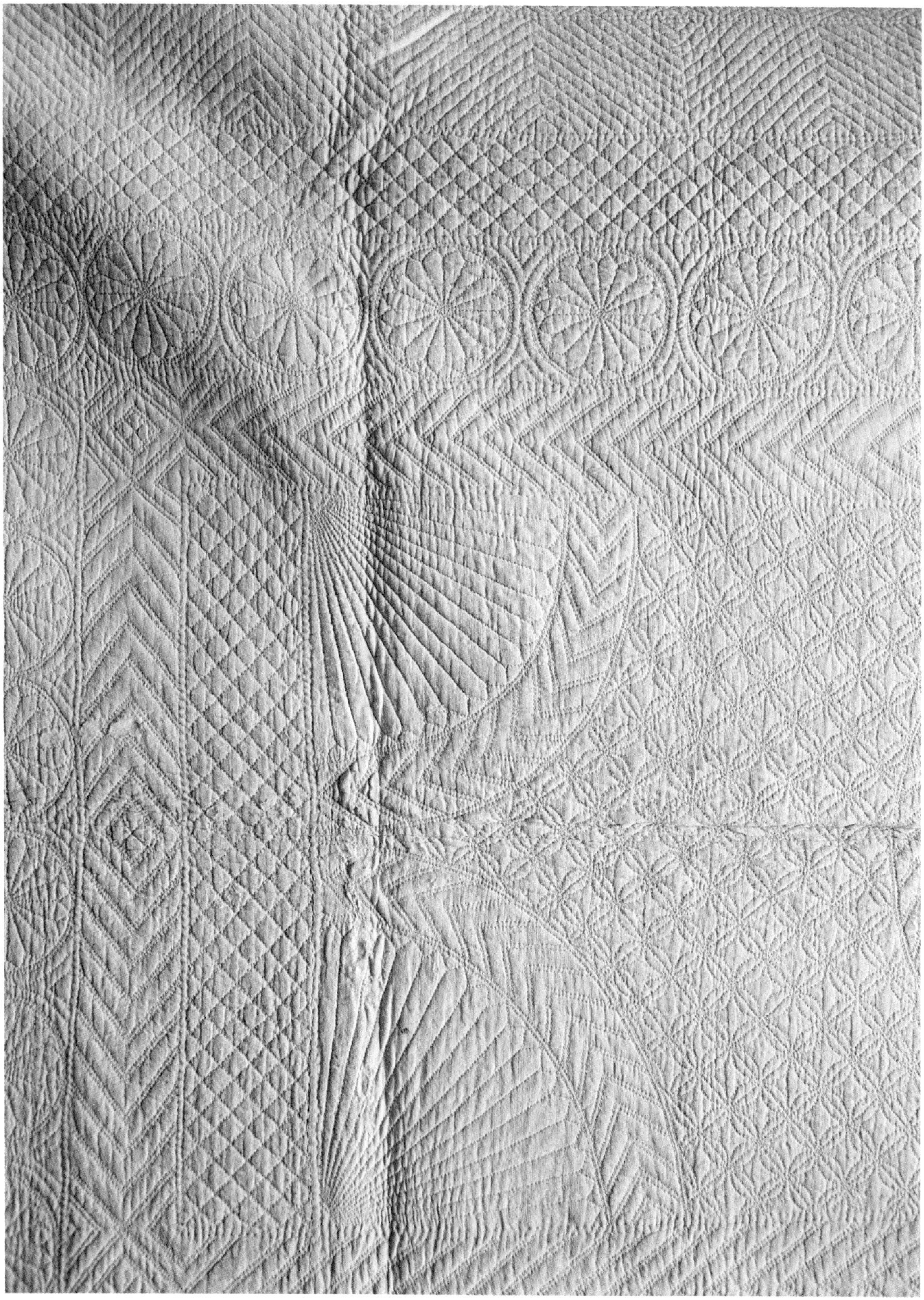

Subhash Sharma has collected some of the most wonderful textile pieces. It would be interesting to review the Jaipur quilts against this background. Sharma is also a collector of antique royal clothing

Antique textile revivalists

His shop Rajasthan Fabrics and Arts is a favourite haunt of collectors and museum curators looking for some of the rarest textiles in India. Subhash Sharma, the owner, who studied political science and law, is passionate, knowledgeable and ready to extend help and advice. He is a collector of antiques himself and keeps a wide range of objects in his shop. There one can find a range of beautiful textiles, art pieces and even prints of old and rare photographs on sale, which are available for a nominal price as well as thousands of euros.

Collectors' haunt

I have known Subhash Sharma and his fascinating store for some time now. I used to visit him while I was in Jaipur and glance through all the antique textiles, garments, ethnic jewellery, silver and brass sculpture and other art objects in his store. He told me the story of his enterprise, of how he started his business along very humble lines by selling tribal skirts sitting under a tree near his present store, how he learnt the tricks of trade and the subtle nuances which drew a line between mediocrity and excellence.

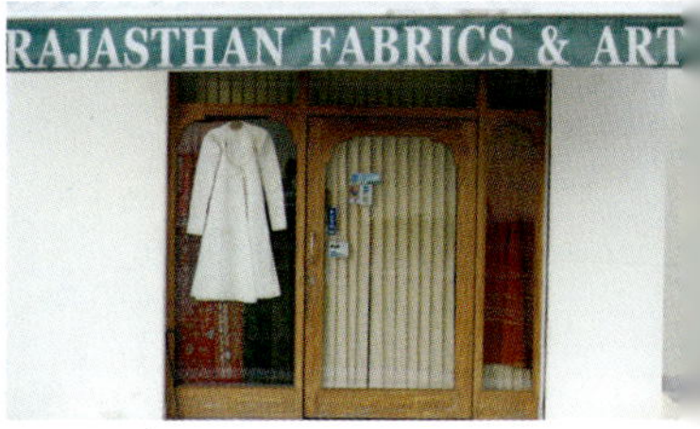

Front door of Subhash Sharma's outlet adjacent to the compound of the City Palace

Facing page: *Antique* sujani *detail, mid-nineteenth century*

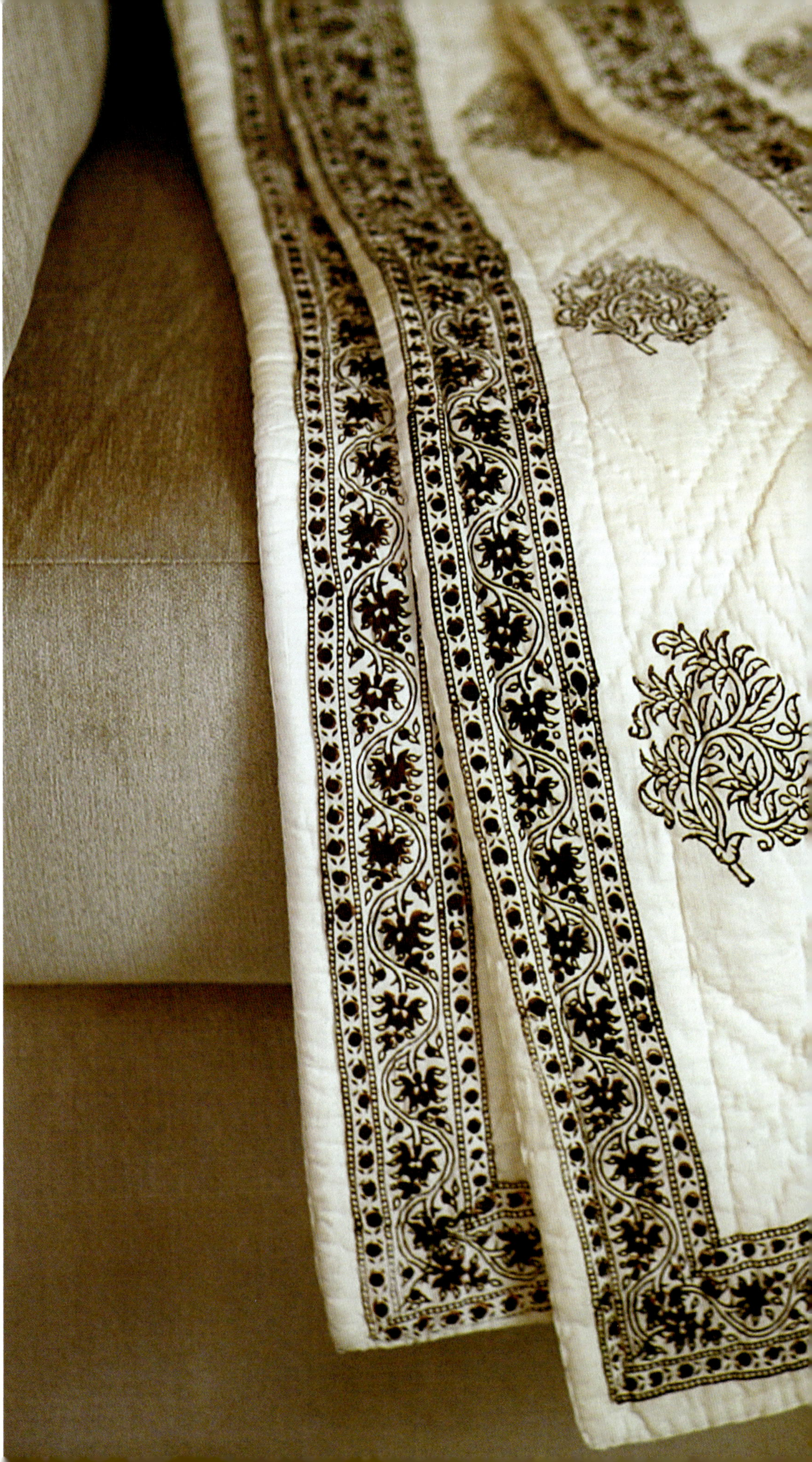

Elegant plain weave in black, white and gold to suit both classical and modern interiors. Quilt from Satayam

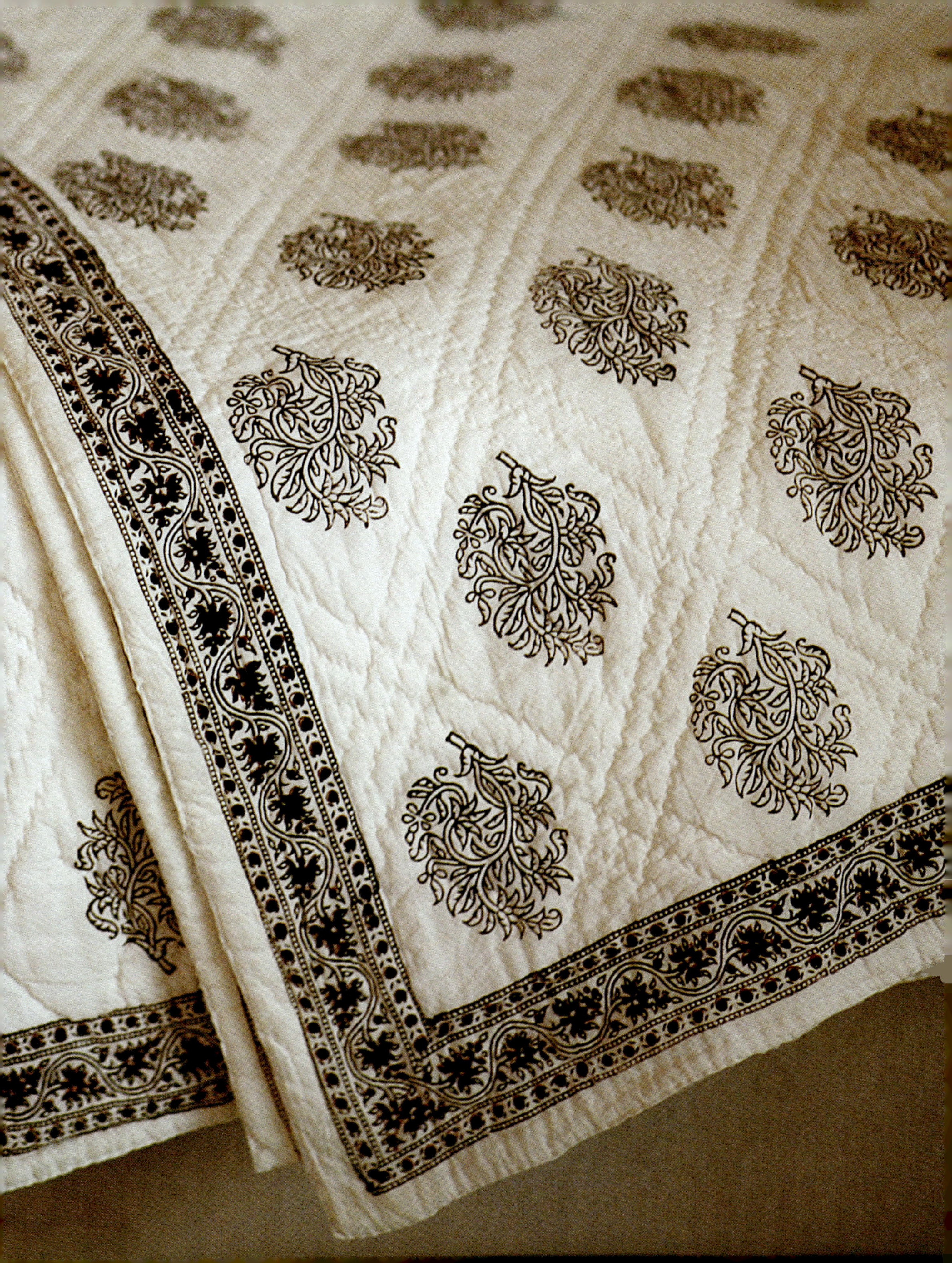

Right: *Colours painted directly on cotton textile from Sanganer*

Below: *The sun-bleached desert landscape from atop Ninder Mahal*

He eagerly learnt from everybody, occasionally also from his buyers. When he started his business in earnest he had suppliers in Delhi. Today people in possession of interesting pieces of antique textile or art flock to his shop from even beyond. Sharma is known to be a great connoisseur of art. They know full well that they will be able to leave satisfied after an honest and smooth transaction.

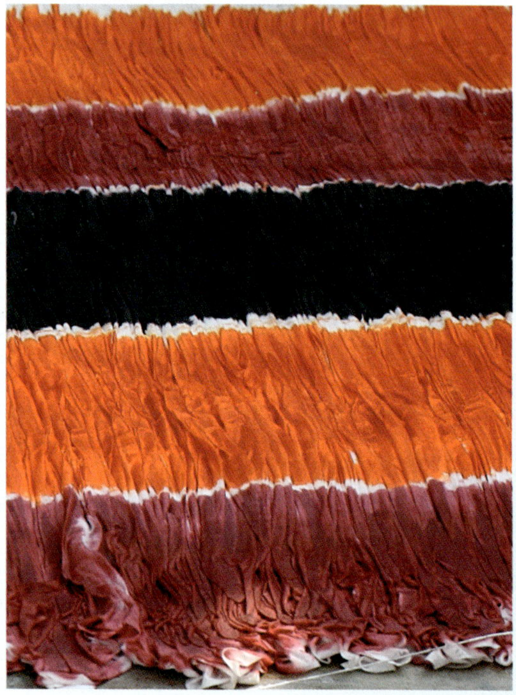

Rajasthan and particularly Jaipur have always been associated with a wide spectrum of colours. The bleak, dry landscape is lit up by the brilliance

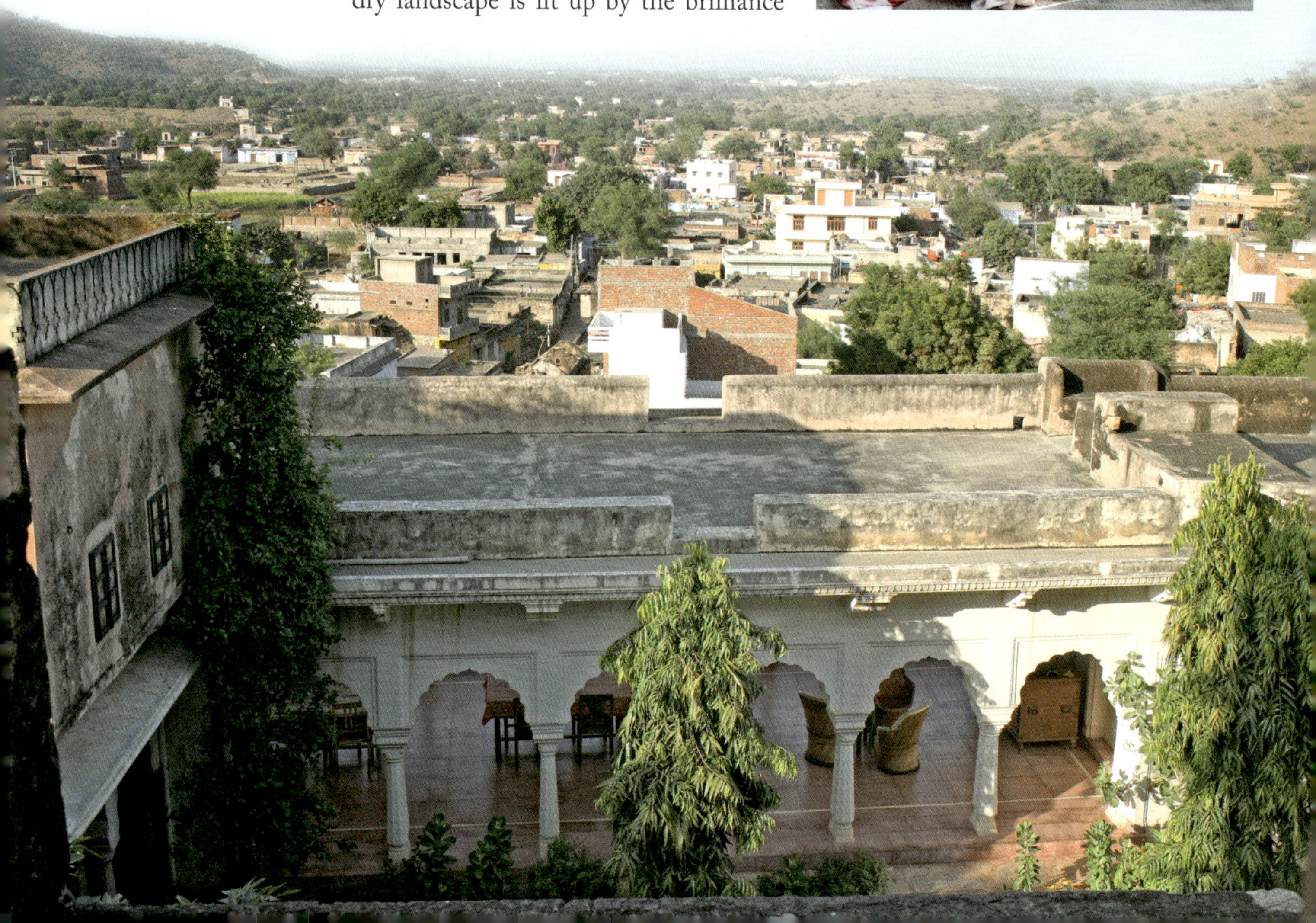

of luminous hues used on textiles and art objects; colour is perhaps the most lasting and endearing impression that visitors carry home after travelling in this state. Canary yellows, emerald greens, vivid purples, electric blues and splashes of brilliant reds matched with a sedate pearl white lend the art objects and textiles a rich but unique look. Shopping for Rajasthani art and artefacts plays a vital role on any tourist's itinerary and Subhash Sharma's store in Laxman Dwara, just outside the City Palace attracts the sophisticated tourist.

Antiquity is another element that lends itself to this region in fitting contours. Subhash's store turned out to be a treasure trove. I decided to see if Subhash could help me with ideas or would let me photograph some of his antique *sujani*s. As soon as I arrived, a cup of coffee drifted in magically and we settled down comfortably for a chat. I told him about my plans. Soon after, some very beautiful antique 'white-on-white' *sujani*s emerged from indoors, accompanied by a few exquisite antique white coats, and quilted fans. He kindly let me photograph what I chose and also let me copy a few of his expensive, sepia-tinted photographs of nineteenth century Jaipur by the famous photographer Raja Deen Dayal. Later we stepped out onto the green lawn outside his store which is situated in a lovely location, just outside the City Palace and in the vicinity of the famous Jaipur astronomical observatory, the Jantar Mantar.

Close-up of a beautiful quilted fan

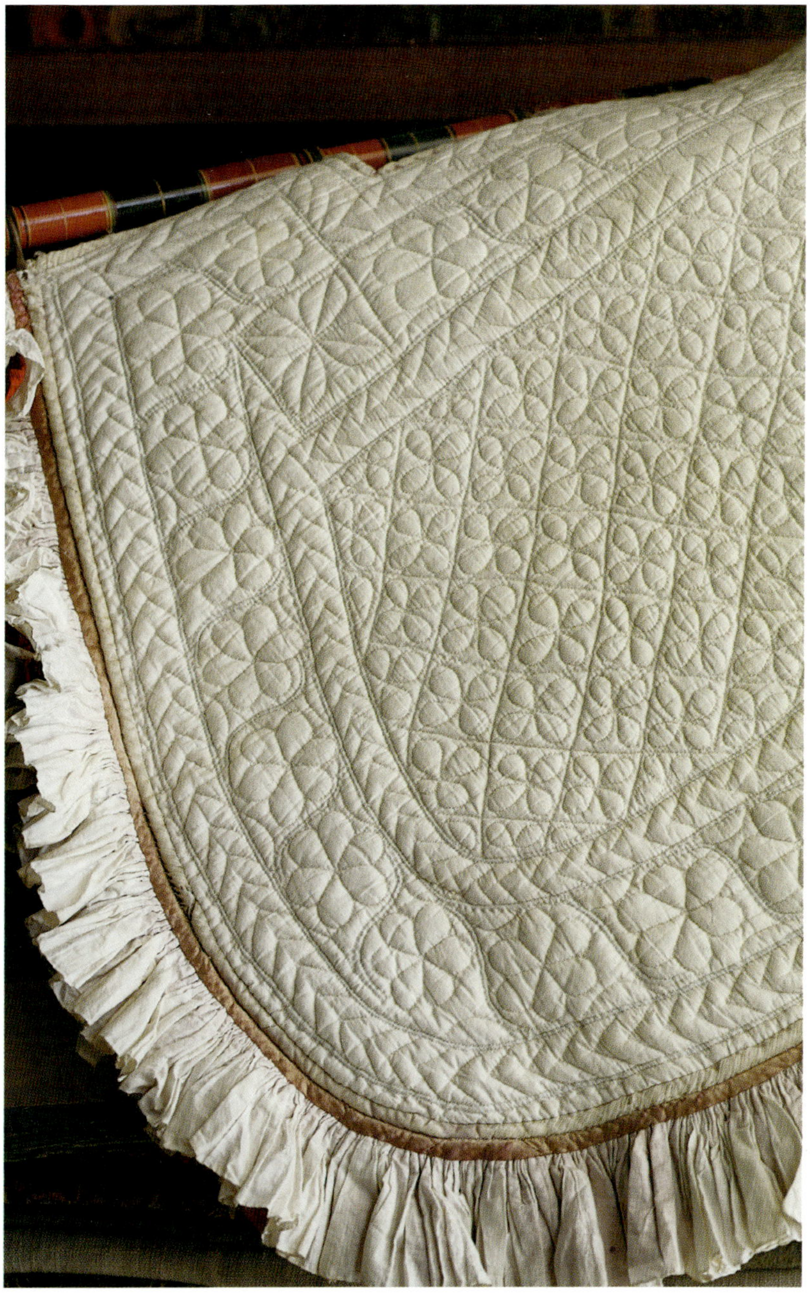

Satayam

We stepped out of Subhash Sharma's shop and walked a few metres to enter his son Jatin's boutique Satayam, which is almost adjacent to Rajasthan Fabrics & Arts. This is one of the best places for original contemporary textiles in Jaipur. One finds nothing here that is not beautiful or interesting in some way. Satayam set off by working in alliance with Christina Kim's Dosa Inc—which also has a small but elegant and well-known boutique in New York, dabbling in organic and recycled clothing. Christina Kim stands apart from the mainstream with her pronounced minimalistic approach and specialises in hand-washable silks and khadi cotton, all of it interchangeable and meant to be worn in layers. The company in its turn worked with design consultant and fine arts lecturer Yoshiko Iwamoto Wada—also an artist, curator and textile designer specialising in traditional Japanese silk embroidery, indigo dyeing and *bandhni* prints. Jatin also worked with the famous company Hermes. So Satayam has an impressive background and I was naturally curious to have a look at the quilts.

Satayam produces its own quilts. Incidentally it was Chinar Farooqui, a student from the famous National Institute of Design (NID), Ahmedabad, who gave them the idea of trying out

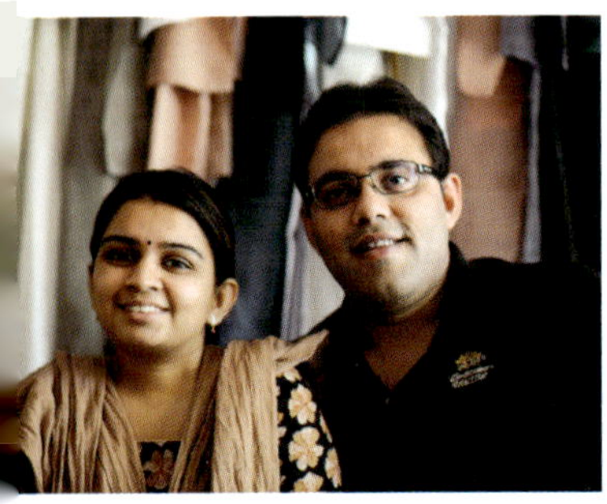

Jatin Sharma, Subhash Sharma's son and owner of Satayam with his wife Ekta

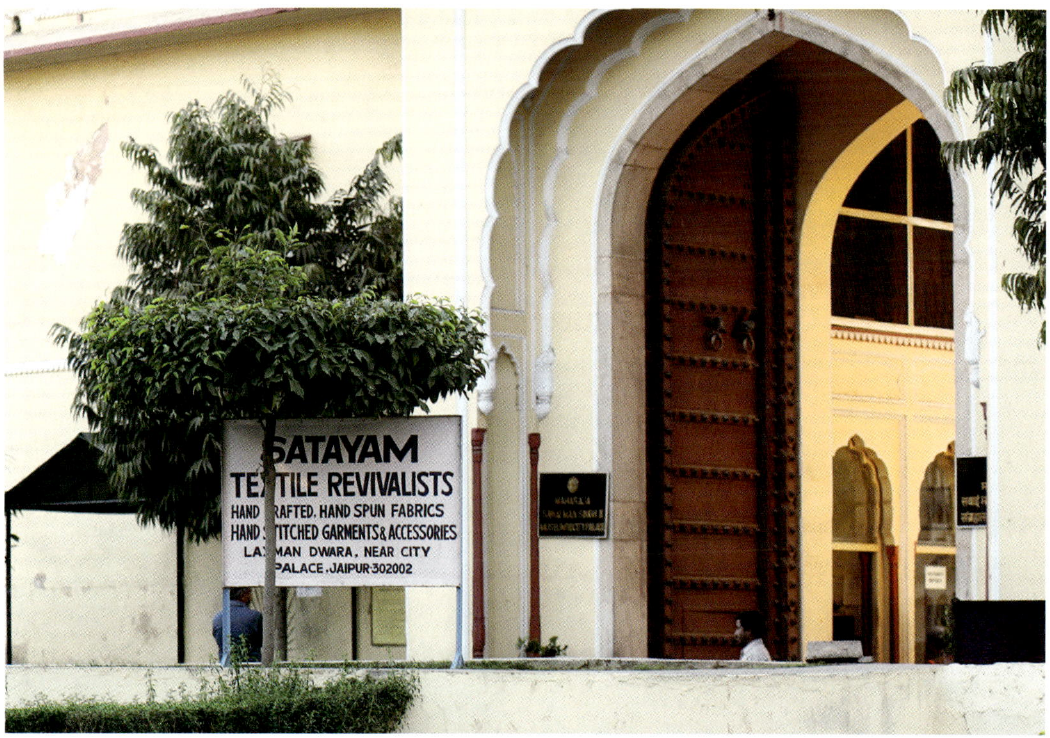

Right: *Entrance to City Palace, Jaipur, with the Satayam sign board*

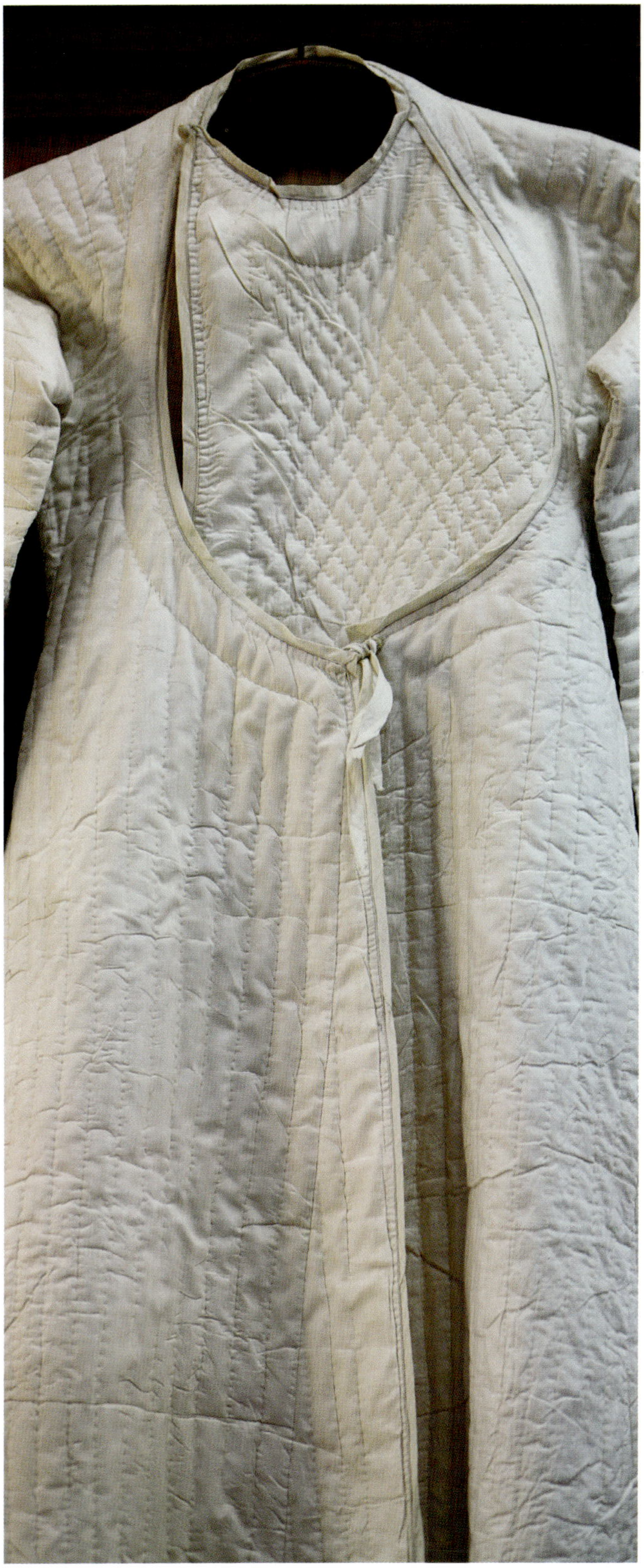

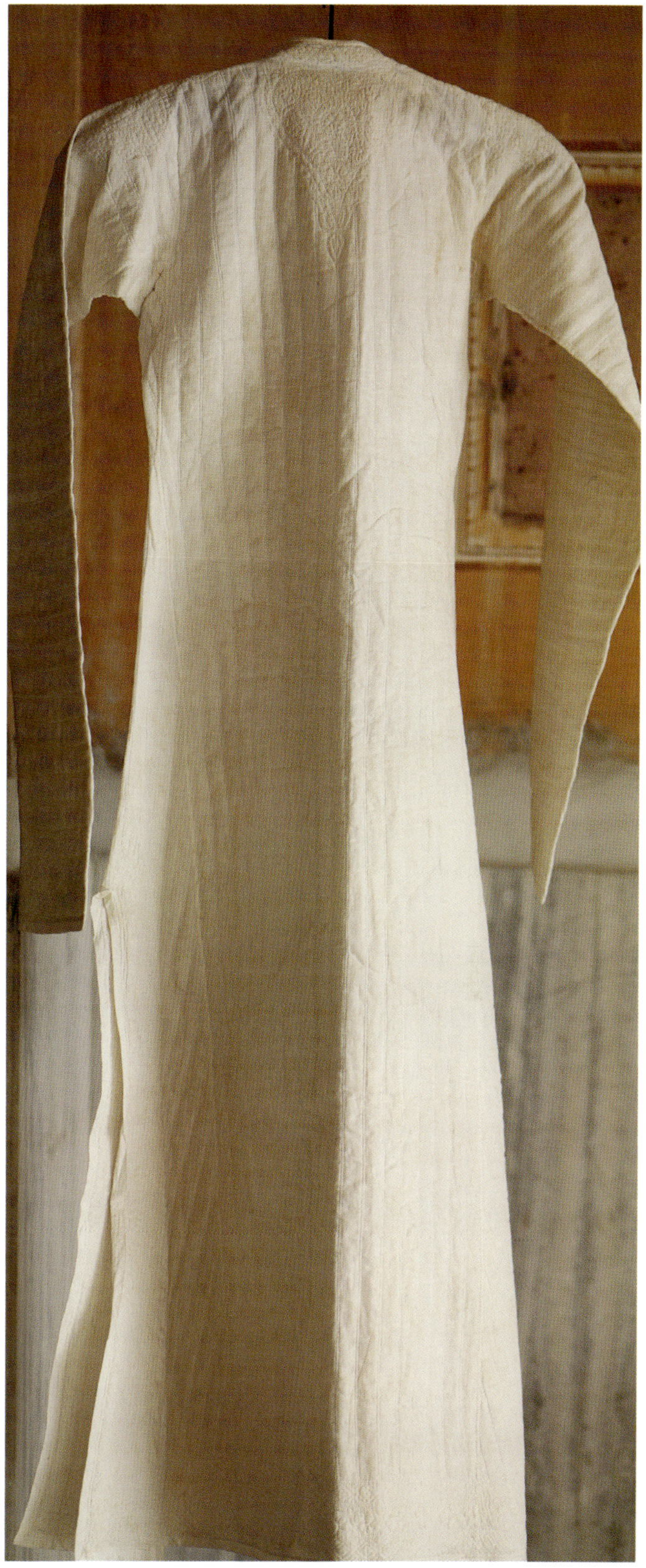

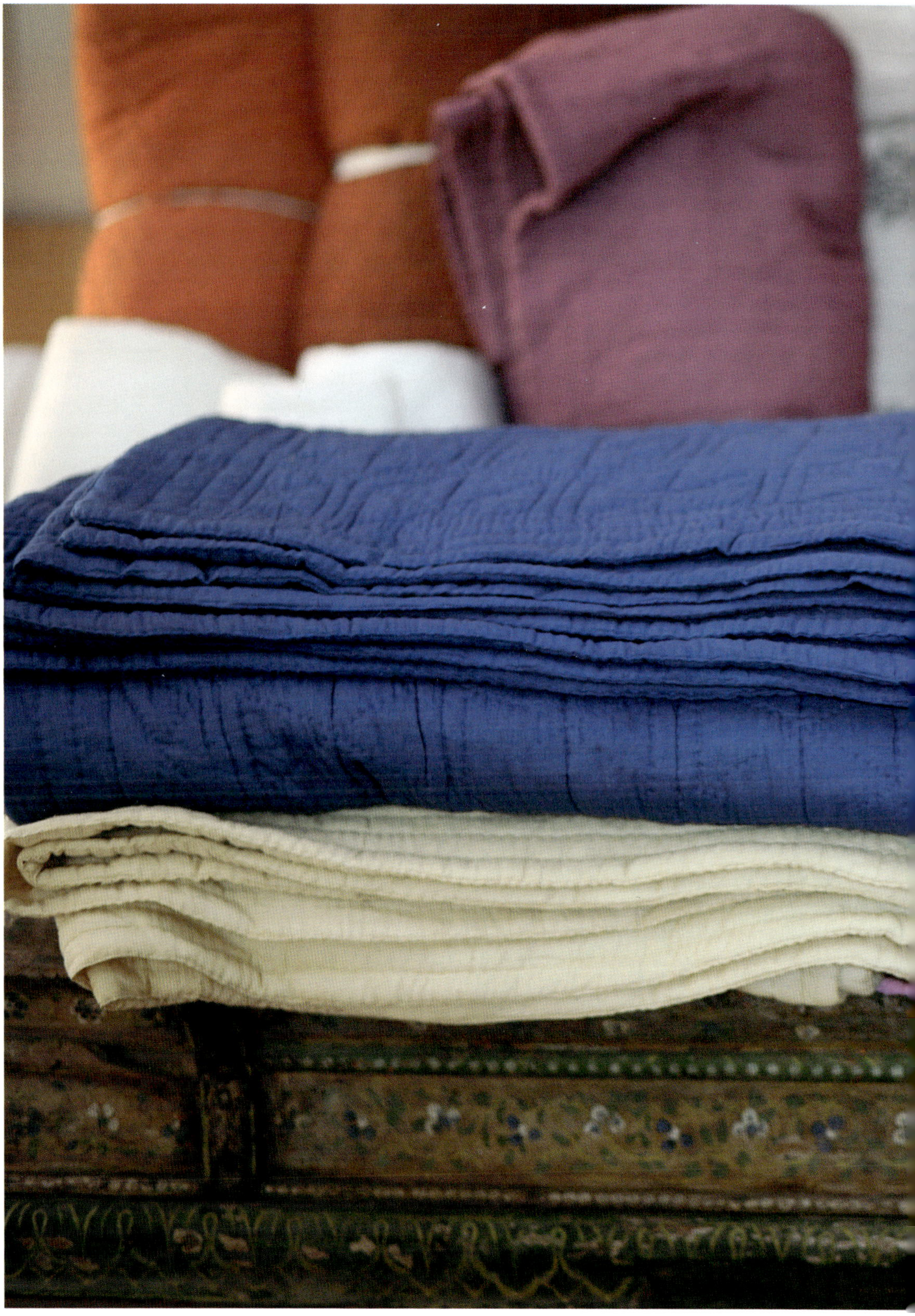

Subdued colours in plain weaves on display

Facing page: *Details on quilted coat sleeves*

Page 147: *Exquisite quilted* angrakhas *in tones of white and cream. The* angrakha *or long coat is the formal wear of the affluent section in Rajasthan. The pastoral and tribal communities may also resort to the* angrakha *on particular occasions. A unique design element of the* angrakha *is sometimes a triangular opening at the front. The inner panel known as the 'purdah' covers the chest. The* angrakha *is usually made of plain silk or brocade. Cotton voile is also used. Front view of* angrakha *with details (left). Back view of the coat in self-coloured quilted stripes and gold embroidery (right)*

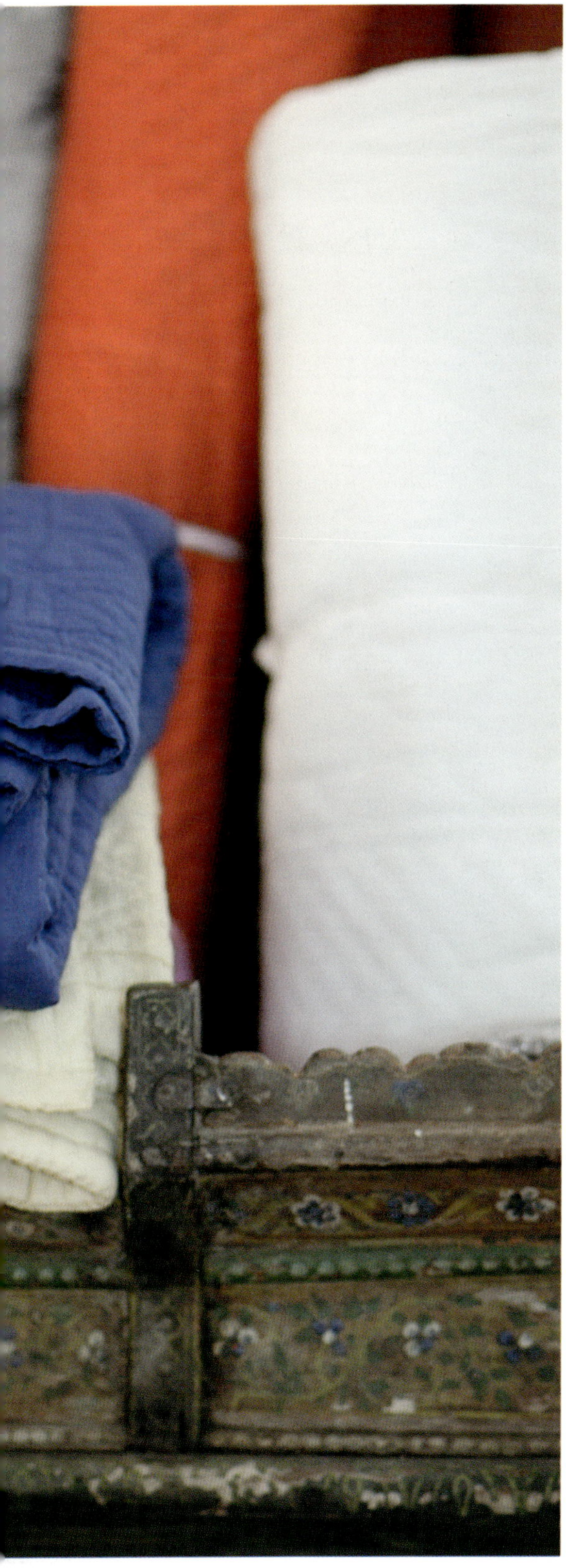

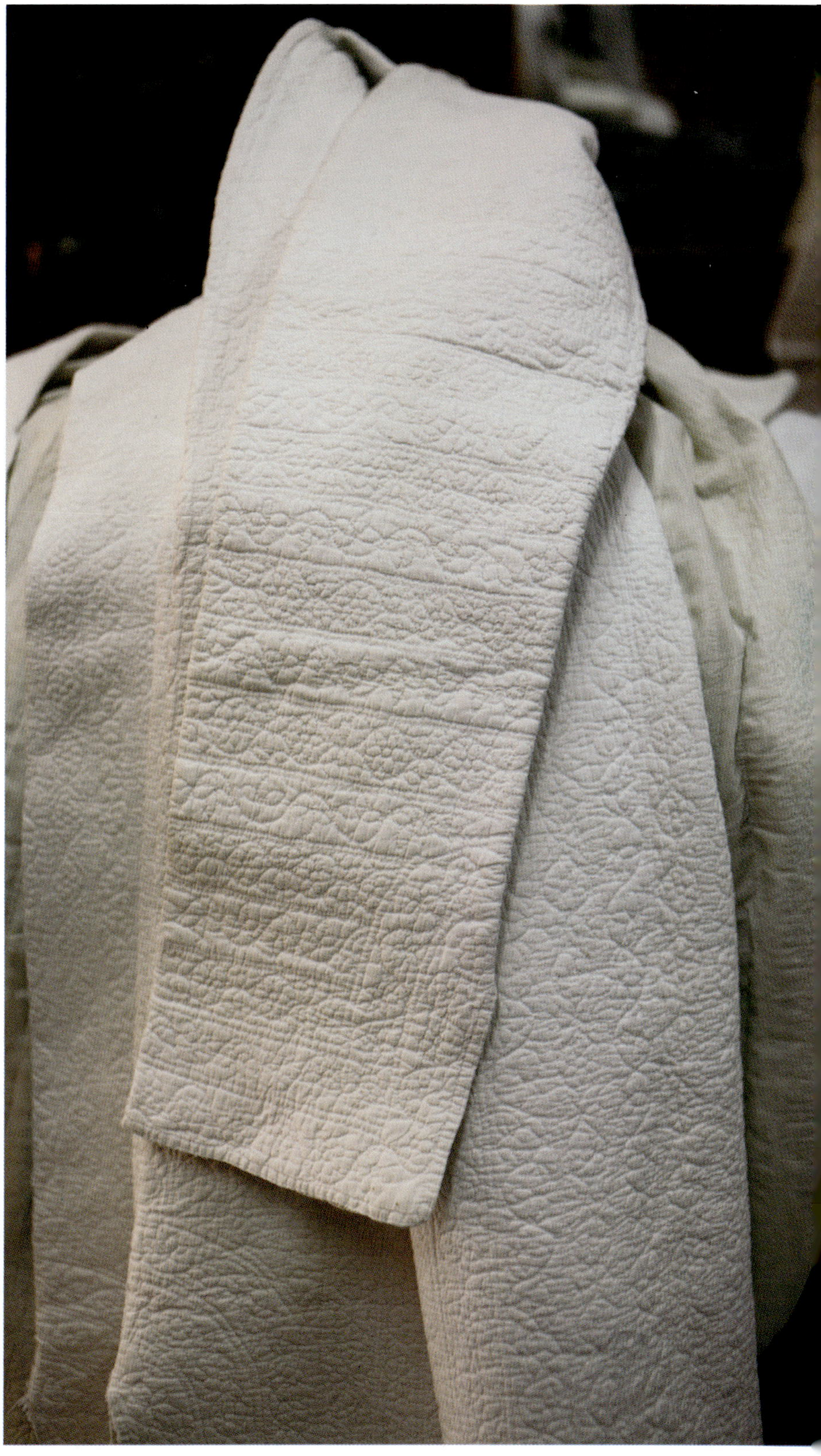

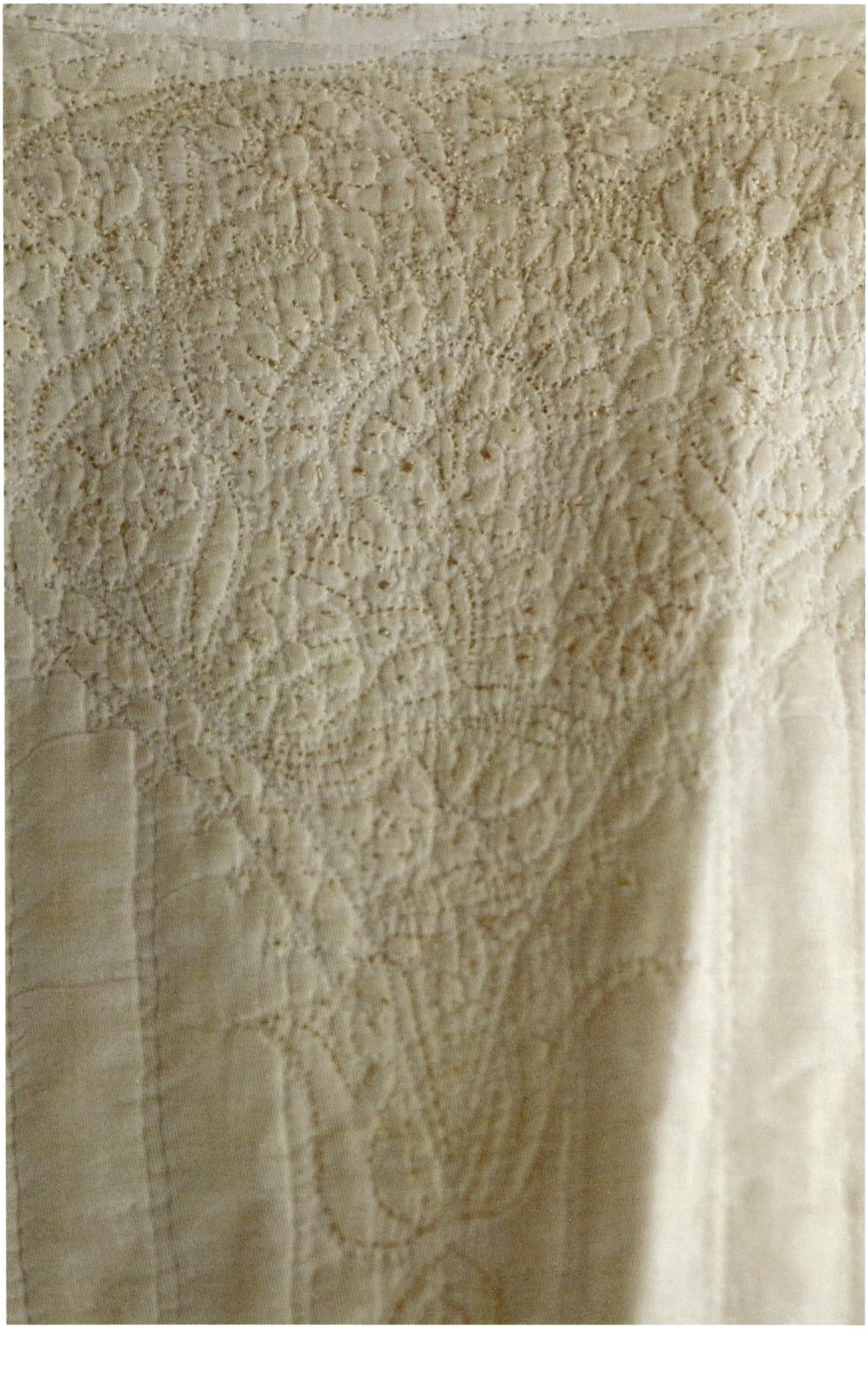

Details of decorative gold embroidery woven within quilted patterns

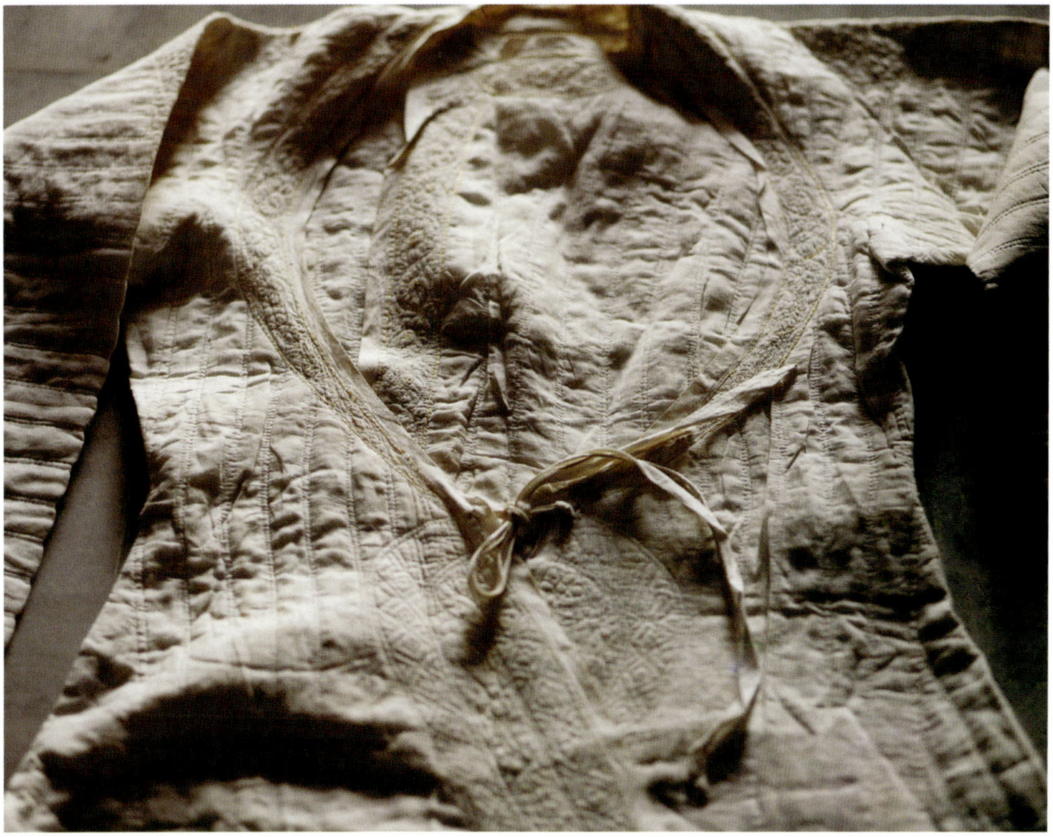

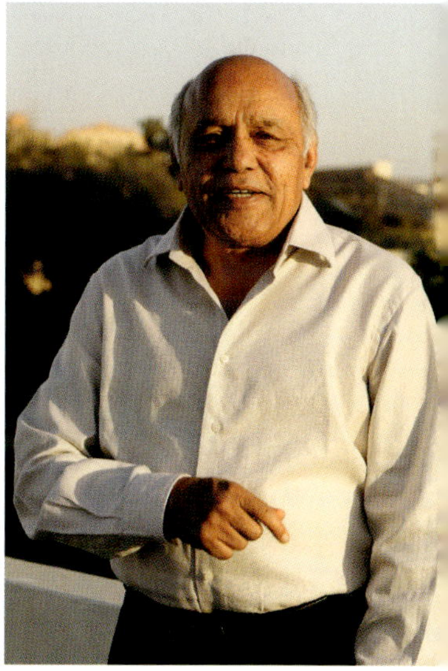

Subhash Sharma, the creator of quilted antique textiles and owner of Rajasthan Fabrics and Arts

Left: *Front view of another beautiful* angrakha

the lovely textile patterns she had been copying in their shop for her own project, for the quilts. These quilts are often white-on-white or have used solid colours; some are decorated with traditional designs executed in a contemporary style with some gold and black elements or subdued colours thrown in for variation. Satayam was greatly inspired by the Jaipur *jalli* work as well as Subhash Sharma's antique *kantha* textiles. Besides the regular mulmul Satayam uses superb khadi cotton, of 300, 400 or 500 thread count, according to proprietor Jatin Sharma. The layer of cotton wool inside the quilt is kept very thin. These two elements when combined help to make their quilts extremely light. I personally weighed their king size quilt, which turned out to be only 1400g. The quilt was also very soft.

The story of the quilt is a little different for every designer or manufacturer. Each shares an exclusive intimacy with the quilt and lends new and unique edges to it. Looking at the variety and quality produced by Satayam, I could well imagine their quilts adorning any and every part of the house with the same amount of ease and grace.

I saw my first quilts in the shops and museums of Arles and other places in the south of France. I admired the antique ones, and discovered the new production. I bought Kathryn Berenson's book *Boutis de Provence*, which is a beautiful book and a great source of information on the Provencal quilts. In real life antique quilts are a rarity; some are made by stitching old pieces of quilted textiles while others are original antique pieces. The quilting style and the patterns are beautiful. Most of the antique quilts are very expensive.

The tradition of needlework in Provence declined in the beginning of the twentieth century. However, the Provencal embroiderers left a priceless heritage of the needlework. The so called *boutis* (quilted work) is one of the most exquisite works in this tradition. Nowhere else do we find the art of quilting so sophisticated and so refined. The sculpted effects and the beauty of the quilted images are amazing.

The new production that I came across in the boutiques lately was very different. It seemed to me as if a certain theme, pattern and colour combination had been decided upon and repeated everywhere. It was called the Provencal style. The quilts are most often machine quilted, to be used as bedcovers. They are pretty and easy to use in western interiors I agree, but I miss the freedom of creation and fantasy that I find in the Jaipur quilts. I also find the Provencal quilts heavier and stiffer than the Jaipur razai. I was initiated into the world of quilts through the Provencal quilts and yet when I later saw the quilts in Jaipur I fell in love with the block-printed designs, which are so important for the embellishment of the Jaipur quilts.

The lightness, warmth and the simple quilting offer many possible opportunities of use too. Somehow the lightness of spirit associated with the making of the Jaipur quilt makes me happy; people love the quilts and use

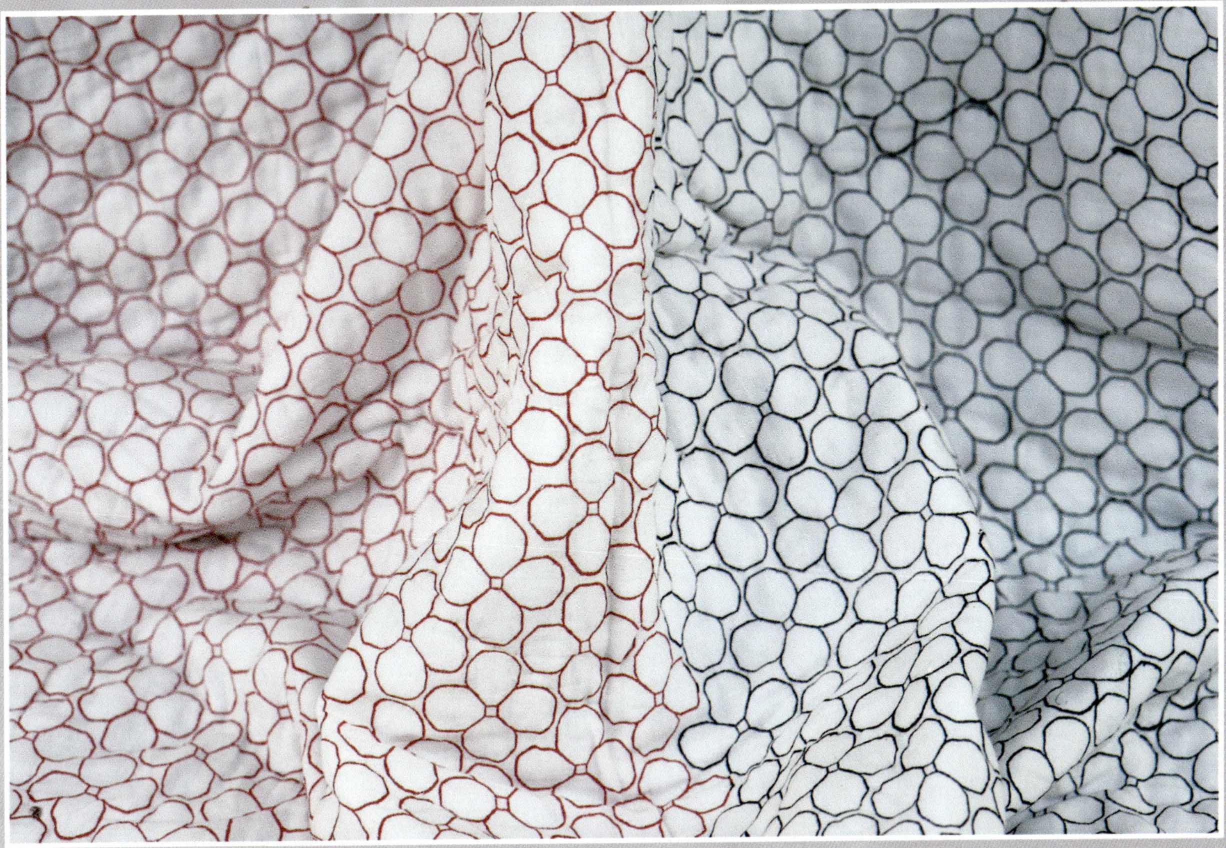

Quilt with stylised flower petals, created by Rasa

them in a simple, intimate way. They are not only expensive and decorative covers on a fine bed. They provide warmth and homely comfort to all and sundry on a cold winter's night. After the *razai* becomes old and frayed after being in use for a long time, new ones are made, with new patterns again. I somehow like this intimacy lining the user-quilt relationship in Rajasthan and particularly in Jaipur.

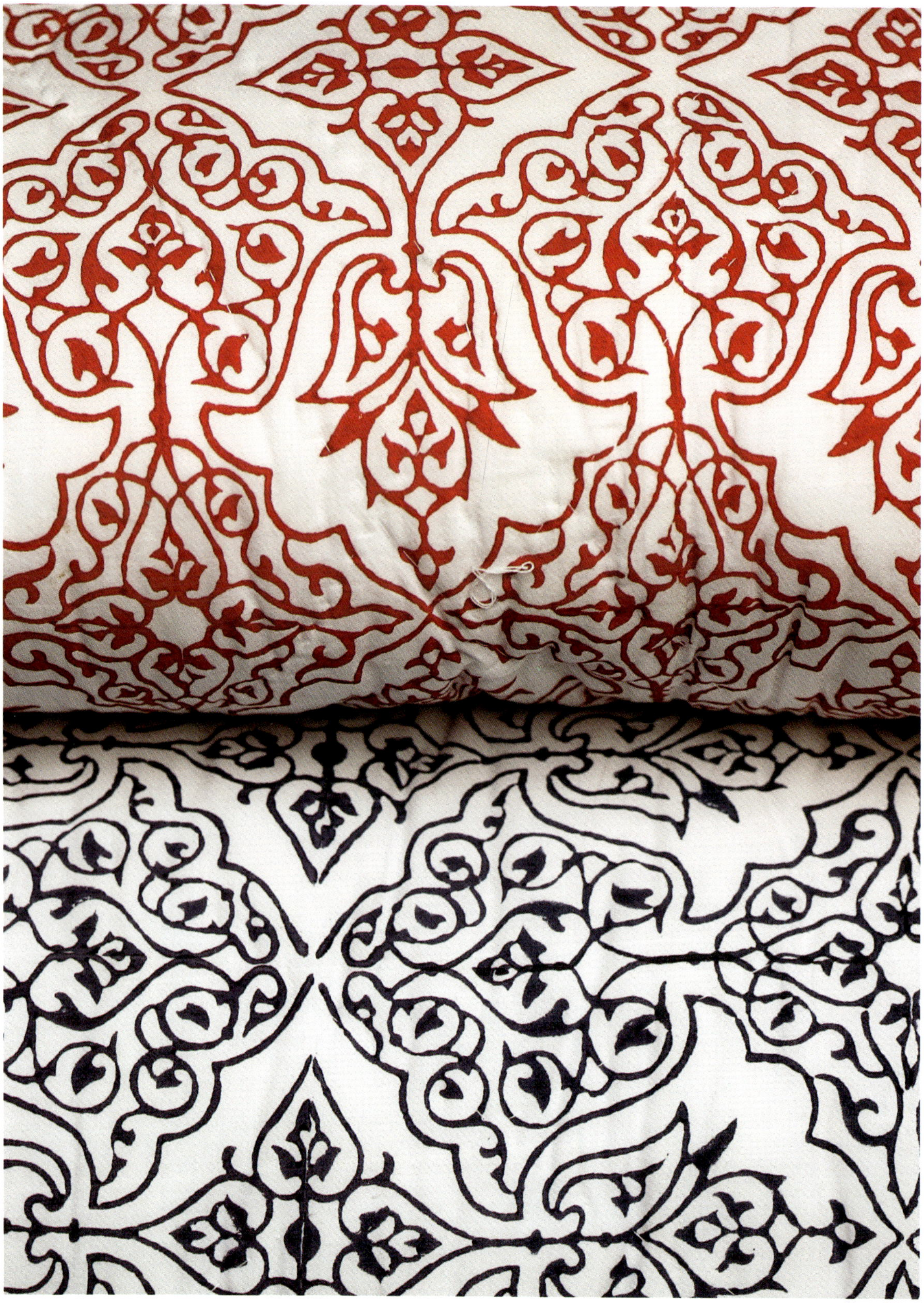

Gitto reminded me of the artists of Scandinavia. I liked her contemporary approach while adapting traditional patterns and motifs in the prints she uses for her quilts and her restrained style

Artist in residence

During one of my visits to Subhash Sharma, he asked me if I knew Gitto, a quilt producer and designer in the city. I did not. As usual all the 'best' addresses in any trade in India (except for the ones which have a window to the customer) are a 'secret' and it often takes time, imagination and endurance to track them down and get an appointment. Should you manage it, you will see that it is worth the effort, because the places and the atmosphere are so different and so much more entertaining than the run-of-the-mill workshops or factory outlets most of us are used to, in Europe. The contact here is built along personal lines. The environment often appears exotic to a foreigner; it may even be very simple. But once you have savoured the ambience, you will never forget it.

I was keen to meet all the eminent quilt makers in Jaipur and expressed my wish to see Gitto's work too. Not much time was lost and I was taken to her factory the same afternoon. Buyers were waiting to place their orders with Gitto and I was invited to return to her workshop later, talk to her and take some photographs.

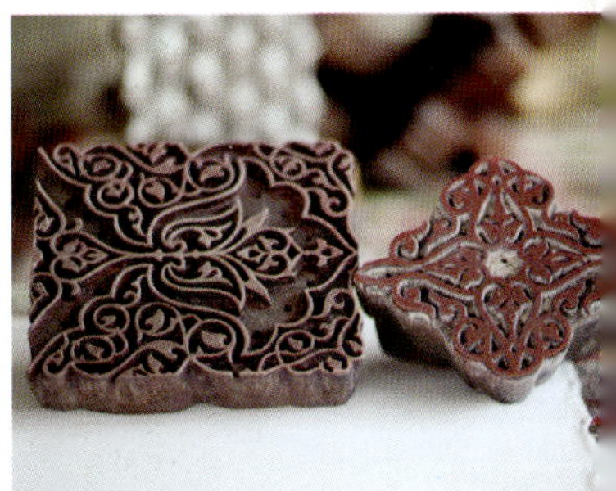

Motif details on Gitto's printing block. Each designer holds exclusive rights over original motifs and printing blocks created at the workshop

Facing page: *Stylised blue and red patterns from Gitto's collection, inspired by traditional motifs*

Madhurima Patni, who is better known in Jaipur and among her customers as Gitto, has a long and impressive CV. She studied at the Fashion Institute of Technology in New York, NID in Ahmedabad and holds a BA in Fine Arts from the University of Baroda, India.

She taught at NID, Ahmedabad for a while, worked as a freelancer and consultant for several export houses including Anokhi, designed for Hemmila Oy, Finland, and also worked as a consultant for Shrishti School of Art, Design and Technology in Bangalore. She is a member of the Governing Board at the Indian Institute of Craft Design in Jaipur.

Gitto's work is very artistic. Her place reminded me of an art school where she was a professor. Her workshop was her second home—her creative lair and a hub of activities, with Gitto in complete charge of everything.

The fabrics lying around were modern and simple. Gitto was smartly dressed in a traditional Indian ensemble of a long kurta (knee-length long shirt) and churidars (slim pants)—which looked quite contemporary on her. She gave the impression of being a strong and independent woman.

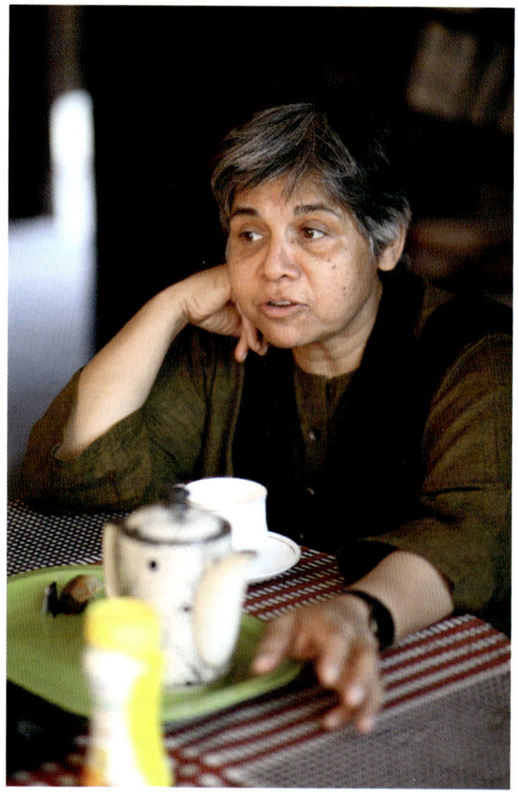

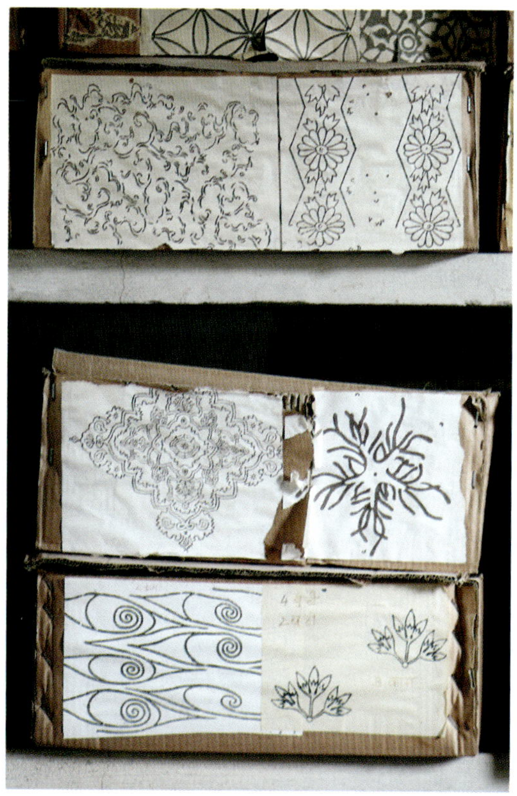

Right above: *Madhurima Patni, the owner of Surabhi Exports is popularly known as Gitto in the world of art and textile designing*

Right below: *Storage boxes, containing printing block sets. The print pasted outside the box confirms the particular motif of the blocks stored inside*

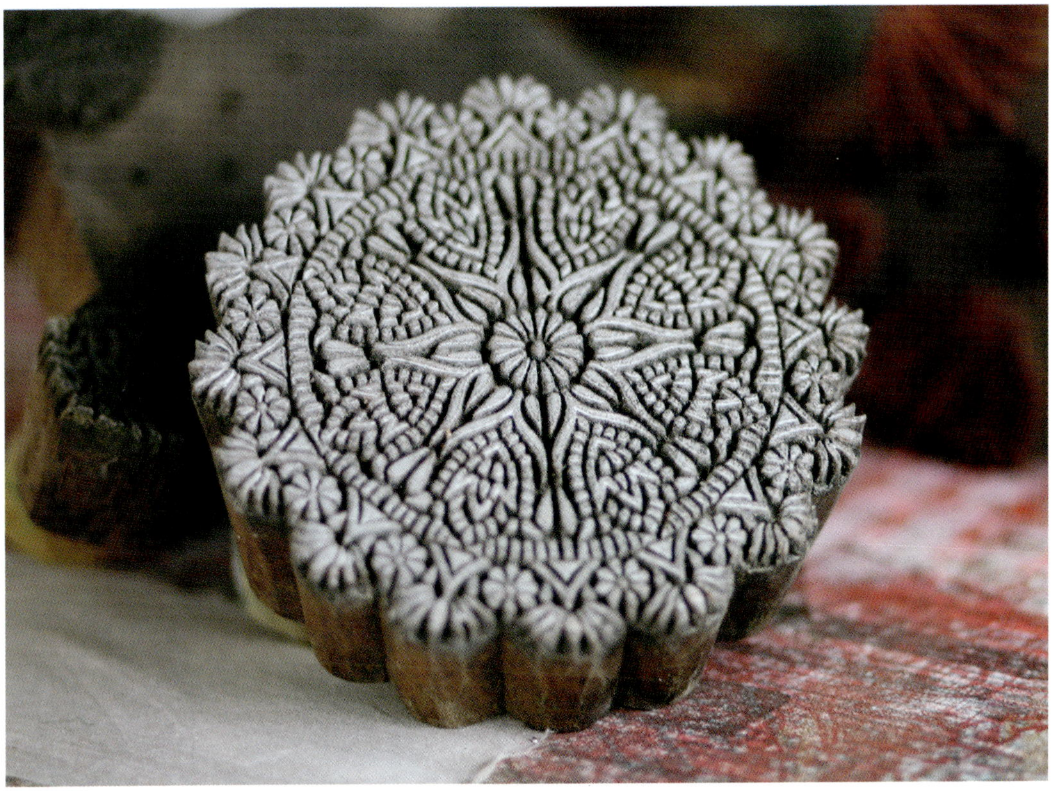

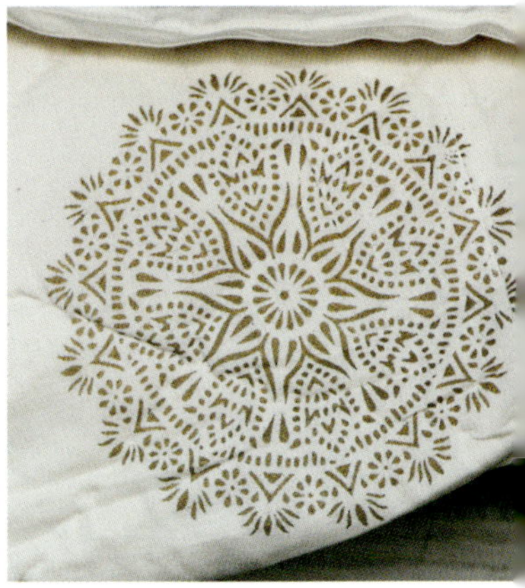

Inside Gitto's factory–Surabhi Exports–two Italian ladies placed their orders and chose designs for fabrics; some British customers followed suit. From one box popped out an absolutely gorgeous fabric and tunics made for a French designer. The pattern was refined with small stylised flowers in very light fuchsia, almost a shade of pink on white. It looked gorgeous; my girl friend and I were fascinated by it. Then I went to the printing room which was piled high with boxes of printing blocks. They lay strewn about as tools of the trade but they were decorative elements as well and made a pretty picture of the factory. A worker showed me around, displaying Gitto's quilts. Again I had before me new creations to admire and enjoy—a set of very elegant and sparse yet resplendent quilts with motifs and designs inspired by traditional art. Simple and sublime compositions mostly in a colour combination of black-on-white, these were modern and beautiful in their own way.

I had another chance to meet Gitto and this time she told me a few stories about her company and her work. She created her own company in order to be independent and be able to control her own work. It all began with little money

Details of a motif on the face of a printing block

Above: *The corresponding print in gold on white lends aesthetic sophistication*

and a lot of learning experience riddled with initial difficulties. She made mistakes and learned on the job but also derived a lot of satisfaction from her work.

Gitto received orders for white quilts from England. To produce them was not an easy task. Since the women quilted at home, the finished products often came back soiled and dirty, sometimes with particularly stubborn spots and marks which were difficult to remove. Gitto remembers having had to extract from them strands of hair, cotton seeds and the like, but the day she discovered a fly in the quilt, she decided enough was enough. 'This fly is here without a visa,' she thought to herself and decided to change it all.

She contacted the man who had organised the group of women who quilted at home. Realising the problems of making export quality quilts from home, he built a large community hall where the women could come without their children and work in peace. Dogs, food and shoes were not allowed inside. The women were also happy to get some relief from housework and the round-the-clock pressing needs of their large families for a while. They listened to music while working, chatted and were generally a happy lot working amidst clean, pleasant surroundings. Gitto let them make small quilts—150 x 150 cm,

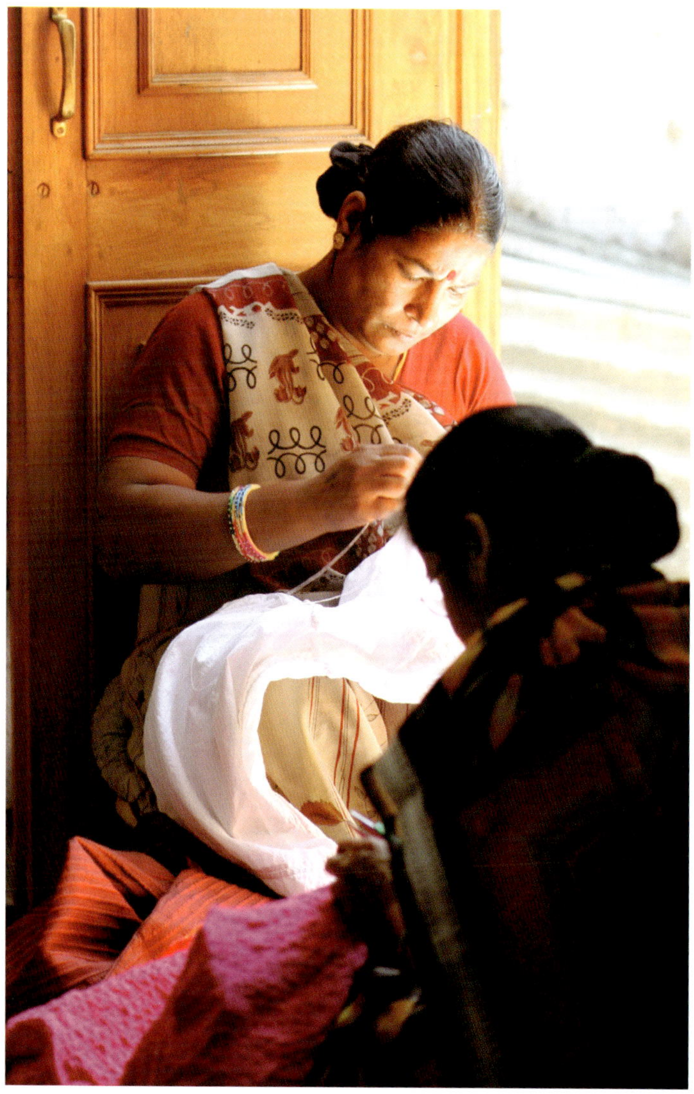

Women quilters at work

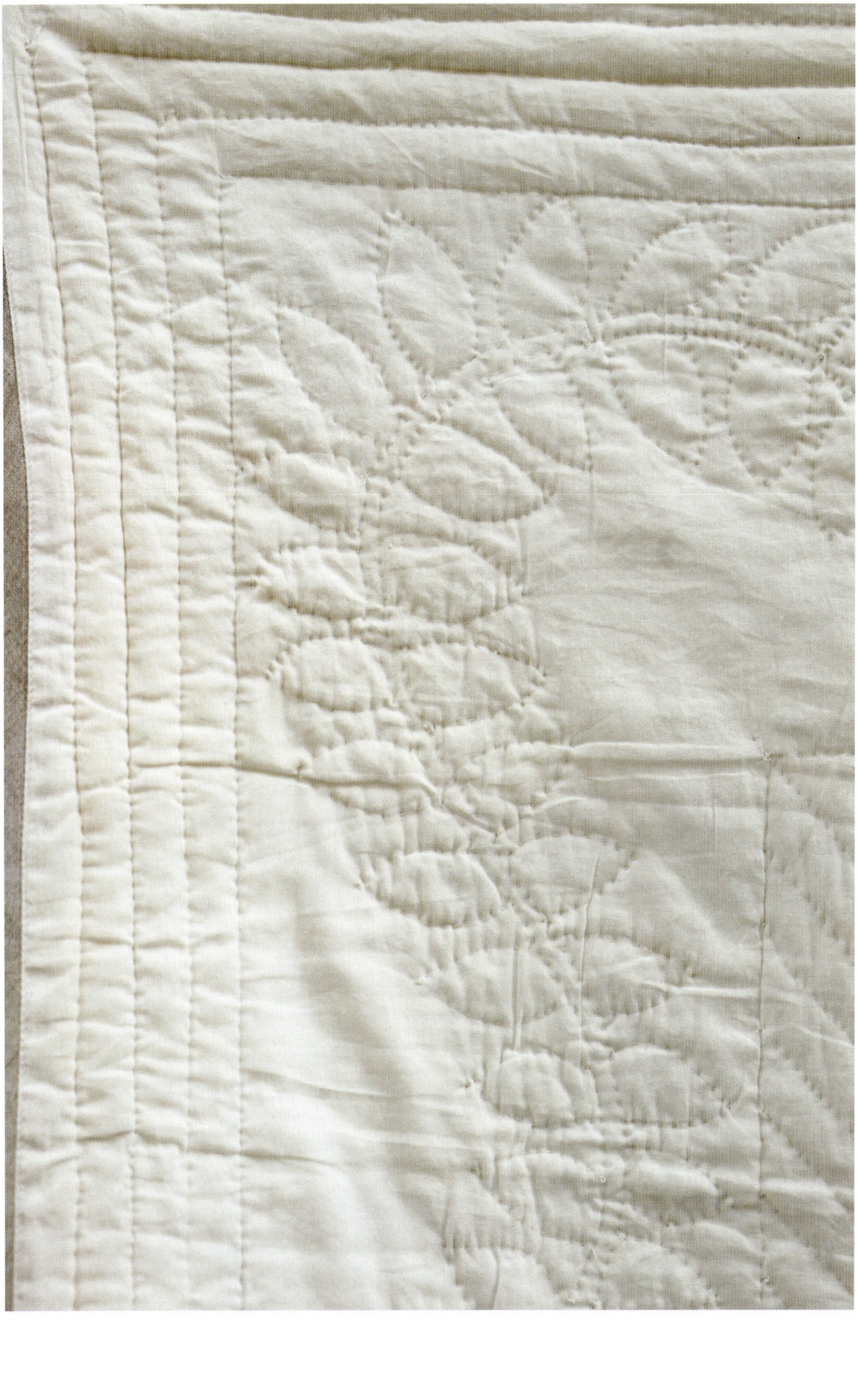

White-on-white quilt details with the quilting stitches and a portion of the pattern in highlight

and create any pattern they wished to. The women did not disappoint her and delivered beautiful work.

Traditionally, quilting was a craft popular among Muslim women but as word got around, young girls from other communities joined them at the community hall to learn the art of quilting. Gitto created botanical patterns but quite unlike the Sanganer designs. They were geometrical shapes. She sought out old patterns and motifs which were more refined and sophisticated than the ones copied many times and used everywhere. Now she often uses the cotton plant flower as her central motif, borrowing abundantly from nature but creating her own contemporary style with minimalism as her leading light. Gitto's colour palette is very elegant and interesting, as she uses both subdued and strong colours.

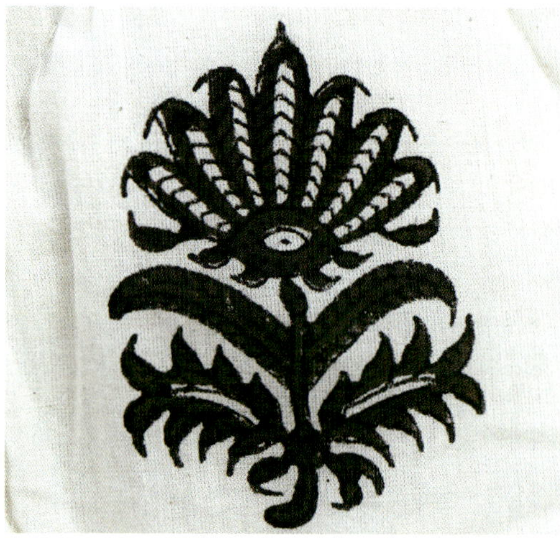

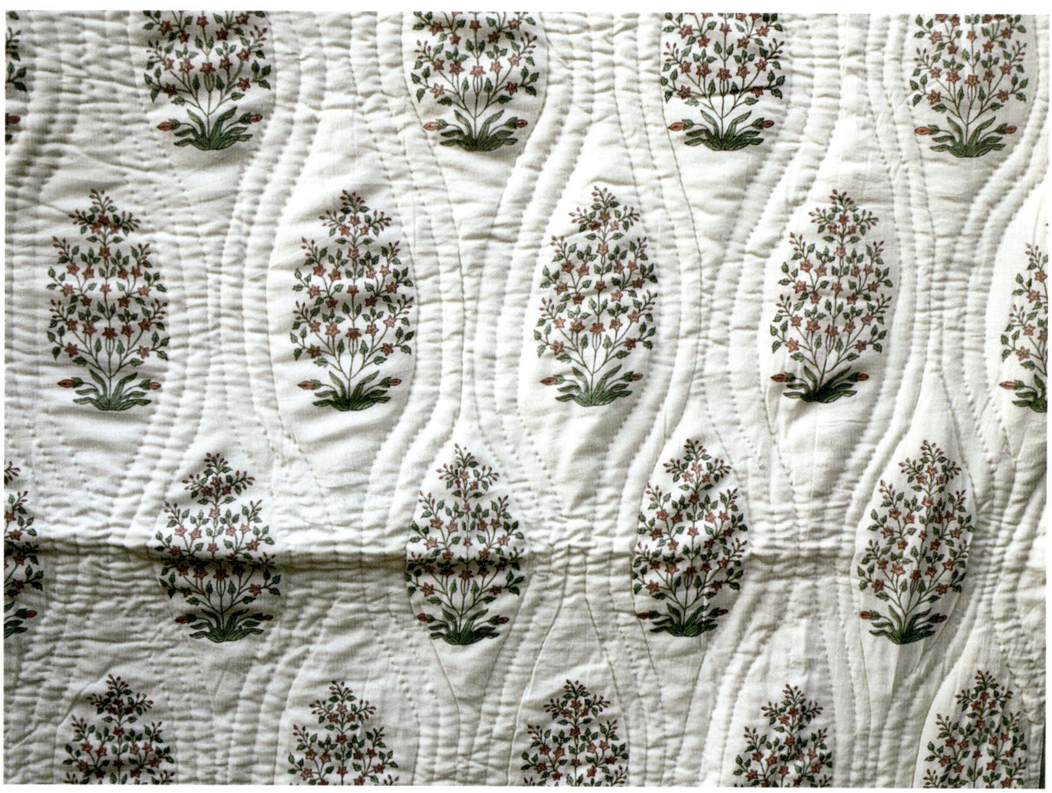

Right: *Gitto's quilt details spell out her signature style*

Above right: *Magnified image of a stylised flower motif*

Gitto's company works largely against orders. It also develops prints and products according to the clients' briefs. Her main products are soft furnishings and clothes and simple accessories like scarves, stoles and bags.

According to Gitto, in older times before the onset of winter in Rajasthan, it was common practice for people to open up their used quilts, wash the cotton, fluff it again and stitch the quilts anew. This was done to ensure that every winter the family had a fresh, warm and fragrant quilt to wrap up in and fight the cold. There are still men who walk the streets every autumn with a fluffing bow, which resembles a musical instrument and sounds like one too. In earlier times, these men would regularly call on all homes to fluff cotton extracted from old quilts and the lazy afternoons would reverberate with the soft metallic but at the same time melodious 'tonk, tonk' of fluffing bows.

Printing with wooden block at Gitto's workshop

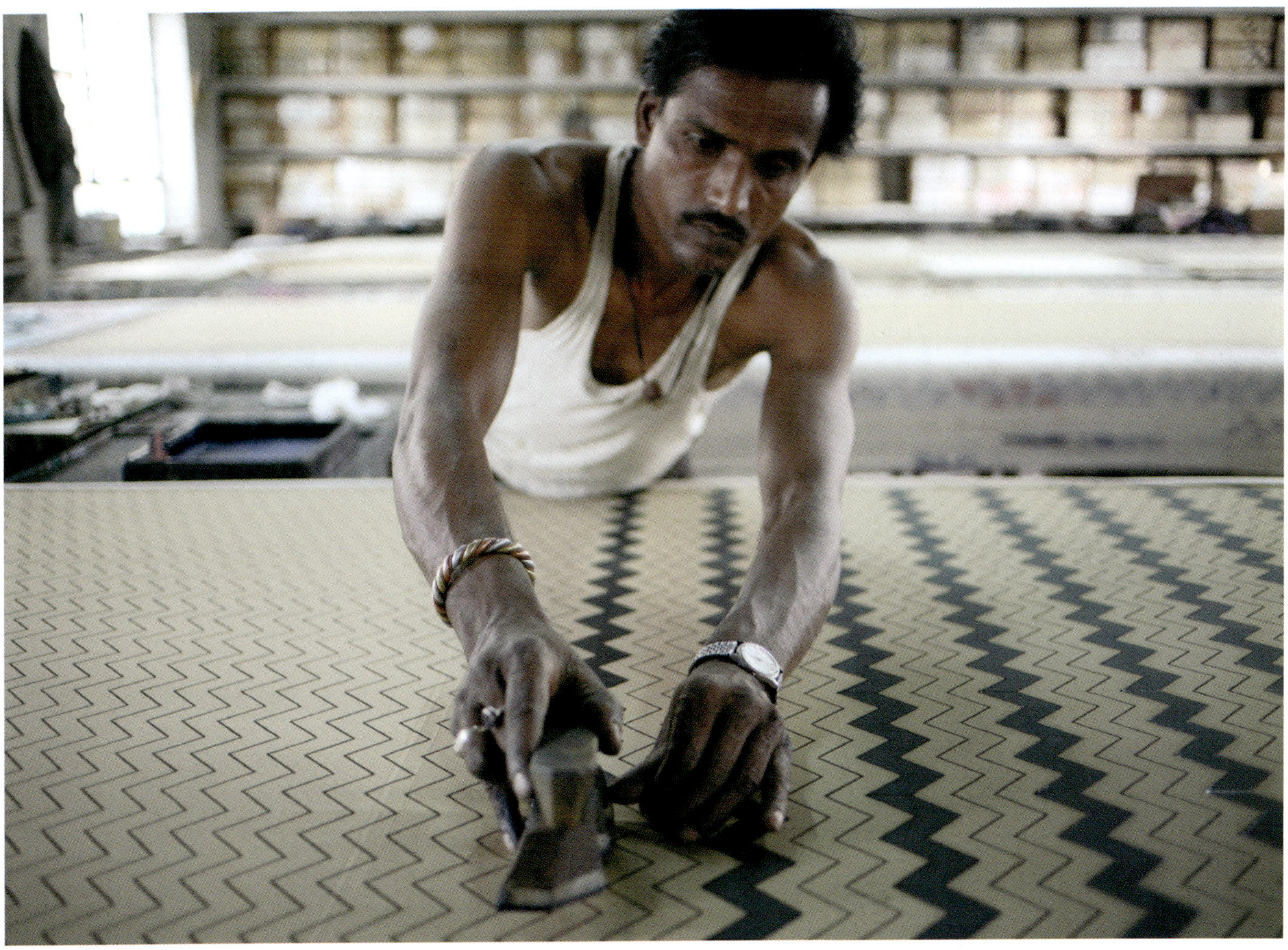

Epilogue

It took much longer to write this book than I had planned. When I returned to Sweden, the realisation of what could have been done differently or better dawned upon me. However, I looked upon writing my book much in the same tune as packing a suitcase before setting upon a long journey. An unscheduled extra day before setting off helps one prepare and pack better. I finally set my own timeline with the book and scheduled it for publishing. Therefore it was necessary to set the book free and let it fly.

I hope that it will reach all relevant corners of the world and that the reader will receive it with interest and joy. I hoped to write a simple, visually appealing and useful book giving basic information about the art and trade of Jaipur quilts. I mainly wished to show the quilts to my readers, recount stories about the people who make them, describe how a quilt is made and help preserve something so unique and precious as the art of quilt-making in Jaipur.

It was quite an effort but it also turned out to be one of the most wonderful and creative periods in my life. I met talented people, made new friends and visited new places which were hitherto unknown to me. While researching, I was also led on to new subjects and received in-depth knowledge about a lot of other things

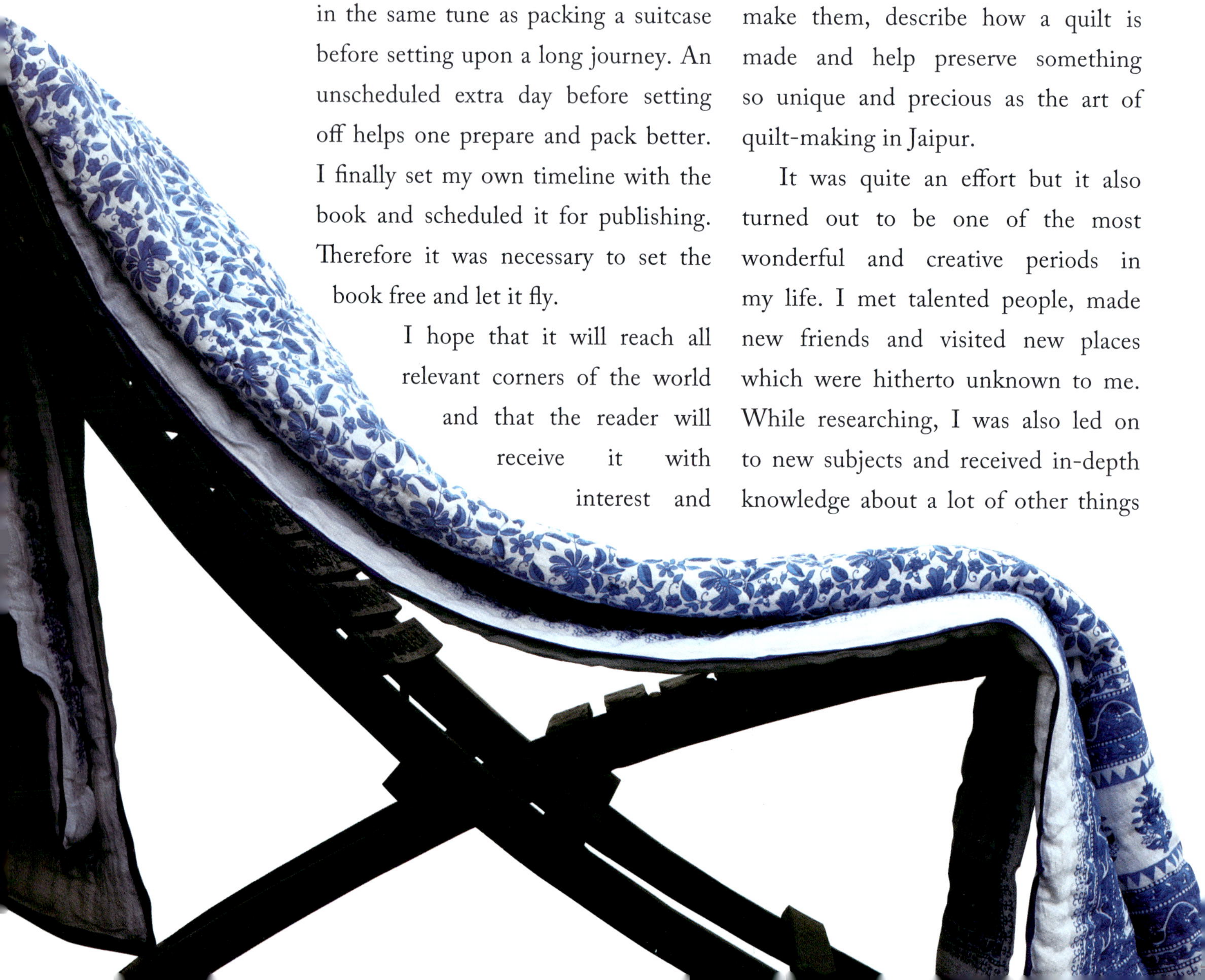

besides quilts. I spent a lot of time in Jaipur, which might seem to be little else than just a popular and historical tourist spot with wonderful shopping possibilities on the surface, but once you learn your way around and into the soul of the city and its people, you begin your own journey of discovery.

I stayed often at the charming Diggi Palace Hotel, where I felt at home. I also stayed for significant lengths of time at Arya Niwas hotel, where life is simple and easy going for designers and business people who look forward to the comfort of pleasant and relaxed surroundings after a day's hard work. I have thoroughly enjoyed all my periods of stay in Jaipur over the years and felt completely at home and at ease in Indian surroundings.

I have never collected mementos from my trips around the world and I like empty spaces, but I cannot resist a beautiful quilt. So I now possess quite a number of beautiful Jaipur *razai*s and I find them a good deal useful, too.

If I ever come back to live another life I would like to learn some creative work using my hands. A gardener has a wonderful job, working in peace, looking at plants and flowers, and creating a perceivable thing of beauty within a span of real time. Watching people create and work with their hands in Jaipur made me realise how natural a phenomenon it was. We have forgotten about it in the West. Everything is ready made, and we have lost the skill to build a house, to bake bread or to sew a skirt. I don't even know how to make a fire. If there is a calamity someday it would really turn out to be a serious catastrophe for people in the western world. But most people in India would face it and survive fairly easily. I watched people weaving, dyeing material, printing on the material, sewing, making jewellery, cutting stones, carving marble or wood, making pots, stitching shoes...And it still is real life, not some figment of imagination or a model workshop set up for the eco-friendly production of handkerchiefs.

On my next visit to Jaipur I shall buy some cloth, go to Sanganer and Bagru and learn how to print on the fabric and then try to make my own quilt or a quilted sheet. Quilted bedsheets usually look very good. You can print the pattern on one mulmul sheet and stitch it together with two other sheets on both sides of the printed sheet. This ensures that the print on the bedsheet

Facing page: *Quilt in blue from Kadar Bux, laid out for display*

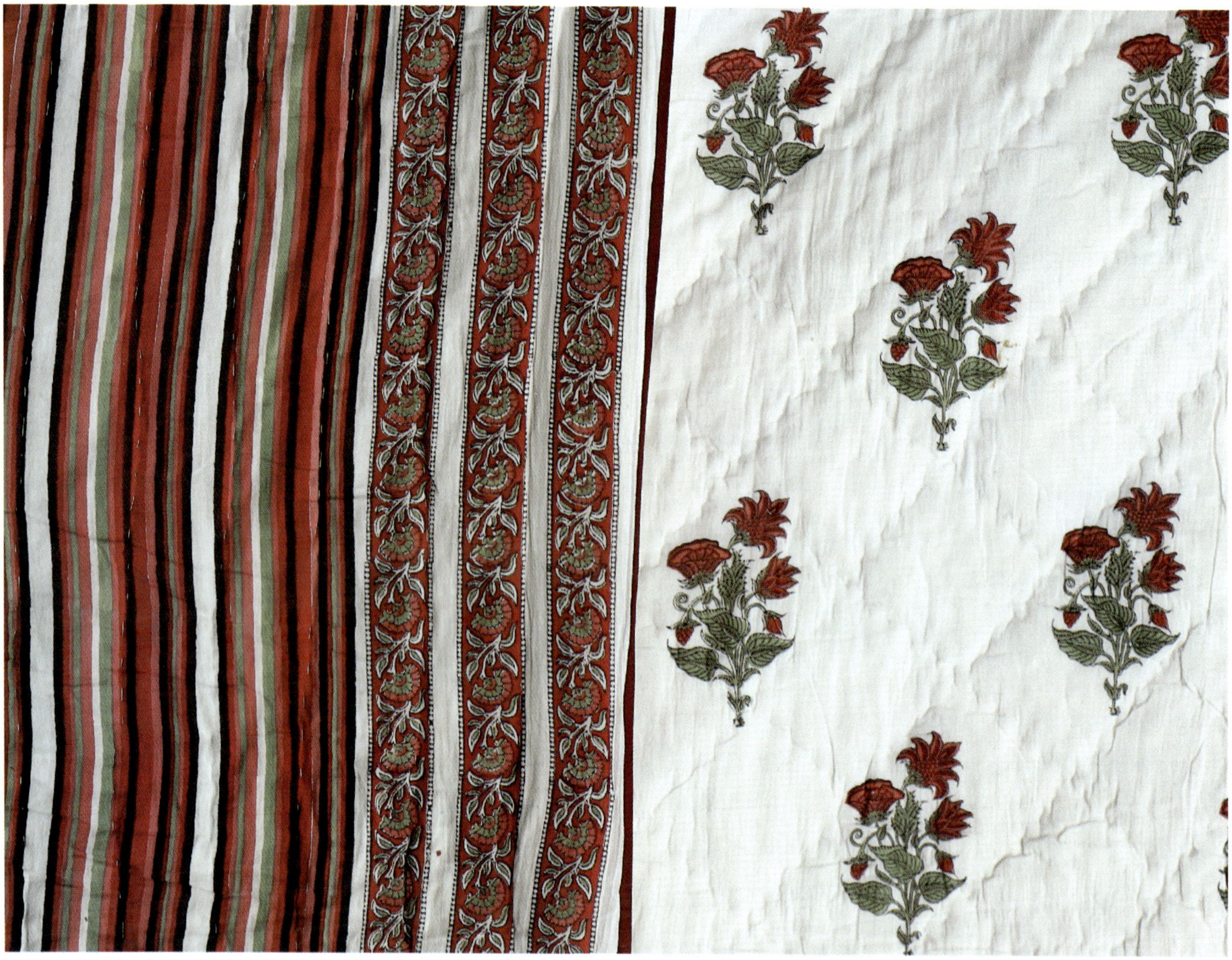

Floral motif entwined with narrow stripes in red and white. A simple yet stylish quilt by Kitty Rae

is not too stark; you can match it easily with other printed bedclothes.

I have met art students in Jaipur, often from Japan, or just regular visitors who had come with their own designs or created them while trying out the printing in Sanganer. They produced very interesting fabrics, shawls, scarves or bags. They felt free to experiment as much as they desired, since they didn't have any pressure on them to make marketable products. They created for themselves and for pleasure. The results were astonishingly good and everything turned out to be truly beautiful. I realised that we are all artists or artisans at heart. We just have to discover ourselves.

Acknowledgements

I would like to thank all those who helped me conceptualise and create this book, especially Kent Gramer who was my lifeline in Sweden while I was researching for the book in India and who also gave me my first professional camera without which this book would not have seen the light of day. Maria Hegborn who executed the first blue print for this book in Sweden and gave it to me as a gift; Dr Chandramani Singh, my mentor and guide, who showed me where to find the material for writing a book on Jaipur quilts.

I would like to thank all the quilt producers and designers in Jaipur—Kitty Rae, Radhakrishnan Nair and his wife Andrée Pouliot, Brigitte Singh, Gitto, Jatin Sharma, the husband-wife team of Madhulika Singh and Manish Tibrewal and the pioneers in this trade: Kadar Bux, Miya Bajaj, Lashkari Textiles, Friends Rooi Mattress and Magic Quilts. They all extended a warm welcome to me when I stepped into their homes and showrooms, patiently replied to all my queries and allowed me to photograph their collections. I specially mention in this respect all the talented artisans who silently work at the workshops.

I owe my gratitude to Pankaj Sharma, curator at the Maharaja Sawai Man Singh II Museum of the City Palace, Jaipur, who let me copy

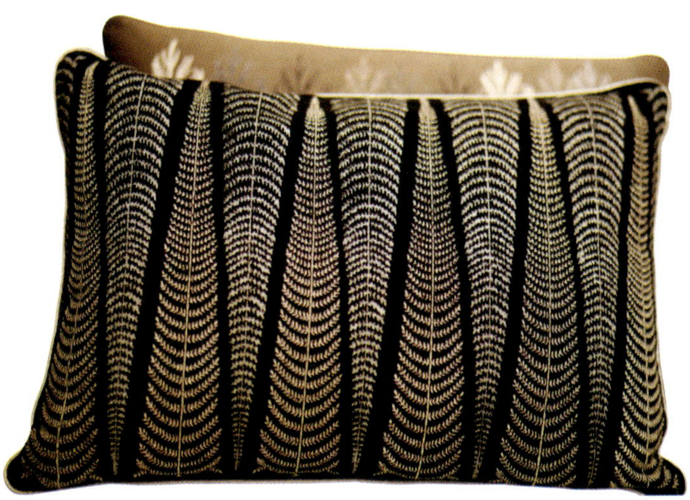

The leafy print in black and gold on a pillow cover has been created by Rasa

pictures from Dr Chandramani Singh's museum catalogue; Subhash Sharma of Jaipur—the well-known and veteran collector of exquisite antique textiles who also kindly let me copy some of his priceless photographs of old Jaipur by Raja Deen Dayal.

Thanks go out to: Col K. Garcha of the Jaipur Polo Club for having patience with me and my editor while exchanging countless e-mails as well as photographs with detailed captions from his personal collection; the manager of the Rambagh Palace hotel in Jaipur for permitting me to take photographs at the hotel; my friends Aparna and Rajiv Sahay who prevented me from starving, supplied medication when I was ill and also helped me understand India and Jaipur by inviting me to different events and leading me on to some important connections in Jaipur; Dharmendar Kanwar for kindly agreeing to write the Foreword for my book, her wise comments on my manuscript and her valuable advice; Arvind Singh and his wife Shweta for their help and showing me around the city of Jaipur; the management of Nana Ki Haveli, where I photographed some quilts; the Diggi Palace Hotel which was often my home in Jaipur as was Arya Niwas hotel. I thank the hotel staff for taking excellent care of me and forgiving my bad moods arising out of exhaustion.

Last but not least my thanks go out to people in Jaipur—my tailor and friend Nanag Ram Saini and the tailors working with him, for making my clothes and always supporting me. And I should not forget the rickshaw drivers. Some of them lived around Diggi Palace and the rest hailed from other parts of the city but they all had helped me find the addresses and locations I was looking for. And I felt safe with them all.

I am glad that I had the good luck to hear about Niyogi Books. I would like to sincerely thank my publisher Mr Bikash Niyogi and his wife Tultul for believing in my book and inviting me to publish with their company Niyogi Books. I appreciated their enthusiasm and generosity.

The Regalia Hotel staff in Delhi was generous and greeted me happily every evening when I returned exhausted from a day's work.

I would like to thank my editor Mohua Mitra for her guidance, for improving my English and assisting me when difficulties arose.

I wish to thank the entire Niyogi Books team for being cheerfully and smilingly accommodating.

Addresses: Designers, Producers and Museums

Miya Bajaj Razai Emporium
Manmohan Miya Bajaj
55 Hawa Mahal Bazaar
Jaipur, India
Ph: +91-141-260 72 61
Mobile: 9829068607

Magic Quilts
Hazai Babu Khan, Manzoor Ahmed & Maqsood Ahmed
1590 Under 2nd Crossing
Parshuram Marg
Khavas Ji Ka Rasta
Jaipur, India
Ph: +91-141-2613298
Mobile: 9829184056

Kadar Bux Textiles
Abdul Fareed & Abdul Haseen
Shop No 11
Hawa Mahal Bazaar
Opp. Old Assembly Hall
Jaipur, India
Mobile 9314563164

Abdul Gafoor & Abdul Aijaz
Shop No 9
Opp. Old Vidhan Sabha,
Jaipur, India

Friends Rooi Mattress
Abdul Gaffur & Abdul Tahir
Topkhana Ka Rasta
Chandpole Bazaar
Jaipur, India
Ph: +91-141-231 20 05
Mobile: 9414323060

Lashkari Textiles
Shri Krishan Lashkari, Dinesh Lashkari & Manish Lashkari
Shop No 70, Opp. Jain Mandir
Chaura Rasta
Jaipur, India
Ph: +91-141-231 17 20

Kin Fabrics
Kitty Rae
D'Villa, Station Road
Jaipur, India
Ph: +91-141-220 45 79

Brigitte Singh
E-mail: brigittesinghms@.com

Soma
Radhakrishnan Nair
Soma House, Khatipura
Jaipur, India
Ph: +91-141-235 51 12
www.somashop.com

Rasa
Madhulika Singh
& Manish Tibrewal

Factory: Keshav Vihar 31,
Vishnu Path
Gopalpura Bypass
Jaipur, India
Ph: +91-141-276 28 49
Mobile: +91-982 906 42 23

Shop: S-55, Ashok Marg
C-Scheme
(adjacent to Shahnaz Herbals)
Jaipur, India
Ph: +91-141-403 85 84
E-mail: rasa_jpr@sify.com

Surabhi Exports / Gitto
Madhurima Patni
FE-8 Malviya Industrial Area
Malviya Nagar
Jaipur, India
Mobile: +91-93145-13809,
+91-93145-62202
E-mail: amitabhpatni@gmail.com

Satayam
Jatin Sharma
174, Laxman Dwara Road
Opp Jantar Mantar ticket window
City Palace
Jaipur, India
Ph/fax: +91-141-260555
E-mail: satayam.gartex@gmail.com
E-mail: jatin55@hotmail.com

Rajasthan Fabrics and Arts
Subhash Sharma
174, Laxman Dwara Road
Opp. Jantar Mantar ticket window
City Palace
Jaipur, India
Ph/fax: +91-141-260 31 31

Useful Addresses

The Victoria and Albert Museum
South Kensington
Cromwell Heath Road
London E2 9PA, UK
Ph: +44-2079422000

The Victoria & Albert Museum in London is the world's largest museum of decorative arts and design.

Museon Arlaten
29 Rue de la République
132 00 Arles, France
Ph: +33-490960823
The Museon was founded by the poet Frédéric Mistral. It serves as a memorial site for the history and culture of Provence.

City Palace Museum
City Palace
The Maharaja Sawai Man Singh II Museum
Jaipur, India
Ph: +91-141-260 80 55
Entrance from Tripolia Gate
It is a fine repository of a variety of textiles, housing the royal formal costumes, sanganeri block prints, embroidered shawls and a few quilts made in Jaipur.

Anokhi Shop
2nd Floor KK Square
C-11 Prithviraj Road,
C-Scheme,
Jaipur, India
Ph: +91-141-400 72 44
Anokhi sells soft furnishings and garments in traditional designs.

Anokhi Museum of Hand Printing (AMHP)
Anokhi Haveli
Khedi Gate, Amber
Jaipur, India
Ph: +91-141-253 02 26

Textorium
Mirza Ismail Road
Jaipur, India
Ph: +91-141-236 11 90
E-mail: info@textorium.com
Textorium sells good quality textiles and pretty silk quilts.

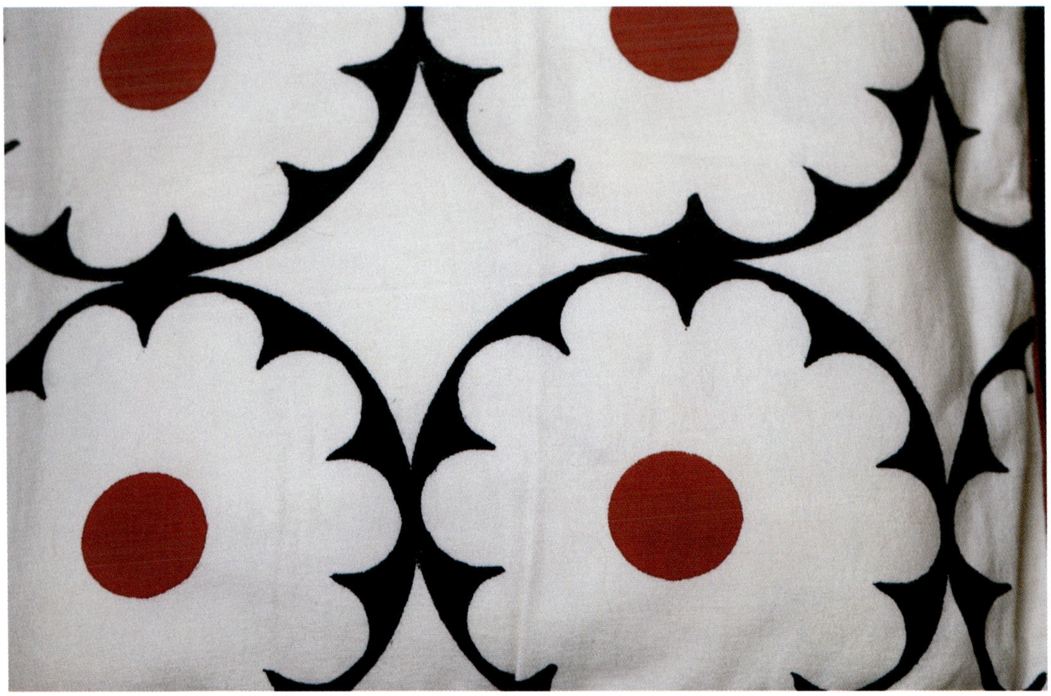

A Kitty Rae pillow cover

Bibliography

Berenson, Kathryn: *Boutis de Provence* (1996). Flammarion, Paris.

Biehn, Michel: *En jupon piquee et robe d'indienne* (1987). Edition Jeanne Laffitte, Paris.

Mainardi, Patricia: *Quilts, the Great American Art* (1978)–*The Feminist Art Journal*, 2, no 1. Miles and Weir Ltd., San Pedro, California.

Parker, Rozsika: *The Subversive Stitch, Embroidery and the Making of the Feminine* (1989). The Women's Press Ltd., London.

Pedersen, Karen & Wilson, J.J.: *Women Artists: Recognition and Reappraisal from the Middle Ages to the Twentieth Century* (1978). The Women's Press Ltd., London.

Singh, Chandramani: *Textiles and Costumes from the Maharaj Sawai Man Singh II Museum* (1979). MMS-II Museum Trust, City Palace, Jaipur.

Wentworth, Judy: *Quilts* (1991). Studio Editions, London.

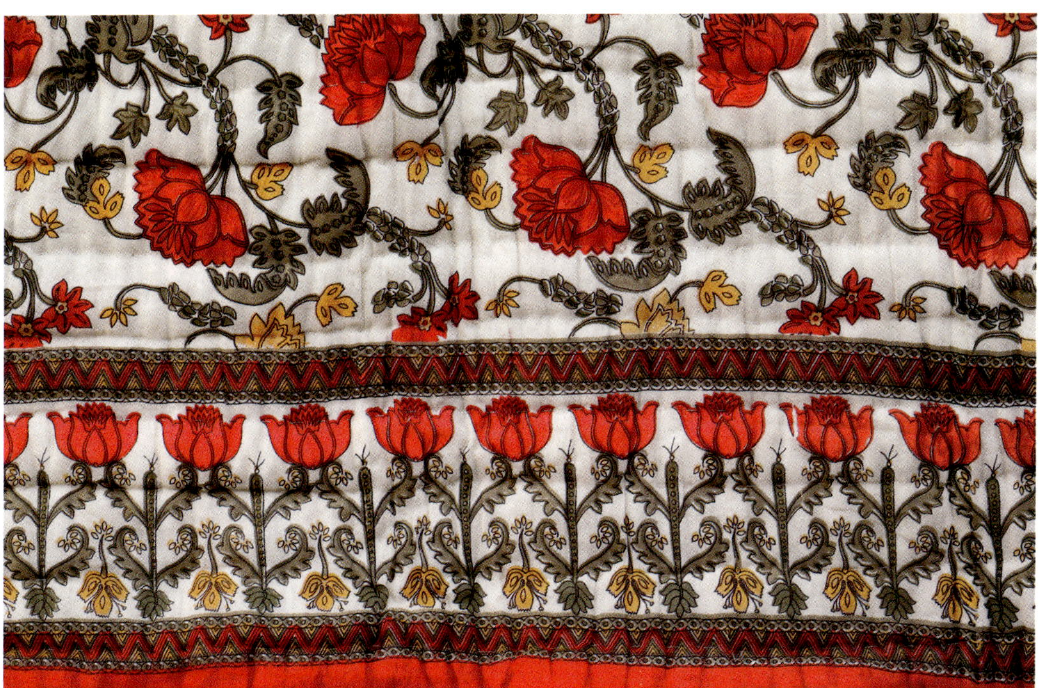

Bright and beautiful in red and yellow, Sanganeri *print. Quilt from Lashkari Textiles*

Glossary

Ajanta Caves
Located in Maharashtra, India, outside the village of Ajintha in the Aurangabad district. They are rock-cut caves and monuments dating from the first century BC, containing paintings and sculptures considered to be masterpieces of both 'Buddhist religious art' and universal pictorial art.

Amber Fort
Also known as Amer Fort, it is located in Amber, 11 km from Jaipur. It was the ancient citadel of the ruling Kachhawa clan of Amber, before the present day Jaipur was made the capital. Amber Fort is known for its unique artistic style, blending both Hindu and Mughal elements.

Much of the present structure is the palace built by Raja Man Singh who ruled from AD 1590-1614. The palace contains several spectacular buildings such as the Diwan-i-Khas and the Ganesh Pol. The old and original fort of Amber dating from the Meena period is what is known in the present day as Jaigarh Fort.

Arts and Crafts Movement
An international design movement that originated in Britain and flourished between 1880 and 1910.

It was initiated by the artist and writer William Morris (1834-1896) in the 1860s and was inspired by the writings of John Ruskin (1819-1900). Its influence reached out to architecture, interior design and the decorative arts, using simple forms and a medieval style of decoration. It advocated truth to traditional craftsmanship.

Benaras
Varanasi, also commonly known as Benaras or Banaras is an Indian city situated on the banks of the River Ganga in the state of Uttar Pradesh, regarded as holy by Hindus, Buddhists and Jains. It is one of the oldest continuously inhabited cities in the world.

Batiste
The softest of the lightweight opaque fabrics. It is made of cotton, silk, wool, spun rayon or a blend.The cotton batiste is sometimes mercerised.

Block Master
A craftsman in the textile printing industry, who carves printing blocks for printing on fabrics.

Brahmin
A class or caste in the Indian sub-continent. Brahmins perform religious duties as priests in Hinduism but they also have a parallel career and have been practising other professions like lawyers, writers, poets, engineers and corporates, etc. Many parts of India were also ruled by Brahmin kings in the ancient days.

Brocade
A heavy fabric interwoven with a rich, raised design. The background may be twill, satin, or plain weave. Brocade is often used for draperies, and upholstery. Benaras is famous for high quality, beautiful brocades.

Cashmere
A fine wool obtained from Cashmere goats.

Cashmere Shawl
A fine hand-woven, and often embroidered, shawl made in Kashmir.

Caufield & Saward
Created *The Dictionary of Needlework*, 1885.

Chintz
Calico cloth printed with flowers and other patterns in different colours. Chintz was originally a wood-block printed, painted or stained calico produced in India from 1600 to 1800 and popular for bed covers, quilts and draperies. The early fabrics were very expensive and rare. Europeans at first produced reproductions of Indian designs, and later added original patterns. A well-known product was toile de Jouy, which was manufactured in Jouy, France, between 1700 and 1843.

City Palace
The Palace with the Chandra Mahal and Mubarak Mahal, forms one of the most famous landmarks in Jaipur. The beautiful palace

was built by Maharaja Sawai Jai Singh II during his reign. The complex covers a big area, which is divided into gardens, courtyards and buildings. The additional grand buildings were constructed later by the succeeding rulers. The Chandra Mahal Palace now houses a museum but the larger part of it is still a royal residence.

Colour Master
A craftsman in the textile industry who mixes colours for block printing on fabrics.

Cotton Wool
The term refers to raw, minimally processed cotton. Cotton wool is combed to remove impurities and then cleaned to sterilise it. Tufts of raw cotton look like chunks of wool, explaining the name.

Dhoti
Traditional dress for Indian men. It is often worn with a kurta—a long loose fitting shirt. It is a rectangular piece of cloth about five yards long, wrapped about the lower body and knotted at the waist.

Dupatta
Lengths of textile in silk, cotton or chiffon of different sizes. Women wear them over the shoulders, cover their heads or sometimes wrap them around the upper part of the body.

Gupta Age
Considered to be the most prosperous era in Indian history, the period evolved with an ancient Indian empire, founded by Maharaja Sri Gupta, existing from approximately the end of the third century AD to the beginning of the seventh century AD, covering much of the Indian subcontinent.

The capital of the Guptas was Pataliputra, present day Patna. This period is called by some scholars as the Golden Age of India in science, art and philosophy.

Jean Arp
Jean Arp/Hans Arp, (1886-1966), was a German-French sculptor, painter, poet and abstract artist in other media.

Krishna
Hindu deity, an incarnation of Vishnu. He was the king of Dwarka.

Levant
The non-European coastlands along the eastern shore of the Mediterranean.

Maharaja
Maharaja is a Sanskrit title for a 'great king'. The female equivalent title Maharani denotes either the wife of a Maharaja or a woman ruling a large kingdom in her own right.

Mughal Empire
An Islamic and Persian imperial power that ruled a large portion of the Indian subcontinent from 1556 and gradually grew in strength and stature to form an empire, transcending political, cultural and aesthetic boundaries. It ruled most of Hindustan by the late seventeenth century and ended in the mid-nineteenth century. The 'Classic period' of the Empire started with the accession of Akbar the Great to the throne in 1556. It ended with the death of Emperor Aurangzeb in 1707. All the significant monuments of the Mughals date to this period. The Mughals brought in influences of Persian literature and culture to India.

Mulmul
Fine, soft muslin.

Muslin
A light cotton fabric, finely woven and typically white. Dhaka in Bangladesh, is famous for muslin.

Nathdwara
Nathdwara is a city in Rajasthan state of western India. This holy town is famous for its temple of Krishna which houses the Shrinathji, a twelfth century 'infant' incarnation idol of Krishna.

Printer
In the textile industry, he is a craftsman who prints with printing blocks on fabrics.

Sari
The traditional and characteristic dress of Indian women today. The sari was probably a southern dress which became popular in northern India in the medieval period.

A long piece of cotton or silk cloth was the principal garment of Hindu women, worn round the waist, one end falling to the feet, and the other crossed over the bosom, shoulder, and sometimes over the head. In southern India a sari measured 8.5 metres, serving also as an undergarment. In northern India a sari was shorter in length, about 5 metres, and was worn with a skirt underneath.

Shiva
A major Hindu deity, and the Destroyer or transformer, forming with Brahma and Vishnu the Hindu trinity. Shiva is usually worshipped in the abstract form of the Shiva *linga*.

Sonia Terk Delaunay
A French artist, (1885-1979), who with her husband Robert Delaunay and others, cofounded the Orphism art movement, known for its use of strong colours and geometric shapes. Her work extends to painting, textile design and stage set design. She had a retrospective exhibition at the Louvre in 1964, and in 1975 was named an officer of the French Legion of Honour. Her work in modern design included the concepts of geometric abstraction, the integration of furniture, fabrics, wall coverings, and clothing.

Sophie Taeuber
A Swiss artist, (1889-1943), painter and sculptor. She collaborated on numerous joint projects with Jean Arp. They married in 1922.

Tristan
One of the main characters of the *Tristan and Isolde* story, a Knight of the Round Table. Son of Blacheflor and Rivalen, and the nephew of King Mark of Cornwall. Tristan was sent to bring Isolde back from Ireland to wed the king. However, he and Isolde accidentally consumed a love potion during the voyage and fell in love. They experienced numerous trials.

Turban
A turban, or head dress, was the most important part of medieval costume in Rajasthan. It was a sign of honour. To remove a turban meant complete submission in those days. Removal of his turban was the most insulting punishment for a nobleman.

Victoria and Albert (V&A) Museum
The Victoria and Albert Museum in London, is the world's largest museum of decorative arts and design. Named after Queen Victoria and Prince Albert, it was founded in 1852. Its collection contains art from ancient times to the present day, in every medium, from Europe, north America, Asia and North Africa.

Vishnu
In Hindu theology, the second god of the trinity (Brahma, Vishnu, and Shiva) known as 'the Preserver'. Of his many incarnations the most famous is as Krishna.

Woodblock Printing
A technique for printing text, images or patterns used widely throughout East Asia and originating in China thousands of years ago, as a method of printing on textiles and later paper.

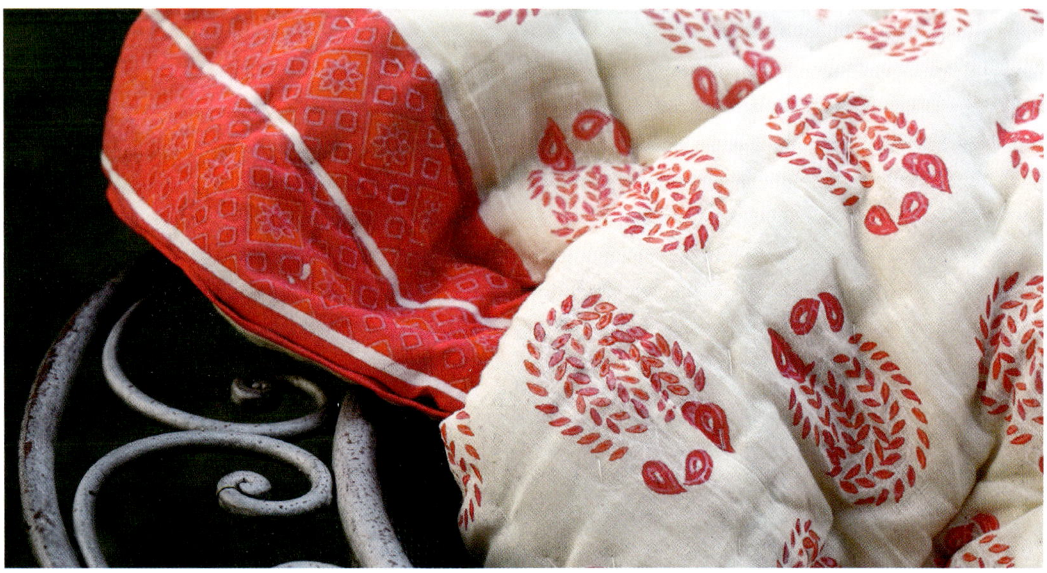

Paisley motif created with leaf prints in delicate pink